LOST GODDESSES

GENDERING ASIA
A Series on Gender Intersections

Gendering Asia addresses the ways in which power and constructions of gender, sex, sexuality and the body intersect with one another and pervade contemporary Asian societies. The series invites discussion of how people shape their identities as females or males and, at the same time, become shaped by the very societies in which they live. The series is concerned with the region as a whole in order to capture the wide range of understandings and practices that are found in East, Southeast and South Asian societies with respect to gendered roles and relations in various social, political, religious, and economic contexts. *Gendering Asia* is, then, a multidisciplinary series that explores theoretical, empirical, and methodological issues in the social sciences.

Series Editors: Wil Burghoorn, Gothenburg University, Sweden; Cecilia Milwertz, NIAS – Nordic Institute of Asian Studies, Denmark; and Helle Rydstrøm, Linköping University, Sweden.

Contact details and other information (including members of the international advisory board) can be found at: http://www.niaspress.dk.

Working and Mothering in Asia
Images, Ideologies and Identities
Edited by Theresa W. Devasahayam and Brenda S.A. Yeoh

Making Fields of Merit
Buddhist Female Ascetics and Gendered Orders in Thailand
Monica Lindberg Falk

Gender Politics in Asia
Women Manoeuvring within Dominant Gender Orders
Edited by Wil Burghoorn, Kazuki Iwanaga, Cecilia Milwertz and Qi Wang

Lost Goddesses
The Denial of Female Power in Cambodian History
Trudy Jacobsen

LOST GODDESSES

THE DENIAL OF FEMALE POWER IN CAMBODIAN HISTORY

TRUDY JACOBSEN

Gendering Asia, No. 4

First published in 2008
by NIAS Press
NIAS – Nordic Institute of Asian Studies
Leifsgade 33, DK-2300 Copenhagen S, Denmark
tel (+45) 3532 9501 • fax (+45) 3532 9549
email: books@nias.ku.dk • website: www.niaspress.dk

British Library Cataloguing in Publication Data
Jacobsen, Trudy
    Lost goddesses : the denial of female power in Cambodian
    history. - (Gendering Asia)
    1. Women - Cambodia - Social conditions 2. Women - Cambodia
    - Political activity - History
    I. Title
    305.4'2'09596

ISBN-13: 978-87-7694-001-0

Typeset by NIAS Press
Produced by SRM Production Services Sdn Bhd
and printed in Malaysia

*This book is dedicated to
the women of Cambodia
in the hope that greater knowledge of their past
can make for a better future.*

Contents

Contents

LIST OF FIGURES

Preface

I met Peou a little before midnight in a Phnom Penh nightclub. She was hovering nervously near the door and appeared not to know anyone in the teeming crowd of predominantly male aid workers, diplomats and tourists, and scores of young Cambodian women. At first I didn't realise what was different about her. Then I saw that unlike the standard *srei bar* uniform of t-shirt and miniskirt or jeans, she was wearing a white, collared blouse, buttoned almost to the neck, such as schoolgirls wear, and a *sampot*, a skirt made from patterned silk or cotton. Usually *sampot* are ankle-length, but Peou's had been cut to just above the knee and neatly hemmed. When Peou discovered I spoke Khmer, she began telling me excitedly about herself. She had come from Kompong Speu province that day at the suggestion of her mother's cousin in order to find work in a factory. She had found none, but had met a very nice older woman in the market who invited her to stay at her house with other girls from the provinces, some of whom were coming to this nightclub and had suggested Peou come too in order to meet a foreign man who would marry her and take her overseas. Wanting to appear unprovincial, Peou had altered her *sampot* into what she perceived as a more fashionable approximation of the Western miniskirt.

Peou has remained in my thoughts over the last five years. I know the trajectory of disappointment, resignation, and despair that her life would have taken. She had few choices. Women are expected to work hard, support their families by whatever means possible, and not complain no matter how they are exploited and abused. When anyone, Cambodian or otherwise, attempts to introduce changes to the lives of Cambodian women, the obstacle of 'tradition' is always asserted as something incontrovertible and inviolate. To change tradition is to meddle in Cambodian cultural identity. But what if the true tradition of Cambodia is not one of male privilege, but dignity, value and agency for women? What if Cambodian women were active participants and agents in the past? Perhaps when Peou's daughters read this book, they will refuse to accept anything less in the present.

This book was begun in 2000 as my doctoral project at the University of Queensland, and subsequently revised with the incorporation of further archival material and ethnographic data collected after the thesis was submitted in 2003. I have lived and worked in Cambodia since 1988. This has presented me with unique opportunities but also bicultural vision in the sense that things that do not seem to me to require explanation are mystifying to those who did not grow up in Cambodia; similarly, some 'universal' Western assumptions are at times painfully oblique to me. Thankfully, I have always had guardians to reorient me toward my proper *dharma*.

The first of these was Ron Poulton, who is responsible for first inculcating a proto-feminist consciousness in me through the medium of Margaret Atwood's *The Handmaid's Tale*. Martin Stuart-Fox, my PhD supervisor, instilled the importance of theory and concise erudition (with debatable success). Helen Creese told me it was fine to use frameworks rather than theory. Barbara Watson Andaya, who has redefined the boundaries of gender history in Southeast Asia, has been consistently supportive of my work and exceedingly generous in her comments. Bob Elson, at a time when my stipend was running out and there were no jobs on the horizon, told me to persevere in academia. I thank them all for their encouragement.

I am very grateful to the Monash University Faculty of Arts for allowing me to use my new employee grant in order to facilitate the production of the book in the final stages. My mentors at Monash, Penny Graham and Marika Vicziany, have been wonderful supporters of my work since I joined them in 2006. Their patience and generosity has kept me going through difficult times.

Thanks are due to all who kept me (relatively) sane in Cambodia – Emi Aizawa, Stephen Close, the Germans (Thomas, Anja, Anne et al), Karen Heyes, Geoff O'Keefe, Paul Matthews, Audrey Riffaud, Lisa Scheel, Antonia Staats, Paul Stewart, Vanessa Tuck, Ken Wilcox; the many fantastic Cambodian and Cambodian-American women I know – Loung Ung, Putsata Reang, Y Dary, Theary Seng, Aing Sokroeung, Ham Samnom, Khun Ravikun, Hou Sopheara, and Hou Bopha to name a few; the ubiquitous Tom Fawthrop; and my mother, Carol Jacobsen, without whom I would never have had the opportunity to know and love Cambodia. The support of colleagues Duncan McCargo, Laura McGrew, Sunait Chutintaranond, Michael Barr, Monica Lindberg Falk, Penny Edwards, and Annuska Derks has been very much appreciated. Alexandra Kent and Cecilia Milwertz and their families deserve special thanks for making me feel welcome during my sojourns at NIAS in 2003 and 2004 and continuing to be interested and engaged in all I do.

Gerald Jackson and Leena Höskuldsson at NIAS Press have been amazing to work with throughout the three years it has taken for my original manuscript to be transformed into this book. Leena has been extremely patient with my Australianisms and lack of proper respect for n-dashes! Gerald has gone above and beyond the call as a publisher, devoting personal time to the project, drawing the maps and applying judicious editorial *droit de dieu* when I was inclined toward author tantrums. His willingness to take a chance on an untried, green academic bolstered my professional self-esteem at a precarious moment and if it were not for his unwavering faith in my work I may not have continued in academia. I certainly could not have completed this book without him.

Yorick Smaal, tea-maker, intellectual foil, talker-down from high ledges, has been a tower of strength throughout the process of writing this book. In a world where nothing is certain, our friendship is my guiding light.

Finally, I am forever indebted to David Chandler, who established the framework for Cambodian history to which I here humbly offer my contribution, and who has been exceptionally generous in reading and commenting on various drafts of this book, providing me with materials from his own collection, and encouraging me in all my endeavours.

Glossary

a	prefix indicating that something is bad; also the title given to non-elite men until the middle of the twentieth century
adthipul	a supernatural energy manifested in spirits and practitioners of magic
ak yeay chastum	elderly women of the palace
Angkar	'Organisation'; name assumed by the government of Democratic Kampuchea (1975–1979)
anuj khshatri	'young queen'
ap	witch
apsara	celestial female spirit
arête	decree issued by the French colonial government
arhat	a person who is very spiritually advanced
bauk	term used to describe gang rape
Bhagavati	one of the names of Lakshmi
bhariya	wife
anuj bhariya	lesser or younger wife
jao bhariya	stolen wife
nea nea bhariya	wife through unusual circumstances
patoe kan bhariya	wife whose father has refused his consent
satru bhariya	enemy wife
sroengkar bhariya	(minor) wife of the king in the Middle Period
tean resey bhariya	wife through charity
bhikkhuni	ordained nun
bodhisattva	a person with sufficient merit to enter Nirvana; a Buddha-in-waiting
bonne femme	good woman, good wife
brai	female spirits, ghosts of dead women

araks brai   wild spirits, inclined toward evil

brai krala plerng ghosts of women who died in childbirth

brai kramom ghosts of women who died as virgins

bunn   merit

cakravartin   'Lord of the earth'; supreme king

cbpab   law; code of conduct

   cpbab chah   'old *cbpab*', written before c. 1790

   cbpab thmei 'new *cbpab*', written after c. 1790

chao adthika   head monk

chen-t'an   defloration ceremony observed by Zhou Daguan in the late thirteenth century

cholop   spy

daun chi   Buddhist nun

devadasi   (female) slave of the gods; temple slave

devaraja   'god-king'

devata   guardian spirit, found at temple doors and archways

dharma   duty; observance of one's correct place in society and the world

dhuli jerng kamsten śri title meaning 'Lord who is the dust of the feet [of the gods]'

encongayment   term used to refer to temporary marriages between the French and local women in their colonies

guha   womb; inner sanctum of a temple complex

huyen quan   Vietnamese title meaning 'princess'

hyang   title meaning 'princess' in early Cambodia

jamdev   title meaning 'Lady'; female equivalent of *oknha*

joal m'lap   'entering the shade'; ceremony marking the entrance of girls into womanhood

kaev hva   title of the Middle Period

kamratan an   title meaning 'Holy, revered'

kamraten jagat 'holy, revered god'

kang chao   title given to women of the palace

kanlong kamraten an title given to deceased women of the royal family during the Angkor period; also a cult devolving upon these women

kanlong theat   widow observing propriety

kantai   woman, women

khloñ, khloñ   title or reference to elite rank

Glossary

khmei khieu	'Blue Khmers'; refers to Cambodians living in diaspora
khsae	'cords', 'threads'; refers to network of patron–client relationships upon which power in Cambodia is based
khum	sub-district
khun preah moneang	title given to women of the palace; denotes rank over others
K'mouch	ghost
koan	child, children
koan kroach	foetus that has been smoked over a ritual fire, worn as a talisman of protection
kram	law, edict
kramar	length of cloth (usually checked cotton) that can be worn as a scarf, a sarong, and used for a variety of purposes
kramom	virgin
krom	group, collective
krom samaki bongko bongkoeun phol	'solidarity production group', implemented during the People's Republic of Kampuchea (1979–1989)
kru khmei	traditional healer; practitioner of magic
krup leakkhana	'full of [good] qualities or virtues'
ku	early Cambodian term meaning 'woman'; also an honorific for non-elite women, including slaves
leang komus	'washing away the stain' of sin through compensation or observance of ritual
loak kru	polite term to use when speaking to a monk or other elite person
lon	title of elite men in early Cambodia
maharaja	'great king'
maharishi	'great poet', 'great scholar'
matra-vamsa	matrilineal family
m'dey doeum	'original mother'
me	'mother'; also polite way to refer to a married woman
me kha	title given to wives who had been slaves
me kong	head of group
me padevat	'mother of the revolution', Khieu Ponnary
me sa	'White lady'; very powerful female spirit
me vat	head of *wat*
meba	ancestral spirits, usually in the female line

meba p'dteah	ancestral spirits dwelling in the house
métis	term of the colonial period used to refer to children of mixed parentage wherein one parent was European
mise en valeur	term used to legitimate the French colonial presence
mission civilisatrice	the perceived responsibility of the French in modernising the countries and peoples it colonised
mit	friend, comrade
mit neary	'female comrade'
mit p'dai	'comrade husband'
mit prapuan	'comrade wife'
mohat	person indentured to serve the royal family
mratāñ	title of lesser princes in early Cambodia
neak	people, person
neak che deung	'people who know knowledge'; group of secular elite patronised by the French
neak khloñ	'people of the *khloñ*'
neak ta	ancestor spirits
neang	young woman; title given to young women
neang chi	Buddhist nun
oknha	official; title meaning 'Lord'

oknha suttanta prachea 'Lord poet of the land'; title given to Ind

omnaich	influence
padhyay	spiritual preceptor
phnom	hill
phum	district
pi doeum	'the time before [the Khmer Rouge period]'; the past
prapuon	wife

prapuon jerng 'end' or 'last' wife; wife of third rank

prapuon kandal 'middle' wife; wife of second rank; also called *prapuon stoeu*

prapuon mecak 'bought wife'; wife of third rank; also called *prapuon touch*

prapuon thom 'big' or 'principal' wife; wife of first rank

Preah	'holy'; prefix to royal or divine titles

Preah ek khsatri 'first princess'; elder sister of the king

Preah moneang title of a rank of royal wife

Preah snang lesser wife of the king

purohita	religious official
quan chua	Vietnamese title given to Queen Ang Mei (r. 1835–1840, 1844–184?)
rajaputri touch	lesser prince, son of a king who had reigned
raks	supernatural being; demon
Ramakerti, Reamker	Cambodian version of the *Ramayana*
Résident Supérieur du Cambodge	highest colonial office
rieong bpreng	folktales
rup, rup araks	medium
sakh	rank, level
śakti	female aspect of Brahmanical gods; female power
samlor trey	soup or stew of fish
sampeah kmouch	ceremony of 'saluting the ancestors' wherein a couple who have offended the *meba* ask for forgiveness
sampot	traditional skirt made from patterned silk or cotton
sampuor	a fruit used by women to wash their hair in the Middle Period
samre	novice monk; novicehood
samsara	cycle of birth and rebirth
sangha	the hierarchical structure of the Buddhist clergy
sati	'virtue'; practice of wives killing themselves by immolation at their husbands' funeral pyres
sauchey	class of female servants in the palace; also a name given to prostitutes in the colonial period
sdec prades raj	title given to a king in the middle period
sena thong	leader of armed forces
setthi manus	human rights
si	honorific given to non-elite men
smir	women who turn into tiger-like creatures when smeared with a certain oil
snang	assistants who interpret the words of mediums; lesser wives of the king
srah	artificial lakes, part of temple complexes
srei	woman, female
srei aht leakkhana	'woman with no qualities or virtues'
srei beer	waitresses who represent a particular beer company

srei kouch   'broken women'; women who have had sex; prostitutes
srei krup leakkhana 'woman full of qualities or virtues'
srei luok khluen 'woman who sells herself', prostitute
srei neak leng 'woman who gambles'
srei rijoh rilenh 'wriggly woman'; prostitute

srok	land; area; country
stridhana	property and goods belonging to a wife
tai	woman; female slave
ten	title denoting elite (female) status
thmup	male witch, sorcerer
ubhayoraj	title given to a king who has abdicated; usually the uncle of the reigning king
uparaj	title given to the heir apparent to the throne
upasaka	devout layperson who observes five, eight or ten Buddhist precepts
vap	title of elite men in early Cambodia
varna	colour; group; line
vatthabandh	length of cloth worn by monks
vihara	structure housing sacred image in temple complexes
vrah kamratan an	'the holiest holy'; title given to royal and divine persons
yaks, yaksini	supernatural being; demon
yeay	'grandmother'; elderly woman
yuan	Vietnam, Vietnamese
yuvaraja	'young king'; heir apparent
yvan	term referring possibly to Javanese, possibly to Cham peoples in early Cambodia

CHAPTER 1

Introducing the Goddesses

O ne often hears of a people who have endured with courage and defiance in the face of complicity and deceit. Typically, the country in which they live has ascribed to them an inferior position of subjugation and passivity. They have been denied a history. All too often, the international community has colluded in their representation as inactive participants because of its own prejudices. Yet there has been no outcry from civil society either to free them from their predicament or to demonstrate their past glory and present consequence. Such a people are the subject of this book. In this case, however, these people are neither a persecuted minority ethnic group nor members of an outlawed religious sect. They are the women of Cambodia.

The original ruler of Cambodia, according to legend, was an unmarried female warrior known as 'Liu Yie' to the Chinese and as 'Soma' in Sanskrit. These names are not learned by young Cambodians along with those of Kings Jayavarman VII and Ang Duong, however, although some Cambodians today believe that 'tradition treated women with strong respect in the past'.[1] This conflicts with sociological and anthropological studies that assert that 'traditionally' Cambodian women were powerless and inferior. Cambodian proverbs such as *broh jee-a daw dail meas, srei jee-a daw dail kotong saw* ('men are like gold, women are like white cloth'), the implication being that gold can be washed clean of dirt whereas white cloth will always bear a stain, are

1

ingrained in the collective consciousness of Cambodians today and further perpetuate the stereotype of Cambodian women as passive and Cambodian society as unequal. The dichotomy posed by these conflicting views raises several queries that must be addressed in order to ground the current relationship of women to power in Cambodia. Who or what is responsible for the denial of female power in Cambodian history? Have Cambodian women ever been powerful? If so, when did this begin to change, and by what agency?

Framing women and power in Cambodia

The first principle outlined in the English version of Michel Foucault's *The order of things* was that the book constituted a study of a relatively neglected field over which other disciplines, themes and subjects had been given precedence.[2] The same is true for the field of gender history in Cambodia (and, in fact, gender history in Southeast Asia). Only one author has run the gamut of the historical period in Cambodia, David Chandler, who in his 1983 work, *A history of Cambodia* (and in subsequent revised and updated editions), established the framework against which themes in Cambodian history, culture and politics are now addressed by other authors. Significantly for historians of Cambodia, in the concluding passages of the second revised edition, he states that, while the female voice is for the most part absent in accepted versions of Cambodian history, this is not necessarily a reflection of the importance or passivity of women.

Cambodia is situated in the Mekong Delta region, one of the few extensive areas of fertile lowland in mainland Southeast Asia. It is thus no surprise that the area was the cradle of Southeast Asian civilisation as well as the place that saw a convergence of influences from India and China (see Fig. 1.1). In 1944 George Cœdès noted the 'high status' of women in early Cambodian societies, especially a perceived tradition of matrilineal success, and extrapolated from these examples – based as they were in the very heart of Southeast Asian cultural genesis – the theory that societies throughout the region could be grouped together on the basis of these shared cultural features.[3]

Yet, despite its importance, no study in existence concerns itself solely with the history of Cambodian women from the earliest historical period to the present day. Existing histories of Cambodia mention women in relation to how they were represented in artistic tradition, their religious participation, and their social function. The purpose of such studies is not to shed

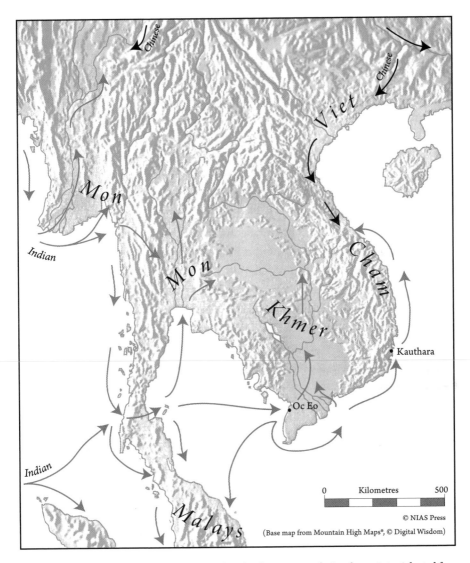

Fig. 1.1: The spread of Indian and Chinese cultural influences in early Southeast Asia. Adapted from Jan M. Pluvier, *Historical Atlas of South-East Asia* and other written sources.

light on the experiences of women but to show how particular institutions functioned in Cambodia. There are only three extant monographs that focus upon Cambodian women; the PhD theses of Judy Ledgerwood, 'Changing Khmer conceptions of gender: women, stories, and the social order' (Cornell, 1990), and Annuska Derks, 'Khmer women on the move: Migration and urban experiences in Cambodia' (University of Amsterdam, 2005), and, most recently, based on her thesis, Mona Lilja's *Power, resistance and women politicians in Cambodia: Discourses of emancipation* (Copenhagen: NIAS Press, 2008). All three of these works are gender studies; they illustrate the impact of the decade of civil war, revolution and subsequent displacement upon gender roles in contemporary Cambodia. Yet only Judy Ledgerwood looks further into the past than the Khmer Rouge era for historical evidence for Cambodian perspectives toward women and power, and then only to the colonial era. While all of these works are essential for understanding current Cambodian social and political norms, none explain how the 'high status' of women in the earliest historical periods gave way to the perceived inferiority of women in the late nineteenth century. A study that shows the extent of female power in each historical period and explains how access to female power has been impeded is long overdue.

Many of the current challenges for women in Cambodia relate back to (false) constructs of earlier periods; at the same time, most Cambodians have no way of accessing the records that would give a more accurate picture. As an example, in recent years certain Cambodian politicians have made remarks about returning to 'traditional social values'. The context of these comments seems to imply a patriarchal society, although Cambodian women are alleged to have enjoyed a high level of autonomy and independence in the distant past. Most Cambodians have little idea of gender relations prior to the nineteenth and twentieth centuries, believing that male pre-eminence has always been a facet of Cambodian society. In reality, it seems that there have always been greater differences between social classes than between men and women within those classes. 'Traditional social values' as a phrase must therefore be used carefully. When does tradition begin? And what 'power' are we talking about anyway?

'Power' is a difficult concept to explain in one's own culture. Ascribing a meaning to the way that people of another culture perceive it is inherently problematic. Most Western political and philosophical thought on power originates from post-Enlightenment reasoning, using specifically European historical examples and contexts. How can Western discourses of power have equal resonance in non-Western societies? Power in Southeast Asia has been, and continues to be, linked to cosmological and supernatural forces, whereas Western ideas of power focus on the ability to control economic production

4

or military might.[4] At the same time, it is not appropriate to assume that all non-Western states will react or develop along similar trajectories because they share the characteristic of being non-Western. As Francis Fukuyama has argued, Europe comprises countries with similar cultural origins and a more or less shared experience in the twentieth century, whereas Asian nations are very different in terms of culture and the experiences of the last century.[5] Similarly, demarcating a difference between what Western authors have taken to be indicative of power and what Cambodians themselves think of as power today is difficult; providing an overview of how these two factors have changed over time would require a separate volume.

Studies of women and power elsewhere in Southeast Asia are helpful in furthering our understanding of the relationship of women and power in Cambodia, however. In the last two decades, a number of edited collections have shown the importance of historical contextualisation and class differences in delineating a powerful female voice in the Southeast Asian past and present.[6] Yet even here, the predilection for transferring Western norms to non-Western cultures is discernible in the view that women in Southeast Asia have 'high status', and therefore 'power', because they often control their family's finances.[7] Narrowly defined, Western meanings of power as solely relating to economic production and political decision-making are not appropriate to a discussion of women in Southeast Asia. Wazir Jahan Karim argued against the relevance of 'unequal power generating gender hierarchies … in non-Western civilisations in Southeast Asia, which derive a theory of knowledge from concepts and values of bilateralism'.[8] Those that insist upon maintaining a Eurocentric approach run the risk of ascribing significance where it does not exist and denying it where is does. When Western gender norms and power structures are applied in this manner, as Chandra Talpade Mohanty warns us, 'sexual difference becomes coterminous with female subordination, and power is automatically defined in binary terms: people who have it (read: men), and people who do not (read: women)'.[9]

The association of power with public leadership has led to the classification of all societies as patriarchal. Once other forms of power are considered, however, 'one can show that in many societies male leadership is balanced by female authority'.[10] The association of power with public leadership furthers the 'public/private space' dichotomy wherein public space is perceived as civilised and male. Private space, on the other hand, is seen as uncivilised and

– by dint of women being involved in the 'primitive' activities of pregnancy and childbirth (areas in which men have had little participation) – female. Maila Stivens has been unequivocally critical of this view, describing it as 'manifestly severely limiting to discuss gender in the context of a supposed private sphere which 'women' are presumed to inhabit'.[11] At the same time, many Western scholars tend to dismiss evidence of the importance of women in areas where political or economic authority is not demonstrated. According to the *Pararaton*, Ken Dedes, queen of Java, was described as having a 'glowing vulva' or 'flaming womb'. This indicated that she was an exceptional woman whose husband would become a *cakravartin* (a 'wheel-turning' king of limitless sovereignty) regardless of his personal shortcomings.[12] Power from a supernatural source resided in the queen. Other examples of authority associated with women in Southeast Asia include the relationship between novice monks and their mothers, and the prevalence of cults devolving upon or officiated by women in mainland Southeast Asia.

In Cambodia, ancestral spirits are known as *meba*; heads of household as *meba p'dteah*; monks in charge of a religious establishment as *me vat*. During the Khmer Rouge period, group leaders were known as *me kong*. Significantly, *me* is also the word for 'mother' or the polite way to refer to a married woman. Instances such as these have not been considered markers of 'power' because of Western preconceptions about the pre-eminence of political and economic power. Yet it appears that although Cambodian women have been represented at different times as 'powerless' in Western analyses, they have continued to exercise authority outside those areas of concern to Western constructs of power.

In the introduction to *Women of Southeast Asia*, Penny Van Esterik used the phrase 'substantial influence' as a metaphor for power.[13] It is this sense of power that I have taken in this book. There are many words for 'power' in the Cambodian language, from the amorphous *adthepul* to the charismatic *baramei* to the moral virtue *selathoa*. The Khmer word corresponding to 'influence' is *omnaich*, which is derived from the qualities of *baramei*, *bunn* ('merit'), and *mean* ('wealth').[14] It should not be confused with *komlang*, a more physical type of power, in the sense of 'strength'; although *komlang* can contribute to the level of *omnaich* wielded by an individual. Moreover, power, in the Cambodian context, rests upon a complex network of social relationships, in keeping with Foucault's general observation that the conditions for political power are determined by other pre-existing power relations.[15] In Cambodia, these relationships are known as *khsae*, literally 'cords', that link people and families. *Khsae* can be familial, institutional, or political, but are usually cemented through marriage or a long-standing patron–client relationship between a family based in the centre and individuals inheriting the relationship on the periphery.

Once *khsae* have been established, there are certain expectations between the contractors. The higher status party will expect their client to pass on a portion of any benefit they receive and support them in their endeavours. In return, the patron is expected to extend their protection to clients, be generous towards them, and privilege them when selecting candidates for positions, especially those that will put the client in a position to benefit financially. Clients accept their position within this framework because elite status is perceived as giving that person natural rights over others due to their higher levels of *bunn*, or the power that results from the performance of meritorious acts. The idea is that the elite would not have been able to achieve this level of authority, or be born to it, if undeserving. *Ipso facto*, their decisions and edicts must be in the best interests of their people. This unquestioning acceptance that certain people are entitled to lead and others to follow must be taken into consideration when considering power relations in Cambodia.

Elisabeth Fox-Genovese persuasively argued that being part of a 'gender system ... as a female means to accept the related but differential participation of males in the same system', and that this 'actively contributes to the prevailing relations of power'.[16] As Cambodian women today negotiate for empowerment in a society that has conflicting constructions of societal norms and gender roles, there is an urgent need for a comprehensive history that recounts the ways that Cambodian women have wielded power in the past. This is in keeping with neither usual historical practice nor recent gender discourse that urges the inclusion of both men and women in order to provide the most accurate representation of the past. Put simply, the historian should not just include women in the historical record, but also relate how the structure of gender relations determined the ways in which men and women interacted in the past. Yet until women have been 'added', in the sense that studies focussing specifically on the female voice have been prepared, compared, and critiqued, we cannot begin to rewrite existing histories more holistically.[17]

Principles for a methodology covering 2000 years

One of the great scholars of Southeast Asia, O.W. Wolters, wrote that 'the scope of gender studies in historical perspective should not be limited to registering, encyclopaedia-style, specific details and maybe stereotyped comments about females and their activities'.[18] Recent trends have taken the gendering of Southeast Asian history further. Barbara Watson Andaya has commented that

> when the national story has already been laid out according to certain accepted formulae, 'women' can only be included as a kind of supplement. This has been especially evident in Southeast Asia, where nationalist movements and the struggle against colonialism or western influence have been infused with masculine pride. Histories already articulated in terms of themes such as the suppressed people, the emergence of leaders, the awakening of popular consciousness, the successful revolution have proved highly resistant to the incorporation of a women's perspective.[19]

Ashley Thompson has argued against Cambodian women's experiences being pushed piecemeal into existing conceptualisations of the past. Instead, she offers two possible approaches. The first is to examine sexual difference in history, 'paying particular attention to feminine roles and voices.' The second approach, described by Thompson as 'the most radical, the most disquieting, the most promising', calls on historians to be engenderers of history, the task being 'one of finding the women lost or abandoned in history but also of writing or cooking up or smelling out history *as* women, or rather as women-and-men.'[20]

The methodological implications of this approach are not as revolutionary in Southeast Asian contexts as they may be in others. Karim pointed out that 'Western themes of feminism cannot envisage a situation where male and female relations are managed in a way as flexible and fluid as they are in Southeast Asia.'[21] What is necessary, then, is a re-examination of the sources in order to fashion new paradigms in which the female voice, or its absence, is integrated. Often, anthropologists and sociologists do not look further back in time than the Khmer Rouge period for explanations of current gender inequity in Cambodia, yet the roots of male chauvinism and gender constructs of women as passive go back to the educational system of the 1950s and 1960s, to the falsely constructed 'natural' place of women in the creation of a nationalist identity, back further to French colonial perceptions of women (which in turn relate to Orientalism as inculcated in the eighteenth century), and to early nineteenth-century Cambodian elite texts authored at the Siamese court. Even those that travel this far do not look beyond this point to the evidence attesting to powerful women in earlier periods. The reason is not to be deliberately obfuscatory, but because the sources for earlier periods are often inaccessible to historians who have been trained in modern history.

It is no longer possible, in the current age of radical amputation of entire departments, disciplines, and programmes by management in commercialised educational institutions, for scholars to cling stubbornly to the discipline in which they have been trained and refuse to diversify or embrace inter- and cross-disciplinary approaches. Perhaps I am representative of my generation in that I never felt that I had to resist, instead welcoming opportunities to use both methodologies in which I was trained, namely history and anthropology. Indeed, history and anthropology are essentially twin sides of the study of people – one using written documents, the other drawing upon the words and actions of people themselves, or analysing, as Clifford Geertz famously described it, 'Culture – this acted document'.[22] History allows us to delve into the past, anthropology the present.

Tradition is a subjective entity, but all must begin somewhere. Studies encompassing vast tracts of time can be either thematic or chronological. Foucault abandoned 'the great divisions that are now familiar to us all'; he looked beyond the recent past – the ascribed wellspring of current trends in knowledge – to the classical age. I have taken a similar approach in this book. It seems sensible to approach the analysis of the relationship of Cambodian women to power chronologically, in order to ascertain when and why it was that the relationship began to change. This approach is especially appropriate in examining Cambodian history, as source genre often corresponds to definitive historical periods as set out by David Chandler and recognised by the majority of other scholars whose focus is Cambodia.

The earliest 'Cambodian' kingdoms (3rd–9th centuries CE) and the classical 'Angkorian' civilisation (9th–14th centuries) left records in the form of stone inscriptions in Sanskrit and Old Khmer. The epigraphy has for the most part been collected, transliterated, translated into French, and annotated by George Cœdès.[23] The inscriptions are supplemented by Chinese dynastic histories and observations in French and English translation. The court chronicles of other mainland Southeast Asian kingdoms and images of women in the art and architecture of preclassical and classical Cambodia are also valuable resources.[24] Taking Stephanie Jamison's approach to analysis of ancient Indian texts,[25] I have re-examined all of these sources for evidence of women, in most cases eschewing conventional translations in favour of a new rendition using my own language training in Sanskrit and Old Khmer. The results have been illuminating. Although these sources have been, for the most part, 'mediated through male mentalities', they allow 'us an opening, to peer behind the relatively homogenous façade that each text type presents individually'.[26] The same is true of the sources for the middle period (15th–18th centuries). Aside from a handful of inscriptions, sources for this period consist of chronicles kept at the Cambodian courts, some passages in the histories of neighbouring kingdoms, legal instruments, and the *cbpab*, or didactic codes for correct behaviour. There is also the Cambodian version of the Rāmayāṇa, known as *Rāmakerti* or *Reamker*. It was also during this period that Europeans first encountered Cambodia, and the observations of travellers such as Gabriel Quiroga de San Antonio and Abel Rémusat provide valuable descriptions.

The nineteenth century fares far better in terms of material. Folk tales from this period have been preserved. This genre is often considered most useful for researching women.[27] From the middle of the 1800s an ever-increasing slew of French travellers' and explorers' tales of their intrepid adventures in the dense Cambodian jungle and their encounters with Cambodians themselves – including women – began to appear. Toward the end of the century and into the next, French official records began to be kept, documenting the bureaucracy of the administration of Cambodia as a *Protectorat*. These are all very useful for understanding not only how Cambodian women were perceived by the French but also for comprehending female access (or lack thereof) to education and employment opportunities in the colonial era. The majority of these are available in the National Archives of Cambodia and the Archives Nationale de France in Aix-en-Provence. Newspapers, magazines, posters, photographs, and French- and Khmer-language popular fiction from the time are also available from these archives. Court chronicles for the period are available on microfilm. Again, I have relied upon my own linguistic capabilities in analysing this material for the purpose of this book.

The period between 1954 and 1975 has been described by the many biographies and autobiographies of King Norodom Sihanouk and the travel commentaries of Western travellers such as Christopher Pym and Maslyn Williams,[28] which provide descriptions of life during the 1950s and 1960s in Cambodia. The series of films produced by, starring and directed by Sihanouk are informative of the roles he wanted women to accept. Government records and publications, photographs, newspapers, journals, and political propaganda have been conserved in the French and Cambodian archives mentioned above. Most government records of the Sangkum and Khmer Republic governments were destroyed by the Khmer Rouge, however, so it is difficult even to provide complete lists of members of the National Assembly or changes to ministerial portfolios. Popular literature from the period is available in the library of the *École Française d'Extrême-Orient* and *Bibliothèque Nationale* in France, the British Library and the library of the School of Oriental and African Studies in London, the libraries of Cornell and Berkeley Universities in the United States, and the library of the Australian National University and the National Library in Australia.

Several autobiographies by women provide valuable sources for the 1970s. The role of women in the resistance movement is difficult to determine from available documentation as such movements are by nature clandestine and membership secret. Some official documentation and publications from the 1970s have survived, however, and have been translated and published in journals and as edited collections.[29] The Documentation Centre of Cambodia (DC-CAM) is the repository for photographs and 'confessions' of men and women tortured and executed by the Khmer Rouge in prison S-21. These confessions ask the victims to set out their names, province of origin, profession before 'liberation' in 1975, and their duties as part of Democratic Kampuchea. Most of this information has been entered into the Cambodian Genocide Biographic Database and is accessible online at www.yale.edu/cgp/databases.html. The period since 1979 is also heavily reliant upon autobiographical and biographical records, supplemented by a large number of government and international aid organisation reports on the condition of women in Cambodia between 1980 and 2000. Cambodian popular literature during this period permits analysis of the experiences of women in post-revolutionary Cambodia. Publications by non-governmental organizations on women's rights, domestic violence, and 'proper conduct' are also useful.

Ethnography comprised a significant component of sources for the later periods covered in this book. I am extremely fortunate in having spent my adolescence and young adulthood in Cambodia between 1988 and 1995; I was therefore able to speak to people without the intermediary of a translator when I returned in 2001 and subsequently for archival research and fieldwork. I began living in Cambodia in the decade of reconstruction following the Khmer Rouge period, before the withdrawal of the Vietnamese presence, the signing of the Paris Peace Accords, and the advent of UNTAC. I experienced, alongside Cambodians, the changes wrought to the country as a result of these events. I believe that this has given me a particular insight into Cambodia's recent past denied researchers who have approached a particular period or issue as outsiders. My long association with Cambodia also gives me a certain legitimacy in the eyes of informants and institutions. A heightened sense of cultural awareness has allowed me to frame questions in more acceptable ways than may otherwise have been the case had I not had such a nuanced understanding of Cambodian society. My analysis of the Cambodian past and present has therefore been much more 'thick description' than perhaps I otherwise would have been able to achieve.

Reading the past in the present

Such a diversity of sources provides for fascinating material. A caveat is in order, however. It is not possible to delineate the experiences of *all* Cambodian women in every period under discussion. The epigraphic material of the earliest periods does not reveal much of women who were neither elite nor enslaved, for example. Similarly, sociological and anthropological reports of NGOs in the 1990s have an urban bias – so we cannot generalise about the situation of Cambodian women in this period, although we can state with some certainty that women in the large cities, for example, were becoming increasingly more likely to abandon wearing the traditional *sampot* in favour of Western-style clothing.

Chapter 2 provides a starting-point for the analysis of women and power in Cambodian history by examining the available evidence for the earliest period of Cambodian history, namely the third to ninth centuries, and establishing what (if any) power and significance women wielded at that time. Chapter 3 undertakes to determine whether this changed during the so-called 'Angkorian' period between the ninth to fifteenth centuries, and if so, by what agency. Chapter 4 represents the middle period in Cambodian history, from the relocation of the capital away from Angkor to the sack of Phnom Penh by the Thai in 1772, and investigates whether the advent of Theravada Buddhism as the religion of the elite explains the devolution in the alleged 'high status' of women in the distant past.

Chapter 5 explores the period of great social and political upheaval from 1772 to the establishment of Cambodian as a French Protectorate in 1864. This period does show some indications of a loss of significance for women in the literature produced by the elite at this time, notably the *Cbpab Srei*, 'Code of Conduct for Women'. This chapter examines some of the potential biases of the authors of the different versions of this text and other literature and changes to the legal code implemented after the middle of the nineteenth century. Although this literature is today considered by many Cambodians to represent 'traditional' Cambodia, the *rieong breng*, 'folktales', and the observations and records of the French from the late nineteenth and early twentieth centuries belie any notion of female powerlessness. This is discussed in Chapter 6.

Chapter 7 addresses the part the French colonial government played in removing women from spheres in which they had exercised agency in the past and the construction of a false notion of the Cambodian past and its gender roles. As Cambodian society at lower levels came to emulate the elite, increasing numbers of Cambodians came to believe that gender roles in a Cambodia free from external influence were predicated along the same lines as those espoused in elite nineteenth-century literature. This included the cohort responsible for developing Cambodia's nationalist agenda and those who have lead the country since independence in 1953. Those educated in the French tradition (including the educational syllabi of post-colonial governments, which changed little) interpreted the ideal societies of nineteenth-century elite literature as the lines along which 'correct' Cambodian society should run with some variation for the peculiarities of individual interpretation or extrapolation, and of course, the exceptions of the royal family and political elite. Chapter 8 demonstrates that underpinning the insistence of correct observance of these so-called traditional values in order to be 'Cambodian' is the need to reconcile them with a society increasingly beset by forces of modernisation in the period after independence. This is true even in the face of intense militarisation of Cambodian society during the Khmer Republic (1970–1975), in the milieu of both mainstream and *maquis*. Chapter 9 shows that, in keeping with global models, once the Khmer Rouge objective was achieved, women who had been co-opted into the struggle were expected to resume roles associated with domesticity.

Chapter 10 details the role that women played in the reconstruction of Cambodia after 1979 and its reintegration into the international community. Chapter 11 discusses the struggle that Cambodian society in the new millennium faces in reconciling the need for gender egalitarianism with the potential loss of cultural identity and the pressures of globalisation. Cambodian cultural identity has undergone many changes in the past fifty years and in many respects it is understandable that yet another revolution would be unpopular. Yet it is also unfair that Cambodian women are hampered from attaining the same levels of education and employment diversification as their brothers and husbands and continue to shoulder the greatest burden in terms of social and familial responsibility because of a conspiracy to make them the repositories of Cambodian tradition. It is significantly more difficult to run toward gender equality in a *sampot*, the traditional long skirt advocated as correct dress for women, than in the Western-style suit trousers favoured by Cambodian men who see themselves as 'modern'.

Chapter 12 draws together the key themes of this book and shows that Cambodian women have always been powerful, although not necessarily in ways that dovetail with Western constructs of power. They are the survivors of a fraudulent enterprise concocted against them. This book will reveal the circumstances of this deceit and identify the perpetrators of the denial of female power in Cambodian history.

Notes to Chapter 1

1   Chhay Yiheang, quoted in *Gender and behaviour towards love*, Phnom Penh: Women's Media Centre, 2000, pp. 6–7.

2   Michael Foucault, *The order of things: An archaeology of the human sciences*, London; New York: Tavistock, 1970, p. ix.

3   George Cœdès, *Histoire ancienne des états hindouisés d'Extrême-Orient*, Hanoi: Imprimerie d'Extrême-Orient, 1944, pp. 7–10.

4   See for example Jalal Alangir, 'Against the current: The survival of authoritarianism in Burma', *Pacific Affairs* 70, 3 (Fall 1997), pp. 333–350; David W. Ashley, 'The failure of conflict resolution in Cambodia: Causes and lessons', in Frederick Z. Brown and David G. Timberman (eds), *Cambodia and the international community: The quest for peace, development, and democracy*, Singapore: Institute of Southeast Asian Studies, 1998, pp. 49–78; Vincent Boudreau, 'State repression and democracy protests in three Southeast Asian countries', in David S. Meyer, Nancy Whittier, and Belinda Robnett (eds), *Social*

movements: Identity, culture, and the state, Oxford; New York: Oxford University Press, 2002, pp. 28–46.

5   Francis Fukuyama, 'Re-envisioning Asia', *Foreign Affairs* 84, 1 (Jan–Feb 2005), p. 75.

6   Jane Atkinson and Sherry Errington (ed.), *Power and difference: Gender in island Southeast Asia* (Stanford, California: Stanford University Press, 1990); Wazid Jahar Karim (ed.), *Male and female in developing Southeast Asia* (Oxford: Berg, 1995); Aihwa Ong and Michael Peletz (ed.), *Bewitching women, pious men* (Berkeley: University of California Press, 1995).

7   Shelley Errington, 'Recasting sex, gender and power: A theoretical and regional overview', in Jane Monnig Atkinson and Shelley Errington (eds), *Power and difference: Gender in island Southeast Asia,* Stanford, California: Stanford University Press, 1990, pp. 5, 41.

8   Wazir Jahan Karim, 'Introduction: Gendering anthropology in Southeast Asia', in Karim (ed.), *Male and female in developing Southeast Asia,* p. 16.

9   Chandra Talpade Mohanty, 'Under western eyes: Feminist scholarship and colonial discourses', *Boundary 2,* 12, 3 (Spring–Autumn 1984), p. 344.

10 Peggy Reeves Sanday, *Female power and male dominance: On the origins of sexual inequality,* Cambridge: Cambridge University Press, 1981, p. 113.

11 See Carole Pateman, *The sexual contract,* Stanford, California: Stanford University Press, 1988, pp. 11–12; Nancy Hartsock, 'Foucault on power: A theory for women?', in Linda J. Nicholson (ed.), *Feminism/postmodernism,* New York and London: Routledge, 1990, pp. 157–175; Maila Stivens, 'Why gender matters in Southeast Asian politics', in Maila Stivens (ed.), *Why gender matters in Southeast Asian politics,* Clayton, Victoria: Centre for Southeast Asian Studies, Monash University, 1991, p. 15.

12 Ann Kumar, 'Imagining women in Javanese religion: Goddesses, ascetes, queens, consorts, wives', in Barbara Watson Andaya (ed.), *Other pasts: Women, gender and history in early modern Southeast Asia,* Manoa, Hawai'i: University of Hawai'i Press, 2000, p. 96; see also Barbara Watson Andaya, *The flaming womb: Repositioning women in early modern Southeast Asia,* Honolulu: University of Hawai'i Press, 2006, p. 1.

13 Penny Van Esterik, 'Introduction', in Penny Van Esterik (ed.), *Women of Southeast Asia,* rev. ed. (De Kalb, Northern Illinois: Center for Southeast Asian Studies, Northern Illinois University, 1996), p. 1.

14 Martin Stuart-Fox and I are submitting for publication a paper outlining the taxonomy of power in Cambodian culture. An earlier draft was presented at the workshop 'Reconfiguring Religion, Power, and Moral Order in Cambodia', held in Varberg, Sweden, 27–29 October 2005, as 'Power in Cambodian texts and contexts: A *ptdaim-mukh* taxonomy'.

15 Michel Foucault, 'Truth and power' [1976], in Michel Foucault, *Power,* vol. 3 in *Essential works of Foucault, 1954–1984,* ed. Paul Rabinow, New York: The New Press, 2000, pp. 122–123.

16 Elisabeth Fox-Genovese, 'Gender, class and power: Some theoretical considerations', *The History Teacher* 15, 2 (February 1982), p. 261.

17   See Ashley Thompson, 'Introductory remarks between the lines: Writing histories of middle Cambodia', in Barbara Watson Andaya (ed.), *Other pasts: Women, gender and history in early modern Southeast Asia*, Manoa, Hawai'i: University of Hawai'i Press, 2000, pp. 47–68; Joan W. Scott, 'Gender: A Useful Category of Historical Analysis', *American Historical Review* vol. 91 (1986), pp. 1053–1075.

18   O.W. Wolters, *History, culture, and region in Southeast Asian perspectives*, rev. ed. (Ithaca, New York: Southeast Asia Program Publications, Cornell University, 1999), p. 166.

19   Andaya, 'Introduction', pp. 1–2.

20   Thompson, 'Writing histories of middle Cambodia', p. 49.

21   Karim, 'Introduction', p. 26.

22   Clifford Geertz, *The interpretation of cultures: Selected essays*, New York: Basic Books, 1973, p. 10.

23   *Inscriptions du Cambodge*, 8 vols., comp. and trans. George Cœdès, Paris; Hanoi: Imprimerie Nationale and Ernest Leroux, 1937–66.

24   *Cūḷavamsa, being the more recent part of the Mahāvamsa*, trans. Mrs C. Mabel Rickmans, London: Pali Text Society, 1973; *The Glass Palace chronicle of the kings of Burma*, trans. Pe Maung Tin and G.H. Luce, London: Oxford University Press, 1923.

25   Stephanie Jamison, *Sacrificed wife/Sacrificer's wife: Women, ritual, and hospitality in ancient India* (New York; Oxford: Oxford University Press, 1996).

26   Jamison, *Sacrificed wife/Sacrificer's wife*, p. 11.

27   Jamison, *Sacrificed wife/Sacrificer's wife*, p. 8.

28   Christopher Pym, *Mistapim in Cambodia* (London: Hodder & Stoughton, [1960]); Maslyn Williams, *The land in between: The Cambodian dilemma* (Sydney; London: Collins, 1969).

29   *Pol Pot plans the future: Confidential leadership documents from Democratic Kampuchea, 1976–1977*, trans. and ed. David P. Chandler, Ben Kiernan and Chanthou Boua (New Haven, Connecticut: Yale University Southeast Asia Studies, 1988); John Marston, 'Khmer Rouge songs', *Crossroads* 16, 1 (2002), pp. 100–127.

CHAPTER 2

Devi, Rajñi, Dasi, Mat*

*D*uring the earliest period for which historical evidence exists – from the third century C.E. to the establishment of the capital at Yaśodharapura ('Angkor') in the tenth century – Cambodia comprised several political entities in mainland Southeast Asia, at times only loosely affiliated. From time to time, one of these kingdoms would exert hegemony over its neighbours. The Chinese, from whom modern scholars have obtained most of their information for this period of Cambodian history, were aware of only two polities, however, which they called 'Funan' and 'Zhenla'. The earlier Funan spanned the lower Mekong delta and the coastline of the Indochinese peninsula. Archaeological evidence suggests that these sites were occupied simultaneously since the late centuries BCE. At different stages, some principalities on the Malay Peninsula appear to have been subjugated by Funan and reduced to tributary status. Funan included the polity known as Vyadhapura in the inscriptions, and probably extended over the sites of Oc Eo, Angkor Borei, Phnom Da, Ba Phnom, and Thapmuoi in modern-day Vietnam. The 'Funanese' appear to have shared many ethnic and cultural features with the Cham and the inhabitants of the Malay Peninsula (see Fig. 2.1).

The inhabitants of 'Zhenla', the Khmer, occupied the middle Mekong valley region, frequently encountering the Mon to the

---

* Goddess, queen, slave, mother [Sanskrit].

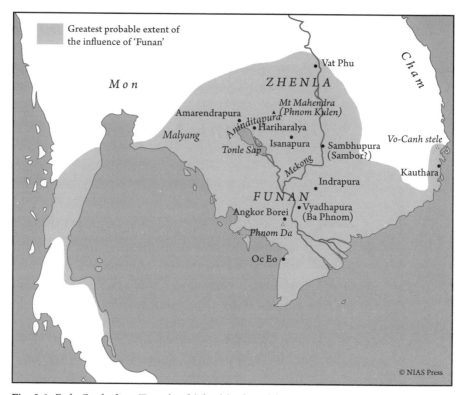

Fig. 2.1: Early Cambodia – 'Funan' and 'Zhenla'. Adapted from Jan M. Pluvier, *Historical Atlas of South-East Asia*.

west and the Cham to the east. An important site for this upper polity was Vat Phu. The Khmer also established themselves in areas to the north and east of the Tonlé Sap. The assumption was, for many years, that 'Zhenla' had been under at least partial Funanese hegemony until the sixth century, when the Khmers rebelled and conquered their overlords, resulting in a unified state. More recently, this theory has been replaced by alternate views. One is that by the time Funan disappeared from the Chinese records its internal economic and political structures had degenerated beyond repair, circumventing the need for an all-out military conquest of the territory by Zhenla.[1] Another argues that the elite of Funan came to rule over the northern polities known as Zhenla.[2] At any rate, there is no campaign recorded in the contemporaneous inscriptions.

Were the women of these early Cambodian polities powerful? If by 'power' we mean an individual exercising authority over others, in the Cambodian context of *omnaich* referred to in the introductory chapter, then the answer is yes; similarly, if we are to entertain 'female power' as events or roles wherein women had significance and agency, in a more Western conceptualisation of power, then the answer is again in the affirmative. This did not apply to *all* women, of course; there has always been a distinct difference between the elite and the non-elite, and between the non-elite and the enslaved, in Cambodian society. At the same time, it is important to preclude any anticipation of a matriarchal society in which men were inferior to women, although an elite woman certainly would have been regarded as being more 'powerful' than a non-elite man. The evidence to substantiate these assertions is discernible in the very earliest records of Cambodian history, preserved by the Chinese and substantiated by inscriptions in Sanskrit and Old Khmer. According to the Funanese creation mythology, the first ruler of a Cambodian polity was female; moreover, she was unmarried, and led her male soldiers into battle.

Mythological role-models

A Chinese diplomat was the first to record the creation myth of Funan around 230 CE. This version was recopied into subsequent dynastic histories with minimal changes.

> Formerly, [Funan] had for its sovereign a woman named Liu Ye. There was a man from the country of [India], Hundien, who dreamed that a spirit gave him two bows, and ordered him to embark upon a merchant ship and take to the sea. Hundien, in the morning, betook himself to the temple of the spirit, and, at the foot of a tree, found the bow. He embarked upon a merchant ship and directed it towards Funan. Liu Ye saw the ship and organised her soldiers to resist it. But Hundien raised his bow and shot an arrow which, penetrating the side of a boat, struck someone. Liu Ye was afraid and surrendered. Hundien then made her his wife. Not happy to see her go naked, he folded a piece of material across her that passed over her head. Then he governed the kingdom.[3]

Mythology is not incontrovertible proof of past social or political custom, but it does potentially demonstrate that in the early centuries CE the inhabitants of Funan believed that a female sovereign had ruled their ancestors. The Funanese were not alone in this belief; the Vo Canh stela, located in what is now the central coast of Vietnam, records the foundation of the late third- or early fourth-century Bhadreśvara temple by a king named Bhavavarman and traces the genealogy of the king back to two progenitors, Kaundinya and Soma.

> Kaundinya, head Brahman of Bhavapura, planted the spear that he had received from the eminent Brahman Asvatthaman, son of Drona. There was a daughter of the king of the Nagas … who established upon the earth the race that bears the name of Soma; she adopted that state and lived in human form … . Kaundinya married her in order to fulfil certain obligations.[4]

Bhavavarman was probably not a Funanese king;[5] the (mythological) events of the inscription cannot be proved to have mirrored society in general. The legend indicates, however, that the executors of the Vo Canh inscription not only traced their lineage back to an original ruler who was female, but also found this perfectly acceptable. Had it not been in keeping with prevailing social attitudes toward women and power, the myth is likely to have been recast. We can infer, therefore, that in the earliest historical period at least two mainland Southeast Asian societies were at ease with the idea of women rulers.

There is other, more tangible evidence to support the notion of a widespread acceptance of female authority in preclassical Cambodia. Goddesses in this period were represented separately from their male counterparts. Often the iconography expressed a martial aspect to their characters. One such example is the popularity of the goddess Durga Mahishasuramardani, 'slayer of the buffalo-demon'. Although there are only two possible extant preclassical epigraphic references to Durga Mahishasuramardani, sculptural images of the goddess abound. All early Cambodian images of Durga Mahishasuramardani depict the goddess standing triumphantly atop a buffalo head (see Fig. 2.2). The popularity of this cult in the preclassical period in Cambodia eclipsed its counterpart in South India, although it is clearly from there that the cult derived. There are examples of buffalo sacrifices, performed by female religious officials, across mainland Southeast Asia.[6] It is likely that the popularity of this goddess stemmed from her similarity to, and subsequent assimilation of, a pre-existing indigenous female deity. David Chandler and Michael Vickery have both suggested that the cultural memory of Durga Mahishasuramardani continues in modern Cambodia. Powerful female spirits are believed to have resided at both Ba Phnom, where an image of Durga was once erected, and at Prasat Neang Khmau, 'Tower of the Black Lady', where an inscription referring to Durga was found.[7]

Other goddess images were represented separately from gods. There were many independent religious establishments dedicated to Lakshmi during the preclassical period, and her name was invoked in the inscriptions as a literary play on royal fortune. Sarasvati, the goddess of speech, was never depicted with her counterpart Brahma, although there is one example of images of the two existing in the same sanctuary.[8] There are inscriptions recording the establishment of images of Sarasvati in the seventh and eighth centuries, but none of the actual sculptures have survived intact to the present day. Similarly, Prajnaparamita, the embodiment of perfect wisdom and counterpart to

Fig. 2.2: Durga as the Slayer of the Buffalo-Demon (Durga Mahishasura-mardini). Sketch by Kyle Jakobsen of a sculpture held in the Mr. and Mrs. John D. Rockefeller 3rd Collection of Asian Art.

Lokeśvara, the Cambodian form of the *bodhisattva* Avalokiteśvara, was also represented separately from the male *bodhisattvas* in this earliest period of Cambodian history. In 693 a doctor erected an image of her under the name Vidhyadharani, and provided goods for the maintenance of the cult.[9] The fact that goddesses were represented as active, often aggressive, and separate from their male counterparts, indicates that in early Cambodia, female authority in the supernatural realm was an acceptable concept.

Queens among men

Political authority, although not irrefutable proof of the level of power enjoyed by an individual or group, is nonetheless a fairly good indicator in most cultures. The Cambodian concept of *omnaich* is most evident in the political sphere. Certain queens in the Cambodian past were autonomous wielders of the ultimate political authority in the land. The first of these queens dates from the early sixth century, in a location that corresponds to the geographical area comprising Funan. An inscription calls upon Vishnu to protect Kulaprabhavati, 'the great queen, principal spouse of King Jayavarman'.[10] The 'Jayavarman' referred to is one of the few early Cambodian kings for whom epigraphical and Chinese records coincide. The *History of the Liang* states that in 514 Jayavarman, king of Funan, died, and 'the son of a concubine, Rudravarman, killed his younger brother, son of the legitimate wife, and ascended the throne'.[11] The name of this younger brother is not given in the text, but Jayavarman did have another son, Gunavarman, who, during the reign of his father, had been placed in charge of a community dedicated to the god Vishnu. As the inscriptions relating to both Kulaprabhavati and Gunavarman are Vaishnavite, it is tempting to infer that the latter was the son of Jayavarman and Kulaprabhavati, and that Rudravarman killed him in order to ascend the throne. On the other hand, it is extremely unlikely that Jayavarman would have had only two sons, given that the usual practice of the elite throughout Southeast Asia until very recent times was to have a number of principal and lesser wives, all of whom could potentially bear children.

Three years elapsed between the death of Jayavarman in 514 and the arrival of the first of Rudravarman's emissaries in China, during which it seems that the throne was contested. Rudravarman himself lamented that there were other elites who did not favour his accession.[12] It is possible that there was a religious dimension to the succession dispute. While the inscriptions of Kulaprabhavati and Gunavarman are Vaishnavite, Rudravarman appears from his name to have been a follower of Śiva. He also took an interest in Buddhism; having found 'Buddha, *dharma,* the *sangha,* each with all their virtues, excellent … [he] fulfilled all the acts of an *upasaka* [lay follower of precepts].'[13] The *History of the Liang* also records that Rudravarman boasted of possessing a hair of the Buddha. Kulaprabhavati's donation to a Vaishnavite community can be construed as an attempt to secure support from Vaishnavite elite families by demonstrating her own adherence to Vishnu. It is unfortunate that there are not more extant examples of Rudravarman's inscriptions; as it is, we must assume that ultimately his supporters, probably Buddhist and Shaivite, were more powerful than those of Kulaprabhavati. In any event, it seems more than likely that upon the death of Jayavarman in 514 there was a three-year struggle for succession between Kulaprabhavati and Rudravarman before the latter succeeded in taking the throne. The Chinese did not record her as having acceded after Jayavarman probably because the Chinese themselves had no tradition of female sovereigns until Empress Wu of the Tang dynasty, nearly two centuries after Kulaprabhavati. Furthermore, emissaries of Rudravarman dispatched to the Chinese court in 517 would not have mentioned their king's difficulty in acceding.

Jayadevi (c. 685–c. 720) is the next queen for whom evidence exists to support an 'autonomous' reign. Her father Jayavarman I (r. c. 657–c. 685) was a very powerful sovereign in preclassical Cambodia. His capital, Purandarapura, was probably to the southeast of the Tonlé Sap. He controlled the territory once ruled by his great-grandfather Iśanavarman, including the polities of both Iśanapura and Vyadhapura, within the area delineated by 'Funan'. His personal conquests extended his territory along the southern side of the Tonlé Sap to the modern province of Battambang (see Fig. 2.3). Initially it was believed that Jayadevi was Jayavarman I's widow, forced to act as regent while a male heir to the throne was found or reached an age where he could govern alone. Historians now largely accept that Jayadevi succeeded her father, with a brief period in which the queen reigned in conjunction with her husband, the king Nrpaditya, also known as Nrpatindravarman, who was originally from the polity of Aninditapura. After the death of Jayavarman I, Nrpaditya and Jayadevi reigned over an extensive combined kingdom, comprised of the territory of Jayavarman I and the polity of Aninditapura. This explains how an inscription located in the southern polity of Vyadhapura

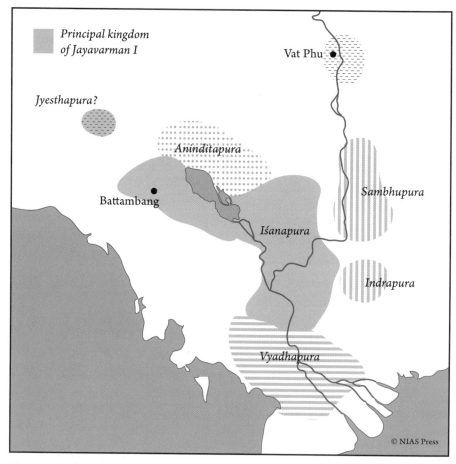

Fig. 2.3: Preclassical 'Cambodian' polities, c. 700. Map adapted from Helen Ibbitson Jessup and Thierry Zephir (eds), *Sculpture of Angkor and Ancient Cambodia: Millennium of Glory*.

could refer to Nrpaditya as the king. When Nrpaditya died, Jayadevi continued ruling alone.

This differs from the usual treatment of the period after Jayavarman I, informed by the theories of George Cœdès and Lawrence Palmer Briggs, who believed that the death of Jayavarman I resulted in civil war.[14] The implication was that a female sovereign was unacceptable to the people and they revolted against her. These scholars have tended to perceive the period immediately following Jayavarman I's last inscription in 681 as anarchistic. A number of factors have contributed to this perception. First, there is a general dearth of inscriptions that contain a king's name after 681; those that are mentioned do not appear in classical genealogies. Moreover, Chinese records assert that the country split into 'Land Zhenla' and 'Water Zhenla' after 707. Finally, there is the evidence of an inscription dated 716, which was believed to record the appearance of a king called Pushkaraksha at Sambhupura. The last known inscription of Jayadevi, K. 904, is dated 713. In the old conceptualisation of early Cambodian political organisation, it would have been inconceivable for two sovereigns to rule simultaneously. The assumption, therefore, was that Pushkaraksha was a contending king who ultimately won out in a struggle for power with Jayadevi because, as a female ruler, she was unable to draw upon sufficient legitimising factors.

None of these arguments is borne out by the epigraphic evidence. Whilst it is true that few inscriptions of the eighth century name a sovereign, a substantial number of dated inscriptions from the late seventh and early eighth centuries do, eleven between 681 (the last known date of Jayavarman I) and 713, the date of Jayadevi's K. 904 inscription. The contents of these eleven inscriptions are interesting when one considers the traditional representation of anarchy and discontinuity that Cambodia was supposedly subject to during this time. Each inscription records either the consecration of a new image in honour of a deity or the donation of slaves or goods to ones already established. It is difficult, therefore, to perceive the years after Jayavarman I as a period of civil war and factional struggles, unless it was one that nonetheless allowed time and resources for patrons to donate to sanctuaries in what would have been elaborate ceremonies.

The division of preclassical Cambodia into 'Land Zhenla' and 'Water Zhenla' after 707, observed by the Chinese in eighth-century histories, was, until very recently, accepted by historians as proof that Cambodia during this period was subject to internal struggles for power. This does not appear to have been the case. As early as 1943 Pierre Dupont concluded that there were many realms within the areas designated Land Zhenla and Water Zhenla, a belief shared by Claude Jacques and Michael Vickery among others.[15] Again, the epigraphic record belies the notion of a major division in preclassical Cambodian political geography. The divisions were already inherent in the geopolitical arrangements of early Cambodian polities.

The appearance of Pushkaraksha at Sambhupura in 716 provided historians, on the basis of an incorrectly translated inscription, with evidence for a chaotic eighth century. A king or a god named Pushkaraksha does appear in two other eighth-century inscriptions. Both are from the Thap-muoi area in Vietnam, which would once have been part of 'Funan'. The earlier of the two records either the establishment of a sanctuary or an image, bearing the name Pushkaraksha, by '*kamratan an* Sambh[u]varman'.[16] The later inscription refers to donations made to the god Pushpavatasvami, to be shared 'in common with the *vrah kamratan an* Pushkaraksha'.[17] Genealogies of the classical period unequivocally refer to Pushkaraksha as a king – and furthermore as the son of another king, Nrpatindravarman, identified above as Nrpaditya, the husband of Jayadevi and ruler of Aninditapura. The conclusion, therefore, must be that there *was* a king named Pushkaraksha in the eighth century, but far from being a potential rival of Jayadevi, he was her son, who ruled from Sambhupura while his mother remained at Aninditapura with his sister Narendradevi (for this and subsequent genealogical discussion see Fig. 2.4).

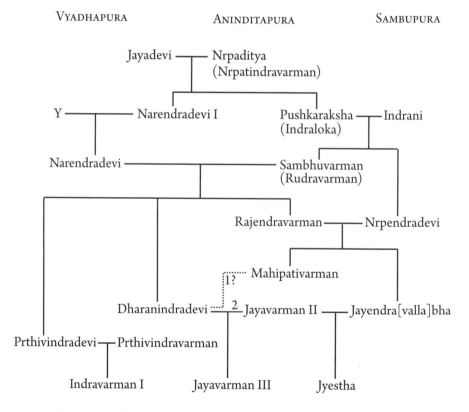

Fig. 2.4: Genealogies of Vyadhapura, Aninditapura, and Śambhupura.

Jayadevi was not the only queen to rule an eighth-century Cambodian polity; the royal women of Sambhupura seem to have done so for generations. Briggs referred to a mysterious woman 'presumed to have been a daughter of the suppositious Sambhuvarman' as the 'first ruler of Sambhupura.'[18] He derived this statement from an inscription dated 803 from Sambor in the modern Cambodian province of Kratie. In the inscription, a queen named Jyestha, 'the elder daughter of *kanhen kamratan an* Sri Jayendra[valla]bha, granddaughter of *kanhen kamratan an* Sri Nrpendradevi, great-granddaughter of *vrah kamratan an* Sri Indraloka' made a donation of slaves.[19] The title *kanhen kamratan an* was used exclusively to denote royal status for women. The inference, therefore, is that these women were princesses or queens. What indicates that Jyeshtha was a queen as opposed to a princess is the title *rajni* that also appears in the inscription.[20] This does not preclude the husband of Jyeshtha – or, indeed, any of the women named in the inscription – from being an important member of the political elite, as Michael Vickery cautions.[21] The important factor is that the women of Sambhupura were designated the important quality in terms of demonstrating genealogical affiliations and legitimacy.

Pushkaraksha, son of Jayadevi, was also known as Indraloka, a posthumous name meaning 'the king who has gone to the realm of Indra'. The inscriptions say that he acquired the throne of Sambhupura through his marriage to the heiress of that polity. A later king, Indravarman I (r. 877–889), erected a statue of 'the queen of Indraloka, Indrani', at the Bakong monument in 881. We can deduce that Pushkaraksha and Indrani were ruling Sambhupura in the middle of the eighth century. They had at least two children, a son named Sambhuvarman, and a daughter, Nrpendradevi (also known in later inscriptions as Nrpatindradevi). Sambhuvarman was sent to the polity of Vyadhapura in order to marry a descendant of Jayavarman I through the female line.[22] The best candidate for this Vyadhapuran princess is Narendradevi, Sambhuvarman's cousin. In a later inscription, a princess Prthivindradevi from Vyadhapura is described as having been 'born into a family where sovereigns succeeded each other, daughter of Rudravarman and daughter of the daughter of Nrpatindravarman'.[23]

There are explanations that account for this seeming contradiction in the two names given to Narendradevi's consort. Sambhu and Rudra are names of similar aspects of Śiva; also, in the hundred years that passed between events and their epigraphic commitment, details may have become blurred. Following this logic, the princess Dharanindradevi, described as the sister of Prthivindradevi in the genealogy of Indravarman I, may also have been the child of Narendradevi and Sambhuvarman. They also had a son, Rajendravarman, who married the heiress of Sambhupura, Nrpatindradevi; she was both his aunt and his cousin.[24]

Deconstructing Jayavarman II

At some point after the middle of the eighth century, according to some sources, a calamity befell the Cambodian court. The *maharaja* of 'Zabag', angered by the boasting and pomposity of the young Cambodian king, invaded Cambodia and had him beheaded, placing a Cambodian court official on the throne.[25] The likeliest candidate for this king is Mahipativarman, the son of Rajendravarman and Nrpatindradevi. In the late 770s, another young prince named Jayavarman returned from the court of 'Java', which may have referred to the island itself or a kingdom in neighbouring Champa, establishing himself as king in Indrapura by 781.[26] This king, known as Jayavarman II, married Jayaendra[valla]bha, who had inherited the sovereignty of Sambhupura from her mother, Nrpatindradevi.[27] Jayavarman II is usually credited with single-handedly 'liberating' Cambodia from 'Java' and uniting a fragmented Cambodia. It is true that between 780 and 824 Jayavarman II established his position as sovereign in the polities of Indrapura, Vyadhapura, Malyang, Hariharalya, Amarendrapura, and on Mount Mahendra (Phnom Kulen). He also married at least six other women. Much is made of Jayavarman II's courage in taking on the rest of the country in order to unite the land under one king. In fact, he seems to have accomplished this remarkable feat relatively bloodlessly, through marriages with women who symbolised the land in these places. The inscriptions relating to Jayavarman II do not name any of the seven women as his principal queen. Indeed, their titles are remarkably similar despite their different cultural and geographical origins.

Who were these women and why did Jayavarman II find it necessary to marry so many of them? Jayendra[valla]bha was the queen of Sambhupura. Another of Jayavarman II's queens was Dharanindradevi, sister of Rajendravarman. Given the propensity for the elite to send their sons to neighbouring polities for marriage, it may be that Mahipativarman was her first husband; or perhaps he had been sent to another nearby polity such as

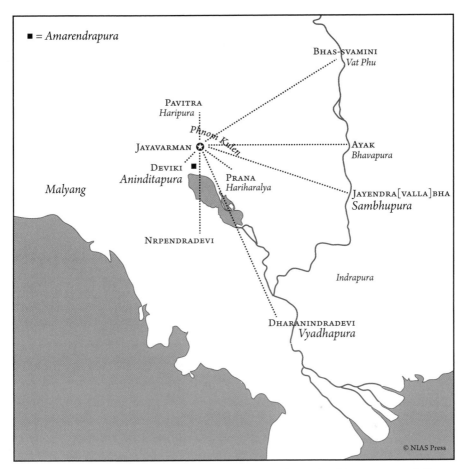

■ = *Amarendrapura*

BHAS-SVAMINI
Vat Phu

PAVITRA
Haripura

JAYAVARMAN

DEVIKI ■
Aninditapura

Malyang

PRANA
Hariharalya

AYAK
Bhavapura

JAYENDRA[VALLA]BHA
Sambhupura

NRPENDRADEVI

Indrapura

DHARANINDRADEVI
Vyadhapura

© NIAS Press

Fig. 2.5: The marriage alliances of Jayavarman II. Map adapted from Helen Ibbitson Jessup and Thierry Zephir (eds), *Sculpture of Angkor and Ancient Cambodia: Millennium of Glory.*

Indrapura. Their other sister, Prthivindradevi, was married to Jayavarman II's right-hand man, Prthivinarendra or Prthivindravarman, who assisted him in pacifying the region of Malyang. Interestingly, yet another of Jayavarman II's queens, Nrpendradevi or *svamini hyang* Amita, was the younger sister of two brothers who also aided Jayavarman II in the conquest of Malyang.[28] This family appears to have been clients of Prthivendravarman, as it was he who commanded the brothers and later asked Jayavarman II to grant titles and land in return for services rendered. Similarly, the father of yet another queen, Deviki or Sarasvati of Aninditapura, was made a fan-bearer at the royal court; a further decree charged his descendants with the responsibility of serving the *purohita* of the *kamraten jagat* of Kaden. The three brothers of Kambujalakshmi (also known as Prana), from the northwest, were made chief of castes, councillor of the royal bedchamber, and private treasurer to Jayavarman II after he married her. Other wives are known from inscriptions: *ten* Ayak of Bhavapura, east of the Tonlé Sap; *hyang* Pavitra of Haripura, to the north; and Bhas-svamini, daughter of a follower of Vishnu from what is now Laos. *Hyang* Pavitra may have married Jayavarman II after the death of her first husband, Vindvardha.[29] These marriages connected Jayavarman II to ruling families in all parts of Cambodia (see Fig. 2.5). All of the women concerned bore elite titles, *sten, ten* and *hyan*. The male relatives of these women, without exception, became court officials.

Jyestha, daughter of Jayendra[valla]bha, described herself as queen of Sambhupura in 803; there seems no reason not to believe that she was Jaya-varman II's daughter, who inherited the sovereignty of the polity from her mother and ruled while Jayavarman II was busy with conquest and marriage elsewhere. Yet the next ruler of Cambodia is conventionally believed to have been Jayavarman III, son of Jayavarman II by Dharanindradevi.[30] No inscription records the details of how Jayavarman III, who ruled between 834 and 877, came to power. All we know is that he was described as 'a wise king' by the *Brahman* family who officiated at legitimation ceremonies for all Cambodian kings between Jayavarman II and Suryavarman I (r. 1002–1050). Yet an inscription dated 860, commissioned during the reign of Jayavarman III, mentions 'the land of *vrah kamraten an* Indrani'.[31] As noted above, Indrani was the queen of Sambhupura during the first quarter of the eighth century. An establishment venerating this queen was still in existence one and a half centuries after her death. Indravarman I (r. 877–889) erected another statue of Indrani before 881.[32] Evidence suggests that Jyestha, Jayavarman III's half-sister, also formed the basis of a funerary cult; in 895 an emissary of the court, sent to clarify a matter concerning some slaves, determined that they were part of the property belonging to 'the *vrah kamraten an*, the lady Jyestha'.[33] The queens of Sambhupura thus continued to be venerated by the male sovereigns of Cambodia.

Prevailing patriarchal attitudes in nineteenth- and twentieth-century scholarship may have biased a reading of the sources toward primogeniture, when actually this was not the key legitimating aspect of political culture. Indravarman I claimed his right to the throne through neither his position as nephew of Jayavarman II nor as cousin of Jayavarman III, but through his relationship to his mother and her sister – and even more significantly, not in the latter's capacity as the wife of Jayavarman II. Indravarman I erected six temples, dedicated to three pairs of ancestors, at the Preah Ko monument. These were Prthivindradevi and Prthivindravarman, his parents; Rajendradevi and Rudravarman, his mother's parents; and Dharanindradevi and Jayavarman II, his mother's sister and her husband. Prthivindradevi's relationship to Vyadhapura provided Indravarman I with necessary legitimation in that locale. An inscription describes Prthivindradevi as 'born into a family where sovereigns succeeded each other … . [She] became the wife of Prthivindravarman, born in a *kshatriya* family, and had for a son the king, venerated by other kings, named king Indravarman.'[34]

Indravarman I gained control of other polities through marriage in the same manner as Jayavarman II, marrying *ten hyang* Narendra, great-niece of Ayak of Bhavapura who had married Jayavarman II.[35] This queen became known as Indradevi after her marriage, literally 'the queen of Indra'. She was the daughter of Rajendradevi and Mahipateśvara.[36] Indravarman I had another wife, Indralakshmi, 'the fortune of Indra'.[37] The inscription mentioning the latter was found in modern Kompong Cham province, to the south of the site of Bhavapura, southwest of Sambhupura, and northwest of Vyadhapura. It could represent a marriage between Indravarman I and the heiress of one of the small polities that emerged or re-emerged as a result of the assassination of Mahipativarman in the 770s. In any event, there is evidence that Indravarman I was married to two women of relatively equal status: the *Umagangapateśvara* at the Bakong monument. This sculpture depicted the king and two of his queens represented as Śiva with the goddesses Uma, and Ganga. In order to demonstrate his sovereignty over the land in both areas, Indravarman I erected an image that illustrated his relationship to the women through whom he accessed the authority to rule in these places.

Women, 'matriliny', and marriage

A handful of inscriptions wherein elite women describe themselves as queens does not indicate that gender was immaterial when it came to the ultimate political authority in early Cambodia. These women were the exception, not the rule. Yet the fact that elite women, like men, could appeal to different factions amongst the elite for support in their quest for legitimation – and seem to have received it – indicates that female authority in the political realm was not anathema in the earliest Cambodian societies. Michael Vickery has suggested that the genealogies related in Cambodian inscriptions represent a 'conical clan' model, in which primacy is conferred upon each (usually male) member of a generation before passing to the person of highest status in the next.[38] Later successions, such as those of the middle period, corroborate this assertion. Some royal wives would have been regarded as more senior in rank due to their own ties to past kings and queens, relationships to powerful political or religious families, or the personal preference of the king. One of these would usually be referred to as the principal queen but – although a Chinese text states that 'only the sons of the queen, legitimate wife of the king, are permitted to inherit the throne'[39] – this did not prevent the children of lesser queens attempting to accede, as in the case of Rudravarman in the early sixth century. The necessity for determining 'highest status' amongst potentially dozens of half-siblings made cognatic or bilateral kinship important amongst the elite (although not always at other levels of society, as will be discussed presently).[40] Thus in their inscriptions, Jayadevi and Kulaprabhavati drew attention to their relationships to the kings that had preceded them. Jayadevi asserted her relationship to Jayavarman I; Kulaprabhavati emphasised the fact that she was the principle wife of Jayavarman.[41] Jyeshtha, although claiming descent from three queens, also established her relationship to her great-grandfather Indraloka (Pushkaraksha).

At the same time, there is no denying that elements of matriliny are constantly encountered in the records of the early Cambodian polities. These should not, however, be confused with the presence or remnants of a matriarchal society; as Judy Ledgerwood has convincingly argued, matriarchy 'must be divorced from the idea of "matrilineality", with which it has so often been jumbled in literature on Khmer culture'.[42] Kinship reckoning according to the female line was present at all levels of early Cambodian society. Matrilineal descent was also the means by which relationships amongst some Brahman families with hereditary religious positions were established.[43] This was necessary for the simple reason that although many of the privileges and responsibilities were hereditary, the functionaries themselves were often required to remain celibate. Sisters of the original operatives were therefore required to provide male heirs in order to maintain the family's hereditary position at court. There are no examples of brothers fulfilling such a role. The inscriptions always record female slaves with their children, for example *ku kandin 1 koan*,[44] '*ku* Kandin (one child)'. The names of the children's fathers were not recorded. Male slaves were almost always listed separately, but some record seems to have been kept of their relation to particular female slaves. A woman named Prabhasoma was released 'with her [unnamed] sons and grandsons' at a ceremony celebrating the establishment of a linga. Presumably she had fulfilled her duties satisfactorily and earned her freedom. There are no equivalent examples of male slaves being released with their families.

Matrilocality seems to have been the norm amongst the elite, with princes travelling between the many polities in order to marry the inheriting princess of any given locale, then remaining to rule with her there. If we are to accept mythology as indicative of prevailing social norms, then we have some evidence for this in early Funan; the *History of the Liang* records that Hundien and Liu Ye had a son who was sent to another kingdom and governed there.[45] As we have seen from the examples cited above, the custom amongst the ruling elite of early Cambodia was to send their sons to other polities for marriages with princesses therein. Although these princesses would become the principal queen, other elite families in the region would send their daughters and sisters to the palace in order to indicate their clan's fealty; these women would become queens of lesser rank. It was not unusual for sisters to be married to the same man simultaneously. Elite women were regarded as representatives of the land in which they were born. Marriage with the princess of highest status therein at once signified a contract of mutual support and assistance between elite families, in other words, initiating or strengthening a *khsae* affiliation, and established the right of the man involved to rule the 'land', as its representative (in the form of the princess) had given him, in theory at least, permission through sexual union. This is one reason that the women of elite families were often subject to stricter control than other levels of society. Opportunistic men could assert a claim to power through marriage. One family took particular care in issuing an interdict upon potential marriages between its female members and persons of 'low caste', stating that should this occur then the women concerned would lose their inheritance rights.[46]

Marriage alliances were far more than the socially sanctioned union of two individuals. They were political tools of great significance. Thus large numbers of women were maintained by elite men in their households. Families who wished to indicate their loyalty sent representatives in the form of their daughters to the households of powerful elite men. The more representatives of 'land' collected in a man's household, the more 'territory' he ruled, and thus the more support he could command should anyone contest his position. Obviously, the king, as the most powerful man in the kingdom, would have maintained the largest household, full of women who represented covenants between their families and the king. The fact that these women were required to fulfil sexual roles has lead to their misrepresentation as sex slaves. Words such as 'harem' and 'concubine', often used in association with women of the palace in Southeast Asia, and which may or may not be appropriate in the Middle Eastern and East Asian contexts in which they were first invoked, conjure up associations with sexual licentiousness and slavery that demean the women involved and devalue their roles as diplomats, administrators, and practitioners of fine arts.[47] The women who were sent to the palace could become principal wives, lesser wives, or servants and guards; regardless of their function, they represented an agreement between their families and the king, and were accorded perquisites denied to their brothers, such as being entitled to ride elephants. Family members would be accorded special rights and privileges as long as their daughter or sister continued to demonstrate her own sexual and political fealty. Kulaprabhavati, for example, described herself as 'making her family prosper through her majesty'.[48]

Families wishing to secure the services or loyalties of the gatekeepers to supernatural powers, namely the Brahmans, used marriage alliances in this regard as well. The epigraphic record attests to a large number of Brahmans residing at the courts of Cambodian sovereigns throughout the preclassical period. Some of these Brahmans came from distant lands in South Asia and the Malay peninsula, others from Cambodian polities, but all were well-versed in religious texts that could summon the protection or assistance of the gods. The sovereigns of preclassical Cambodia held Brahmans in high esteem, due to their knowledge of the texts that could consecrate land, access the power of the cosmological realm, and provide legitimation for their reigns. Anxious to secure their services, men would marry their daughters to them, thus providing a familial basis for support. The Chinese described a fifth-century polity of the Malay Peninsula, subject to 'Funanese' hegemony, as having over a thousand resident Brahmans from India married to local women.[49] Sobhajaya, daughter of Jayavarman I and sister of Jayadevi, married the Brahman Sakrasvamin, held in high esteem by that queen.[50] The Brahman

34

Durgasvamin was 'honoured by King Isanavarman by the gift of his daughter'. The same inscription goes on to say that the Brahman, 'showered with riches on the occasion of his marriage,' erected a linga in the name of the king.[51] The arrangement was beneficial to all concerned – the Brahman earned wealth and status, the sovereign could access supernatural, legitimating forces. Only the princess may have had reservations. Yet the women who entered into these arrangements had been raised to see their function as more than pawns; they were representatives of their families, who could be called upon to argue their families' interests, state their families' positions on policy, and act as intermediaries.

Beyond the elite

O.W. Wolters debated the propriety of using 'autonomy' to describe preclassical and classical Southeast Asian women, as sources tend to describe the experiences of the elite rather than societies as a whole. Furthermore, the extent to which the sources represent idealised versions rather than common practice cannot be determined.[52] Little is known of the people who existed in the world between the elite and the enslaved. Women in the families of free farmers, artisans, merchants, administrative officials, and scholars most probably participated in the activities associated with these professions, although the historical sources do not furnish details of their exact roles. We do know that for amusement they could attend cock- or pig-fights; their houses were built on stilts and had roofs made out of palm leaves; and communal living was the norm, with up to ten families sharing a pond for water and bathing purposes. Men and women both owned property, including slaves. Women appear to have been able to choose when to bestow property and when not to. The *acharya* Vidyavinaya 'jointly with his wife, gave to the Śivalinga all that he possessed that he had received from Śivadatta'. In another inscription, however, the wife seems to have baulked at handing over all her possessions: a Brahman 'gave to Siddhesvara all the goods he had legally acquired, except the *stridhana* of his wife'.[53] The *stridhana* (literally 'wife goods') seems to have been the absolute property of the wife, usually bequeathed to her daughters. Most abhorrent to the fastidious Chinese, 'boys and girls follow their inclinations without reprisal'.[54] This is perhaps not unexpected in a matrilineal (or bilateral) society, where any children would be absorbed into the maternal family as contributing members.

The duties and conditions of women designated 'slaves' by epigraphists were varied. Although the term 'slave' in the Western sense is probably inappropriate, there is no doubt that these people were not free, as they could be exchanged for land. Those attached to temples could be 'freed', thereby indicating that they were not before. Some people seem to have become slaves through the failure to pay debts; others were taken by force from hill tribes and as prisoners of war. The Chinese recorded that the fifth-century Funanese took 'by force the inhabitants of nearby towns that do not pay them tribute, and make them into their slaves'.[55] This resulted in peoples who were not Funanese or Khmer serving in Cambodian households and temples. K.76 includes in its list of temple workers the following phrases: *knyum rman ta si* 'Mon slaves that are male' and *knyum rman ta kantai* 'Mon slaves that are female'.[56] There appears to have been very little difference between female slaves, the *ku*, and their male counterparts, the *va*. Usually inscriptions listed them separately, as 'slaves that are male' followed by a list of *va*, and 'slaves that are female' with a list of *ku* and their *koan*, 'children'.[57] Occasionally the term *kantai gui koan* (name or number of children) was used in a list of male slaves to indicate that his wives and children accompanied a male slave. The ratio of male to female slaves was approximately 1:2, indicating that polygamy may have operated in this social stratum as well as in that of the elite.[58] Both men and women toiled in the rice paddies, picked fruit in the orchards, and harvested crops in the fields. As a group they appear to have had ties to particular people rather than places, as donors gave, removed and redistributed them to religious personages and communities at will. Those with particular talents might find themselves employed in cooking, weaving, spinning, singing, dancing, or playing musical instruments.[59] Female singers, dancers and musicians received elegant names such as Vasantamallika, 'Jasmine blossom', and Rohini, a goddess. Some women were called names like 'Born-for-love', 'She-who-laughs-for-penis' and 'She-who-eats-penis', although it is unclear whether these were due to the characters of the persons so named or a reference to the acts they performed. If the latter, there is evidence to suggest that sexual duties were not universally popular; one inscription records a *ku* known as 'Penis-hater'. Male slaves also received names of this type, such as 'Catch-him-if-you-want-him' and 'Mischievous-penis'.[60]

A special subset of female 'slaves' has been difficult to define: the *kantai kloñ*,[61] 'assigned' to duties within religious establishments throughout the sixth, seventh and eighth centuries. They have no equivalent male cohort. *Kantai* translates as 'female' or 'women'. *Kloñ* implies elite status. The most likely translation of *kantai kloñ* is 'women belonging to the *kloñ*',[62] although Cœdès once translated the term as 'female slaves of the *kloñ mratāñ*'.[63] Furthermore, these women were 'donated' to deities by an elite male functionary.[64] Two inscriptions list *kantai* who have elite status indicator suffixes.[65] In at least two inscriptions it seems clear that the *kantai kloñ* acted as substitutes for the *mratāñ* within the religious community.[66] It has been suggested that the kantai kloñ may have been women related to or otherwise associated with the principal donor, who occupied ritual positions within the temples. One of these may have been the pouring of libations upon sacred fires.[67] The practice of women entering religious communities through the offices of a male relative may reflect a social convention whereby superfluous womenfolk with poor marriage prospects or no means of their own were absorbed into the temples. In this way the burden of their maintenance would be removed from their relatives. Or perhaps these women were required, through meditation and the performance of rituals, to create merit, which was then directed to their benefactor. These are merely suggestions, however, as there is nothing in the inscriptions to support or contradict such assertions. Apart from this one institution, there seems to have been little difference in gender roles, rights and responsibilities beyond the elite. In fact, it appears that in the earliest periods of Cambodian history, women at all levels of society were seen as necessary and vital components, with important skills and abilities, and ideological significance.

Notes to Chapter 2

1   Michael Vickery, 'What and where was Chenla?', in F. Bizot (ed.), *Recherches nouvelles sur le Cambodge*, Paris: École Française d'Extrême-Orient, 1994, p. 199; O. W. Wolters, *Early Indonesian commerce*, Ithaca, New York: Cornell University Press, 1965, pp. 152–153.

2   See Michael Vickery, 'Funan reviewed: Deconstructing the ancients', *Bulletin de l'École Française d'Extrême-Orient* [hereafter *BEFEO*] 90–91 (2003–2004), pp. 101–143.

3   Paul Pelliot, 'Le Fou-nan', *BEFEO* 3 (1903), p. 256. The *History of the Southern Qi* records her name as Liu Ye, 'Willow Leaf', although the dynastic histories vary slightly, for example Ye Ye, 'Coconut Leaf'. Interestingly, willows do not grow in Cambodia.

4   Louis Finot, 'Les inscriptions de Mi-son', *BEFEO* vol. 4 (1904), pp. 897–977, III, lines 16–18.

5   Ian Mabbett and David Chandler make the point that this inscription was found in an area that is recognised as a key site of Champa (*The Khmers,* Oxford; Cambridge,

Massachusetts: Blackwell, 1995, p. 71). This does not necessarily mean that it was a Cham inscription, however. An explanation could lie in that there are at least two kings named Bhavavarman in the preclassical epigraphy of Cambodia; it appears, therefore, to have been a popular name for kings. Furthermore, the extents of the territories of respective sovereigns have never been successfully delineated. It is not impossible that the author of the Vo Canh stela was a Bhavavarman who was the king of another preclassical Cambodian polity such as Sambhupura, perhaps unknown from any other source.

6   Vickery cites Tai peoples in Chiang Mai, Thailand, and the Nung in southern China and northern Vietnam (*Society, economics, and politics in pre-Angkorian Cambodia: The 7th–8th centuries,* Tokyo: The Center for East Asian Cultural Studies for UNESCO, 1998, p. 253, note 148).

7   David P. Chandler, 'Royally sponsored human sacrifices in nineteenth century Cambodia: The cult of *nak ta* Me Sa (Mahisasuramardini) at Ba Phnom', *Journal of the Siam Society* 67 (1979), pp. 54–62 (also in *Facing the Cambodian past: Selected essays 1971–1994,* St Leonards, New South Wales: Allen & Unwin, 1996, pp. 119–136); Vickery, *Society, economics, and politics,* p. 157.

8   There is no extant evidence in Cambodia for the existence of a Brahma cult, although the god was honoured in conjunction with Śiva and Vishnu, and even, very rarely, alone.

9   K. 132, verse 1, *Inscriptions du Cambodge,* 8 vols, Paris and Hanoi: Imprimerie de l' *l'École Française d'Extrême-Orient* and Imprimerie Nationale [hereafter *IC*], vol. 2, p. 85.

10   K. 875, verse 1, in George Cœdès, 'A new inscription from Fu-nan', *Journal of the Greater India Society,* vol. 4 (1937), pp. 112–121.

11   Pelliot, 'Le Fou-nan', p. 270.

12   K. 40, verses 1, 4, in George Cœdès, 'Études cambodgiennes 25: Deux inscriptions sanskrites du Fou-nan', *BEFEO* vol. 31 (1931), pp. 1–12.

13   K. 40, verse 6.

14   Cœdès, 'Stèle du bàrày occidental (K. 904)', *IC* 4, p. 55; Lawrence Palmer Briggs, *The ancient Khmer empire,* Philadelphia, Pennsylvania: The American Philosophical Society, 1951, p. 57.

15   Pierre Dupont, 'La dislocation du Tchen-la et la formation du Cambodge angkorien (VIIe-IXe siècle)', *BEFEO* 43 (1943–46), p. 54; Claude Jacques, ''Funan', 'Zhenla': The reality concealed by these Chinese views of Indochina', in R.B. Smith and W. Watson (eds), *Early Southeast Asia: Essays in archaeology, history, and historical geography,* New York and Kuala Lumpur: Oxford University Press, 1979, p. 376; Mabbett and Chandler, *Khmers,* pp. 79–80; Vickery, 'What and where was Chenla?', p. 210.

16   K. 7, lines 2–5, George Cœdès, 'Etudes cambodgiennes 31: A Propos du Tchen-la d'eau: trois inscriptions de Cochinchine', *BEFEO* 36 (1936), p. 272.

17   K. 6, lines 1, 7–9, Cœdès, 'A propos du Tchen–la d'eau', p. 274.

18   Briggs, *Ancient Khmer empire,* p. 58. It is interesting to speculate upon how x(a) could have been the first ruler of Śambhupura if that polity was founded by Śambhuvarman,

as Briggs asserts – surely the person who established the polity could reasonably be expected to rule it?

19 K. 124, verse 1, lines 3–7, *IC* 3, pp. 170–174.

20 K. 124, line 23.

21 Vickery, 'What and where was Chenla?', p. 208.

22 Digraphic Inscriptions, verse 3. The Digraphic Inscriptions comprise twelve identical inscriptions (K. 42, K. 45, K. 47, K. 57, K. 95, K. 101, K. 110, K. 223, K. 309, K. 323, K. 346, K. 362) commissioned by Yaśovarman I (r. 889–912) erected in 889. The inscription referred to in this instance is K. 323, in *Inscriptions sanscrites du Cambodge*, ed. and comp. Auguste Barth, vols. 1 & 2 in *Notices et extraits des manuscrits de la Bibliotheque nationale et autres bibliotheques, publies par l'Institut national de France faisant suite aux notices et extraits lus au comite etabli dans l'Academie des inscriptions et belles-lettres*, Paris: Imprimerie Nationale, 1885, pp. 391–411.

23 K. 713, verse A4, *IC* 1, pp. 18–29.

24 For a more detailed treatment of this section, see Trudy Jacobsen, 'Autonomous queenship in Cambodia, 1st–9th centuries AD', *Journal of the Royal Asiatic Society*, n.s. 3, vol. 13, 3 (November 2003), pp. 357–375.

25 Briggs, *Ancient Khmer Empire*, p. 69. No Cambodian sources record this event so it is perhaps best to regard the decapitation as a metaphor for a particular Cambodian polity's loss of political autonomy.

26 George Cœdès, 'Piédroits de Lobōk Sròt (K. 134 et 135)', *IC* 2, p. 92; Claude Jacques, 'La carrière de Jayavarman II', *BEFEO* 59 (1972), pp. 194–220.

27 Vickery, 'What and where was Chenla?', p. 208.

28 K. 95, verse 12, R.C. Majumdar, *Inscriptions of Kambuja*, Calcutta: The Asiatic Society, 1953, p. 77; K. 713, verse A4; K. 989, lines B8–B11, B14, K. 989, face B, lines 8, 10–11, *IC* 7, p.175; K. 449, verses 12, 13–14, 27–28, in George Cœdès, 'Études cambodgiennes 11: La stele de Palhal', *BEFEO* 13, 6 (1913), pp. 43–52.

29 K. 382, verses 5 and 9, *IC* 6, pp. 270–271; K. 956, lines 9, 15–17, *IC* 7, pp. 128–135; K. 449, verse 12; K. 277, verse B3, verses A2–A6, *IC* 4, p. 155.

30 O.W. Wolters, 'Jayavarman II's military power: The territorial foundation of the Angkor empire', *Journal of the Royal Asiatic Society*, vol. 36, 1 (1973), p. 25.

31 K. 774, lines 1–7, *IC* 4, pp. 64–65.

32 K. 806, verse 32, *IC* 1, pp. 73–137.

33 K. 774, lines 8–12.

34 K. 713, verse A4.

35 K. 956, lines 7–14.

36 Briggs was convinced, due to the similarity of the names, that Mahipateśvara was the Mahipativarman beheaded by the king of 'Zabag' in the 770s. This is not likely, however. Indradevi would have had to be born, or at least conceived, before 775. The earliest date

that Indravarman I could have been born was around 825. This would make Indradevi fifty years older than Indravarman I and around seventy years old when Yaśovarman I was born. Clearly, Indradevi could not have been the daughter of the king beheaded in the 770s. An alternative explanation could be that Indradevi was the name by which Narendra was known after her marriage to Indravarman I. *Indradevi* translates as 'queen of Indra'. There is no reason that Pavitra and the *kamraten an vrah mula, ten hyang* Narendra's parents, could not have been Rajendradevi and Mahipateśvara. In fact, there is very good reason for identifying the *kamraten an vrah mula* with Mahipateśvara. *Kamraten an vrah mula* can be interpreted as 'the *kamraten an* of the royal [or holy] family'. The implication is that he was the chief of a royal or sacerdotal family. Mahipateśvara can mean 'great lord Śiva', possibly a reference to the name of a political leader, or the name of the principal officiant of Śaiva cult. See Briggs, *Ancient Khmer empire*, p. 98.

37 K. 91, lines A17–B1, *IC* 2, pp. 126–136. Although Cœdès believed that the use of this term implied that Indralakshmi was the principal queen, there is no evidence that this was the case. For his comments see 'Stèle de Kok Trapan Srok (K.91)', p. 131.

38 Michael Vickery, 'The reign of Suryavarman I and royal factionalism at Angkor', *Journal of Southeast Asian Studies* 16, 2 (1985), p. 243.

39 Ma Duanlin [12th/13th century], *Ethnographie des peuples étrangers à la Chine, ouvrage composé à XI siècle du notre ère*, vol. 2, Geneva: Mueller, 1883, p. 479.

40 An additional factor in legitimation was the need to establish the claimant's superior ability to draw upon supernatural forces.

41 K. 259, lines 32–34, *IC* 7, pp. 50–57.

42 Judy L. Ledgerwood, 'Khmer kinship: the matriliny/matriarchy myth', *Journal of Anthropological Research* 51, 3 (1995), pp. 247–262 at p. 255.

43 See for example K. 49, line 3, *IC* 2, pp. 183–185; K. 762, verses 6–10, *IC* 1, pp. 13–14; Thomas A. Kirsch, 'Kinship, genealogical claims, and societal integration in ancient Khmer society: An interpretation', in C.D. Cowan and O.W. Wolters (eds), *Southeast Asian history and historiography: Essays presented to D.G.E. Hall*, Ithaca, New York; London: Cornell University Press, 1976, pp. 190–202 at p. 199. The kinship term *kanmoy kamton* may also designate a nephew through the female line. See George Cœdès, 'Stèle de Vàt Thleñ (K. 1)', *IC* 1, p. 30, note 6.

44 K. 430, line 10, *IC* 6, p. 44.

45 Pelliot, 'Le Fou-nan', p. 265.

46 K. 444, ll. B2–B4, B7–B9.

47 See Barbara Watson Andaya, *The flaming womb: Repositioning women in early modern Southeast Asia*, Honolulu: University of Hawai'i Press, 2006, pp. 172–178; Tamara Loos, 'Sex in the Inner City: The fidelity between sex and politics in Siam', *Journal of Asian Studies* 64, 4 (November 2005), p. 884.

48 K. 875, verse 2.

49 Pelliot, 'Le Fou-nan', 279.

50   K. 904, verses 3–4.

51   K. 436, verses 2, 3–4, *IC* 4, p. 27.

52   O.W. Wolters, *History, culture, and region in Southeast Asian perspectives*, rev. ed., Ithaca, New York: Southeast Asia Program Publications, Cornell University; Singapore: Institute of Southeast Asian Studies, 1999, p. 167.

53   K. 54, section 1, verse 3, lines 5–6, 7, *IC* 3, p. 159; K. 77, verse 4, *IC* 5, p. 47.

54   Pelliot, 'Le Fou-nan', pp. 261, 270.

55   *Ibid.*, p. 261.

56   K. 76, lines 2, 5, *IC* 5, p. 8.

57   For example, K. 109n, lines 12, 17, *IC* 5, p. 43.

58   K. 726 (*IC* 5, p. 83) records the donation of one male and two females with a package of rice fields, cultivatable land and oxen. The sense is that this was a family unit of a husband and two wives.

59   K. 134, lines 14–17; K. 138, line 13, *IC* 5, p. 19; K. 557e, lines 1–2, *IC* 6, p. 22; Jacob, 'Pre-Angkor Cambodia', p. 409.

60   K. 557e, line 3, *IC* 6, p. 23; K. 66, line 12, *IC* 2, p. 53.; K. 74, lines 5, 6, *IC* 6, p. 18; Vickery, *Society, Economics, and Politics*, p. 250; Jacob, 'Pre-Angkor Cambodia', p. 412.

61   In K. 137 they are referred to as *kloñ kantai* (*IC* 2, p. 116). Some scholars refer to them as *kantai khloñ*.

62   Cœdès, K. 562, *IC* 2, p.107, translation lines 1–2.

63   George Cœdès, 'Inscription d'Angkor Bórĕi (K. 557 et 600), *IC* 6, p. 23.

64   K. 600, line 9, *IC* 6, p. 22; K. 137, line 5; K. 66, face B, lines 1–3; K. 54/55, line I.11; Vickery, *Society, Economics, and Politics*, p. 217.

65   K. 137, lines 6–9; K. 816, lines 1–2, *IC* 6, p. 64.

66   K. 66, face B, line 6; K. 137, lines 6–8.

67   Louis Malleret, *La Culture du Funan* vol 3 in *L 'archéologie du delta du Mékong*, Paris: École Française d'Extrême–Orient, 1959–1963, p. 294; Vickery, *Society, Economics, and Politics*, p. 217.

CHAPTER THREE

Behind the Apsara

*I*n the ninth century, the Cambodian court was relocated to a site on the northern side of the Tonlé Sap, in what is now Siem Reap province. Originally called Yaśodharapura after the king who caused it to be built, Yaśovarman I (r. 889–912), over time the city became known as *Maha-Nagara*, 'Great City', gradually distorting to 'Angkor'. At first glance it would appear that in this classical age between the ninth and fifteenth centuries we find the origin of the decline in power for Cambodian women. The inscriptions reveal no autonomously ruling queens. The Khmer origin myth dating from this time depicts the female protagonist as passive and dependent upon her male relatives. The inscriptions and epigraphy represent goddesses as inferior to their male counterparts. Yet women of the classical period continued to enjoy similar social rights and roles to those they had had in the preceding period, including property ownership, important positions at court, education, participation in economic and religious life, and a relaxed attitude towards female sexuality at the non-elite level. Most significantly, women continued to be perceived as human manifestations of the land. In fact, once the importance of women in classical Cambodian political legitimation is recognised, the problems of succession that have confused scholars are removed.[1]

A fall from grace?

Goddesses began to lose their autonomous representation in the ninth century and became increasingly depicted with their male

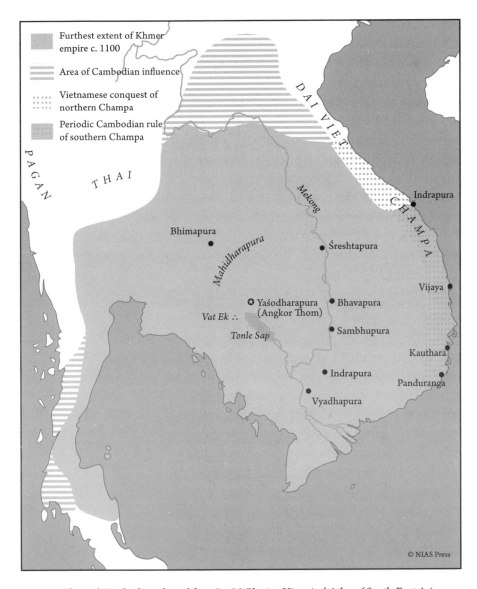

Fig. 3.1: Classical Cambodia. Adapted from Jan M. Pluvier, *Historical Atlas of South-East Asia*.

counterparts. Images of goddesses were erected not for the glory of the goddess, but to honour the god upon whom her existence depended. The *śakti*, or female aspect, of the god was acknowledged, and inscriptions often invoked both male and female divinities' goodwill and protection. Yet the goddess's position as a wife, subject to the will of her husband, was emphasised. There was never an autonomous *śakti* cult in classical Cambodia; the status of a goddess was represented as inferior to that of the god. For example, Uma was never represented as Durga Mahishasuramardani after the eighth century. Instead, she was increasingly perceived as either acting in concert with Śiva or as dependent upon him. Lakshmi and Sarasvati also became increasingly identified as dependent upon their male counterparts during the classical period. A dual form of Śiva and Uma, expressed as *Bhavau* or *Iśvarau* and known from Indian *Purana* texts, was particularly popular in Cambodia during the tenth century; at this time pairs of gods and goddesses were common (see Fig. 3.2).[2] This complementary representation of the male and female aspects of the divine soon devolved into depictions of the male as superior, however. Furthermore, the term *kpoñ*, an honorific preceding the goddesses perceived

Fig. 3.2: *Gauriśvara*, a dual form of Śiva and Uma riding the bull Nandin. Banteay Srei temple, 10th century. (Photograph by the author.)

44

as having local origins such as Durga Mahishasuramardani and Sarasvati, disappeared from the epigraphic record after the ninth century.[3] This is further evidence of a move away from earlier cultural traditions.

The representation of goddesses as correlative or dependent upon male gods was accompanied by a growing emphasis on the value of physical beauty in the inscriptions.[4] Physical perfection was a woman 'of slender and pale body, of white breasts, shining like the Ganga'.[5] Nowhere was this ideal represented as obviously as in the development of the *apsara*, a category of female divinity able to change shape at will and move between the celestial and mundane worlds, in Cambodian art and architecture. Prior to the ninth century, *apsara* were unknown in the Cambodian artistic tradition. Indravarman I inaugurated their incorporation into temple decoration, accompanied by *devata*, female door-guardians. *Apsara* were depicted in the *bas*-reliefs of temples as celestial dancers, renowned for grace, beauty and lust. They congregated near sites associated with death, in order to capture the souls of the dead men. Rambha, in some ways the original *apsara*, having been engendered by the churning of the milky ocean, was described as lurking at the battlefield in wait for the dead.[6] The only other *apsara* named in Cambodian epigraphy is Tilottama, mentioned in an inscription extolling the virtues of the queen Vijayendralakshmi.[7] According to mythology, Tilottama was created for the express purpose of arousing desire in the *asura* ('demon') brothers Sunda and Upasunda and causing rivalry between them. The capacity to arouse desire, and thus exert control over men, can be interpreted as an aspect of female power. A Banteay Srei pediment depicts the *asura*s fighting over the right to possess Tilottama.

Fidelity, chastity, and the observance of duty were the desired qualities in women, according to the inscriptions. Wives were supposed to be devoted to their husbands and their gods, industrious, and of good conduct.[8] One inscription implied that Lakshmi, Sarasvati and Uma were changed by their consorts in order to become more pleasing to the men. The goddesses acted as role models for their mundane counterparts. Despite these admonitions for fidelity and right conduct, the inscriptions relate that it was often difficult for women to restrain themselves upon observing the splendid specimens of manhood that were the classical Cambodian kings. 'It was hard for pretty women to conduct themselves in a virtuous manner when he gave them a glance' says an inscription of Suryavarman I. A mixture of sex and violence pervades many of the inscriptions. Jayavarman V was 'inflamed by [Lakshmi]' yet 'virtuous'; he 'tried to prevent others from ravishing the women of his supporters' yet could not resist their charms himself. Elsewhere a king 'wore on his body the marks of amorous games that his courtesans tore.' Suryavarman I seemed to have approached territorial conquest with the same enthusiasm as he approached his consorts. 'Toward the enemy army he was as towards a beautiful young woman, without blemish, who was given ... for his amusement'; 'in battle, the violent blows that the enemy dealt him with all their might affected him as if they were the bites and scratches of women'; and 'in combat for the conquest of Lakshmi, the sharp sword with which the enemy struck him with excited his sensibilities, as if it was a woman's tooth.' The wives of the kings' enemies were the recipients of particular violence in the inscriptions. An especially esoteric inscription describes Jayavarman VII 'in the pleasure of battle, in voluptuous contact with the erect tusks of those women who are the elephants of the enemies.'[9]

Tenth-century and subsequent representations of women in the celestial realm mirror the shift toward female dependence in mythology. As we have seen, early Cambodian goddesses were perceived as autonomous wielders of power, independent from male deities. In preclassical versions of Cambodian origin mythology, the female protagonist participated in political activities at her own inclination and without the intercession of a male figure. In the classical period, the women of the legend were represented as passive appurtenances of their male counterparts. The Khmer creation myth, although similar to that of Funan and the Vo Canh inscription, differs significantly. The female protagonist, Mera, was described as 'most renowned of beautiful deities', but not as an active participant in events. The *maharishi* Kambu Svayambhuva arrived from 'Aryadesa' and encountered the Naga-king who 'owned' the land. Kambu was invited by the Naga-king to remain in the land due to their common veneration of the god Śiva. Later, Kambu married Mera, who had been given 'as a daughter' to the Naga-king by Śiva. After the marriage, Kambu ruled over the land, which came to be called after him (*Kambuja*, 'born of Kambu', evolving to *Kamboja*).[10] At the end of the thirteenth century, the Chinese observer Zhou Daguan reported that the king of Cambodia was required to copulate each night with a serpent-spirit that appeared in the guise of a beautiful woman. If he failed to maintain the tradition, catastrophe would befall the kingdom.[11]

46

The theme of a foreign male marrying the female heiress or guardian of the land in order to rule is familiar from the earlier mythology. However, unlike Liu Ye or Soma, Mera never ruled the land herself. Furthermore, Mera is repeatedly 'given' from one male actor to another. Śiva bestowed Mera upon his loyal adherent, the Naga-king, in order to establish an alliance with Kambu as a fellow Śaivite. Mera, therefore, was never autonomous. Her importance existed only in her relationship to the men of the story and the bond she created between them. Yet, like Liu Ye and Soma, the power of sovereignty resided in Mera, for Kambu was only able to rule the land *after* his marriage.

Rajendravarman II (r. 944–968), Jayavarman V (r. 968–1001), and Jayavarman VII (r. 1181–c. 1220) all traced their lineage to both Soma/Kaundinya and Mera/Kambu. This reinforces the assertion that the Funanese and the Khmer to the north were acknowledged as ancestors of later Cambodians. This raises questions, however, regarding the legitimacy of the Kambu/Mera legend as an established creation myth in preclassical Cambodia. If it existed, why were there no epigraphic references to Kambu and Mera from preclassical Khmer kings such as Viravarman, Mahendravarman, Bhavavarman II and Iśanavarman I? Why was Mera depicted as passive and dependent when Liu Ye and Soma were represented as active and autonomous? Is this a metaphor for an imposition of patriarchal values on a more egalitarian society?

The absence of preclassical references to Kambu and Mera does not mean that this legend was not part of the earlier cultural heritage of the Khmer. There is no evidence, however, that it was the means by which preclassical Khmer rulers established their legitimacy. The legend must therefore be considered in its classical context. The first time that the Kambu/Mera legend was incorporated into a genealogy was during the reign of Rajendravarman II. Five kings reigned between the death of Yaśovarman I in 912 and the accession of Rajendravarman II, all of whom were the latter's cousins or uncles. Moreover, other relatives could claim sovereignty through the same lines. Rajendravarman II required additional support for his accession. A claim to sovereignty on the basis of a relationship to the original possessor of sovereignty would have been a significant legitimating factor. Jayavarman V incorporated this legend into his own genealogy, as he was the son of Rajendravarman II and could reasonably be expected to reiterate his father's legitimacy as his own.

Two and a half centuries later, Jayavarman VII claimed descent from Kambu and Mera in the genealogy legitimising his accession.[12] Like Rajendravarman

II, Jayavarman VII faced obstacles to his accession. His brother, Yasovarman II (r. c. 1160–c. 1168), had been assassinated by a court official who assumed the throne under the name Tribhuvanadityavarman (r. c. 1168–1178). Jayavarman VII did not accede until 1181, although Tribhuvanadityavarman had been killed during the Cham invasion of 1178. This could be interpreted as further evidence that Jayavarman VII had to establish his claim to the throne by extraordinary means. Again, claiming descent from the initial possessor of sovereignty would have bolstered the aspiring ruler's claim to the throne.

When the Kambu–Mera union was invoked in genealogies of the classical period, Kambu was portrayed as active and Mera as passive. The name of the male protagonist, Kambu Svayambhuva, translates as 'Kambu, the self-creating' or 'self-existent', clearly a metaphor for autonomy. He was also described as powerful. Mera, in contrast, was described more as an ornament than a person. Beautiful and celestial, she was 'elevated to the highest heaven as the queen' of Kambu.[13] Liu Ye and Soma were not described in terms of physical beauty. In fact, nothing is recorded about their appearance at all – although one version of the legend preserved in the Chinese annals states that Liu Ye was 'young and strong, and resembled a boy.'[14] However, this is more likely a reflection of prevailing Chinese constructs of masculinity and femininity than those of preclassical Cambodia. In the classical period, no reference was made to Soma as an independent sovereign before her marriage to Kaundinya. Clearly, something happened after the ninth century that affected Cambodian perceptions of women as expressed in the origin myth.

Indian Brahmans had settled in Southeast Asian courts, bolstering the claims of local sovereigns to the throne by conferring religious legitimacy. Indian Brahmanical society did not accept autonomy for women. In fact, in the words of the classical Indian pandit Manu, women should be transferred from their fathers to their husbands to their sons. Similarly, Mera was transferred from the 'protection' of the god Śiva to the Naga-king to Kambu. At no stage did she exhibit independent thought or choice. She was, therefore, the model of obedient womanhood as espoused by Brahmanical literature. The origin myth of the Khmer elite in the tenth century reflected the patriarchal tenets of Brahmanical religion that served to legitimise (male) rulers of the classical period.

In the previous chapter we saw that Jayavarman II successfully established himself as the king of at least six early Cambodian polities through marriage alliances with inheriting princesses or queens, making their male relatives important members of his court and bestowing land and titles upon their families. He further bolstered his position through the protection of super-natural forces. Thus Jayavarman II ordered his trusted official and brother-in-law Prthivinarendra to perform a ceremony that ensured the autonomy of Kambuja from Java. The Sdok Kak Thom inscription of 1052 relates that

> Parmeśvara invited [the Brahman named Hiranyadama] to officiate at a ritual by which it was made impossible for Kambuja-deśa to submit to Java, as by this he made possible the existence of a sole master of the earth, who was a *cakravartin*.[15]

Hiranyadama passed the secret legitimation ritual to another Brahman, Śivakaivalya, and 'declared that the line of Śivakaivalya should officiate at the *devaraja* [ritual], saying that is was forbidden for others to do so'.[16] Control over the legitimating ritual was effectively transferred to the power of Śivakaivalya and his descendants. They maintained this control for over two hundred years. When this particular family was superceded, however, another Brahman was placed in charge of the legitimating ritual. Cambodian kings therefore had good reason to remain on good terms with their Brahmans, which is why so many marriage alliances were transacted between royal and sacerdotal families.[17] These legitimating and familial relationships would have made it difficult for kings to reject Brahmanical values or their commitment in the epigraphy and iconography of their reigns.

This, then, is the explanation for the apparent decline in female autonomy and agency after the ninth century. Inscriptions of the classical period contend that kings succeeded to the thrones of Vyadhapura and Śambhupura, whereas the preclassical epigraphy indicates that some queens ruled. This was overlooked when the classical kings came to commit their genealogies to stone. As was the case with the passivity of Mera in the creation mythology espoused during the classical period, it is likely that the later genealogies reflect the influence of a more patriarchal social perspective. Yet it is incorrect to assume that the absence of women from positions of power and autonomy in the inscriptions and sculpture of the period meant a corresponding loss of significance for elite women.

The kanlong kamraten an

Yaśovarman I (889–912) demonstrated his right to rule bilaterally, as represented in the Lolei monument, built in 893. Two of the six towers were never completed, but the other four are dedicated to Indradevi and Indravarman I, his parents, and Rajendradevi and Mahipateśvara, his mother's parents. Like his predecessors, Yaśovarman I maintained the tradition of honouring his relatives from his mother's side. Jayayudha, an official at the court of Yaśovarman I, erected an image of *kanlong kamraten an* Jayamaheśvari in the 'field of victory', probably a battlefield. The same inscription refers to victory over 'Champa and others'. The stela itself was found at the monument of Prasat Tasar Sadam in what is now Siem Reap province. A later inscription may refer to this queen under the name *kamraten an śri jayakshetra* – literally, 'holy queen of the field of victory'.[18]

Jayamaheśvari cannot have been Yaśovarman I's mother, as her image at Lolei, under the name Indradevi, was given 'a dwelling, flowers and jewels' by Jayayudha at the same time.[19] Similarly, Jayamaheśvari was not Yaśovarman I's grandmother Rajendradevi. The only other contenders for an elite female relative of Yaśovarman I would be his wives and his sisters. No inscriptions record the names of Yaśovarman I's wives. The names of two of his sisters are known, however. Jayamaheśvari was probably Yaśovarman I's elder sister Mahendradevi (see Fig. 3.3). Her husband, Mahendravarman, was descended from the rulers of Aninditapura.[20] Their son, Rajendravarman II, claimed sovereignty through his mother and father, not through his relationship to Yaśovarman I. Historians, with a few exceptions, never emphasise this point; and yet once this is accepted the succession methodology of classical Cambodia becomes clear.

Many royal women of the classical period were posthumously entitled *kanlong kamraten an*. Usually they were not referred to by name but by place, underscoring the relationship between women and the land. One particularly popular funerary cult, known from many inscriptions, refers to the focus of veneration as '*kanlong kamraten an* Anve Tonlé'. This 'queen of the lake' was particularly associated with the reigns of Rajendravarman II and his son, Jayavarman V. In 952, during the reign of Rajendravarman II, a *mratan* offered land to 'the god of Lingapura and the *kanlong kamraten an* Anve Tonlé'. The land had originally been given to the two previously and had fallen into disuse. The impression of the inscription, therefore, is that the funerary cult had already been in existence for some time. More donations followed during the reign of Jayavarman V. In 972 the deceased queen, designated 'the elder', gave gifts to 'the other statues' of her sanctuary. Jayavarman V gave the

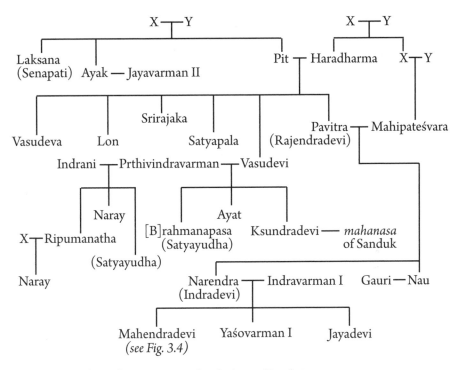

Fig. 3.3: Antecedents of Yaśovarman I, Mahendradevi and Jayadevi.

kanlong a gold leaf in 974. In 978 Yogeśvara offered the *kanlong kamraten an* Anve Tonlé a palanquin of gold. The following year, 'a Bhagavati Mahishasura was erected there in the image of the *kanlong kamraten an* Anve Tonlé'. This is one of the two known references to Durga Mahishasuramardani that occur in the classical period. It cannot be a coincidence that this powerful queen was immortalised in the tradition of early Cambodian autonomous goddesses. During the reign of Jayaviravarman an admonition was added to a stela in the area re-emphasizing the claims of the *kanlong kamraten an* Anve Tonlé to a forest donated in 952. Later still, an inscription of Harshavarman III (1066–1080) recorded that land was restored to the *kanlong kamraten an* in 1071.[21]

Jayavarman IV, husband of Jayadevi and father of Harshavarman II, is not mentioned in any of Rajendravarman II's inscriptions, although the maternal relatives of Rajendravarman II received apotheosis. Rajendravarman II erected an image of 'the daughter of the mountain … in the likeness of Jayadevi, mother of King Harshadeva [Harshvarman II], and younger sister of his mother'.[22] He also established a statue in honour of his younger cousin, Harshavarman II, who died after reigning for one year.[23] There is, therefore, an excellent reason for attributing the identity of Jayamaheśvari to Mahendradevi. Clearly, the women of that area were regarded as representatives and emanations of the land. We may go one step further and identify Jayamaheśvari as the *kanlong kamraten an* Anve Tonlé. Who was Rajendravarman II likely to accord such respect, if not his own mother, through whom he laid claim to sovereignty? Furthermore, the sepulchre of the *kanlong kamraten an* Anve Tonlé was also known as the Rajaguha, 'royal cave'. It cannot refer to the cult of Narendradevi, who died in 968, as an inscription dated between 958 and 967 speaks of a slave and his parents as having been born 'in the vicinity of the Rajaguha'.[24] Goods were offered to this *kanlong kamraten an* by high-ranking court officials in 966 and 967.[25] There is probably a pun in the use of Rajaguha; *guha* can also mean 'womb'. The meaning of Rajaguha could therefore be construed as 'royal womb'.

The tradition of immortalising royal women from this family continued for the next two generations. In 979 Jayavarman V directed three dignitaries and an elite religious instructor to donate their land along the river to other elite persons so that they could establish villages and erect images of deities and members of their family. The persons whose images were erected were Rajapativarman, a general and brother-in-law of Jayavarman V; an unnamed *ten kamraten an*, mother of Narapativiravarman and Jayayudhavarman, the commissioners of the images; and a *ten* Tvan, who was the mother of the *ten kamraten an*, Rajapativarman, and Jayavarman V's wife. K. 356 mentions these people, but adds that Narapativiravarman was the elder brother of Udayadityavarman I (1001–1002). It seems clear that Jayayudhavarman was Udayadityavarman I. Following the end of Udayadityavarman I's reign, a king named Jayaviravarman appeared. He issued an inscription in the year of his accession asserting the rights of the *kanlong kamraten an* Anve Tonlé to a piece of land under dispute.[26] Jayaviravarman was none other than Udayadityavarman I's elder brother, Narapativiravarman.

The *kanlong kamrate an* Anve Tonlé was joined by Narendradevi, chief queen of Rajendravarman II, almost immediately after the death of her husband in 968. The princess Indralakshmi, their daughter, 'erected with love' an image of her mother during this year. A ceremony commemorating the death of Narendradevi was carried out by Divakara, husband of Indralakshmi, in 972. Indralakshmi herself died in this year and was incorporated into the funerary cult. Narendradevi was recorded as offering slaves in this year to the *vrah kam-raten an* of Dvijendrapura and to her daughter, 'the image of princess *kamraten an* Indralakshmi'. At the time of her death Divakara erected 'an image ... of his dear Indralakshmi' and the *kanlong kamraten an* Anve Tonlé gave gifts to the other statues of the temple – clearly, Narendradevi and Indralakshmi.[27]

The funerary cult of one *kanlong kamraten an* thrived into the eleventh century. In 1037, functionary named Rajapativarman commissioned an inscription asking the incumbent king, Suryavarman I, to take into consideration the merits of the head of a family of scribes from what is now the province of Preah Vihear.

> He conserved with zeal the list of goods received ... he had a family who guarded the writing concerning the family of Kambu and the diverse departments of royal service, the writing concerning the high acts of sovereigns, since King Śrutavarman, until those of his majesty ... related to King Indravarman ... and the queen Viraralakshmi of Vrac Vrah Sruk, of the royalty [i.e. the family] of King Harshavarman who has gone to Rudraloka, and King Iśanavarman who has gone to Paramarudraloka ... . The collection of these holy writings commemorate on leaves the goods that are deposited at [two *kamraten jagat*] and at the *kanlong*.[28]

This inscription is illuminating for several reasons. The author of the inscription was called Rajapativarman – the second we have come across associated with apotheosis of elite women in this area. He claimed that he was the grandson of 'Rajapativarman the elder of Avidhapura'.[29] The funerary cult of at least one of the *kanlong kamraten an*, therefore, was alive and well in 1037, despite civil war and dynastic alteration. The family of scribes had recorded the deeds of all the sovereigns in the area since the first king, Śrutavarman. The inscription also named the incumbent king, Suryavarman I, descended from Indravarman I, and his queen Viralakshmi, descended from the kings Harshavarman I and Iśanavarman II. Finally, the inscription allows a glimpse of Cambodia after the wars that attended the accession of Suryavarman I. Once peace arrived, the functionaries of previous kings assured the new ruler of their worth and fealty, as is illustrated in the famous oath of allegiance sworn by around 4,000 Cambodian officials in 1011.[30]

Suryavarman I claimed his right to rule in Yaśodharapura through his mother, who was related to Prthivindradevi, mother of Indravarman I; he was also related to Prana, a lesser wife of Rajendravarman II. He was first recorded ruling in eastern Cambodia in late 1001 or early 1002. From the dates of his inscriptions it appears that he made progress toward the capital over the next eight years, reaching Yaśodharapura in 1006, although Jayaviravarman did not vanish from the epigraphic record for another four years. Significantly, the family of Suryavarman I's chief wife was associated with the funerary cult of a deceased queen. K. 380 calls her 'Viralakshmi of Vrac Vrah Sruk'[31] – a place name corresponding to 'district of the holy place'. Another inscription says that Viralakshmi (who was also called Narpatindralakshmi) and her brother Narapatindravarman were the *kamratem an*, or elite, of a polity named *Vrai Kanlong*, 'forest of the *kanlong*'.[32]

According to the epigraphic evidence, Suryavarman I 'offered a tiara, earrings, clothes of gold, and all sorts of finery, and he also offered a covered palanquin of gold' to Viralakshmi in order to win her hand in marriage.[33] Her brothers were also made the recipients of wealth and honour through the marriage alliance.[34] The title of Narapatindravarman was retained within the family; in 1071 another Narapatindravarman, a descendant of the first, restored a foundation established by his ancestor. Bhuvanaditya, younger brother of Narapatindravarman and Viralakshmi, was made prince of Vanapura. Narapatindralakshmi was accorded particular status after the marriage. Her name is one of the elite persons addressed by Suryavarman I concerning land rights at Thpvan Rman.[35] Clearly, the family of Vrai Kanlong had something that Suryavarman I wanted. They were compensated with extraordinary honours, titles and riches in exchange, for Suryavarman I was able to lay claim to the land through this marriage. As Michael Vickery and Claude Jacques contended over twenty years ago, Suryavarman I was not a usurper, as is usually thought.[36]

Jayaviravarman – 'the victorious Viravarman' – was the nephew of the first Rajapativarman. He either died or was exiled around 1011 as a result of Suryavarman I's conquest of Cambodia.[37] It cannot be coincidence that the woman who was the key to sovereignty for Suryavarman I was named Viralakshmi, 'the fortune of Vira', nor that her merits and the rights of a *kanlong* associated with her were the concern of another Rajapativarman, grandson of the first. It is highly likely that Viralakshmi, recorded in the inscriptions as a relative of Harshavarman I, was the daughter of Jayaviravarman, and therefore the cousin of the second Rajapativarman. Moreover, the Rajaguha venerated by Rajendravarman II and Jayavarman V was located in the district

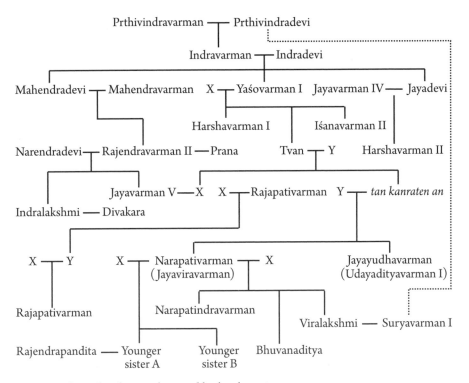

Fig. 3.4: Relationships between kings and *kanlong kamraten an*.

of Jrai Garyyak. The Narapatindravarman of 1071, Viralakshmi's nephew or
great-nephew, was also called 'the *vap* of the *vrah* ['holy' or 'venerated'] Jrai'.[38]
There was clearly a familial connection between the persons associated with
the *kanlong* of the tenth century (see Fig. 3.4). There is no better candidate for
the link between Viralakshmi and Harshavarman I than through the *ten* Tvan
whose image was erected by Jayaviravarman and Udayadityavarman. In the
most likely scenario, she was a sister of Harshavarman I and Iśanavarman II.

Most historians have avoided the ancestry of Udayadityavarman II, stating simply that he was the successor of Suryavarman I. In all likelihood, he
was the younger brother of Viralakshmi, Bhuvanaditya, who had been made
prince of Vanapura, 'city of the forest', when Suryavarman I married his sister.
K. 208 recorded that a king who was probably Udayadityavarman II erected a
Bhagavati in the image of his mother in the town of Rajendrapura. Although
the name of the woman was obscured, she was entitled *ten*, the usual term used
to describe a daughter of an elite family in polities with matrilineal traditions.

Udayadityavarman II was able to draw upon the support of two of the most powerful families known from the epigraphy. Suryavarman I had removed the incumbent *purohita* of the *devaraja*, Śadaśiva (a descendant in matrilineal lines from Śivakaivalya, the original *purohita* that assisted Jayavarman II in the inauguration of the *devaraja*), and married him to a younger sister of queen Viralakshmi, giving him the title Jayendrapandita. Udayadityavarman II bestowed a sizeable tract of land and its tenants to Jayendrapandita and his family in perpetuity. He also inherited the services of Rajendravarman, an elite official under Suryavarman I, raising him to *senapati*, 'commander-in-chief'.[39] It is unlikely that the family of Vrai Kanlong would have entertained the advances of an outsider, and still less likely that they would have allowed him to wield sovereignty over their land without sufficient legitimation.

Harshavarman III (1066–1080) was the brother of Udayadityavarman II. An inscription of Jayavarman VII furnishes some details as to the antecedents of Harshavarman III's queen, Kambujarajalakshmi, 'the fortune of the king of those born of Kambu'. Kambujarajalakshmi was a princess of Śreshtapura, northeast of Yaśodharapura, in modern-day Laos. The sacerdotal families from this area were patrilineal. Suryavarman I replaced the matrilineal family of *purohita*s descended from Śivakaivalya with a patrilineal family connected to *hyang* Pavitra, Jayavarman II's queen in Haripura.[40] Udayadityavarman II bestowed gifts of land and titles on persons disenfranchised by the appointments they had made. Perhaps Harshavarman III did not continue to placate his relatives to their satisfaction, as Cambodia was beset by civil unrest for most of his reign.

The kings who reigned after Harshavarman III had no pre-existing ties to Yaśodharapura. The first of these kings was Jayavarman VI. He came from Mahidharapura, a polity to the northwest of Yaśodharapura and north of the Dangrek mountains. The polity had existed at least from the early tenth century and was fairly extensive; an inscription records a court official of Mahidharapura offering servants from Bhimapura (Phimai) in 921. In the late eleventh century, the incumbent sovereigns were Hiranyalakshmi and Hiranyavarman. They had at least four children, the eldest of whom was Dharanindravarman I, followed by Jayavarman VI, and a third son known only by his title, *yuvaraja* 'crown prince'. Their daughter, whose name has not come to light in any inscription, was the grandmother of Suryavarman II.[41] In 1109, a large group of elite persons donated goods to 'the god of Lingapura and the *kanlong kamraten an*.[42] If a relationship had existed linking the house of Mahidharapura with the women of Yaśodharapura it would have been asserted in the epigraphy as a basis for sovereignty. We may deduce that neither Hiranyalakshmi nor Hiranyavarman had ancestral links to Yaśodharapura. It is therefore highly unlikely that Hiranyalakshmi would have been interred in the heartland of Yaśodharapura, let alone become a focus for veneration.

The other woman of significance to the Mahidharapuran kings was Vijayendralakshmi. Described as 'the receptacle of riches, beauty, eloquence and affection',[43] she married all three of the Mahidharapuran princes. Her first husband was the *yuvaraja* of Mahidharapura.

> Between her and the celestial Lakshmi, there was no difference, and neither of them could prove their superiority over the other. It was from this thought that the *yuvaraja*, about to set forth for the heavens, gave her to his brother, King Jayavarman [VI]. As a result of familial affection, when King Jayavarman followed his ancestors and the *yuvaraja* to the heavens, he gave her to Dharanindra[varman I].[44]

Although remarriage was common in classical Cambodia, no other woman in the epigraphic record married two kings in succession, let alone three. There must have been something extraordinary about Vijayendralakshmi. The inscription says that she had an elder brother who obtained the name Nrpendradhipativarman for his services as head of the army. He was described as 'brother-in-law of his friend the *yuvaraja*, then favourite of Jayavarmadeva'. Vijayendralakshmi herself appears to have been compensated for agreeing to these successive marriages: 'She obtained, through the favour of the king named Jayavarmadeva, and in accord with the promise of the *yuvaraja*, Amalakasthala, which was her birth-place'.[45]

The most likely interpretation of events is that Jayavarman VI of Mahidharapura was assisted by Nrpendradhipativarman in a campaign against Harshavarman III or his successor. It could be that Nrpendradhipativarman and Vijayendralakshmi were the children of Udayadityavarman II or one of the two younger sisters of Viralakshmi. In order to cement the alliance and claim sovereignty over Yaśodharapura, the *yuvaraja* married Vijayendralakshmi. When the *yuvaraja* died – unexpectedly, as he was the younger brother of Jayavarman VI – sovereignty over the land was maintained by marrying Vijayendralakshmi to Jayavarman VI. Upon the death of the latter, the eldest Mahidharapuran prince, Dharanindravarman, sustained the alliance by be-

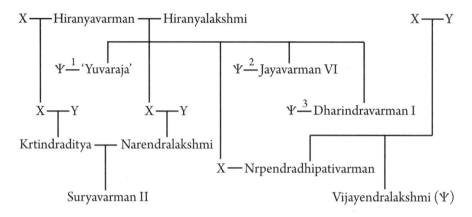

Fig. 3.5: Relationships between the people listed in inscriptions of the Mahidharapuran kings.

coming Vijayendralakshmi's third husband (see Fig. 3.5). Her eulogy reveals her importance to the Mahidharapuran kings: 'Because she was considered the fruit of Fortune and Victory [*lakshmi* and *vijaya*], she bore the name Vijayendralakshmi'.[46]

There is insufficient extant evidence to discern whether the practice of the *kanlong kamraten an* continued after Dharanindravarman I, but Jayavarman VII (r. 1181–c. 1220) traced his descent bilaterally in the inscriptions and in the architectural arrangement of the 'Buddhist triad', representing his father as the *bodhisattva* Lokeśvara, his mother (Chudamani, daughter of a King Harshavarman) as the *tara* Prajnaparamita, and himself as the Buddha. His principal wives, however, were connected to pre-Mahidharapuran sovereigns. Jayavarman VII married two sisters, Jayarajadevi and Indradevi, well-educated Buddhists, daughters of 'kshatriyas, amongst the elite of the royal family'. Indradevi claimed that their father was 'Ja … ', descended from 'Rudravarman' and a woman entitled 'queen', and that their mother was descended from Rajendradevi.[47] It is tempting to see a paternal connection with Vyadhapura and Śambhupura and a maternal link to Bhavapura, but there is insufficient evidence either to support or contradict such an assertion. The most we can establish from the reign of Jayavarman VII is that cognatic legitimation was still in force amongst the Cambodian elite at the end of the twelfth century, and important figures therein were both male and female.

What are we to make of the *kanlong kamraten an*? Do they represent, as Éveline Porée-Maspero hypothesised, a 'lunar race' descended from the

Kaundinya–Soma line of Funan that all would-be kings of Cambodia were required to marry into in order to reign?[48] Michael Vickery dismissed the notion of the 'succession féminine' as an inventive idea that Porée-Maspero attempted unsuccessfully to force on facts. He also made the point that the identities of the women concerned in the succession genealogy were largely unknown. Had they been crucial to the legitimatory process, surely they would have had a greater presence in the epigraphic record.[49] Now that some of the women have been identified, it could be suggested that they did constitute a significant ideological force for the ruling elite families between the ninth and twelfth centuries. The fact that the establishments devoted to the *kanlong kamraten an* occurred in 'natural' phenomena – lakes, caves, forests – instead of in the man-made structures housing the *devaraja* does not necessarily imply that they were less important.

The existence of the *kanlong kamraten an* indicates that elite women, although their importance may have diminished in the official political record, continued to be seen as representatives of the land, and were honoured as such. The classical inscriptions abound with anthropomorphisations of the land as the bride of a particular king, for example 'the land ... took that unique husband, treasure of all the virtues'. The same inscription says that the earth chose her own husband. A similar inscription says of Yaśovarman I that 'the land, having obtained that king for a husband, was full of virtue, pleasure, and profit, and fecund.' The city of Yaśodharapura – Angkor Thom itself – was described as 'adorned with powder and jewels, burning with desire, daughter of a good family' and married to Jayavarman VII 'in the course of a feast at which nothing was lacking'.[50] In the thirteenth century, Zhou Daguan remarked that the king was bound to fulfil a covenant between the female 'guardian-spirit' of the land and the male rulers of Cambodia:

> Out of the palace rises a golden tower, to the top of which the ruler ascends nightly to sleep. It is a common belief that in the tower dwells a genie, formed like a serpent with nine heads, which is lord of the entire kingdom. Every night this genie appears in the shape of a woman, with whom the sovereign couples ... . Should the genie fail to appear for a single night, it is a sign that the king's death is at hand. If, on the other hand, the king should fail to keep his tryst, disaster is sure to follow.[51]

It is significant that the serpent – the true ruler of the kingdom – appeared as a woman, and that it was necessary for the king to unite with her in order to maintain harmony in the kingdom. There was a parallel of this concept in thirteenth-century Java; queen Ken Dedes conferred the status of *cakravartin,* 'lord of the earth', upon her husband, King Ken Angkrok, through the consummation of their marriage.[52] The symbolism of sexual union giving a man the right to rule the land meant that the sexual activities of elite women were more rigidly controlled than their less elevated counterparts. In 1296, the incumbent ruler was the son-in-law of his predecessor, who,

> devoted as he was to his daughter, gave her the chance to steal the golden sword of office and give it to her husband, thus depriving her brother of the succession. This brother strove to stir the soldiery to revolt, but the king, hearing of this, cut off his brother-in-law's toes and threw him into a dark dungeon.[53]

Elite women were thus gateways to power and had to be carefully guarded lest an opportunist seek to elevate himself, as was the case when a lesser son of a provincial family 'took a woman from the royal family' and lived with her in an ashram.[54]

Women of the palace

Marriage alliances continued to be important in maintaining political fealty in the classical period. According to a thirteenth-century observer, 'when a beautiful girl is born into a family, no time is lost in sending her to the palace'.[55] In one case, a queen's mother was given to the service of her son-in-law the king.[56] Officials also offered their sisters and daughters.[57] This resulted in hundreds and even thousands of women living in the palace.[58] Numbers of women entitled 'queen' varied. At the end of the thirteenth century, it was the custom for the principal queen to live in the central palace, lesser queens residing at each of the four cardinal points.[59] There were also lesser wives of varying ranks and a great number of other women, described by Zhou Daguan as 'palace servants', numbering two thousand at the end of the thirteenth century. They had a distinctive hairstyle, shaved high in front and with three red marks on their foreheads. These women were married, with homes outside the palace, to which they went at the end of every day, 'moving in an unbroken stream through the streets in front of and behind the palace'.

They performed a diverse range of activities, some proceeded, 'gaily dressed, with flowers in their hair and tapers in their hands ... other girls carrying gold and silver vessels from the palace and a whole galaxy of ornaments, of very special design'.[60] Some women were midwives (see Fig. 3.6).

Fig. 3.6: Woman in childbirth and attendant midwives, Bayon, 13th century.

Madhyadeśi, 'because of her beauty and her intelligence', arranged flowers in the palace. She was apparently very diligent: 'Because of her fear of the ocean of transmigrations, she was not guilty of any transgressions in the observance of her duty'. Maliniratanalakkha, 'a pious *upasika* ... gifted in good works and other virtues', was keeper of the royal jewels under King Śrindravarman. Prana, consort of Rajendravarman II, served the next king, her stepson Jayavarman V, in an administrative capacity. Other women appear to have occupied a martial role in the palace. Zhou Daguan related that in a royal procession the male army went first, then flags, banners and musicians, followed by girls who were 'the bodyguard of the palace, holding shields and lances'. The king travelled either by elephant or in a golden palanquin carried by women of the palace. Two women were responsible for lifting the curtain that separated the king from his court each day when he seated himself on the royal lion's skin in preparation for addressing matters of state.[61]

Women favoured by the king appear to have been influential. A *ten hyang*, the daughter of the Prthivinavarman who had assisted Jayavarman II in the pacification of Malyang, became a wife of the chief cook of the province of Sanduk. Indravarman I gave her the title and name of *ten kamraten an* Kshitindradevi.

Some years later, Kshitindradevi asked the king to order her brothers Satyayudha and Ripunathana to erect an image named Gapatikshitindra. Another woman bearing the same title was given 'the command of the servants gathered in the land of Suvarnapura' by Jayavarman III. Maliniratanalakkha, keeper of the royal jewels, implemented public works of King Śrindravarman, namely rebuilding a *vihara* and excavating a ditch and a pond. In 1309 she erected a statue of the Buddha and donated slaves and goods on behalf of the king. Women of the palace were accorded privileges; only they were permitted to stain the soles of their feet and the palms of their hands red with henna. This was forbidden to men. All women that served in the palace, regardless of their role, were allowed to wear material patterned with a particular arrangement of flowers, but administrative officials were the only men allowed to wear this pattern.[62]

Elite women seem to have received religious and literary education, as some inscriptions refer to gifts given to the *guru* of a queen or princess. Two queens acted as religious instructors themselves. Indradevi, elder sister of Jayarajadevi, wife of Jayavarman VII, 'initiated [Jayarajadevi] into the peace and tranquillity of the teachings of the Buddha, away from the fire of torment'. Her conversion gave Jayarajadevi the inspiration to become a teacher herself. She 'took for her own daughters members of a group of girls who had been abandoned by their mothers … [and] entered them in the religious life with clothes and gifts, according to the prescribed rites'. The queen then trained the girls to perform scenes from the *Jataka* as a means of instruction for others.[63] Indradevi married Jayavarman VII after the death of her sister and was appointed head of Nagendratunge, Tilakottare and Narendraśrama, three 'colleges' that taught Buddhist doctrine and other sciences. Narendraśrama seems to have been an educational community for women, including those from elite families. Women destined for the service of the king were among those who received religious instruction. Madhyadeśi gave land, silver and gold to her teacher; at his instigation she performed a *brahmayajna* sacrifice. Women were instructed in astrology and how to calculate days of auspiciousness. Zhou Daguan related that the women of Cambodia were the merchants, adding that 'for this reason a Chinese, arriving in the country, loses no time in getting himself a mate, for he will find her commercial instincts a great asset'.[64]

Social strictures and daily life

It appears that women in classical Cambodia were not as powerless in real life as the Brahmanical mores of the epigraphy would suggest. Women continued to make donations of land, goods and slaves to gods and religious communities during the classical period, as they had during the preceding centuries. Women therefore remained entitled to ownership of land, its produce and its tenants.[65] Those who served in the royal palace, despite their often humble origins, were entitled to own and dispose of property. Konti, wife of Kavindrarimathana, palace servant of Rajendravarman II, and niece of Virendravikhyata, inherited the latter's 'divine power, his land, his fields and his gardens'.[66] Ordinary women also owned property. Most property-owing non-elite women were entitled *me*, which designated a woman who was or who had been married.

Matrilineal reckoning also continued to be practised. Harshavarman I 'had a younger brother, born of the same mother'. Viralakshmi, chief queen of Suryavarman I, was named as 'the ancestor in the *matra-vamsa* ['maternal family'] of Harshavarmadeva'. Most elite families, particularly those with hereditary religious functions, were matrilineal. Udayadityavarman II gave the land of Stuk Rman, 'district of the Mon', its produce and slaves, to Jayendrapandita, as the original owners of the land, a group of women entitled *ten* and one *lon*, 'had no children nor grandchildren and their line was extinguished'. The king also decreed that the maternal line of Jayendrapandita would possess the land and its produce in the future. A similar inscription from another place stated that 'the *varna* of *vrah kamraten an* Rajendrapandita … in maternal lines are designated to guard the foundation of Prasat Khtom'.[67]

Amongst slaves, kinship continued to be reckoned solely according to matrilineal descent. In the reign of Yaśovarman I, a woman named *me* Nem bought a *tai* ('female slave') named Kantem. The inscription records that 'the ownership of the *tai* was given until her death, likewise that of her children and grandchildren'.[68] Any children of a female slave would automatically become slaves themselves. The fathers of slave children could have been either other slaves or the owners of the female slaves, or even others to whom the slave-owner offered the sexual services of their slaves. This is contrary to Zhou Daguan's observation that

> it would be unheard of for the master of a house to have sexual relations with [slaves] … if by chance a Chinese, arriving in the country after long abstinence, should assuage his appetite with one of the women slaves, and the fact becomes known to her owner, the latter would refuse to be seated in the presence of a man who had defiled himself with a savage.

Another interpretation is that the owner of the slave was annoyed that his permission was not sought in the first instance. If a female slave became pregnant, the mother would have no claims to the fortune of the father of the child, regardless of the latter's status; the child would remain with its mother, thus increasing the number of slaves 'owned' by the household.[69] Almost everyone, except the very poor, had 'at least a dozen' slaves at the end of the thirteenth century. They appear to have been within the means of most people. A *tai* and her three children were 'bought for the price of a paddy, a slave and a boat'. Some slaves were of foreign extraction. K. 105 records a *tai* bought in exchange for silver from a *yvan* in 987 CE.[70] *Yuan* is the modern Cambodian ethnic appellation for 'Vietnamese', although the term could apply equally to the Cham in the classical period. Zhou Daguan related that slaves could be members of hill tribes or otherwise 'of a wholly separate race'.[71]

As in the preceding period, male and female slaves undertook similar roles in the service of the temples, cooking, manufacturing palm leaf books, brewing perfumes, dancing, singing, and playing musical instruments. A functionary of Suryavarman II donated 'for the clear fortnight, nine slaves: six women and three men; for the obscure fortnight, four women and six men' to perform tasks in the temple. Higher-ranking temple personnel were also referred to as 'slaves' of the god they served. One inscription refers to '*tai* Harikela and *si* Takkara, the servants of the holy *linga* and of the sacred fire'. Men and women of this higher class were responsible for officiating at temple ceremonies. The highest temple officiants were men, although one inscription states that in the event of a lack of male heirs, women of the line would be allowed to officiate. In the time of Jayavarman II, a royal decree charged the descendants of '*sten* Rau', of the '*varna* of Aninditapura', to assist the *purohita* of *kamraten jagat* Kaden in performing temple duties. It continued: 'For want of male descendants, the royal order prescribes that the *avyah* women, virgins or not, enter into religion in the capacity of *bhagavati*, and that they be charged with the puja of the *kamraten jagat* of Kaden'.[72] It was therefore important that a particular family, be its members male or female, continue to officiate at the temple of this god.

The reference to *bhagavati* probably refers to a religious order, not unlike the *kantai kloñ* of the preclassical period, who were called *neak khloñ* in classical Cambodia. Again, there was no equivalent male cohort. In the preceding chapter it was established that *kantai khloñ* could be most likely translated as 'women of the *khloñ*'. These women were, at least in two cases, elite, and acted as substitutes for an elite male within the temple community. During the classical period, one woman was given to a temple in order that she perform sacrifices in place of the *ten* Tvan of Vnur Jas. The exact role of the *neak khloñ* is difficult to decipher from the epigraphy, but they were clearly important and entrusted with significant duties. The women of a family from modern-day Kompong Thom province were prohibited from performing the functions of *neak khloñ* for persons of low caste. If they did, they would forfeit their inheritance rights. An inscription of a middle-ranking official says that after marrying a woman he was ordered, by her grandfather, to 'place her among the servants of the temple, because the *neak khloñ* there acted with good conduct'. These women were not nuns in the sense of *bhikkhuni,* or ordained nuns. Zhou Daguan reported that neither Buddhist nor Brahmanical nuns existed in the capital.[73] It is possible that the *neak khloñ* were a variation of the Indian *devadasi,* although clearly in the Cambodian context women could be married whilst fulfilling their temple obligations. Regardless of their specific function, it is clear that women were not precluded from acting as religious officiants.

Cambodian society below the level of the royal house accepted similar, even complementary, roles for men and women. Both sons and daughters shaved their heads as a sign of mourning for a deceased parent. Zhou Daguan noted that men and women bathed together without apparent impropriety: 'If all the bathers [of mixed gender] are of the same age, they ignore ceremony; the women hide their sex with the left hand as they enter the water'. Men and women both wore bracelets of gold on their arms and scented themselves with perfumes made from sandalwood and musk. To the immense disgust of the Chinese, 'some of the women make water standing up – an utterly ridiculous procedure'.[74]

Punishments for men and women appear to have been relatively the same. Zhou Daguan commented that punishment was usually carried out through a system of fines, although for the worst crimes the perpetrator was buried alive outside the West Gate of Yaśodharapura. Less serious crimes were punished by amputation of hands, feet, or nose; yet to Zhou Daguan's surprise, no lasting punishment was prescribed for adultery. 'If the husband of an adulterous woman is informed of what is going on, he has the lover's feet squeezed between two splints of wood till the pain grows unendurable and he surrenders all his property as the price for his liberation.' Squeezing the head or feet in a vice appears to have been a popular form of punishment. *Me* Ayak, in conjunction with four men, sold land that was not lawfully their own. Upon the discovery of the fraud, the men and Ayak had their heads and feet placed in a vice and squeezed as punishment. Two of the men died. Punishment for one member of a family often resulted in punishment for all. A slave called Varuna ran away from the cult of the Ragaguha. When caught, the religious and civil administrators of the area cut off his nose and ears and offered him and his mother and father into the service of the *kanlong kamraten an*. This may have been why the parents of *me* Ayak above, upon hearing of their daughter's offence and subsequent punishment, 'frightened, ran off to hide' rather than suffer the same fate.[75]

Women were able to exercise a significant degree of choice in their lives. They appear to have been able to remarry with comparative ease – in some cases, before the death of their first husband. A woman named Thun was entitled *dhuli jerng kamsten śri*, the highest title that could be awarded, when she was first married. Some years later, during the reign of Rajendravarman II, she was given in marriage to a second man, a *mratan khloñ*. We do not know whether her first husband had died, or whether this second marriage better suited the political purposes of her family. A widow, Sok, took it upon herself to arrange her second marriage. She asked the man concerned 'to become the master of her house'; her grandfather gave him a horse and other goods, four umbrellas for the man's father, and Sok went to pay her respects to him. When all was settled, Sok's name was changed to *me* Mani and she was married to the man of her choice. Zhou Daguan recorded that in the thirteenth century, when a daughter was born, it was customary for the parents to exclaim 'May the future bring thee a hundred, a thousand husbands!'[76] This could, of course, refer to future existences, but even in this context it is interesting that good wishes did not exhort that the girl be reborn as the partner of her husband.

Of course, remarriage was probably encouraged because of the role it played in facilitating alliances between families. This may also have been why *sati*, the practice of consigning a widow to her husband's funeral pyre, was not practised in classical Cambodia. There is only one extant reference to an occurrence of *sati*, in an inscription of the late tenth or early eleventh century which names a *tan kamraatn an* Sativarti. Cœdès was convinced that the woman was a princess, due to her title, and that she immolated herself at the cremation of her husband. However, the name could equally mean 'the virtuous one' without necessarily referring to immolation. There are abstract references to *sati* in the inscriptions. One described lack of faith as 'the same as a stupid woman, who on the point of entering in the fire to die there, asks herself whether all this torment will get her anywhere'. Another related that when 'the wife of Kama [the god of love] saw the unparalleled beauty of the body of the king [Suryavarman I] ... she did not want to subject herself to the fire' of her husband's funeral pyre.[77] Perhaps *sati* was never popular due to the benefits that remarriage of the widow could bring her family; gifts of textiles and other goods were given to the families concerned as part of the marriage celebrations.

Sexual autonomy seems to have been exercised by women to a high degree, at least amongst women who were not born into the royal family. Zhou Daguan was told that Cambodian women were not likely to remain faithful in the absence of their husbands:

> Everyone with whom I talked said that the Cambodian women are highly sexed. One or two days after giving birth to a child they are ready for intercourse: if a husband is not responsive he will be discarded. When a husband is called away on matters of business, they endure his absence for a while; but if he is gone as much as ten days, the wife is apt to say, 'I am no ghost; how can I be expected to sleep alone?' Though their sexual impulses are very strong, it is said some of them remain faithful.[78]

This is at odds with the inscriptions, which stress the importance of fidelity of women after marriage. Virginity is also the subject of conflicting views. One inscription speaks of a king's infatuation with a woman 'of perfect body, of irreproachable face' waning when he realised that she was 'already deflowered'. Jayavarman VII was pleasurably aroused by 'a virginal and enchanting wife, awkward in revealing her charms'. According to Zhou Daguan, however, brides and grooms often had pre-nuptial intercourse without social reprisal.[79] There was one rule for the elite and another for the rest of society.

A ritual defloration practice called *chen-t'an* by the Chinese was popular at the end of the thirteenth century. Conducted by both Buddhist monks and Brahmans, according to the religious orientation of the girl concerned, once a year authorities selected a day auspicious for the ceremony and notified families that had girls between seven and eleven years old. Such families would then engage the services of a priest of their choice – elite families usually securing more senior officials. These were permitted to perform one defloration per year. They were presented with gifts including rice, wine, cotton, silk, areca nuts, and silver plate. The amount given corresponded to the means of the family. Wealthy persons seeking to acquire merit would sponsor very poor girls.

> Two pavilions hung with brilliantly coloured silks have been set up; in one of these is seated the priest, the maiden in the other. Words are exchanged between the two, but they can scarcely be heard, so deafening is the music, for on such occasions it is lawful to shatter the peace of the night. I have been told that at a given moment the priest enters the maiden's pavilion and deflowers her with his hand, dropping the first fruits into a vessel of wine. It is said that the father and mother, the relations and neighbours, stain their foreheads with this wine, or even taste it. Some also say that the priest has intercourse with the girl; others deny this … . At daybreak the priest is escorted back home with palanquins, parasols, and music, after which it is customary to buy the girl back from the priest with presents of silk and other fabrics; otherwise she becomes his property forever and cannot marry.

There are echoes here of the prescribed ritual of purification following the consummation of marriage in classical India, wherein the Brahman was presented with the bloodstained bed cloth. He alone could absorb the dangerous impurities of the blood; if he did not, the groom faced destruction. Yet in the Cambodian context it appears that the ritual of defloration marked a coming of age. Zhou Daguan concluded his description of the defloration ritual by saying that, whereas before the ceremony the girl and her parents had always shared a bedroom, afterward 'the room was closed to the young woman, who went wherever she pleased, with no constraint'. This is hardly in keeping with the Brahmanical maxim that 'women must be particularly guarded against evil inclinations'.[80] There were clearly differences between what was acceptable for women of the royal family, as representatives of the land who through access to their bodies permitted the land to be 'ruled', and the habits of those in other divisions of society.

∿

It may appear that women in classical Cambodia lost some of the power and significance they had previously enjoyed, but the patriarchal timbre of the epigraphic and sculptural record after the ninth century did not impact greatly upon the status of women relative to either men or their counterparts in the preceding period. Elite women continued to be perceived as the intermediaries by which access to the land was granted. The women of the palace had a variety of important roles and functions for which they were well compensated in social standing and material assets. In fact we may interpret the women of the palace and the *neak khloñ* as institutions that provided women with an avenue for enhanced status and privilege denied to men. Women continued to own and dispose of land and goods, including slaves. Matrilineal reckoning persisted in society, overlaid with bilateral variations when necessary to establish political legitimation. Men and women were active members of Cambodian society, participating in religious and economic life; slaves were not treated with any discernible degree of difference according to gender, and punishments for men and women were similar. A contrast existed between the ideal society, as depicted by the conservative Brahmanical elite in inscriptions and sculpture, and the reality of everyday life in the classical period.

Notes to Chapter 3

1 Most histories of Cambodia that touch upon the classical period indicate that the kings after the tenth century were usurpers or otherwise unrelated. See for example George Cœdès, *The Indianized states of Southeast Asia,* trans. Susan Brown Cowing, Honolulu: East–West Center Press, 1968, pp. 114–122, 134–139, and D.G.E. Hall, *A history of South-East Asia,* 4th ed., London: Macmillan, 1981, pp. 120–127. The latest edition of David Chandler's *A history of Cambodia,* however, incorporates new insights into the possible antecedents of these kings drawn from recent epigraphic analysis (4th ed., Colorado: Westview Press, 2007, pp. 42–61).

2 K. 214, verses A6–A7, *IC* 2, pp. 202–206; K. 772, verse 2, *IC* 7, pp. 104–105; K. 111, verses 44–45, *IC* 6, pp. 195–211; K. 230, verses A2–A4, *IC* 6, pp. 241–242; K. 225, verses 2–4, 14, *IC* 3, pp. 66–69.

3 Michael Vickery, *Society, economics, and politics in pre-Angkorian Cambodia: The 7th–8th centuries,* Tokyo: The Center for East Asian Cultural Studies for UNESCO, 1998, p. 140.

4 K. 263, verse C14, *IC* 4, pp. 118–139; K. 286, verse s10, *IC* 4, pp. 88–101; K. 263, verse A4.

5 K. 675, verse s7, *IC* 1, pp. 61–68.

6 K. 834, verse B72, *IC* 5, pp. 244–269.

7 K. 191, verse B29, *IC* 6, pp. 300–311.

8 K. 485, verse 48, *IC* 2, pp. 161–181; K. 205, verse 5, *IC* 3, pp. 3–11.

9   K. 218, verse 10, *IC* 3, pp. 45–53; K. 263, verse C3; K. 111, verse 16; K. 692, verse C39, *IC* 1, pp. 227–249; K. 661, verses A19, A22, A24, *IC* 1, pp. 197–219; K. 287, verse 24, *IC* 4, pp. 235–253; K. 834, verses 61–63; K. 485, verse 6, *IC* 2, pp. 161–181.

10 K. 286, verses 11 and 12.

11 Zhou Daguan, *The customs of Cambodia*, trans. J. Gilman d'Arcy Paul, 2nd ed., Bangkok: Siam Society, 1992, p. 5.

12 K. 273, verses 6–7, in George Cœdès, 'La stèle de Ta Prohm', *BEFEO* vol. 6 (1906), pp. 44–81.

13 K. 286, verses 11 and 12.

14 *History of the Liang*, in Paul Pelliot, 'Le Fou-nan', *BEFEO* vol. 3 (1903), p. 256.

15 K. 235, verse 71, in George Cœdès and Pierre Dupont, 'l'Inscription de Sdok Kak Thom', *BEFEO* vol. 43 (1942–1943), pp. 57–134.

16 K. 235, verses 70–77.

17 K. 162, verses n10–n11, *IC* 6, pp. 101–106; K. 989, ll. B18–B19; K. 989, ll. B33–B34, *IC* 7, pp. 164–189; K. 842, verses A13–A14, *IC* 1, pp. 147–157; K. 263, verse C24; K. 258, verse C4.

18 K. 832, verse 6; K. 276, ll. 17–19, *IC* 4, pp. 153–154.

19 K. 832, verse 9.

20 K. 806, verses 6–8, 12–13, *IC* 1, pp. 73–137.

21 K. 143, ll. A2–A6, *IC* 6, pp. 218–223; K. 143, ll. B15–B17; K. 669, ll. D25–D26, *IC* 1, pp. 159–186; K. 444, ll. B20–B23; K. 276, ll. 4–6; K. 257, ll. s29–s31, *IC* 4, pp. 140–150; George Cœdès, 'Inscriptions de Banteay Prav: Inscription du piédroit nord du la tour centrale (221)', *IC* 3, p. 57.

22 K. 806, verse 280.

23 K. 806, verse 281.

24 K. 231, ll. 7–13, *IC* 3, pp. 72–75.

25 K. 231, ll. 7–13, 38–43, 44–53.

26 K. 257, ll. s7–s11; George Cœdès, 'Inscription de Prasat Car ((K. 257)', *IC* 4, p. 140; K. 143, ll. B15–B17.

27 K. 263, verse C24; K, 669, ll. B1–B9, *ICI*, pp. 167–168; K. 263, ll. B16–B17; K. 669, ll. D37–D3; K. 263, verse C30; K. 669, ll. D25–D26.

28 K. 380, ll. w11–w21.

29 K. 380, l. e3.

30 George Cœdès, 'Études Cambodgiennes 9: Le serment des fonctionnaires de Suryavarman I', *BEFEO* vol. 13, no. 6 (1913), pp. 11–17; Michael Vickery, 'The reign of Suryavarman I and royal factionalism at Angkor' *Journal of Southeast Asian Studies*, 16, 2 (1985), pp. 226–245.

31 K. 380, l. w18.

32 K. 782, l. n1–n6.

33 K. 989, ll. B31–B33.

34 K. 782, ll. n1–n6; K. 989, verse A26.

35 Cœdès, 'Inscription du piédroit nord du la tour centrale (K. 221)', p. 57; K. 660, ll. 4–6, *IC* 1, pp. 195–19; K. 989, ll. B5–B8.

36 Vickery, 'Reign of Suryavarman I', p. 244.

37 One argument is that Jayaviravarman went to Bali, where his brother Udayadityavarman, or Udayana as he was known in the Balinese context, was ruling.

38 K. 380, ll. w11–w21; Lawrence Palmer Briggs, *The ancient Khmer empire*, Philadelphia, Pennsylvania: The American Philosophical Society, 1951, p. 148; K. 222, ll. 6–7, 9, *IC* 3, pp. 61–64; K. 221, l. 20, *IC* 3, pp. 57–61.

39 K. 208, verse 13, ll. 58–59, *IC* 6, pp. 287–292; K. 235, verse 74; K. 219, ll. 6–13, *IC* 7, pp. 45–47; K. 208, ll. 48–50.

40 K.273, verses 8–11.

41 K. 271, ll. s1–s2; George Cœdès, 'Études Cambodgiennes 24: Nouvelles données chronologiques et généalogiques sur la dynestie de Mahidharapura', *BEFEO* vol. 29 (1929), p. 169; K. 384, ll. 3–11, in Cœdès, 'Nouvelles données chronologiques et généalogiques sur la dynestie de Mahidharapura', p. 172.

42 K. 249, ll. 9–10, *IC* 3, pp. 97–99.

43 K. 191B, verse 28.

44 K. 191B. verses 31–32.

45 K. 191, verses B39, B46, B33.

46 K. 191, verse B28.

47 K. 485, verses 100; 33–34.

48 Éveline Porée-Maspero, 'Nouvelle etude sur la nāgī Somā', *Journal Asiatique* 238 (1950), pp. 237–267.

49 Michael Vickery, 'Funan reviewed: Deconstructing the ancients', *BEFEO* 90–91 (2003–2004), p. 118.

50 K. 287, verses 20–21; K. 491, verse 11, *IC* 2, pp. 183–185; K. 287, verse 76.

51 Zhou Daguan, *The customs of Cambodia*, p. 5.

52 Ann Kumar, 'Imagining women in Javanese religion: Goddesses, ascetes, queens, consorts, wives', in Barbara Watson Andaya (ed.), *Other pasts: Women, gender and history in early modern Southeast Asia*, Honolulu: University of Hawai'i Press, 2000, p. 96.

53 Zhou Daguan, *Customs of Cambodia*, p. 72.

54 K. 449, verses 44 and 45, in George Cœdès, 'Études Cambodgiennes 11: La stèle de Palhal', *BEFEO* vol. 13, no. 6 (1913), pp. 43–52.

55 Zhou Daguan, *Customs of Cambodia*, p. 13.

56   K. 956, ll. 42–44, *IC* 7, pp. 128–135.

57   K. 92, verse 10; K. 989, verse A26.

58   K. 158, verse A13. K. 989, ll. B33–B34. K. 989, ll. B14–B16. K. 692, verse B29.

59   Zhou Daguan, *Customs of Cambodia*, p. 13.

60   Zhou Daguan, *Customs of Cambodia*, pp. 13, 33.

61   K. 216, verse 4; K. 754, verses 5–7; K. 136, verse A20, *IC* 6, pp. 284–286; K. 158, l. A4; Zhou Daguan, *Customs of Cambodia*, pp, 72–73.

62   K. 956, ll. 46–49; K. 956, ll. 52–56; K. 774, ll. 1–7; K. 754, verses 5–7; Zhou Daguan, *Customs of Cambodia*, p. 7.

63   K. 258, verse C7; K. 485, verse 59; K. 485, verses 79–80; K. 485, verse 73.

64   K. 485, verses 98–99; K. 216, verses 6–7; K. 216, verse 5; Zhou Daguan, *Customs of Cambodia*, pp. 30, 43.

65   K. 54/55, verse I.3, ll. 5–6, 7, *IC* 3, pp. 157–163; K. 77, verse 4, *IC* 4, pp. 47–48; K. 89, ll. 13; K. 128, l. 7, *IC* 2, pp. 87–88; K. 240, ll. 6–9, *IC* 3, pp. 76–77; K. 774, ll. 1–7; K. 270, ll. s1–s2, *IC* 4, pp. 68–73; K. 669, ll. C31–C32; K. 214, verses A6–A7; K. 370, ll. 7–8, *IC*7, pp. 58–59.

66   K. 157, verses A9–A10, B11–B13, B19, *IC* 6, pp. 123–127; K. 754, verses 5–7, in George Cœdès, 'Etudes Cambodgiennes 32: La plus ancienne inscription en Pali du Cambodge', *BEFEO* vol. 36 (1936), p. 16; K. 216, verses 8–9.

67   K. 675, verse s17; K. 660, ll. 4–6; K. 165, ll. n4–n7, n17–n20; K. 219, ll. 6–13; K. 450, l. 11; K. 887, verses 6–7, *IC* 5, pp. 153–155; K. 956, ll. 7–32; K. 989, ll. B13–B14; K. 230, C & D.

68   K. 158, ll. C8–C16.

69   Zhou Daguan, *Customs of Cambodia*, p. 20; K. 221, ll. 2–9; K. 222, ll. 7, 8–9; K. 89, ll. 28–29, *IC* 3, pp. 164–169; K. 222, ll. 2–3.

70   K. 105, ll. 28–29.

71   Zhou Daguan, *Customs of Cambodia*, p. 20.

72   K. 139, ll. B11–B13, *IC* 3, pp. 176–179; see also K. 192, ll. 6–17, *IC* 6, pp. 128–130; K. 238, ll. B4–B6 (left), *IC* 6, pp. 119–122; K. 105, l. 25; K. 832, verse 10; K. 221, ll. 15–17; K. 713, verses A28, A35–A36; K. 61, verse A4, *IC* 7, pp. 20–22; K. 254, ll. B25–B28; K. 143, ll. C1–C3; K. 89, ll. 18–19; K. 989, ll. B8, B10–B11; Zhou Daguan, *Customs of Cambodia*, pp. 20, 21.

73   The term *nak*, in Malay, translates as 'child'. K. 137, ll. 6–9, *IC* 2, pp. 115–118; K. 66, l. B6; K. 89, ll. 24–25; K. 444, ll. B2–B4, B7–B9; K. 245, ll. 10–15; Zhou Daguan, *Customs of Cambodia*, p. 11.

74   Zhou Daguan, *Customs of Cambodia*, pp. 13–14, 39, 69.

75   Zhou Daguan, *Customs of Cambodia*, pp. 33, 67; K. 158, verse A27, B31–B32; K. 231, ll. 1–6; K. 231, ll. 7–13; K. 158, verse A27, B31–B32.

76 K. 989, ll. B24–B26; K. 245, ll. 10–15; Zhou Daguan, *Customs of Cambodia*, pp. 18–19.

77 K. 468, l. n11; George Cœdès, 'Inscriptions des Prasat Khlon', *IC* 3, p. 227; K. 111, verse 88; K. 218, verse 13.

78 Zhou Daguan, *Customs of Cambodia*, p. 15.

79 K. 56, verse B18; K. 485, verse 6; Zhou Daguan, *Customs of Cambodia*, p. 19.

80 Zhou Daguan, *Customs of Cambodia*, pp. 15, 19; Werner F. Menski, 'Marital expectations as dramatized in Hindu marriage rituals', in Julia Leslie (ed.), *Roles and rituals for Hindu women*, London: Pinter, 1991, p. 57; *Laws of Manu*, 9, verse 5.

CHAPTER FOUR

Goddesses Lost?

*T*he royal court moved away from Yaśodharapura in the middle of the fifteenth century and was relocated repeatedly in the ensuing centuries until the sack of Phnom Penh by the Thai in 1772. The intervening period has received relatively little attention from historians, largely due to the paucity of sources.[1] No magnificent temples were constructed; inscriptions gave way to palm-leaf records, few of which survived into the colonial period. The perception of these centuries as a period of political and cultural decline is expressed in the term usually employed to describe it, 'post-Angkorian'. The implication is that the centuries after the capital had been moved elsewhere had no character of their own, that they can be defined only in relation to the classical 'Angkorian' period. More broadly, Southeast Asia between the fifteenth and eighteenth centuries is designated 'early modern', yet this is not appropriate in the Cambodian context.[2] Whilst new religions and technologies were brought to Cambodia by the first Europeans in the sixteenth century, these did not usher in an era of modernisation, as occurred elsewhere in Southeast Asia. A better alternative for the period, as advocated by Ashley Thompson, is 'middle Cambodia', first used over thirty years ago by Saveros Pou to describe the language of Cambodia during this time, and later re-employed by Khing Hoc Dy to describe a historical period.[3] Although Theravada Buddhism became the dominant religion and Europeans became tangentially involved in Cambodian politics at this time, very little changed for women in Cambodia; in fact, a female presence is more clearly discerned than in the preceding period.

Theravada Buddhism

The shift from Brahmanical religions to Theravada Buddhism had been occurring gradually in Cambodia for some time before the middle period. It was during the middle period, however, that Cambodian ways of life began to reflect predominantly Buddhist beliefs and traditions. The 'conversion' of Cambodia to Theravada Buddhism at first only added a thin veneer of Buddhist beliefs to Cambodian culture. The role of the king as intermediary between mundane and celestial worlds was unchanged. Brahmans continued to occupy important positions at the courts of Theravada Buddhist and Muslim kings in Southeast Asia. In Cambodia, existing architecture and sculpture were converted into spaces for Buddhist iconography. Thus in the fifteenth century, a reclining Buddha was carved into the rear of the Baphuon temple at Angkor, a monument originally constructed to house the golden *linga* that represented the sovereignty of Udayadityavarman II (r. 1050–1066). The earliest extant Cambodian literature from the middle period reflects similar Buddhist characteristics. This comprises the royal chronicles, the Cambodian version of the *Ramayana*, called the *Ramakerti* or *Reamker*, and the *cbpab*, normative poems that described the correct way for society and its members to act. It does not necessarily follow, however, that the *cbpab* recorded for the first time in the middle period reflect a Middle Cambodian innovation.[4] In all likelihood, codes of conduct existed in earlier periods, when they would have embodied Brahmanical notions. As shown in previous chapters, admonitions for correct behaviour are discernible in the subtext of many early inscriptions, yet Cambodian society does not appear to have followed them verbatim. Nevertheless, *cbpab* constituted the key texts for Cambodian pagoda schools and in state education curricula well into the twentieth century, although they enshrined the values of a minority – their elite (male) authors.

The *cbpab* provided models for a harmonious society, predicated upon the correct observance of action for all its members.[5] Everyone had their particular *dharma*, or duty:

> The sangha must devote themselves to the holy *vinaya*,
> Women should be devoted to a high standard of conduct,
> People must always strive never to commit evil.[6]

Many *cbpab* were concerned with ensuring domestic accord. *Cbpab Preah Rajasambpir* describes a good man as 'having a happy wife and home, children who obey their father, slaves who bring themselves to their master to hear his orders'. The text goes on to advise householders that 'three things sully a home: the deeds and behaviour of a wife who loses her temper beyond rea-

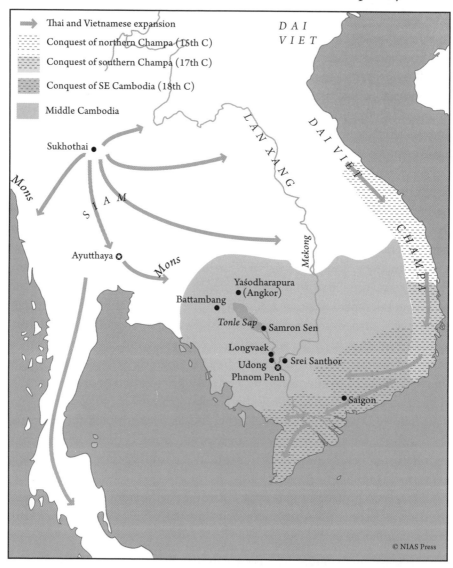

Fig. 4.1: Middle Cambodia. Adapted from Jan M. Pluvier, *Historical Atlas of South-East Asia* and other written sources.

son; precocious children who do not follow advice; a slave who hides so that he cannot be ordered to work'. This maxim is reflected in a contemporaneous inscription. In 1702, an *oknha*, or high-ranking official, listed the existences that he would like to avoid in his future incarnations. One of his demands was that he 'avoid a bad wife and a home without peace that would make me very

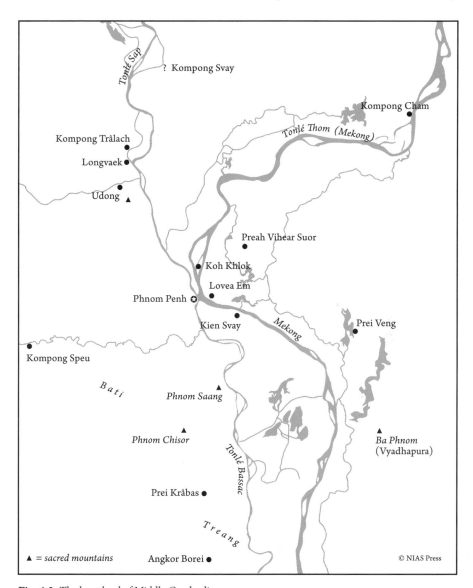

Fig. 4.2: The heartland of Middle Cambodia.

unhappy'. According to *Cbpab Trineti*, a wife 'organises the household with a firm and loving hand. Goods acquired by hard work may be placed in her hands; she minds them with economy and without any loss'. This appears to be a Cambodian version of the duties of a wife as described by the historical Buddha; the *Rajabhisek* of Jai Jettha II also warned women that to act in ways that made them *kheadak bhariya, jao bhariya,* and *satru bhariya* (menacing, thieving or enemy wives) would cause them to go to hell.[7]

Cambodian Buddhist texts, like those throughout South and Southeast Asia, are ambiguous in their representations of women, at times seeming to consider them forces for good, at others designating them corruptors of society. 'Good' women, according to the *cbpab*, were virtuous wives and nurturing mothers. This was also reflected in the court chronicles. King Paramaraja III (r. 1599–1600) attempted to seduce the wife of another by offering her wealth and status, and when these inducements failed, used physical force. She resisted, thinking 'it is not proper to allow [a woman] to unite herself to a second man after a first, or she will not be a woman who is virtuous, grateful and faithful to her husband'. 'Bad' women, on the other hand, were wanton, sexually preoccupied, and immoral, incapable of attaining enlightenment themselves and seeking to distract others – namely diligent men – from their own spiritual journey. 'Women who have lost their virtue' were unable to follow the path of Buddhism. Perhaps, as Alan Sponberg has argued in the South Asian context, these seeming contradictions carried 'a multiplicity of voices, each expressing a different set of concerns current among the members of the early community'.[8]

One of these voices in middle Cambodia articulated a significant role for female figures in Theravada Buddhism. Cambodian *Jataka*, stories of Buddha's lives, depart from Indian models in depicting women for the most part as intelligent, active, and dignified, and detailing the consequences for men who do not treat women as their equals. Adhémard Leclère described a very old text he had discovered in a Cambodian pagoda at the end of the nineteenth century that spoke of a female *bodhisattva,* sister of the Buddha Tibangkar, who earned her status for her meritorious acts toward her brother. In his footnotes, he said that this was a tenet peculiar to the Cambodian context; he had never come across such a prediction in any other country or literary tradition. Buddha images themselves could become infused with 'femaleness'; a wooden statue of the Buddha, dating to the seventeenth century, was

said during the colonial period to have become the dwelling-place of a female *neak ta* or ancestor spirit called *Neang* Khmau, 'black lady'. Cambodia is one of the few places where the earth goddess, Preah Neang Dharani, has enjoyed enduring popularity (see Fig. 4.3); excised from iconography elsewhere, she has maintained a presence from at least the late twelfth century in Cambodia, when the king Jayavarman VII caused her image to be included with other members of the Buddhist pantheon in four of the temples erected during his reign.[9]

This egalitarian approach to gender translated into the mundane realm as well. Buddhist women in middle Cambodia seem to have been perceived as spiritually equal to their male counterparts. One of the *cbpab* says that 'in being born human, *dharma* is the only concern to men and women'. Another suggests that gender is immaterial: 'Whether you are born male or female in this world, the wise say to obey your masters, to ensure that unclean substances do not touch you and contaminate you, and that you must endure the consequences of your actions'. Further evidence of spiritual equality is the fact that spouses performed meritorious deeds in tandem, the merit accruing to both or to other persons. Kalnyakesar, a

Fig. 4.3: Neang Preah Dharani (photograph by the author).

jamdev or high-ranking lady of the court, accomplished meritorious deeds in order that the merit might transfer to her deceased husband. The inscription reveals that she expressed a wish that she be reunited with her husband in each reincarnation until she obtained the level of *arhat* and was able to enter enlightenment. This may indicate that Theravada Buddhism in Cambodia reflected very early Buddhist practice in India, when women were not precluded from attaining the highest spiritual level of *arhat*, although in later times rebirth as a woman indicated punishment for bad deeds in the previous life.[10]

Mothers and fathers were both accorded great respect in the *cbpab*. One *cbpab* speaks of the difficulties in being 'affectionate and protective mothers and fathers'. Another advises children to 'listen to the words and recommendations of your parents'. Mothers, however, were accorded special consideration in connection with novice monks. *Cbpab Kram* advises novice monks to act in accordance with the rules of the sangha so that merit could be acquired by their *padhyay* (spiritual preceptor) 'with your mothers as well as your fathers'. Novices were also admonished against arguing or contradicting their *padhyay* as 'he is equal to your mother'. The special relationship between mothers and novices was reflected in the practice of entering 'adopted' sons into the monastic life. Six people, three men and three women, donated one golden and three silver statues of the Buddha and a banner to a temple. Then, 'filled with sympathy and compassion', they committed a young slave boy to the monastery. One of the three donors adopted him 'as if he were a son of her own'. Not only did merit accrue from the act of releasing a slave from bondage; the act of placing the boy in a monastery resulted in significant merit for the adoptive mother. Eleven years later, the same woman travelled across the Tonlé Sap with her family in order to visit relatives living at Angkor. In addition to making donations of statues and banners, they placed two more children in the monastery in order to receive instructions as novices. IMA 39 records that an *oknha* gave his son Kan to Buddhism and then paid for his immediate release. The congregation was asked to record the merit of those that entered into religion.[11] Merit, then, was something that both men and women could acquire through various activities.

Women could also be 'entered into religion'. Although the *bhikkhuni* order, in which women were ordained as counterparts to monks, is conventionally believed to have died out in Sri Lanka around the twelfth century, and a century later Zhou Daguan commented that there were no nuns of any sort in Cambodia, there appears to have been a contemporaneous tradition of female asceticism in that endured in Southeast Asia. The Thai chronicles speak of 'Nak Chi', in Ayutthaya, who was originally of Cambodian extraction. *Neak chi* today means 'holy person' in Khmer. There is a reference in middle Cambodian inscriptions to elite women 'entering into' religion. Some time after 1747, an *oknha* and his wife, aunt, sister-in-law, and two nieces travelled to Angkor, where they made donations to the monks. Then the women – but not the *oknha* – were 'entered as *neang chi*'. Saveros Pou and David Chandler both translated this term as 'nuns'. There is no other reference to *neang chi* or *daun chi*, the term given to lay nuns in modern Cambodia, in any other middle Cambodian text. The merit that the women received for having spent this time as *neang chi* was transferred to the spiritual benefit of others.[12] There is a resonance between this practice and that of the *kantai kloñ* of the preceding periods. Perhaps this was the purpose of the *kantai kloñ* as well – to make merit for someone else, who would then attempt to progress in *samsara*, the cycle of birth and rebirth, to a greater degree than they would otherwise have been entitled to. It appears, therefore, that a social institution for Cambodian women continued without cessation for over a thousand years.

There were also male and female *upasika*, laypersons who observed precepts and did good deeds. At times husbands and wives would perform pious acts together. One such couple, Naga and Pan, paid for the construction of a temple compound complete with a college for monks. The complex was called *Wat Me Pan* after Pan herself, who was described as 'a slave' of Buddhism. Another spousal endowment came from Abhayaraj and his wife Dhamm in 1566. They manufactured images of the Buddha in gold, silver and stone, restored a *chedi*, planted a grove of sacred trees, and commissioned copies of Buddhist texts. It was also common for women to perform good deeds alone. Manumission of slaves was a popular method of acquiring merit. The dying wish of a woman of high rank was that a certain slave be freed. Two other women, 'their hearts full of *dharma*', freed another slave in 1698. Phnom Penh itself was alleged to have been established as a consequence of an act of Buddhist piety by a woman named Penh, who lived on the banks of the confluence of the Tonlé Sap and Bassac rivers. One day, after the flood-waters had receded, she found four statues of the Buddha and one of Vishnu in a *koki* tree. She brought them to her house and established a shrine for them there, exhorting the neighbouring people to construct a small *phnom* (hill) near her house and a sanctuary on top of it. She placed the four Buddha statues in the sanctuary, the statue of Vishnu at the foot of the hill, to the east, and invited monks to come and establish a monastery at the foot of the hill on the opposite side.[13] A statue of *Me* Penh is today honoured at Wat Phnom (see Fig. 4.4).

Neang Hiem, 'inspired to accomplish good deeds', invited monks to perform a ceremony at Angkor Wat in order to drive away misfortune and obstacles and ensure the prosperity of the beneficiaries. Twenty years later, Hiem completed another act of piety, this time freeing a slave. Another woman, *Neang* Paen, had performed good deeds 'from the age of sixteen to her present age [44]'. These acts included the construction of seventeen statues and one painting of the Buddha in diverse materials; the making of nine banners, three platforms, and an umbrella; the construction of over a thousand stupas; the ordination of nine youths; the fabrication of five religious texts; the offering of five monks' robes and forty monks' *vatthabandh*, lengths of

Fig. 4.4: *Me* Penh (photograph by the author).

cloth worn over the robe; and providing candles and combustible materials for the use in temples and monasteries.[14]

Elite women were particularly zealous in the accomplishment of meritorious acts, undoubtedly due to their greater resources. An inscription dated 1577 was executed at the command of the queen mother:

> I here profess my good works ... I, the queen mother Mahakalynavatti Sri Sijhata, princess of noble birth, devout *maha-upasika* [lay Buddhist]. I prostrate myself at the noble lotuses that are the feet of the revered Triple Joy who is our lord, our supreme refuge ... . My heart full of *dharma,* I have regularly accomplished many pious acts, up until the present, that is to say the year of the Ox 1499 *śaka.*[15]

These pious deeds included using her influence to convince her son the king to restore Angkor Wat. Having meditated on the impermanence of existence and the physical form, she cut off her 'luxuriant hair' and burned it, scattering the ashes over the statues of the Buddha. In 1684, a consort of King Jai Jettha III (r. 1677–1702) erected gold, silver and leaden statues of the Buddha, had a banner and a dais made, and caused five manuscripts to be copied, all of which she gave to a monastery. She also gave furniture, clothing, food, and utensils for the monks' use. The merit of these acts she directed to her husband. One maxim of *Cbpab Preah Rajasambhir,* therefore, reflected reality: 'In order to form an estimate of a queen, one must look at her pious acts'.[16]

The widespread acceptance of Theravada Buddhism during the middle period did not result in a wholesale privileging of male interests to the detriment of women. Pre-existing traditions prevailed. Women continued to make donations to religious establishments, alone and in conjunction with their husbands and families, according to their means. Male and female slaves continued to serve in religious establishments. Women continued to be 'entered in religion', perhaps in a continuation of the *kantai kloñ* tradition of the pre-classical and classical periods. The only discernible difference was that the establishments were Buddhist, not Brahmanical. Similarly, despite the textual construction of women as dangerous forces, this is no different from earlier, Brahmanical codes of conduct that stressed virginity and fidelity. The *cbpab,* written by elite men, often monks, reflect the way that the authors believed a correct society should operate. It is difficult to judge to what extent their influence was effective, but the available evidence contradicts any notion of inferiority or submission on the part of Cambodian women.

Patron princesses, querulous queens

Elite men and women at court acted as patrons for poorer relatives and rural clients. Women were thus integral members of the *khsae* networks upon which power depended. Rural elite and their dependents would offer respect, services and gifts to their patrons at court in return for assistance, protection, and accommodation. Keo Keng Nya, the Cambodian wife of the Lao king Fa Ngum, was the 'benefactress and protector' of the companions-in-arms of the king, many of whom were Cambodian. Patrons spoke for their clients when they brought suit. In the middle of the seventeenth century, Chong Damrey, a *mohat* or indentured servant of the *preah ek khsatri* (first princess, elder sister of the king), was selling cucumbers in Phnom Penh when he was set upon by a gang of youths. He told them that he was a *mohat*; a woman nearby, frightened, told them to beat him to death so that there would be no reprisal. He eventually escaped and told the princess, who complained to her brother the king. An inquiry was put in motion and the perpetrators brought to justice. The woman who had urged them to kill the *mohat* had her mouth mutilated for daring to speak against a servant of the royal family.[17] At other times, a patron might be of financial use to their client. In 1738, the ill-fortune of a young prince was reversed by a wealthy female patron:

> In the year of the Snake ... a tragedy occurred; [the nephew] found himself completely impoverished. His aunt, *jamdev* Ratnakanya, and her niece, *Neang* Sa, made a *sambal hul* and a jacket which they dispatched to the prince at the fortress of Longvaek. [As soon as he had received these] the latter travelled hastily to rejoin his family as Samron Sen ... . There he re-encountered his aunt and relations to the seventh degree of kinship. He then married *Neang* Bau, a young woman of means and with masses of clients and slaves, after which he returned to the capital ... . [The king] generously promoted the prince to the rank of *oknha* Surendradhipati and *Neang* Bau to the rank of *jamdev* Sriratnakesar.

Neang Bau, who had 'masses of clients' of her own, was probably *Neang* Sa, daughter of the prince's aunt mentioned earlier in the passage, as the title bestowed upon her by Dhammaraja incorporated elements of the titles borne by the prince's aunt and mother.[18]

Clients, in their turn, supported their patrons in their endeavours, even when this meant turning against the king. Queen Ang Li Kshatri, forced to marry Padumaraja II (r. 1672–1673), had him assassinated by Cham and

Malay clients whom she had inherited through her mother, herself of Cham or Malay extraction. Pretending to be sick, she asked the king for permission for a group of her retainers to be admitted to the palace, so that they might prepare medicines and attend to her in the night. Padumaraja II agreed. Once the king had retired, Ang Li Kshatri ordered the contingent of Cham and Malay people to find and kill the king as he slept.[19] An *anuj khshatri*, 'young queen', established a court at Samron Sen in the eighteenth century, attended by members of the royal family, the children and nephews and nieces of the king. When King Jai Jettha IV died in 1729, his son Dhammaraja was at the Thai court, where he had been since 1710. Ang Im, married to Dhammaraja's sister, ruled with Jai Jettha between 1710 and 1722. He then abdicated in favour of his son, Sattha, married to his wife's half-sister, another daughter of Jai Jettha, named Sijhata. Ang Im took the throne again in 1729 but abdicated the following year. Sattha ruled from Longvaek until some time after his father's death in 1736, when Sijhata and her relatives sought to oust him. Thai and Cambodian sources indicate that Sijhata was in Samron Sen around the time of events recorded in IMA 39. There seems little doubt, therefore, that the *anuj khshatri* was Sijhata.[20]

The same inscription speaks of a *maha-kshatri*, 'great queen', who was 'born the daughter of the king *kaev hva*'. An *oknha* was instructed to march against the *maha-kshatri* in 1747. He was successful, 'routing her completely. ... He captured the lady and a mass of goods, and escorted her to the king in order to prostrate herself and offer her slaves and her belongings.' The chronicles are silent on this episode. The inscription relates that in 1737 a *kaev hva* who was a *rajaputri touch* ('lesser prince') was at Longvaek. He was well-disposed towards supporters of Dhammaraja. Chandler proposed that this *kaev hva* was Cun, a nephew of Dhammaraja, and the *maha-kshatri* was his daughter. He suggests that Cun's relatives were offended when his title, *kaev hva*, and his widow were distributed to two of Dhammaraja's own sons when Cun died in 1743, and that his daughter led them in a rebellion against Dhammaraja.[21] Pou and Chandler both translate *maha-kshatri* as 'princess' in their studies of the inscription, although, if we are to understand *anuj khsatri* as 'young queen', the meaning of *maha-khsatri* is 'great queen'. The implication is that the *maha-kshatri* was more powerful than Sijhata had been.

Ang Im (r. 1710–1722 and 1729–1730) had been given the title *kaev hva* by his wife's father, King Jai Jettha, in 1699. Although he assumed the title of *ubhayoraj*, 'former king', when he abdicated in 1730, he was usually referred to as *kaev hva*. A daughter of Ang Im old enough to lead a rebellion in 1747 must have born by 1727, before Ang Im became the *ubhayoraj*. She would have been, therefore, 'born the daughter of the king *kaev hva*', as it says in the inscription.[22] Such a daughter would have a basis for legitimation through her mother, a daughter of King Jai Jettha, and her father, who had clearly been a popular ruler, as he reigned twice and his death resulted in immediate rebellion. The *maha-kshatri* posed a considerable threat to Dhammaraja's attempts to establish his own legitimacy; thus, he ordered his *oknha* to eliminate her. The Cambodian chronicles, composed in the court of the victor, would not be expected to mention the fact that Dhammaraja had encountered political opposition from his half-sister. It does indicate, however, that as had been the case in earlier periods, royal women who represented the interests of certain factions were recognised as legitimate rulers.

The most powerful woman at court was undoubtedly the mother of the king, who could determine succession. This was not a peculiarly Cambodian phenomenon; Queen Maha Thevi ruled the Lao kingdom of Lan Xang from behind the throne for nearly a decade following the death of her husband, 'making and murdering a succession of puppet kings'. Queen Devikshatri, chief queen of Paramaraja I (r. 1556–c. 1570), orchestrated the accession of two of her grandsons. The Thai sack of Longvaek in January 1594 had thrown middle Cambodia into confusion. King Sattha (r. c. 1570–1594), son of King Paramaraja I (r. 1556–c. 1570) and queen Devikshatri, had moved to Srei Santhor in 1593, leaving Longvaek in the hands of his half-brother, Suriyobarna. The Thai king took Suriyobarna and his court to Siam. Ram Jerng Prei, a lesser member of the royal family, took the opportunity to attack Sattha at Srei Santhor in 1594, seizing the throne. Sattha fled to Laos with his two eldest sons, Jettha and Ton, and died there in 1596. The following year, with the help of Spanish and Portuguese soldiers, Ram Jerng Prei was killed and Ton took the throne, reigning under the name Paramaraja II. The latter died in 1599, upon which the youngest son of Paramaraja I, An, acceded under the name Paramaraja III. He reigned until the end of 1600. Devikshatri then proposed that her sixteen-year-old grandson, Nom, a third son of King Sattha, ascend the throne. The ministers and court officials concurred and he took the throne under the title *kaev hva*. Three years later she turned upon her grandson. After consulting with the *oknha*, she sent a message to the

Thai king, asking that her husband's second son, Suriyobarna, be returned to Cambodia, as he would make a better king. The Thai king complied and supported Suriyobarna in winning over the populace. Devikshatri 'called all the ministers together and consulted with them … [then] stripped her grandson prince Nom of sovereignty, gathered the royal family and the court, and offered the throne to Suriyobarna', who reigned under the name Paramaraja IV (r. 1603–1618).[23]

Powerful and effective queen mothers seem to have had their rights enshrined in law during their lifetimes. The 1596 *Cbpab kram chakrei* ('Law regarding elephants'), composed when Devikshatri was at the height of her power, states that the only people who were permitted to own elephants, in addition to the king himself, were 'the queen mother; the *ubhayaraj*, the uncle of the king; the brother, son, or daughter of the king; the queen or a titled wife; a prince or princess of a *preah moneang*; or an aunt or uncle of the king'. Jai Jettha III, who ruled five or six times between 1677 and 1702, abdicated in 1687 in favour of his mother Queen Tey. She remained there for a matter of months before returning the throne to her son. In 1693, immediately after her short reign, two laws were composed, *Kram srok* ('Law of the land') and *Kram seh* ('Law of horses'). These list the most important people in the country as the king, the king's father, the queen mother and the *uparaj*, and state their entitlements to certain privileges and revenues.[24] Queen mothers were usually the daughters of previous kings. A staggering number of liaisons, marriages and re-marriages between kings and the daughters of other kings – usually their sisters, nieces or aunts – were recorded in the chronicles.

One story, referring to events that are legendary rather than historical, related that Prince Padum, son of King Cakrabattiraj, was told that in order to perpetuate the royal line, he must leave the monastery and conceive a son with princess Sobhavatti, who was either a half-sister of Padum himself or a sister (and possibly a lesser wife) of his father. Once the child was born, he returned to his religious pursuits.[25] Jai Jettha II (r. 1618–1627) wished to unite his son, Dhammaraja, and daughter, Ang Vatti, half-siblings, but the marriage was postponed until Dhammaraja completed his monkhood. Upon Jai Jettha II's death, his younger brother, the *ubhayoraj* Paramaraja Udaiy, married Ang Vatti, renaming her Mae Your Vatti. A century later, Prince Cun's widow was remarried to a son of the incumbent king, Dhammaraja. There are many other examples of such unions between royal siblings in Cambodia, although elsewhere in Southeast Asia first cousinship was the closest degree permitted. Such marriages were desirable because marriage with a royal princess gave the groom a legitimate claim to the throne, and usurpers, on occasion, took this avenue. Thus Ram Jerng Prei (r. 1594–1597) 'was seized with ambition and wished to dispute the throne to take the consorts and wives' of King Sattha. Suriyobarna, later King Paramaraja IV (r. 1603–1618), 'secretly had sexual relations' with Sujata, his younger sister, making her his principal queen. Another of these situations had arisen in the sixteenth century, when a Malay official in charge of the coast during the reign of Paramaraja II (1597–1599) 'seriously offended the king by surreptitiously taking with him one of the king's sisters and living with her against the king's will'. The king ignored this transgression as he was relying on the official to keep the coast safe for the Spanish emissaries whom he had dispatched to Manila for military aid. The official was described 'a very malicious man' who was waiting for an opportunity to kill the king 'and to stir up the kingdom to revolt'.[26]

Princesses had to be carefully watched lest they provide an avenue for an upstart to gain the throne. This was why, as the *Rajaphisek* of Jai Jettha II related in 1618, the queen was the first of the seven treasures that marked a *cakravartin*. The chronicles recounted a story in which a fifteen-year-old princess allowed a fisherman to come to power. Suvarnamali, sister of King Suvarna Padum, a legendary king, fell in love with the sixteen-year-old son of the chief of a fishing village and took measures to ensure that her brother the king could not interfere with her choice, imperiously informing the boy and his family of her wishes, constructing a fortified palace and placing soldiers at the ready to protect her and her bridegroom. She also bestowed a title, *sdec prades raj*, on her husband, paying no heed to the protestations and advice of her counsellors. Happily, 'the king eventually forgave his sister her transgression' and after his death the court decreed that her husband should ascend the throne.[27]

Royal women were accorded particular posthumous honour in the middle period, perhaps in a continuation of the *kanlon kamraten an* of earlier times. Upon the death of the queen of the legendary King Cakrabarti, her son erected a pavilion in which her body lay in state for five days. After the cremation, the king took his mother's ashes to the temple of Lolei, where they were interred. Another version of the chronicles relates that this king, 'thinking of the merits of the royal lady his mother,' ordered statues erected on Phnom Roung in the likeness of his mother and the Buddha contemplating *nirvana*, 'enlightenment'. The name of the statue of the queen mother was *Srei Krup Lakkhana*, 'Lady full of virtues'. When Sobhavatti died, her two sons held funeral ceremonies for her 'in the popular tradition'. The same text adds that 'in that place, under the reigns of the subsequent kings, people gave offerings to the revered royal queen'. Many other examples of such treatment of royal women are referred to in the chronicles. Others, however, were not so lucky; according to Hann So, King Ang Non III (r. 1775–1779) had one of his *oknha* killed. The *oknha's* mother incited her remaining four sons in the provinces to rebel against the king in retaliation. The *oknha* Baen allegedly captured her, tethered her 'like a cow', and forced her to crawl on all fours and eat grass until she died.[28]

There are numerous accounts of royal princesses travelling to and from Southeast Asian kingdoms in order to cement political alliances between courts.[29] A Cambodian princess became the principal queen of Fa Ngum, founder of the Lao kingdom of Lan Xang. King Sattha (r. c. 1570–1594) fled to Laos with his two eldest sons following a disastrous rout by the Thai. According to Gabriel Quiroga de San Antonio, the Lao king 'greeted him warmly, showed him deep friendship and, as a gesture of close alliance and in order to ratify mutual good will, the Cambodian king's eldest son married the Lao king's eldest daughter. The kings, princes, and, generally speaking, the whole kingdom were very satisfied'.[30] A Nguyen princess, Ang Chuv, was married to the Cambodian prince Jai Jettha in order to form an alliance. Towards the end of his reign, Suriyobarna (Paramaraja IV) (r. 1603–1618) summoned his *oknha* and expressed his fear that the Thai would again invade Cambodia unless an alliance was made with Hué.

> 'It is proper that we contract an alliance with the kingdom of the Vietnamese and that we ask for the hand of Ang Chuv, the daughter of the Vietnamese king, to be the royal wife of Jai Jettha. Thus, our friendly relationship will be strengthened. If the Siamese raise troops to come and attack us, we will take troops from the Vietnamese kingdom to help us make war'. Accordingly, envoys and gifts were dispatched to the Vietnamese court. The Vietnamese king consulted with his advisors, saying 'If our royal daughter was to become the wife of the son of the Khmer king, and if she had a son and if he ascended the throne, he would submit to our will, as he is part of our line'.[31]

Members of the Cambodian royal family would be 'invited' to the Thai court, ostensibly for education or protection, following events in Cambodia that necessitated an incumbent ruler seeking assistance from Siam. The reality was that the co-operation of Cambodian kings would be assured as long as their wives, sisters, and children were at the mercy of the Thai king. After the sack of Longvaek in 1594, the Thai king asked the Cambodian prince, Suriyobarna, 'to assemble his wives, princes, princesses, advisors and ministers, in order that they accompany him to the Thai capital in a gesture of goodwill.' Although reluctant, Suriyobarna agreed, his ministers advising him that there was nothing else to be done if peace with Siam was to be preserved. Accordingly, most of the court, including the two crown princes, Jai Jettha and Udaiya, and a princess, Eng Chanda Bopha, went to Ayutthaya. The Thai king had suitable accommodation erected to house the Cambodian court,[32] which consisted not only of the Cambodian royal family, but their retainers and courtiers. For this reason it was inevitable that some cross-cultural assimilation occurred amongst the Thai and Cambodian elite.

Marriages between Cambodian princesses and the first Europeans to become embroiled in Cambodian politics can also be seen as political alliances of this nature. The first European to visit Cambodia was a Portuguese missionary, Gaspar de Cruz, in the 1550s. A Spanish priest, Antonio de Magdalena, visited Angkor around 1585 or 1586. He recounted his experiences to Diogo do Couto, the official historian and archivist in Goa at the end of the sixteenth century, who wrote them into a history of Asia around 1611. The Spanish and Portuguese accounts indicate that King Sattha (r. c. 1570–1594) was particularly well-disposed towards the Europeans, especially Diego Veloso and Blas Ruiz. The chronicles relate that he called them his 'adoptive sons'. This amicability undoubtedly stemmed from Sattha's fear of the Thai, who had launched a moderately successful attack on Longvaek in 1583. The Portuguese and Spanish had gunpowder technology and the latter reserves of soldiers stationed in the Philippines. Sattha's eagerness to please the European contingent is evident from his expression of a wish to convert to Catholicism. He entreated the Spanish and Portuguese to go to Manila 'to request for and to bring friars for that purpose as well as soldiers if necessary'. The king pressed copious gifts upon the Portuguese and Spanish, marrying Diego Belloso to one of his cousins and giving him and his heirs jurisdiction of the province of Ba Phnom. Ruiz received the province of Treang.[33] Gifts of wealth and land, elevated titles, and alliance through marriage were what a Cambodian *oknha* would receive as a reward for his services.

Life at court

The necessity of establishing and maintaining alliances through marriage, as we have seen in the previous chapter, resulted in large numbers of women residing in the 'women's apartments' of kings, princes and officials , usually of differing ethnicities, backgrounds and appearances (see Fig. 4.5). King Jai Jettha II (r. 1618–1627) had Vietnamese, Lao, and Cambodian queens. Women at court were given titles and ranks according to their birth and the status of their family. A document describing the coronation of Suriyobarna in 1603 spoke of women titled *preah snang,* the *preah moneang,* the *sroengkar bhariya,* the *ak yeay chastum,* and the *jamdev khoneang,* 'clothed in magnificent *sampot,* in ivory, wearing the crown of their rank'.[34] The accession of a new king must have been an anxious time for the court; it was within the scope of the new king, the day after his own coronation with the principal queen, to withdraw, confirm or redistribute ranks and entitlements amongst the nobility and the women of the palace, including the wives of officials. *Cbpab khon sala,* devised in 1723, stated that 'those who have received titles and marks of honour from the king and who have never given any service' and wherein inheritance of titles and land was devolved upon a *jamdev,* 'the deci-

Fig. 4.5: Women of the palace. Mural, Royal Palace, Phnom Penh.

sion is left to the king'. The court ladies greeted him upon his return from the coronation by prostrating themselves at the king's feet and saying 'We pray of you, receive us; we are always at your feet, and we come to offer you our bodies and our lives, we place ourselves under your authority until the end of our lives'. The women who had comprised the king's household before his coronation were elevated to new titles as a matter of course. The four *preah snang thom*, the highest level of royal wife after the queen, received the title *preah moneang*; the second rank of *preah snam* became *preah neang*; the third rank, *neak moneang*; and the fourth, *neak neang*. The queen, known as *preah socheat kshatriya eng* ('first princess') before the coronation, would be known as *samdech preah pheakka vati srei socheata* ('royal revered flower, the virtuous lady') afterward, although this varied from king to king.[35]

The king Viroraj married a princess, *Neak Neang* Des, and bestowed upon her the new name and title *preah* Mandadevi *sobha lakkhana maha-kshatri*. Paramaraja III, seeking to seduce the wife of a provincial official, elevated her to the rank of *preah moneang* in an attempt to persuade her to co-operate. Ang Chuv received the title 'royal lady Bhagavatti vara-kshatri'. It was also possible to have two principal queens simultaneously. Padumaraja II (r. 1672–1673) made his own wife, Dhita, 'left-hand' queen; the widow of the previous king, Ang Li Kshatri, he took as his 'right-hand' queen. The female relatives of kings also benefited. Ramadhipati gave his mother a title and permission to use a gong to summon the elderly to the door of her palace; he also gave her an elephant named Kraysasey for the park, a three-tiered throne, four umbrella bearers, and sixteen men for her entourage. Ang Li Kshatri was elevated to a higher rank of nine *sakh* by her nephew in 1659, and authorised to have two bearers, four men to carry her umbrella, and eight men for each her right- and left-hand entourage. The families of women raised to new ranks in this manner would benefit as they would be in a better position to offer patronage – in other words, they would become imbued with more potential to effect change through their close relationship with the king.[36]

The 'favourite' of the king was not necessarily the consort of highest birth. The favourite would remain in that position as long as no younger and prettier claimant came along. Anna Leonowens, writing of the Thai court in the 1770s, said that the consort that loved King Mongkut the most, Thiang, 'contrived to be always in favour with the King, simply because she was the only woman among all that vast throng who really loved him, though at no period of her life had she ever enjoyed the unenviable distinction of being the favourite'. The favourites were always described as beautiful. According to the chronicles, such was the power of the favourite that other women concocted potions and charms that would enable them to outshine their competition. They also seem to have resorted to poisoning their rivals, as a special tribunal was charged to examine matters involving women of the palace who were suspected of being *ap* (witches) or poisoners.[37]

Some royal women were charged with conducting judicial inquiries, such as Ang Li, who was authorised to investigate a case in which a woman, *me* Loeu, and her husband, *a* Ngoun, were decapitated by another man on the pretext that they were practitioners of black magic, after which he confiscated their belongings. On another occasion she sent *oknha* to judge a matter in the provinces on her behalf. Such was Ang Li's renown for legal matters that in 1693 her nephew the king asked her to recount all she knew of past judicial custom so that they might compose a new law code for the future; she 'declared that she was very happy that her nephew wished to know the ancient laws' and suggested he then call together all the astrologers, teachers and wise persons at the court to restore the law.

Other women of the palace played diplomatic roles. Hong Lysa observed that in the Thai court 'palace women were positioned at the interstices of the domestic domain and the sphere of court affairs'. This was also true of the Cambodian court in the middle period. A *neak moneang*, 'lesser queen', sent girls who were 'instructed, intelligent and trustworthy' in order to persuade her brother Kan to cease his rebellious ways and return to her husband's court. In 1600, Paramaraja III attempted to seduce *Neang* Dev, wife of a provincial official. When she rejected his advances, the king had her imprisoned and chained, ordering the women of the palace to speak with her and convince her to comply with his wishes. Dhammaraja I (r. 1627–1632) 'charged elderly ladies who knew how to speak to take [a letter] to princess Mae Your Vatti, without the knowledge' of her husband. Women of the palace also acted as chaperones and attendants. At the time of her marriage, Ang Chuv was attended into the palace by 'one hundred elderly ladies, one hundred young girls, daughters of court officials, and also a certain number of royal consorts and women of the palace.' Older women were also sent on pilgrimages with queens.[38]

At times, however, their role was more ceremonial. At the coronation of Suriyobarna in 1603 'male dancers, female dancers and orchestras played throughout the first seven days'. The *srei snang*, followed by *srei kanha* (young, unmarried girls), 'were all clothed in brocaded cloth of red and sequins of ivory, covered in rings, golden bracelets and gold chains' and proceeded in two columns before the king on his way to the coronation. In the bedchamber, women were to enter bearing items signifying prosperity, including plates of betel, cigarettes, gold trays, *sampot*s, goblets, jewellery and perfumes; the four wives of *preah snang* rank then each busied herself with her particular task. One would present him with a cat of three or more colours; the others would bring a statue, an elephant tusk or rhinocerous horn, and the fourth would wash his feet. Upon the death of a king, the women of the palace were ordered to cry continuously and to play the death-drums.[39]

Despite the privileges that came with becoming one of the king's consorts, women in the Cambodian court were required to observe a strict prohibition on their interaction with men. Sexual infidelity was more than a betrayal of a woman's personal obligations as spouse of the king; it was political treason, as these women were also ambassadors of their family's fealty and interests. It was illegal for anyone except the king to have sexual relations in or near the palace and heavy penalties were in place for those who transgressed. A man named Krak was caught fornicating with the wife of an employee of the royal treasury; he had to pay a fine of 3 *anching* and 17 *damlong*. The same rules were in place for officials of the king. Around 1660 *oknha* Yos chased a bird into the apartments of *neak neang* Bos, who had him arrested. The judge determined that he was at fault and should be executed; the king intervened and spared his life as he was unarmed. A scale of punishments were in place for women of the palace who dared to entertain lovers, or even to communicate by 'fluttering eyelashes' with men in the world outside. This does not seem to have deterred them, however. A special tribunal could be convened to try not only erring women who quarrelled and spoke ill of the queen or other wives of the king, but the *ak yeay chastum* (old women of the palace) and others who acted 'as go-betweens and panderers for women of the palace'.[40]

Elite women were active participants in political and social life of middle Cambodia, deciding matters of succession, acting as diplomats and confidantes, and orchestrating policy. They continued to own property and donate to religious establishments, despite the overtly patriarchal timbre of the royal chronicles and didactic literature. Although, as occurred elsewhere in Southeast Asia, the court records imply that the involvement of women in the political realm had ill effects for the kingdom,[41] careful reading of the sources reveals a continuing equality between women and men of the same social bracket in middle Cambodia.

Beyond the palace walls

The evidence indicates a relatively egalitarian existence between men and women beyond the palace walls. Everyone, irrespective of gender, who lived outside the palace or the provincial forts, was at the mercy of those within. At any time, men might be called up for corvee labour or military service; women might be required to accompany armies as supply personnel. Pretty girls were destined for presentation to the households of powerful local elites as signs of fealty; these could then send the women on to the king as a sign of their own loyalty, or keep them in their own service. When a new king came to power, *oknha* actively scouted for favourable additions to his retinue. Two *oknha* reported to the legendary king Paksiy Cham Kru that the daughter of the Cham king Sendra II was 'very pale and very beautiful. The princesses of the royal palace have nothing like her equal.' They went on to relate that the princess had two ladies-in-waiting who had already been approached by the *oknha*'s envoys and were kindly disposed towards them. It was virtually impossible for ordinary Cambodians to refuse the demands of the elite. King Nom (r. 1600–1603), who ascended the throne at the age of sixteen, sent his *oknha* and servants to nearby villages in order to bring back the daughters and wives of the inhabitants for his pleasure. If the women resisted him, he ordered them imprisoned; if one of them did not please him, he would 'order a page to unite himself to her in front of her husband's very eyes'. His grandmother, Queen Devikshatri, removed him from power for his behaviour. In 1600, Paramaraja III forgot 'his royal consorts and the ladies of the palace; he forgot his reputation and all criticism' in his pursuit of Dev, allegedly trying 'to seduce Dev in different ways'. The chronicles describe the four kings who ruled Cambodia before Paramaraja IV (r. 1603–1618) as 'menacing young girls and women'.[42]

Women seem to have been constantly at risk of seduction and interference, given the detailed punishments for transgressions against them laid out in the legal codes of the middle period. One wonders, indeed, if men had anything else on their minds; *Cbpab tous bhariya* ('Law on matters concerning wives'), derived from a very old Pali text, mentions, amongst other ill deeds, the man 'who goes to another's house, and, seeing the wife of that man, mimes urinating in speaking to his wife so as to tempt her' and he who 'seeing a woman go into the forest to empty her bowels' attempts to take advantage of the remote location. Men who violated 'the daughters of others in an isolated place' were to pay a fine of 1 *anching* and 5 *damlong* 'so that other men will be less audacious and less tempted to follow this example'. When the women involved were *kramom*, girls who had reached puberty but were still virgins, the penalties were higher. At particular risk were the girls indentured in the houses of wealthy men. Women were regularly placed in the households of the local elite as collateral against loans taken out by their parents and other relatives. Their work would pay the interest on the loan until the sum was repaid in full. The laws were explicit as to the prohibition concerning masters taking advantage of women in their employ. If an unmarried girl was violated against her will, the law allowed her to leave the house without her relatives having to repay the loan. If the woman was married, she could leave and her husband bring suit against her master for compensation.[43]

Sexual activity that took place outside a 'legitimate' union was regarded as an outrage against the girl's *meba*, a term that can refer to parents and relatives more generally, but in this context means 'ancestors', specifically of the maternal line. Usually the displeasure of the *meba* was manifested in a sudden and serious illness befalling a male relative of the girl concerned. He would only recover once the *meba* had been appeased. This could occur through marriage of the offending parties (even when intercourse occurred through force). If the man refused to marry the girl, he would be invited to *sampeah kmouch*, 'salute the spirits', in a ceremony in which both the man and girl made offerings to the *meba* and asked for forgiveness, or by *leang komus*, 'washing away the stain', wherein the man would pay a fine of varying amounts depending on whether a child resulted from the union, the status of the girl, and so on. *Cbpab khon sala* relates a case in which a girl stole the *sampot* of her lover and offered it to the ancestors by way of appeasement, after which her master, cured of his illness, compensated the man double the value of the *sampot*. *Cbpab tumnam boran* warned of dire consequences for those who transgressed against the *meba*. Chan, a free man, refused to appease the *meba* of Pou, his lover; her brother Kong fell ill. Ney, Kong's wife, begged Chan to make an offering to the *meba* but he continued to ignore her pleas. Kong died and Ney complained to the king, who ordered Chan to assist with the funeral and to pay 30 *damlong*, two-thirds of which went to the widow, the remainder to Pou; he was then placed in the king's slave retinue as punishment for his bad conduct.[44]

Marriage gave women status and legal protections. Those that persisted in flaunting social convention and living with a man without her *meba's* permission were completely in his power. There were three categories of legitimate wife, differentiated by the type of ceremony and the status of the woman. The *prapuon thom,* 'principal wife', was the wife of first rank. She would be married in a large wedding ceremony, attended by both sets of parents, and elaborate and numerous gifts given to the bride's family. After her marriage, she would be referred to as *Neang,* a polite title designating her marital status. *Prapuon thom* seem to have been virgins upon their marriage. This characteristic put them at risk in their first pregnancy if their husbands happened to be evil men. In the second, third or fourth month of gestation, the father of the child might trick his wife into saying the words 'this is your child, do with it what you will'; he would then take her to a remote part of the forest and remove the fetus, killing the mother in the process. He would then dehydrate the fetus, known as *koan kroach,* 'smoked child', over a ritual fire and wear it around his neck in a small bag, from where it would advise him of potential danger. The frequency of *koan kroach* occurrences is not recorded, but the penalties for the men who made use of their wives in this way were severe. Perhaps the egalitarian nature of the law in middle Cambodia encouraged women to speak out against their husbands. *Cbpab tumnam pi boran* tells of a woman who discovered that her husband had stolen Buddha statues from a nearby *wat* and informed on him. The king rewarded her with clothes and a family of slaves. Women could also stand in for their husbands in court, as 'the law says "a husband and wife are the one person" and that "what is won or lost by one is won or lost by the other".'[45]

Free women who were not eligible to be *prapuon thom* were known as *prapuon stoeu, prapuon kandal,* or *anuj bhariya,* 'middle' or 'lesser' wife. Although the law codes are not explicit, *prapuon kandal* were probably women who had been married before or who had been married under irregular circumstances such as abduction or a premarital sexual liaison. The *meba* could solemnise a union after the fact, in which case the wife was known as a *nea nea bhariya,* 'wife by alternative means' or *tean resey bhariya,* 'wife out of charity'. Should a father refuse his consent but the couple obtain it from the woman's mother, she was known as a *patoe kan bhariya,* 'wife in spite of objections'. The only difference between *prapuon thom* and *prapuon kandal* lay in the degree of ceremony involved; *prapuon kandal* could be obtained simply by a gift of goods to her relatives, with no official ceremony.[46]

The final category of spouse was the *prapuon jerng* or *prapuon touch*, 'end' or 'least' wife. *Prapuon jerng* were women who had been taken as the spoils of war, members of ethnic minorities, relatives of rebellious *oknha* whose punishment was the enslavement of their family, convicted criminals, or those who had been born to a slave. Women within this category would serve the household as cooks, cleaners, preparing food, manufacturing cloth, sewing, tending to small-scale agricultural and animal husbandry, and assist in marketing good produced. Female slaves would also be offered to household guests in gestures of hospitality and goodwill. As numbers of European merchant ships and their crews increased in Southeast Asia in the seventeenth and eighteenth centuries, female slaves became commoditised, sent out from the household to engage in sex-for-cash transactions, the proceeds of which were returned to their master or mistress. No doubt many were ill-treated by their masters. *Cbpab tumnam pi boran* tells the story of a slave, Sok, who made her master Som a *samlor trey*, or fish stew. Upon discovering a frog in his food, he became angry and beat her until she bled. Sok ran away but was retrieved by an *oknha* who returned her to her master.[47]

The law may have frowned upon masters taking advantage of their female slaves, stating that women who were violated were free to leave, but it was not always possible for them to do so. In the early seventeenth century, a girl named Ou was placed in the household of a provincial official as surety for the sum of 100 *anching* her parents borrowed. When they went to repay the *oknha* and reclaim their daughter, he refused to see them, instead sending an intermediary to tell them that Ou was busy weaving. They returned the next day but this time the *oknha* said that he could not allow Ou to leave as one of his slaves had died and he was very sad. The third time, he said that he was troubled because his children were sick and Ou was needed to tend to them. Finally, after the king and queen had intervened, the *oknha* was forced to pay an enormous fine to the court and Ou was released to her parents without having to repay the 100 *anching*. *Cbpab tous bhariya*, whilst stipulating that women who were abused were permitted to leave, adds that 'if, despite the outrages of her master, the woman stays in his house', the master could then decide whether or not to marry her. This was also the case if the brother, son or nephew of her master was involved. The laws are contradictory on whether or not it was necessary to appease the *meba*. *Cbpab tumnam pi boran* stated that it was; thirty years later *Cbpab khon sala* was equally clear that men were not required to fulfil this obligation unless illness arose, because 'if the girl has been pawned or sold, she is called *me-hang* [servant] and cannot be dishonoured'. If he decided to marry her, however, any sum owed by the woman's relatives was expunged; similarly, they would not expect him to give gifts or goods as would be the normal procedure. Married women who had been slaves were titled *Me-kha* or *Me*.[48]

Should a man enter into a relationship with a woman who was the slave of another man he was usually obliged to purchase her from her master. Such women were also known as *prapuon mecak*, 'bought wife'. An *oknha* confiscated slaves from a Chinese merchant named Lak and had a sexual relationship with one of them, Pou, promising her that he would marry her. He also gave her gifts of a sash and a *sampot*. When Lak reclaimed his slaves, he noticed that Pou was wearing unfamiliar clothing and asked her where she had obtained them. Pou confessed that the *oknha* had given them to her and had promised to marry her. Lak complained to the king and the *oknha* was obliged to buy Pou for 3 *anching* and 17 *damlong*. The sum varied according the remaining debt owed by the woman or her family, or the value placed upon her life. When a free man, Ney, refused to marry *Me* Preas despite her pregnancy, the judge ordered him to support her until her delivery. If she died as a result of the pregnancy or during childbirth he was obliged to pay her master a sum that would allow *Me* Preas to be replaced; if she survived, he was to pay 10 *baht* to expiate the shame for the ancestors, and 5 *damlong* to her parents, because they were of the same status as he. Once married, despite her origin, the *prapuon jerng* was no longer considered a slave.[49]

Many Europeans took *prapuon jerng* as temporary wives. The Cambodian chronicles and foreign observers' accounts refer to a large multicultural population in and around the court during the seventeenth and eighteenth centuries, consisting of Portuguese, Spanish, Dutch, English, Japanese, and Chinese merchants and officials. The literature of almost every Southeast Asian polity is peppered with references to alliances between local women and foreign men during this period.

> Once they agree about the money (which does not amount to much for so great a convenience), she comes to the house, and serves him by day as his

maidservant and by night as his bedded wife. He is then not able to consort with other women or he will be in grave trouble with his wife, but the marriage lasts as long as he keeps his residence there, in good peace and unity.[50]

Barbara Watson Andaya suggested that this practice was more prevalent amongst non-royal families, as the purpose of alliances between royal families was to establish long-lasting ties. Obviously, mercenaries and traders would not be permanent fixtures in the region. Women arranged their own temporary marriages in some places. Cambodian women, as was the case in most parts of early modern Southeast Asia, were responsible for day-to-day economic transactions. A popular Cambodian maxim from the middle period was 'do not argue with women, do not make deals with government officials, and do not enter into a lawsuit against Chinese.' The mercantile skills of local women were an asset to a foreign trader, but there were other benefits of acquiring a temporary wife, ranging from clean clothes to translation. Temporary marriages were conducted in the same manner as a permanent union. Partners were expected to behave with respect and fidelity towards each other. Local rules applied to these marriages, with the relatives of the women concerned prepared to act on their behalf should they be mistreated at the hands of their husband.[51]

The presence of more than one wife inevitably led to jealousy and competition in the household. If the law codes are to be believed, women took out their frustrations by quarrelling, murdering, and poisoning each other. Women who committed adultery with the husband of another were required to 'take three bottles of rice wine, a sampot, areca and betel, a brass vase and go to beg pardon of the wife of her lover and promise her that she will never have relations with him again'. If she denied the allegation and it was later proved to be true, she would be whipped in public and promenaded through the streets for three days with a basket on her head, proclaiming 'Yes, truly, I am guilty'. This ridicule was meant to deter other women from following her example. The law was, however, lenient toward wives who were deceived. If a married man had relations with another woman and the wife caught them and killed them in a fury, she was not guilty, according to *Cbpab kaul batoup*, because 'wives do not like it when their husband has another lover'. Another law stated that should 'a husband with many wives, *prapuon thom, stoeu, mekha*, have relations with another woman, and his wives are very angry, and one finds them and kills the lover with her own hand, one may punish the husband and confiscate his goods'. *Kram puok*, written in 1697, stated that women who catch their husbands with another woman were entitled 'to spoil the face of the lover, whether with a small knife, or with a piece of broken pottery'.[52]

Divorce was a relatively simple process for both men and women in middle Cambodia, although in most cases both parties had to agree. There were ten reasons to initiate divorce: the prolonged absence of a husband; the abandonment of the wife by the husband; an incompatibility of character, acknowledged by both parties; the introduction of a second wife into the marital home without the consent of the first wife; the disappearance or re-peated absconding of the wife; adultery of the part of the wife; justified aban-donment; the refusal of the husband to please his wife; the sale of the wife by her husband without her consent; and the sale of the husband by himself, without the consent of his wife.[53] *Kram sauphea thipdey*, 'Law for magistrates', said that

> if a husband does not love the *prapuon thom* he has taken, whatever her rank, if he does not show her any consideration or he abandons the bed of his wife for eight months and takes himself off to romance other women, the aban-doned wife, if she wishes to divorce, must address a judge. Once that is done, she may leave her husband's house and marry another man. If the *prapuon stoeu* or *touch* does not want to stay with him, she must inform the *sauphea*; that done, she may leave.[54]

The extent to which a wife's unhappiness was accepted as justification for divorce is debatable; *Cbpab Rajaneti* warns of the possible disruption to social harmony that would ensue should a jealous wife make plain her dislike of her husband's favourite slave-girl. Abandonment was taken very seriously in the law courts as women could go berserk in the case of a prolonged hiatus from sexual fulfilment. An absence of between eight and twelve months constituted an appropriate length of time for a wife to await her husband; after this, she could consider herself a widow. She was prohibited from marriage for another three years, the usual period that elapsed between death and interment. Should a husband reappear after this, he would have to pay for a new wedding ceremony. Men could also abandon their wives if they took refuge in the house of another for more than a day, or if their wives were charged with a crime and the husband refused to stand by her. In the latter circumstance, women could seek assistance from another man, and, if they were acquitted, could marry him without delay. Men who abandoned their wives, or women they impregnated, relinquished all rights to their children as they had not 'tended the mother, nor brought firewood [for the ceremony of 'smoking' the mother after childbirth], nor hot and cold water which the woman needs, nor necessary medications'.[55]

Temporary wives taken by foreigners could thus consider themselves abandoned or widowed after the prescribed length of time had elapsed, and remarry. The length of a temporary marriage could last for months or years; when the husband returned to his own country or left for duties elsewhere in the region, he gave her 'what ever is promised, and so they leave each other in friendship'. The status of women who had been temporary wives actually may have increased, as upon the dissolution of the union she would have been in possession of a lump sum of capital, business connections, and probably linguistic skills. Multiple sexual partners did not decrease the social worth of women in most parts of Southeast Asia in the pre-modern period, at least amongst the non-royal families. Widows were, however, to refrain from taking another husband or a lover until their husband's bones had been safely interred. If she were to wait another seven months from this point, she would be known as a *kanlong theat*, 'good widow'. Women were also enjoined to prostrate themselves, 'cry, and behave sadly'.[56]

ᘒ

Little seems to have changed for women in Cambodian society in the middle period. Theravada Buddhism wrought changes to the outer form of religion in Cambodia; the content remained remarkably similar to that of preceding, Brahmanical periods. The social mores espoused in the *cbpab* differed little from earlier codes, either in the representation of women as alternatively nurturing and corrupting, or to the extent that these values were embraced by Cambodian society as a whole. Elite women continued to have influence and resonance, as is evidenced by the establishment of satellite courts, the involvement of women in matters of succession, and their presence within *khsae* networks. The continuing significance of women of royal blood as living embodiments of sovereignty is reflected in the numerous remarriages, incestuous liaisons, and status-elevating unions detailed in the chronicles. Women outside the palace seem to have received the same treatment as their male counterparts. A European presence does not seem to have resulted in a devaluation of women in Cambodian society; on the contrary, Europeans were assimilated into pre-existing Cambodian political and social frameworks. Although an increase in the numbers of foreign men undoubtedly led to a commoditisation of sex in Cambodia, as occurred throughout Southeast Asia, and the people required to provide this commodity were women, Europeans were not responsible for the sexualisation of enslaved women; they had been accommodating their masters and household guests in the same manner for centuries. We must conclude, therefore, that the middle period was not the epoch in which power was denied to Cambodian women.

Notes to Chapter 4

1   The Cambodian sources for the period between the fifteenth and late eighteenth centuries are somewhat problematic. There are a handful of inscriptions which relate a significant degree of detail concerning specific events. The earliest *cbpab*, didactic codes outlining correct behaviour, were written at this time, and furnish some idea of how Cambodian society operated. Extant literature is rare, although a written version of the Cambodian *Ramayana*, the *Reamker*, dates from the sixteenth or seventeenth century. Some law codes from the seventeenth and eighteenth centuries have survived. The *bangsavatar*, court chronicles, although purporting to record events from the beginning of Cambodian history, must be used with care, as they were regularly updated upon the succession of a new king, and could therefore be expected to undergo some revision in favour of the new incumbent. The earliest portion of a court chronicle available dates from 1796. It is probably best to regard the events described in the chronicles to the sixteenth century as fictional, as Michael Vickery cautions ('Cambodia after Angkor: The chronicular evidence for the fourteenth to sixteenth centuries', PhD thesis, Yale University, 1977, vol. 1, p. i). The *rioeng breng* or folktales, although doubtless indicative of earlier custom, have not been used as sources in this chapter as they cannot conclusively be said to provide a description of Cambodian society prior to the nineteenth century.

2   Ashley Thompson, 'Introductory remarks between the lines: Writing histories of middle Cambodia', in Barbara Watson Andaya (ed.), *Other pasts: Women, gender and history in early modern Southeast Asia*, Honolulu, Hawai'i: Center for Southeast Asian Studies, University of Hawai'i at Mânoa, 2000, pp. 280–281, note 3.

3   Saveros Lewitz, 'Textes en kmer moyen: Inscriptions modernes d'Angkor 2 et 3', *BEFEO* 57(1970), pp. 99–126; Khing Hoc Dy, *Contribution á l'histoire de littérature khmère*, vol. 1: L'époque classique (XVe–XIXe siècle), Paris: l'Harmattan, 1990, p. 24; Thompson, 'Introductory remarks', pp. 47–68.

4   There are two categories of *cbpab*: *Cbpab chah*, 'old *cbpab*', written before the end of the eighteenth century, and *cbpab th'mei*, 'new *cbpab*'. The latter are usually compilations of earlier versions, although *Cbpab Srei*, 'Code of conduct for women', will be discussed in greater detail in subsequent chapters.

5   David P. Chandler, 'Normative poems (*chbap*) and pre-colonial Cambodian society' [1982], in *Facing the Cambodian past: Selected essays 1971–1994*, St Leonards, New South Wales: Allen & Unwin, pp. 45–60.

6   *Cbpab Trineti*, verse 41, in Saveros Pou and Philip N. Jenner, 'Les *cpap*' ou <codes de conduite> Khmers VI: *Cbpab Trineti, BEFEO* vol. 70 (1981), p. 151.

7   *Cbpab Preah Rajasambpir*, verses 30 and 40, in Saveros Pou and Philip N. Jenner, 'Les *cpap*' ou , <codes de conduite> Khmers IV: Cpap Rajaneti ou cpap' brah Rajasambhir', *BEFEO* vol. 65 (1978), pp. 374–375; IMA 38, verse 98, in Saveros Pou, 'Inscriptions modernes d'Angkor 34 et 38', *BEFEO* vol. 62 (1975), p. 302; *Cbpab Trineti*, verse 30, in Pou and Jenner, 'Les *cpap*' ou <codes de conduite> Khmers VI',p. 149; Adhémard Leclère, *Les codes cambodgiens*, Paris: Ernest Leroux, 1898, t. 1, pp. 59–60.

8   Barbara Watson Andaya, *The flaming womb: Repositioning women in early modern Southeast Asia*, Honolulu: University of Hawai'i Press, 2006, p. 78; *Chroniques royales du Cambodge*, Paris: École Française d'Extrême-Orient, 1981–1988, vol. 3: *De 1594 à 1677*, trans. and ed. Mak Phoeun [hereafter *Chroniques* 3), pp. 79, 175; *Cbpab Koan Cao*, verses 41, 51, in Saveros Pou and Philip N. Jenner, 'Les *cpap* ou <codes de conduite> khmers III: *cpap ' kun cau'*, *BEFEO* vol. 64 (1977), pp.177, 179; *Cbpab Preah Rajasambpir*, verses 4, 6, 24, in Pou and Jenner, 'Les *cpap*' ou <codes de conduite> khmers IV', pp. 369–370, 373; Alan Sponberg, 'Attitudes toward women and the feminine in early Buddhism', in J.I. Cabeson (ed.), *Buddhism, Sexuality and Gender*, Albany, NY: State University of New York Press, n.d., pp. 3–4.

9   Muriel Paksin Carrison (comp.), *Cambodian folk stories from the Gatiloke*, trans. Kong Chhean, Rutland, Vermont; Tokyo, Japan: Charles E. Tuttle, 1987, p. 16; Adhémard Leclère, *Le Buddhisme au Cambodge*, Paris: Ernest Leroux, 1889, pp. 223–224, note 6; Ang Chouléan, 'Le sacré au féminin', *Seksa Khmer* 10–13 (1987–1990), pp. 7–9; Madeleine Giteau, 'Note sur les frontons du sanctuaire central du Vatt Nokor', *Arts Asiatiques* 16 (1967), pp. 136–137. See also Elizabeth Guthrie, 'Outside the sima', *Udaya: Journal of Khmer Studies* 2 (2001), pp. 7–18.

10   IMA 11, line 5, in Lewitz, 'Inscriptions modernes d'Angkor 10–16c', p.224; IMA 17, lines 5–6, in Lewitz, 'Inscriptions modernes d'Angkor 17–25', p. 164; IMA 19, lines 4, 16, in Lewitz, 'Inscriptions modernes d'Angkor 17–25', pp. 173–174; IMA 21, lines 14–15, in Lewitz, 'Inscriptions modernes d'Angkor 17–25, p. 179; IMA 29, line 2, in Lewitz, 'Inscriptions modernes d'Angkor 26–33', p. 215; IMA 34, lines 1–5, in Lewitz, 'Inscriptions modernes d'Angkor 34 et 38', p. 284; IMA 37, lines 5–6, in Lewitz, 'Inscriptions modernes d'Angkor 35, 36, 37 et 39', p. 309; Sponberg, 'Attitudes towards women and the feminine in early Buddhism', p. 8; Andaya, *Flaming womb*, p. 76.

11   IMA 23, lines 8–12, in Saveros Pou, 'Inscriptions modernes d'Angkor 17, 18, 19, 20, 21, 22, 23, 24 et 25', *BEFEO* 60 (1973), p. 184; Barbara Watson Andaya, 'Localising the universal: Women, motherhood and the appeal of early Theravada Buddhism', *Journal of Southeast Asian Studies*, 33, 1 (February 2002), pp. 1–30; IMA 12, lines 4–11, in Saveros Pou, 'Inscriptions modernes d'Angkor 10, 11, 12, 13, 14, 15, 16a, 16b et 16c', *BEFEO* 59

(1972), p. 226; IMA 39, lines 64–70, in Saveros Pou, 'Inscriptions modernes d'Angkor 35, 36, 37 et 39', *BEFEO* vol. 61 (1974), p. 321.

12 Andaya, *Flaming womb*, pp. 76–77; Helen Creese, *Women of the* kakawin *world: Marriage and sexuality in the Indic courts of Java and Bali*, Armonk, New York; London: M.E. Sharpe, 2004, pp. 188–192; David P. Chandler, 'An eighteenth century inscription from Angkor Wat', *Journal of the Siam Society* vol. 59, no. 2 (July 1971) p. 23; Pou, 'Inscriptions modernes d'Angkor, 35–39', p. 324.

13 *Chroniques royales du Cambodge*, vol. 1: *Des origines legendaires jusqu'à Paramaraja Ier*, trans. and ed. Mak Phoeun [hereafter *Chroniques 1*], p. 283; *Chroniques royales du Cambodge*, vol. 2: *De Bona Yat à la prise de Lanvaek (1417–1595)*, trans. and ed. Khin Sok, Paris: École Française d'Extrême-Orient, 1988 [hereafter *Chroniques 2*], pp. 102–105; IMA 4, A, lines 6–15, in Lewitz, 'Inscriptions modernes d'Angkor 4, 5, 6 et 7', p. 108.

14 IMA16a, lines 11–12, in Lewitz, 'Inscriptions modernes d'Angkor 10–16c', p. 236; IMA 35, lines 11–14, in Pou, 'Inscriptions modernes d'Angkor 35, 36, 37 et 39', p. 302; Cœdès, 'La fondation de Phnom Pen', p. 8; IMA 26, lines 4–11, in Saveros Lewitz, 'Inscriptions modernes d'Angkor 26, 27, 28, 29, 30, 31, 32, 33', *BEFEO* vol. 60 (1973), p. 206; Lewitz, 'Inscriptions modernes d'Angkor 26–33', p. 207, n. 17; IMA 28, lines 1–4, in Lewitz, 'Inscriptions modernes d'Angkor 26–33', p. 212; IMA 32, lines 20–27, in Lewitz, 'Inscriptions modernes d'Angkor 26–33', p. 227.

15 IMA 2, lines 1–10, French translation, in Lewitz, 'Textes en kmer moyen: Inscriptions modernes d'Angkor 2 et 3', pp. 103–104.

16 IMA 2, lines 3–9, 16–21, in Lewitz, 'Inscriptions modernes d'Angkor 2 et 3', pp. 102–103; IMA 30, lines 2, 11–16, in Lewitz, 'Inscriptions modernes d'Angkor 26–33', pp. 216–217; *Cbpab Preah Rajasambhir*, verse 37, in Pou and Jenner, 'Les *cpap* ou <codes de conduite> Khmers IV', p. 375; Justin J. Corfield, *The royal family of Cambodia*, Melbourne: The Khmer Language & Culture Centre, 1993, p.16.

17 Probably Princess Eng Chanda Bopha; *Cbpab tumam pi boran*, in *Codes cambodgiens*, t. 1, p. 128.

18 *Chroniques 1*, pp. 51–54; *Chroniques 2*, p. 103; IMA 39, lines 14–21 (French translation), in Pou, 'Inscriptions modernes d'Angkor 35, 36, 37 et 39', p. 322; Chandler, 'An eighteenth century inscription from Angkor Wat', p. 19.

19 An earlier king took steps to ensure that he would not have to convert to Islam before marrying a Cham princess. According to a lesser chronicle, 'he did not want to ask for the hand of the princess in the usual manner as he would have to enter the religion of the Chams. A *neak ta* accordingly spirited the princess two *sin* to the west of her father's palace at midnight, whereupon the king, acting on the advice of the five pages, entreated her to come with him. She accepted.' The Cham king was killed in the ensuing battle and the Cham princess became the principal queen. *Chroniques 3*, pp. 188–190, 192, 201, 207–208.

20 I have not seen the original inscription, but it seems clear that this is a corruption of *kshatri*. Pou translates this phrase as 'the princess who was the younger sister of the king' ('Inscriptions modernes d'Angkor 35, 36, 37 & 39', p. 322). Chandler translates it as

'young queen' ('An eighteenth century inscription from Angkor Wat', pp. 18, 22). Both are correct, as Sijhata was the half-sister of Dhammaraja. See also IMA 39, lines 17–20, in Pou, 'Inscriptions modernes d'Angkor 35, 36, 37 et 39', p. 319.

21 IMA 39, lines 11–13, Lewitz, 'Inscriptions modernes d'Angkor 35, 36, 37 et 39', p. 319; Chandler, 'An eighteenth-century inscription from Angkor Wat', pp. 17–21.

22 IMA 39, lines 38–39, in Pou, 'Inscriptions modernes d'Angkor 35, 36, 37 et 39', p. 320, and comments pp. 323, 324; Chandler, 'An eighteenth century inscription from Angkor Wat', pp. 18, 20–23.

23 *Chroniques 1*, pp. 51–54; Martin Stuart-Fox, 'Who was Maha thevi', *Journal of the Siam Society*, vol. 81, no. 1 (1993), p. 103; *Chroniques 2*, p. 213; Bernard P. Groslier, *Angkor et le Cambodge au XVIe siècle, d'après les sources portugaieses et espagnoles*, Paris: Presses Universitaires de France, 1958, p. 19; *Chroniques 3*, pp. 76, 82–84, 88–89.

24 *Cbpab kram chakrey*, in *Codes cambodgiens*, t. 1, p. 428; Ian Harris, *Cambodian Buddhism: History and practice*, Honolulu: University of Hawai'i Press, 2005, p. 43; Hann So, *The Khmer kings*, San Jose, California, n.p., 1988, p. 24; *Kram srok*, in *Codes cambodgiens*, t. 1, p. 120; *Kram ses*, in *Codes cambodgiens*, t. 1, p. 444.

25 *Chroniques 1*, pp. 117–118; 241. Another version of this story states that while Padum was meditating an 'invisible god' told him that he was predestined to conceive a son with the princess Sobhavatti (*Chroniques 1*, p. 241, f.n. 5). The discrepancies between the two texts are significant. In the official version a Buddhist context has been transposed onto an earlier event; forest animals talk about the Buddha as opposed to a mysterious 'god' referring to predetermined events, which precludes karma.

26 *Chroniques 2*, pp. 186, 214–215; *Chroniques 3*, pp. 149, 152–153, 155, 168, 186; Creese, *Women of the kakawin world*, pp. 120–132; *Chroniques 2*, pp. 186, 214–215; *Chroniques 3*, pp. 149, 152–153, 155, 168, 186; *Chroniques 1*, p. 121; Gabriel Quiroga de San Antonio, *A brief and truthful relation of events in the kingdom of Cambodia*, based on the 1914 translation of Antoine Cabaton, Bangkok: White Lotus, 1998, pp. 31, 38.

27 The other six treasures were 'his horse, his elephant, his vehicle, his wise counsellor, his trusted confidante, and the *preah khan* [sacred sword]'. *Rajaphisek of Jai Jettha* [1618], in *Codes cambodgiens*, t. 1, p. 58; *Chroniques 1*, pp. 51–54; Stuart-Fox, 'Who was Maha thevi', p. 103.

28 *Cbpab Koan Cao*, verse 66, in Pou and Jenner, 'Les *cpap*' ou <codes de conduite> Khmers III', p. 182; *Cbpab Preah Rajasampir*, verse 3, in Pou and Jenner, 'Les *cpap*' ou <codes de conduite> Khmers IV', p. 369; *Cbpab Kram*, verse 10, 16, in Saveros Pou and Philip N. Jenner, 'Les *cpap*' ou <codes de conduite> Khmers V: *Cpap' Kram*', BEFEO vol. 66 (1979), pp. 136, 137; *Nigrodhamiga-jataka*, in *The jataka, or stories of the Buddha's former births*, vol. I, trans. Robert Chalmers, Cambridge: Cambridge University Press, 1957, p. 40; *Chroniques 1*, pp. 106, 242, 272 (57/8,c); *Chroniques 2*, p. 215; *Chroniques 3*, pp. 118, 177; Hann So, *Khmer kings*, p. 28.

29 Creese, *Women of the kakawin world*, p. 46. See also Leonard Y. Andaya, 'Cultural state formation in eastern Indonesia', in Anthony Reid (ed.), *Southeast Asia in the early modern*

era: Trade, power, and belief, Ithaca, New York; London: Cornell University Press, 1993, pp. 37–39.

30 Stuart-Fox, 'Who was Maha thevi?', p. 103; Quiroga de San Antonio, *A brief and truthful relation,* p. 29; Groslier, *Angkor et le Cambodge au XVIe siècle,* p. 19.

31 *Chroniques 3,* pp. 120–121.

32 *Ibid.; Chroniques 2,* p. 213.

33 Groslier, *Angkor et le Cambodge au XVIe siècle,* pp. 64–67, 155; *Chroniques 2,* p. 213; *Chroniques 3,* pp. 72–73; Quiroga de San Antonio, *A brief and truthful relation,* pp. 11, 31.

34 These can best be translated as royal wives of first rank, wives of lesser rank, elderly women who had been wives or lesser princesses of previous kings, and ladies-in-waiting. *Preah Reachea Kroet Prapdaphisek du Preas Sauriyobarn,* in *Codes cambodgiens,* t. 1, pp. 45–46.

35 *Cbpab Khon Sala,* in *Codes cambodgiens,* t. 2, p. 3; *Preah Reachea Kroet Prapdaphisek du Preah Sauriyobarn,* in *Codes cambodgiens,* t. 1, p. 51.

36 *Chroniques 1,* p. 47; *Chroniques 2,* p. 112; *Chroniques 3,* pp. 78, 126, 131–132; *Chroniques 1,* p. 63; *Cbpab tumam pi boran,* in *Codes cambodgiens,* t. 1, pp. 125–126.

37 *Chroniques 2,* p. 136; *Chroniques 3,* p. 207; Anna Leonowens, *The romance of the harem* [1872], ed. Susan Morgan, Charlottesville: University of Virginia Press, 1991, p. 155; *Cbpab Khon Sala,* in *Codes cambodgiens,* t. 2, p. 32; *Kram preas dhamma anhunhnha,* in *Codes cambodgiens,* t. 2, p. 10.

38 *Cbpab tumam pi boran,* in *Codes cambodgiens,* t. 1, pp. 123, 133, 140, 175; Hong Lysa, 'Of consorts and harlots in Thai popular history', *Journal of Asian Studies,* vol. 57, no. 2 (May 1998), p. 341.

39 *Preas Reachea Kroet Prapdaphisek du Preas Sauriyobarn,* in *Codes cambodgiens,* t. 1, pp. 43, 45, 51; *Chroniques 2,* pp. 99, 158; *Chroniques 3,* p. 127.

40 *Cbpab tumam pi boran,* in *Codes cambodgiens,* t. 1, p. 127, 137; *Kram preas dhamma anhunhnha,* in *Codes cambodgiens,* t. 2, p. 22.

41 Andaya, *Flaming womb,* p. 169.

42 *Chroniques 1,* p. 273 (58/3); *Chroniques 2,* pp. 82, 238; *Chroniques 3,* pp. 78, 88–89, 113; *Cbpab tous piriyea,* in *Codes cambodgiens,* t. 2, p. 537.

43 *Cbpab tous piriyea,* in *Codes cambodgiens,* t. 2, pp. 515, 523, 529, 536.

44 *Kram sauphea thipdey,* in *Codes cambodgiens,* t. 2, p. 504; *Cbpab tous piriyea,* in *Codes cambodgiens,* t. 2, p. 541; *Cbpab Khon Sala,* in *Codes cambodgiens,* t. 2, pp. 37–38; *Cbpab kaul bantop,* in *Codes cambodgiens,* t. 2, pp. 492–493; *Cbpab tumam pi boran,* in *Codes cambodgiens,* t. 1, p. 156.

45 *Kram sauphea thipdey,* in *Codes cambodgiens,* t. 2, p. 504; *Cbpab khon sala,* in *Codes cambodgiens,* t. 1, p. 233; *Kram preas dhamma anhunhnha,* in *Codes cambodgiens,* t. 2, pp. 12–13; *Cbpab tumam pi boran,* in *Codes cambodgiens,* t. 1, p. 148; *Kram Tralakar,* in *Codes cambodgiens,* t. 2, pp. 88–89.

46 Adhémard Leclère translated this as 'concubine'. In Pali *ña ña* means 'different' or 'various'. *Kram sauphea thipdey,* in *Codes cambodgiens,* t. 2, pp. 502–503; *Cbpab tous piriyea,* in *Codes cambodgiens,* t. 2, p. 505.

47 *Cbpab tous piriyea,* in *Codes cambodgiens,* t. 2, p. 505; *Cbpab tumam pi boran,* in *Codes cambodgiens,* t. 1, p. 151. See also Barbara Watson Andaya, 'From temporary wife to prostitute'.

48 *Cbpab tumam pi boran,* in *Codes cambodgiens,* t. 1, p. 149–150; *Cbpab tous piriyea,* in *Codes cambodgiens,* t. 2, p. 529; *Cbpab Khon Sala,* in *Codes cambodgiens,* t. 1, p. 233 and t. 2, pp. 37–38. There was a group of male slaves known as *kha-luong,* 'servants of the palace'; the sense of *me-kha* also connotes servitude.

49 Khing Hoc Dy, *Contribution,* p. 66; *Cbpab tumam pi boran,* in *Codes cambodgiens,* t. 1, pp. 153, 155; *Cbpab kaul bantop,* in *Codes cambodgiens,* t. 2, p. 479.

50 van Neck, *De vierde schipvaart der Nederlanders naar Oost-Indie,* p. 225.

51 Andaya, 'From temporary wife to prostitute', pp. 11–12, 14; William Dampier, *A new voyage around the world* [1697] (New York: Dover, 1968), p. 269; Jacob van Neck, *De vierde schipvaart der Nederlanders naar Oost-Indie onder Jacob Wilkens en Jacob van Neck (1599–1604),* ed. H.A. van Foreest and A. de Booy, vol. 1, The Hague, Linschoten-Vereeniging, 1980, p. 225 (I am grateful to Gertrude van Hest for her translations of this and other passages of this book); Alexander Hamilton, *A new account of the East Indies* [1727], London: Argonaut Press, 1930, p. 96; King Hoc Dy, *Contribution,* p. 74.

52 *Kram preas dhamma anhunhnha,* in *Codes cambodgiens,* t. 2, pp. 4, 22; *Cbpab tous piriyea,* in *Codes cambodgiens,* t. 2, pp. 491, 531, 540; *Kram Puok,* in *Codes cambodgiens,* t. 2, pp. 571, 596.

53 The exceptions were the consorts of the king, as the number of women that a sovereign was able to maintain was indicative of his wealth and status. See Khing Hoc Dy, *Contribution,* pp. 66–67.

54 *Kram sauphea thipdey,* in *Codes cambodgiens,* t. 2, p. 504.

55 *Cbpab Rajaneti,* verse 8, in Pou and Jenner, 'Les *cpap* ou <<codes de conduite>> Khmers IV', p. 370; *Kram Tralakar,* in *Codes cambodgiens,* t. 2, pp. 88–90; *Cbpab tous piriyea,* in *Codes cambodgiens,* t. 2, pp. 505, 510, 521; *Cbpab Khon Sala,* in *Codes cambodgiens,* t. 2, p. 36.

56 Dampier, *New voyage around the world* [1697], p. 269; Reid, *Lands below the winds,* p. 154; van Neck, *De vierde schipvaart der Nederlanders naar Oost-Indie,* p. 225; Andaya, 'From temporary wife to prostitute', pp. 14, 19; *Cbpab tous piriyea,* in *Codes cambodgiens,* t. 2, p. 515.

CHAPTER FIVE

Hostages, Heroines and Hostilities

*A*fter the somewhat vague sources of the fifteenth to eighteenth centuries, the nineteenth century is well documented, often furnishing three perspectives on the same event. The beginning of the century saw Thai and Vietnamese involvement in Cambodian political affairs lead to the almost total loss of Cambodian sovereignty (see Fig. 5.1) and the eradication of Cambodian social norms; by its close, the French were firmly in control. The years between the restoration of Cambodian 'independence' in 1848 and the establishment of the French Protectorate in 1863, when Ang Duong reigned, are perceived by many Cambodians as a 'golden age',[1] paralleled only by the classical 'Angkorian' period and the Cambodia of the 1950s and early 1960s. The nineteenth century poses a dichotomy from the perspective of women and power. On one hand, an unmarried queen ruled Cambodia for over a decade; on the other, the *Cbpab Srei*, 'Code of conduct for women', was composed and a tradition of misogynist literature begun.

Thai forces burnt Phnom Penh to the ground in 1772 and virtually wiped out the Cambodian royal family. The Thai king 'captured and cleared out families in the territories of Barai and Phothisat [Pursat], and took captive Cambodian nobles ... for a combined total, including other families, of ten thousand persons, all sent back to Thonburi ... [and] ordered that the Cambodian

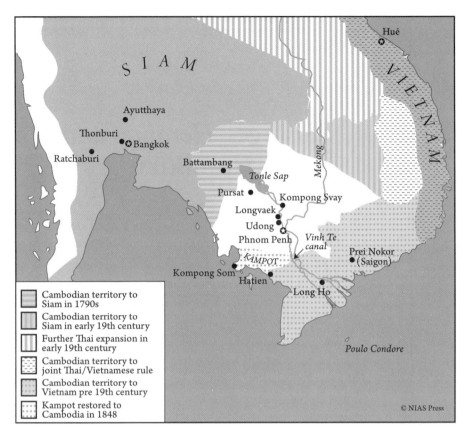

Fig. 5.1: Cambodia in the nineteenth century. Adapted from Jan M. Pluvier, *Historical Atlas of South-East Asia* and other written sources.

families taken captive be settled at Ratchaburi.'[2] There are earlier examples of the Thai relocating Cambodians in this fashion, and Cambodian monarchs in their turn regularly moved thousands of people from Thai territory.[3] After the razing of Phnom Penh, a Cambodian prince, Ang Eng (1772–1796 or 1797), was placed on the throne at Udong at the age of seven, under the patronage of the Thai king.[4] The ensuing period was marked by internal dissentions between *oknha* who supported either a Vietnamese prince, Nguyen Anh (later to rule as Gia Long), or the Tayson rebels of Central Vietnam.[5] Despite Ang Eng's precipitate death at age 24, he had nonetheless managed to sire six children: Ang Chan (1792–1834), Ang Phim (1793–1798), Ang Snguon (1794–1822), a princess, Meatuccha, whose dates of birth and death are unknown, Ang Im

(1794–1844), and Ang Duong (1796–1859).[67] Like his father, Chan was crowned king of Cambodia at the Thai court, in 1806; but the new king was not well disposed toward the Chakri dynasty.[8] Instead, he sought the goodwill of the Nguyen court at Hué. When Snguon, supported by Thai forces, rebelled against him, Ang Chan fled to Prei Nokor (Saigon), where the governor of southern Vietnam provided shelter and maintenance for Chan and his entourage until 1813, when the Thai withdrew to Battambang. The Cambodian royal family was thus polarised in subservience: Snguon, Im and Duong owing fealty to the Thai, and Chan indebted to the Vietnamese.

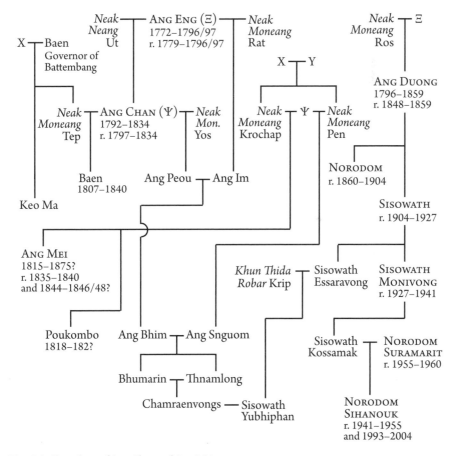

Fig. 5.2: Genealogy of Ang Chan and Ang Mei.

Note: Titles of women of the royal family indicated their status in relation to each other. A *neak neang* is, in this case, superior to a woman entitled *neak moneang*. Those entitled *khun* were lesser wives, often of Thai descent.

The reign of Queen Ang Mei

King Ang Chan died in 1834, leaving four daughters; Baen, Mei, Peou, and Snguon (see Fig. 5.2).[9] Although Ang Chan's surviving brothers, Ang Im and Ang Duong, immediately laid claim to the throne, the Vietnamese and possibly the Cambodian *oknha* wished to install one of Ang Chan's eldest daughters as sovereign. Three reasons are usually given as to why the eldest daughter, Baen, was passed over: she was sympathetic towards Thai interests; she refused to marry the son of the Vietnamese emperor; or the *oknha* would not allow her to enter into such an alliance.[10] The records are similarly inconsistent towards the next princess in line for succession, Ang Mei. A Thai document relates that the Vietnamese forced the *oknha* to accept Mei as their queen, whereas the Vietnamese sources assert that the *oknha* proposed Mei as an alternative to Baen. Walter F. Vella cited a Thai manuscript that stated that the Vietnamese had tried to persuade Mei to marry the son of the Nguyen emperor in order to facilitate the incorporation of Cambodia into the Vietnamese state, but gave way 'in view of strong objections from Cambodian nobles.'[11] Khin Sok also alleges that an alliance between a Cambodian princess and a Vietnamese prince was the means by which the Vietnamese sought to gain control of Cambodia. In any event, Hué bestowed the title *quan chua*, 'princess', upon Mei in May 1835, and her three sisters were given the title *huyen quan*, 'chief of sub-prefecture'.[12] The Vietnamese kept a close guard on the Ang princesses. Mei had two companies of soldiers, 100 men in total, assigned to her for her protection. The other three Cambodian princesses were each assigned thirty soldiers. Ostensibly for their safety, the guards were, in reality, to ensure that they did not escape.

The 'Vietnamisation' of Cambodian society, already underway during the reign of Ang Chan, continued during the reign of Ang Mei. All women were ordered to grow their hair long in the Vietnamese style and to wear trousers instead of skirts.[13] Cambodian dance assimilated elements of Vietnamese and Chinese traditions. The markets sold only Vietnamese food. Cambodian officials had to don Vietnamese ceremonial dress when summoned to Vietnamese officials. A form of Vietnamese had to be spoken to Vietnamese officials. Cambodian administrative and military officials were replaced by Vietnamese ones. At least 5,000 Vietnamese relocated into Cambodia each year. Places received new Vietnamese names. Vietnamese notions of Confucian piety were applied to Cambodian society; an edict from the

Vietnamese emperor Ming Mang exhorted Mei and her sisters to be loyal to their father's memory, a Confucian virtue. Princess Baen's mother, Queen Tep, was deemed 'disreputable' and 'immoral' by the Vietnamese as she was living in Battambang with a Thai official, having deserted her husband's family – contravening another standard of Confucian piety. Masses of Cambodians were forced into corvée labour for Vietnamese construction projects. There was some resistance to the changes wrought by the Vietnamese during this period, however. Kompong Svay revolted in 1836, led by the *oknha* Nong. The following year two brothers in Kompong Som followed suit, eventually seeking refuge in the Thai court. A Cambodian local official in an ethnically Khmer district of southern Vietnam who refused to implement regulations enforcing Vietnamisation policies was executed.[14]

Princess Baen met a similar fate for her resistance to the Vietnamese. In 1840, the Vietnamese discovered that the princess had been in contact with her mother, Tep, and uncle, Ang Im, who were living in Battambang province, and was planning to escape to them. Charged with collaborating with the enemy, Baen was imprisoned in Vietnamese military barracks in Phnom Penh pending her trial. The Vietnamese emperor, Minh Mang, demoted the other Ang princesses to low-ranking titles in the civil service. In August or September 1840, Mei, Peou and Snguon, and other members of the court, including two of Ang Chan's queens, were enticed onto a barge, their retainers plied with alcohol and rendered incapacitated, and taken off to Vietnam. Around the same time, princess Mom, daughter of Ang Duong (r. 1848–1860), another half-brother of Chan, and his principal wife Ong, were captured by the Vietnamese and imprisoned on the island of Poulo Condore. Thai and Cambodian sources state that the Vietnamese drowned Baen in the Mekong river after her sisters had been taken to Saigon, although Khin Sok, citing the Veang Thiounn version of the chronicles, states that Baen was taken to Long Ho and tortured to death by the Vietnamese general, after which her body was placed in a sack and thrown in the river.[15]

Many Cambodian *oknha* and their followers had already revolted against Vietnamese policies; the unrest worsened with the arrest of Baen and the prolonged absence of Mei. Vietnamese officials in Phnom Penh called for Mei to be returned to Cambodia as queen in order to quiet the rebellion, but the Vietnamese emperor refused. The Vietnamese official in charge of Cambodia, Truong Ming Giang, reiterated this request in March 1841. Minh Mang, alarmed and bemused at the continued civil unrest, allowed Mei, Peou, Snguon, and queen Ros, one of Ang Eng's wives and the mother of Ang Duong, to return at the end of April 1841. Upon her return to Phnom Penh, Mei issued directives embossed with the official royal seal of Cambodia, appointed new officials and issued letters to provincial officials and leaders asking for their support of her reign. At the same time, Duong was issuing similar calls for support from Udong. Mei was reinstated as queen and her sister Peou appointed the heir apparent in 1844. Towards the end of that year, the Vietnamese distributed letters stating that Mei and her sisters were the sovereigns of Cambodia and that any dissenters would be executed. Most of the Cambodian court remained under Vietnamese control until October 1846, when the Vietnamese released Ros, a daughter of Ang Duong, and 34 other members of the Cambodian court and allowed them to join Ang Duong in Udong. Discussions were underway between the Thai and Vietnamese for the resolution of the Cambodian problem, resulting in a compromise whereby both Ang Duong and Ang Mei would rule as co-sovereigns. Simultaneous coronations were held in Bangkok and Phnom Penh in 1848, although Cambodian sources record only Duong's accession. The chronicles do not mention Mei after 1848, although she was still living in Udong in the 1870s.[16]

Mei's story is told dispassionately in the Cambodian chronicles, where she is portrayed as a puppet of Vietnamese emperors and officials; some later writers do not even mention her at all, glossing over the period of her rule as one in which Emperor Gia Long made Cambodia into a colony. This is because her reign has been perceived as synonymous with the Vietnamese 'occupation' of Cambodia, a period that left deep scars upon the Cambodian psyche. Khin Sok calls the period encompassed by her reign 'la périod calamiteuse'.[17] The first half of the nineteenth century remains a deeply reviled period in the collective Cambodian consciousness to this day; it is hardly surprising that the sovereign during that time, seen as collaborating with the enemy, would be perceived in a negative context by later generations. A typical example of the association between Mei and Vietnamese dominance can be seen on an Internet forum for Cambodians in diaspora in a blog dated 22 August 2002. A photograph of Prince Norodom Sihanouk being embraced by Vo Nguyen Giap at Hanoi Airport in 1969 had superimposed upon it the following dialogue:

Sihanouk: Guess who will succeed me in 2003?
Giap: Your cousin, descendant of Ang Mei![18]

The connection between Mei and Vietnamese annexation of Cambodia partly facilitated the identification of female political power with national humiliation. As Chandler has shown in his analysis of a chronicle composed in 1856, Cambodians seem to have regarded the time prior to the coronation of Ang Duong in 1848 as one of 'homelessness, barbarism, and the loss of status', a great contrast to the subsequent period, one of 'harmony, propriety and elegance'. Ang Duong himself took care to emphasise the association between Mei and the Vietnamese, blaming 'Samdech Pheakanyea [Ang Mei] who ruled during the Annamite period' for the loss of indentured slaves, who, he implied, having behaved themselves during the reigns of Ang Eng and Ang Chan, took the opportunity of lax (female) rule to escape to the forest. Most histories of the period imply that the *oknha* and Cambodians in general acquiesced to Mei as their sovereign reluctantly, holding out – 'forlornly' – for Duong or for both Im and Duong to return as sovereigns. Walter F. Vella implies that the Vietnamese used a pre-existing negative association between women and political power in order to weaken Cambodian internal politics. There was even a rumour that she was engaged in an affair with Truong Ming Giang, the Vietnamese governor in Phnom Penh. Jean Moura consulted *oknha* and women of the palace who had had positions at the court during the reign of Ang Mei and independent observers who told him that the rumour was not true.[19] Yet historians continue to construct Mei as a passive victim, hardly legitimate in the eyes of her own people.[20]

Bun Sun Theam represents Mei as failing to garner popular support in Cambodia because the general population preferred Duong, as he was male. This is also the line pursued by Nguyen-o Thu-uong. Khin Sok alleges that the Cambodian populace 'turned naturally towards Ang Duong' in order to lead the uprising that would resuscitate the fortunes of the kingdom, which were 'practically in the abyss' during the Mei incumbency.[21] Her reign is seen as completely negative, during which Cambodian territory, culture, and independence were almost lost. A 52-year-old *chao adthika* in Kampot province described her as

> greedy for power. She let the *yuon* eat Cambodia, and for what? So she could be a *neak thom* and live a comfortable life. She didn't care about the people, what they suffered. We had to speak their language and eat their food and they destroyed our wats because they want our culture to die.[22]

Whilst it cannot be denied that the Vietnamese were in control of Cambodia during Mei's reign, she inherited a country that had already been mortgaged to Hué by her father, King Ang Chan. Almost immediately after his coronation, Chan sent word to Gia Long of his coronation and received in return a letter that gave him 'permission' to rule. He was also advised to follow 'civilized models of government', meaning those of the Vietnamese. A period of dual fealty, paying tribute to both Vietnam and the Thai, ensued until 1830, but Chan grew increasingly anti-Thai, refusing to travel to Bangkok to attend the funeral of Rama I. He also refused Thai demands for troops to assist in the campaign against Burma. Fearful of reprisal, he asked the Vietnamese for assistance and in answer they sent a small naval force to Udong in 1810, where it remained until 1812.

The reign of Ang Chan, not Ang Mei, was the beginning of Vietnamese interference in the social, political and economic life of Cambodians; they had already been in control of the Cambodian territory around Prei Nokor for over fifty years. Unlike the Thai, who were content to allow Cambodia to retain its traditions (which in any case differed only slightly from their own), the Vietnamese sought to impose their own customs. Ang Chan was ordered by the Vietnamese to relocate his capital from Udong to Phnom Penh, where Vietnamese storehouses and barracks were constructed. By 1816, Gia Dich Thong Chi, a Vietnamese advisor in Cambodia, reported that Cambodia had adopted Vietnamese clothing styles, which aggravated the *oknha*. Thai records relate that the Vietnamese forced Cambodians to dismantle their Theravada Buddhist *wat*s and *viharas*.[23] In 1816, Ang Chan was ordered to recruit 5,000 workers to excavate a canal linking Chaudoc and Hatien, some seventy kilometres apart. The 500 supervisors were solely Vietnamese, who beat some of the workers to death for infractions. One Cambodian man was decapitated and his head placed on a stake in order to intimidate other Cambodian workers. Conditions such as these only exacerbated the resentment that many Cambodians felt towards the Vietnamese for usurping Cambodian territory, and may have contributed to the rebellion against them, led by a monk, Kai, in 1820.[24]

Mei was crowned sovereign of a kingdom in which the Vietnamese were already in charge. It is difficult to ascertain what course of action other than acquiescence was available to her. Mei seems to have sought a peaceful solution to the factionalism in her country, telling envoys sent by Duong that she wished for a return to peace and amicability, and hoping that 'we would be able to live together with our uncle'. This may, of course, have been a diplomatic response; the Vietnamese annals described her as 'an intelligent young lady' at the time of her accession. Nothing – sudden flights to Vietnam, the murder of her elder sister, and continual changes in her status – seems to have induced hysterical or untoward behaviour. Perhaps Mei would have fared better in Cambodian collective memory if, like her sister Baen, she had actively resisted the Vietnamese. She does not seem to have been despised by the *oknha* in Cambodia; during her exile in Udong Jean Moura spoke with women who had been members of Mei's court during her reign and who remained devoted to her.[25] Furthermore, as we have seen above, in 1844 it was Mei, rather than Ang Duong, who was crowned sovereign of Cambodia, after a campaign in which both attempted to garner support from the Cambodian *oknha*. If Mei had been genuinely unpopular due to her gender, the *oknha* would not have countenanced her accession.

The misogyny of Ang Duong

It is highly likely that Ang Duong harboured some personal resentment towards Ang Mei for not stepping aside as Cambodia's sovereign so that he could ascend the throne. He never attempted to liberate his nieces; in fact, he had to be prompted by the Vietnamese to send a contingent to escort them and the other members of the court to Udong. Once there, Ang Mei was probably ostracised, and possibly imprisoned or tortured. In 1874 she was found by Jean Moura, 'old … and mad … long since removed from power and the world', living 'almost alone in the furthest corner of the old capital'. She died soon after his visit.[26] Yet an underlying thread of misogyny is discernible throughout the life and works of Ang Duong, before and after his accession.

A series of new laws were promulgated when Ang Duong came to power, as, according to the king, 'the ancient laws, for a long time, have not been revised, neither by kings, nor officials, nor the wise' and had not kept pace with regional developments like 'those from Siam, Laos, China, Annam, Europe and Malaya'. In this he was following the normal course of action for kings upon their accession and reassuring his people that the disorder of previous decades was past. One of the first new laws altered the way in which Cambodian princesses could marry, which probably reflected a fear that an *oknha* would marry Mei or one of her surviving sisters and attempt to claim the throne. Another decree was issued in 1857 regulating the succession of princes and princesses in relation to their mothers. These changes ensured that titles could by issued and revoked by the king alone; they were no longer inherited according to the status of the queen or princess. Again, it is likely that Ang Duong feared a challenge to his position, from a child of one of his nieces or brothers' children. Royal women were effectively removed from their previous positions of significance in relation to sovereignty. The only woman to continue to hold any permanent authority, at least until the colonial period, was the queen mother.[27]

Outside the palace, some laws of Ang Duong privileged male interests. Sons born to slave women but fathered by free men inherited their father's status. Divorce was made more difficult for women to initiate. All that men were required to do was present their wives with a document bearing their mark. Women were required to keep this document so that they could prove their status if they wished to remarry. Much more forbearance was necessary for unhappy wives. Even complaining about their husbands was frowned upon; a woman who 'speaks against, injures, or denounces her husband to the law' was an offence in law.[28] Only after repeated attempts to dissuade her spouse from his evil ways was a woman permitted to seek recourse from the courts:

> When, amongst the ordinary people, a married man is a thief, a smoker of opium, a habitual gambler, if his wife, numerous times, reproaches him, tries to correct his behaviour, and he does not heed her, but continues to gamble and smoke, and if his wife is afraid that his debts will fall upon her, the judges must receive her request for divorce and consider that the husband is a bad and obstinate subject.[29]

A woman who took matters into her own hands and dared to beat or otherwise wound her husband was 'fined and put in chains and shackles, then condemned to strangulation and the confiscation of all her goods, which will be divided between the husband of said woman and the royal treasury'. Punishments were generally very harsh during the reign of Ang Duong; although Jai Jettha II had revised *Kram Jao* in 1621 because he considered some of the punishments therein too barbaric, Ang Duong reversed some of these amendments. The punishments for women in the revised *Cbpab tous bhariya* were similarly ruthless, including the use of shackles and impalement.[30]

Ang Duong did not confine his views on female behaviour to legal texts. He was also an author of didactic literature. One of his earliest of works is

Neang Kaki, written in 1813, derived from two *jataka* stories, *Kakati Jataka* and *Sussondi Jataka*, both of which deal with the theme of a king experiencing difficulty in controlling his wife. Women, in these stories, are described as inherently promiscuous, and their energies must be channelled into pious activities lest their sexuality rage out of control, bringing dishonour to the king, and therefore the kingdom. In Ang Duong's *Neang Kaki*, a *raks* ('demon') with whom the king plays chess is consumed with lust for Queen Kaki and devises a scheme by which he may possess her. The *raks* assumes the form of the king and summons Kaki to his bedchamber (or, in some versions, visits her in her own), where she is obligated to fulfil the desires of her 'husband'. When the real king discovers what has occurred, Kaki is thrown out of the court in disgrace for her infidelity. The moral of the story is that women are to blame for their transgressions, even when they have been deceived into committing them. This theme is also discerned in Ang Duong's laws; *Kram bier*, 'Treatise on gaming', held that women who frequented public houses could not be dishonoured in word or deed as they were *srei neak leng* ('women who gamble') and thus were not respectable.[31]

The Cbpab Srei

Correct behaviour for women is set out in the *Cbpab Srei*, 'Code of Conduct for Women', the best-known of the *cbpab thmei*. Authorship of the *Cbpab Srei* is somewhat contested. Khing Hoc Dy states that the *Cbpab Srei* was composed by Ang Duong in 1837. Judy Ledgerwood describes a 'more recent version' of the *Cbpab Srei* as having been authored by a Minh Mai, and another version altogether as the work of the poet Ind in the late 1800s. Judith Jacob, renowned scholar of Cambodian literature, does not include Ind as having written a *Cbpab Srei*, but lists three extant manuscripts of the *Cbpab Srei*, one of which is attributed to a pandit named Mai, a poet of the late eighteenth to mid-nineteenth centuries, and another to Ang Duong. Léang-Hap An attributed a *Cbpab Srei* to the court poet Nong, but the manuscript itself is not well described. Nong was a court poet during the reigns of kings Ang Eng and Ang Chan and tutor to all of Ang Eng's surviving sons after their father's death. He also accompanied Ang Duong and Ang Im to Bangkok for their education. Ang Duong made Nong his personal advisor and secretary, employed him as tutor to his own children, and gave him land. It is perhaps inevitable that Ang Duong's literary style would imitate his tutor, and this may have contributed to a confusion of their work.[32]

The *Cbpab Srei*, like all *cbpab*, provided guidelines for acceptable behaviour. In the 'Minh Mai' text (the best known of the *Cbpab Srei* manuscripts) the narrative takes the form of Queen Vimala instructing her daughter Indrandati in necessary information that will be of use throughout her life before she leaves her parents' kingdom. The key thrust of the text is that it is the responsibility of wives to ensure the good reputation of the family by maintaining a harmonious image of the home, regardless of what occurred behind closed doors. This was best achieved, according to the *Cbpab Srei*, by total obedience to one's husband:

> If you do not believe your husband or ignore him, conflict will arise;
> Happiness will be destroyed, your reputation will suffer, discord will continue without ceasing.
> This means you are not ladylike, but a low person, with the heart of a 'golden flower' [immoral woman or prostitute].[33]

Women are also advised in the text not to tell their mothers if their husbands mistreat them, nor to gossip in general. More prosaic are warnings not to touch one's husband's head in order to look for lice without 'respectfully bowing and informing him', not turning one's back on one's husband in bed or misfortune will befall the household, and to busy oneself with useful activities beneficial to the household, such as weaving. Wives should speak with a gentle voice and walk softly so as not to draw attention to themselves. If a husband becomes angry, regardless of whose fault it is (the *Cbpab Srei* even makes allowances for drunkards who spend all of the family money on gambling), she should 'retire for the night and think about the situation, then speak softly to him and forgive him'. If a man takes a mistress, a wife should not be upset or angry, as 'if she allows him to wander where he wants, he will return to her'. Harsh words, that might affront the dignity of a man, are never to be used, or it will appear that the wife is more potent or powerful. A woman must never think herself as superior to her husband in any respect, but consider him, 'the lord of the chamber, as your leader; never forget it'.[34]

Like the sentiments encapsulated in the Brahmanical inscriptions of the preclassical and classical periods in Cambodia, all versions of the *Cbpab Srei* embody the *ideal* society as perceived by a particular author. As we have seen, controlling and disempowering women seems to have been a popular theme for Ang Duong in his literary efforts and in his administrative reforms. It may not have been coincidental that *Cbpab Srei* was written almost immediately after Ang Mei was crowned by the Vietnamese; one can almost see a frustrated and angry Ang Duong sitting down to furiously write a treatise on the correct behaviour for women in the face of his own niece's perceived obstinacy. Yet there was another source of inspiration for Ang Duong and other members of the Cambodian elite at the Thai court during the late eighteenth and nineteenth centuries: the more conservative strain of Buddhism that became known as the Dhammayut sect. In 1788, Rama I (r. 1782–1809), believing that Buddhism had been corrupted by the involvement of the sangha in political machinations in the middle of the eighteenth century in Siam, sponsored the ninth Buddhist council. The subsequent 'purifying' of Buddhist texts could not have failed to influence the young Cambodian princes, Ang Im and Ang Duong, sequestered at the Cambodian court during this time, especially as Cambodian monks were amongst those involved in the work. Rama I also issued seven decrees aimed at raising the level of morality in the sangha in order to 'restore its prestige and authority'. Three more decrees were issued in 1779, 1794, and 1801. The last expelled 128 monks for 'ignoble behaviour', one characteristic of which was associating with women.

This more austere Buddhism was transmitted to Cambodia, at first slowly, as members of the Cambodian community returned to Udong and Ang Duong pursued his agenda of *wat* restoration and other pursuits aimed at increasing his stores of merit. In 1854, his reign established, Ang Duong asked the Thai court to send him a complete version of the new, 'pure' *Tipitaka* and a number of monks who were well versed in the new form of Buddhism. Ang Duong was sufficiently devoted to this more conservative sect that he imported it to Cambodia, and it was he (not Norodom) who established it, contrary to Adhémard Leclère's account. It is not surprising, therefore, that Ang Duong inculcated elite Cambodian society with models of correct behaviour that reflected the conservatism of the Thai court in which he had grown up, and to which he owed his position as king of Cambodia. There is little doubt that Ang Duong drew inspiration from Thai texts; *Neang Kaki* was modelled on the work of a Thai court poet.[35]

The inspiration of Minh Mai is less readily explained due to the lack of information on his life, but if he was indeed a court poet of the late eighteenth and nineteenth centuries he would have been subject to the same conservative influences as Ang Duong. Most elite men would have spent some years as monks. The author of the third and most recent *Cbpab Srei*, Ind, was ordained at the age of twenty, having studied as a novice under *Preah kru achar* Sok at Wat Kaev in Battambang. He then went to Bangkok, returning seven years later and taking up a position in Wat Kandal, where he remained for a decade. In 1896 Ind voluntarily defrocked and married. According to Tauch Chhong,

> the people of Battambang knew him well. He was called Achar In [*sic*]. Everyone in Battambang praised his works and speeches. While Cambodia had no printed books, the people of Battambang borrowed his work from one another, copying them out by hand to keep and distributing them one to the other for reading. Some people memorized many pages of his poems.[36]

When Battambang was returned to Cambodian control in 1907, Ind was invited to remain under the new administration, with the title *oknha sut-tanta prachea*, 'lord poet of the land', which he held until his death in 1924. Amongst his many works were *Gatilok ru cbpab tumnam khluon* [Guidelines for one's behaviour], *Supasit cbpab srei* [Maxims of the *Cbpap Srei*], and *Neang Chhantea*, a translation of a Thai manuscript in which a wicked woman attempts to deceive her *bodhisattva* husband. Ind's *Cbpab Srei* is thematically similar to the other two versions. The challenge of adhering to the code was admitted but readers entreated to apply themselves with diligence and persevere. Women were enjoined to 'sit modestly, when speaking do not shake with laughter; a woman who is timid has high prestige. Please pay attention to the circumstances appropriate to one's rank'.[37]

The extent to which these texts, and others like them, permeated Cambodian society is debatable. Probably, few people could read and write at the non-elite level; even provincial *oknha* may have been illiterate, maintaining a few educated staff for administrative purposes within their own retinues. It is highly likely that the literature written by Ang Duong and Minh Mai circulated within the court alone. No doubt Ang Duong's work was received favourably as it was written not only by the king, but a king who had saved Cambodia from absorption into Siam and the cultural hegemony of the Vietnamese. Those who had not supported Duong in his bid for the throne would have taken care not to displease him once he came to power through overt criticism of either his religion or his literary pursuits. Similarly, Ind was lauded for being not only a gifted writer, but a *Cambodian* writer who 'demonstrated that while Thailand could interfere with the domain of administration, it could not interfere with the Khmer mind in Battambang'.[38] Reading the work of these authors was far more than mere literary appreciation for the Cambodian elite; it signified political allegiance and collective identity.

Revisionist (female) histories

The negative perspective toward women and power in the didactic literature of the nineteenth century is echoed in contemporary court chronicles' explanations for earlier events. Kings, it seems, were not responsible for any of their actions. Instead, women were implicated as causal agents for events that led to upheaval and disharmony in the kingdom, including civil war, Vietnamese territorial encroachment, and the renunciation of Buddhism.

In 1627 Paramaraja Udaiy married his niece Mae Yuor Vatti, although she had been promised to her half-brother Dhammaraja. The siblings, meeting by accident, fell in love. Mae Yuor Vatti deceived her husband and fled to her lover. A war ensued and Mae Yuor Vatti was captured by Paramaraja Udaiy's Portuguese mercenaries, returned to her husband's court, and sentenced to death by his *okhna*. Even though the authors imply that Paramaraja Udaiy acted incorrectly in marrying Mae Yuor Vatti because she was betrothed to Dhammaraja, and although the half-siblings are depicted as being genuinely (and appropriately) in love, Dhammaraja is represented as being led astray by his passion whereas Mae Yuor Vatti is calculating and deliberate. She asked her husband if she could take a pleasure trip to the lakes and stay there for one or two nights. Having received permission, she went at once to her half-brother's palace at Udong. Her eventual death is portrayed as a fitting punishment for transgressing her duty to her husband and causing the war that resulted in Dhammaraja's death. Before dying, Dhammaraja realised the error of his ways. He is recorded as saying to the Portuguese mercenaries: 'Because of a woman, I am in a detestable state … . Because of passion, I am now facing death. Better to go to my death, in order to once more know *dharma*!'[39]

Ang Chuv, the Nguyen princess who married King Jai Jettha II around 1620, is held responsible for the loss of Prei Nokor (Saigon) and its surrounds and the subsequent permeation of Vietnamese influence in the Cambodian court. In 1623, the Nguyen emperor at Hué asked that the lands of Prei Nokor and Kompong Krabei be handed over to Vietnamese authority. Jai Jettha II consulted with his *okhna* and members of the royal family. They determined that 'if we do not accept … amicability will cease and the royal lady the queen will be annoyed. In this matter, it is proper to give them what they ask'. The

Cambodians were described as reluctant to refuse for fear of upsetting Ang Chuv, who had 'extraordinary powers, on the one hand a result of being the royal Vietnamese princess and on the other being the royal queen'. The implication was that Ang Chuv, not the king and his advisors, was responsible for the Vietnamese presence. Even though Ang Chuv was instrumental in overthrowing a deeply unpopular king, Ramadhipati I (see below) in 1659, by summoning Vietnamese troops to aid her stepsons, her part in this was written dismissively. Far from being portrayed as a heroine, some chronicles describe her as base in nature, consumed by an insatiable sexual appetite. This story alleges that Ang Chuv discovered an aphrodisiac commissioned by her husband the king when she was clearing out his rooms after his death. Unsure what it was for, she tested the potion, which caused her to have 'men to come one by one, continuously. But if a page did not please her, she would drive him away or have him killed to prevent him from talking'. She eventually took a permanent lover, Dham.[40] Thus the memory of Ang Chuv preserved in the Cambodian court histories is of an immoral woman who delivered her adopted country into the hands of the Vietnamese.

Perhaps the most significant event in which a woman is described as having led a Cambodian king astray is the conversion of Ramadhipati I (r. 1642–1659) to Islam. The chronicles relate that while taking a pleasure-trip along the river in the 1640s, the king saw a young Cham girl going down to the river and fell in love with her. He called the people of the village, who were Cham and Malay, to ask them who she was. Her name was Neang Hvah. The king summoned the girl's mother and asked if Neang Hvah could stay on his launch and serve him. The king 'was very pleased' with her and asked her mother if he could take her to the palace. Agreeing, the mother called together the people of the village. The elders of the village performed a series of enchantments that would make the king progressively more in love with Hvah. The king made her his 'queen of the left' and appointed Cham and Malay officials to govern all Cham and Malay peoples in the kingdom. A Malay religious official, 'using magical formulae', convinced the king to convert to Islam. He ordered the court, including the royal family, to do likewise. Carool Kersten suggests that Ramadhipati's conversion to Islam was actually a political strategy in order to form an alliance with the Cham and Malay peoples in the country. This was because he was in a somewhat precarious position with the Cambodian *oknha*, having murdered members of his own family to lay claim to the throne, and as a form of spiritual bulwarking, as he had been led to believe that Islam would expiate these sins whereas Buddhism and Catholicism would not. Nevertheless, the court chronicles specifically detail that it was, firstly, the beauty of Neang Hvas, then her complicity in applying the magic potions, that caused Ramadhipati to take this drastic, most un-Cambodian step.[41]

∿∿

The Cambodian chronicles written after Ang Duong came to the throne depict Ang Mei as a lesson, bitterly learned, in the consequences of women exercising direct power in the political arena. By contrast, the reign of Ang Duong (1848–1859) is a 'golden age' in Cambodian history. This is especially true of Cambodian dance and literary styles, which he is seen as restoring to their pre-'Vietnamisation' glory. He is credited with the 'liberation' of Cambodia from Thai and Vietnamese encroachment and the restoration of Cambodian culture for a brief period of independence before foreigners once again subjugated Cambodia.[42] Historians ascertain their information from written records; the problem, however, is that the Cambodian sources for this period were written in the courts of Ang Duong and his descendants, in whose interests it was to represent Ang Mei as an ineffectual ruler. This was easy to do by playing upon the hatred Cambodians felt (and still feel) for the Vietnamese, dating back to their annexation of Prei Nokor in the early seventeenth century – for which another woman, Ang Chuv, was blamed. The precedents for women and political power, within living memory, led to increasing Vietnamese dominance; the influence of others led Cambodian kings to turn against each other and the holy path of Buddhism. The association between women being in charge and Cambodian subjugation was virtually assured through the 'scapegoating' of women in the chronicles. This was buttressed by the literature written by the conservative elite in the late eighteenth and nineteenth centuries and the legal reforms of Ang Duong which placed women in a position of inferiority in relation to men. As was the case with correct models for behaviour set out in earlier periods, the didactic literature of the nineteenth century did not make much of an impact upon ordinary Cambodians; indeed, if we are to accept late nineteenth and early twentieth centuries as indicative of 'traditional' Cambodia, it was customary for women to have significance and agency.

Notes to Chapter 5

1 David Chandler, 'Going through the motions: Ritual aspects of the reign of King Duang of Cambodia (1848–1860)'[1979], in *Facing the Cambodian past: Selected essays 1971–1994*, St Leonards, New South Wales: Allen & Unwin, 1996, p. 115.

2 *The dynastic chronicles of the Bangkok era – the first reign*, trans. and ed. Thadeus and Chadin Flood, vol. 1: *Text*, Tokyo: The Centre for East Asian Cultural Studies, 1978, pp. 21–22.

3 *Chroniques royales du Cambodge*, vol. 2: *De Bona Yat à la prise de Lanvaek (1417–1595)*, trans. and ed. Khin Sok, Paris: École Française d'Extrême-Orient, 1988 [hereafter *Chroniques* 2], pp. 213, 216; Bun Srun Theam, 'Cambodia in the mid-nineteenth century: A quest for survival, 1840–1863', PhD thesis, Australian National University, 1981, p. 77; *Dynastic chronicles of the Bangkok era*, vol. 1, p. 21.

4 Justin J. Corfield, *The royal family of Cambodia*, Melbourne: The Khmer Language & Culture Centre, 1993, p.15. Corfield says that Ang Eng was the 'sole surviving member' of the Cambodian family but in fact three of his sisters survived and accompanied him to the Thai court.

5 *Dynastic chronicles of the Bangkok era*, vol. 1, pp. 25–26, 35.

6 Corfield, *Royal family of Cambodia*, pp. 16–22. The Thai chronicle gives slightly different dates for the births of these children and does not record princess Meatuccha at all (*Dynastic chronicles of the Bangkok era*, vol. 1, p. 219).

7 David Chandler intimates that Ang Chan, aged five, was sanctioned as the next ruler of Cambodia, and *talaha* Pok appointed to act as his regent until the prince reached his majority, but the Thai chronicle states that Pok was in fact instructed to act as regent for all five princes, as 'the king intended to select the most intelligent and suitable one among them to reign in Cambodia.' The Vietnamese, however, seem to have seen Ang Chan as the next king of Cambodia, as their mission of 1805 was directed at him and his advisors. See David P. Chandler, 'Cambodia before the French: Politics in a tributary kingdom, 1774–1848', PhD thesis, University of Michigan, 1973, p. 81; *Dynastic chronicles of the Bangkok era*, p. 220.

8 *Dynastic chronicles of the Bangkok era*, p. 287.This disgruntlement is not evident in the Thai chronicle, but the fact that Ang Chan demanded that his paternal aunts, Y and Phao, who had accompanied Ang Eng to the Thai court in 1782 and who had subsequently married the heir to the Thai throne before his death, be returned to Cambodia, can be interpreted as an act of defiance, and his anger at the refusal of this request may be why Chan did not go in person to Bangkok when Rama I died in 1809 (Bun Srun Theam, 'Cambodia in the mid-nineteenth century', p. 32).

9 Peou is usually a name given to the youngest child in Cambodian families, but all of the references to the princesses place Snguon last, implying that she was the youngest.

10 Bun Srun Theam, 'Cambodia in the mid-nineteenth century', pp. 58–59; Michael Vickery, 'Cambodia after Angkor: The chronicular evidence for the fourteenth to sixteenth centuries', PhD thesis, Yale University, 1977, p.126. Khin Sok says that Baen 'judged the sug-

gestion insupportable'. See Khin Sok, *Le Cambodge entre le Siam et le Vietnam (de 1775 à 1860)*, Paris: École Française d'Extrême-Orient, 1991, p. 87).

11 Chandler, 'Cambodia before the French', p. 127; Walter F. Vella, *Siam under Rama III, 1824–1851*, Locust Valley, New York: J.J. Augustin, 1957, p. 100, fn 17.

12 Khin Sok, *Le Cambodge entre le Siam et le Vietnam*, p. 88; Bun Srun Theam, 'Cambodia in the mid-nineteenth century', p. 59. It will not escape the notice of astute readers that this title is very similar to *hyang*, 'princess', a title of the preclassical and classical periods in Cambodia.

13 Vickery, 'Cambodia after Angkor', pp. 137–138. In the late 1840s, envoys of Ang Doung encountered a group of Cambodian courtiers living in exile in Vietnam. The men of the party were dressed and had their hair styled in the Vietnamese fashion, but the women of the party had retained Cambodian traditional dress and hairstyles (Bun Srun Theam, 'Cambodia in the mid-nineteenth century', p. 114).

14 Tep was the daughter of *oknha* Baen, who had been given the governorship of Battambang province by the Thai. Bun Srun Theam, 'Cambodia in the mid–nineteenth century', pp. 58–59, 62, 67; Khin Sok, *Cambodge entre le Siam et le Viêtnam*, pp. 89–91;Vickery, 'Cambodia after Angkor', pp. 128–129, 133, 137–138.

15 Bun Srun Theam, 'Cambodia in the mid-nineteenth century', pp. 71–72; Chandler, 'Cambodia before the French', p. 151; Corfield, *Royal family of Cambodia*, p. 23; Khin Sok, *Cambodge entre le Siam et le Vietnam*, p. 94. The latter makes the point that drowning was a form of capital punishment reserved for members of the Cambodian royal family (f.n. 288).

16 David Chandler, 'Songs at the edge of the forest: Perceptions of order in three Cambodian texts', in *Facing the Cambodian past*, p. 92; Khin Sok, *Cambodge entre le Siam et le Vietnam*, p. 95.

17 *Mémoire du Cambodge sur ses terres au Sau-Vietnam (Cochinchine)*, Phnom Penh: Imprimerie du Palais Royale, [1954], p. 2; Julio Jeldres, *The royal house of Cambodia*, Phnom Penh: Monument Books, 2003, p. 10; Khin Sok, *Le Cambodge entre le Siam et le Vietnam*, p. 87.

18 www.3.sympatico.ca/nearori/potins9.html.

19 Chandler, 'Songs at the edge of the forest', pp. 93–94; *Kram Preas Reachea Khant*, in Adhémard Leclère, *Codes cambodgiens*, Paris: Ernest Leroux, 1898, t. 2, p. 613; Chandler, 'Cambodia before the French', p. 126; Vella, *Siam under Rama III*, pp. 99–100; Jean Moura, *Le royaume de Cambodge*, 2 vols, Paris: Leroux, 1883, vol. 1, pp. 233–234.

20 See for example John Tully, *France on the Mekong: A history of the Protectorate in Cambodia, 1863–1953*, Lanham, Maryland; New York; Oxford: 2002, p. 13.

21 Bun Srun Theam, 'Cambodia in the mid-nineteenth century', p. 188; Nguyen-vo Thu-huong, *Khmer-Viet relations and the third Indochina conflict*, Jefferson, North Carolina; London: McFarland & Company, 1992, p. 9; Khin Sok, *Cambodge entre le Siam et le Vietnam*, p. 95.

22 Fieldnotes, 2005.

23 Bun Srun Theam, 'Cambodia in the mid-nineteenth century', p. 40; Chandler, 'Politics in a tributary kingdom', p. 93.

24 As discussed in the preceding chapter, in 1623 the Vietnamese had asked formal permission from Jai Jettha II to set up a customs post in Prei Nokor (Saigon) in order to collect customs duty and other taxes. They were sure of his acquiescence, as a Vietnamese princess, Ang Chuv, had been married to the king three years earlier. The Vietnamese then began sending settlers into the area later known as Cochinchina. See David Chandler, 'An anti-Vietnamese rebellion in early nineteenth century Cambodia' [1975], in *Facing the Cambodian past*, p. 64.

25 Bun Srun Theam, 'Cambodia in the mid-nineteenth century', p. 112; Vickery, 'Cambodia after Angkor', p. 127; Moura, *Le royaume du Cambodge*, p. 232.

26 Moura, *Le royaume du Cambodge*, pp. 233–234.

27 *Kram bamnol* [1853], in *Codes cambodgiens*, t. 1, pp. 458–459; David Chandler, 'Going through the motions: Ritual aspects of the reign of King Duang of Cambodia (1848–1860), in *Facing the Cambodian past: Selected essays 1971–1994*, St Leonards, New South Wales: Allen & Unwin, 1996, pp. 100–118; Jeldres, *Royal house of Cambodia*, p. 15.

28 *Kram dasa kamokar* [1853], in *Codes cambodgiens*, t. 1, p. 386; *Kram Sanghkrey* [1853], in *Codes cambodgiens*, t. 1, p. 309.

29 *Kram Preas Reachea Khant* [1850], in *Codes cambodgiens*, t. 2, p. 616.

30 *Kram Sanghkrey* [1853], in *Codes cambodgiens*, t. 1, p. 309; *Kram Chor* [Jao] [1860], in *Codes cambodgiens*, t. 2, p. 296; *Kram tous piriyea* [1853], in *Codes cambodgiens*, t. 1, p. 235.

31 Ang Duong, *Rieong Kaki* [1813], Phnom Penh: Buddhist Institute, 1997; *Kram Bier* [1853], in *Codes cambodgiens*, t. 2, p. 476.

32 A *Cbpab Srei* ostensibly authored by Ang Duong was published by the Buddhist Institute in 1962. It lists the types of wives and their characteristics in a similar fashion to the Minh Mai text and to *Kram tous bhariya*. Khing Hoc Dy, *Contribution à l'histoire de la littérature khmère*, Paris: l'Harmattan, 1990, p. 90; Judy L. Ledgerwood, Changing Khmer conceptions of gender: Women, stories, and the social order, PhD thesis, Cornell University, 1990, pp. 82, 86; Judith M. Jacob, *The traditional literature of Cambodia: A preliminary guide*, Oxford: Oxford University Press, 1996, p. 70.

33 *Cbpab Srei*, verses 83–85. This and all subsequent quotations are from *Cbpab srei- broh*, Phnom Penh: Phsep pseay juon koan khmei, 2001. A transliterated version with French translation can be found in Saveros Pou (comp. and ed.), *Guirlande de cpāp*, Paris: Cedorek, 1988.

34 *Cbpab Srei*, verses 7, 24, 53–54, 65–80, 100, 107, 108, 115.

35 Yoneo Ishii, *Sangha, state, and society: Thai Buddhism and history*, trans. Peter Hawkes, Honolulu: The University of Hawai'i Press, 1986, p. 64; Somboon Suksamran, *Political*

Buddhism in Southeast Asia: The role of the sangha in the modernization of Thailand, New York: St Martin's Press, 1976, p. 26; J. Kathirithamby-Wells, 'The age of transition: The mid-eighteenth to the early nineteenth centuries', in Nicholas Tarling (ed.), *The Cambridge history of Southeast Asia*, vol. 2: *From c. 1500 to c. 1800*, Cambridge: Cambridge University Press, 1999, p. 248; Meas Yang, *Le Bouddhisme au Cambodge*, Brussels: Thanh Long, 1978, p. 38; Klaus Wenk, *The restoration of Thailand under Rama I, 1782–1809*, trans. Greeley Stahl, Tucson, Arizona: University of Arizona Press, 1968, pp. 39–41; Chandler, 'Going through the motions', pp. 104–105; Adhémard Leclère, *Le bouddhisme au Cambodge*, Paris: Leroux, 1903, p. 403; Klaus Wenk, *Thai literature: An introduction*, trans. Erich W. Reinhold, Bangkok: White Lotus, 1995, p. 30; Judith Jacob, 'Some observations on Khmer verbal usages', in David A. Smyth (ed.), *Cambodian linguistics, literature and history: Collected articles*, London: School of Oriental and African Languages, University of London, 1993, p. 154.

36 Tauch Chhong, *Battambang during the time of the lord governor*, 2nd ed., trans. Hin Sithan, Carol Mortland and Judy Ledgerwood, Phnom Penh: Cedorek, 1994, p. 99.

37 Tauch Chhong, *Battambang during the time of the lord governor*, pp. 98–100; 'Supasit cbpab srei', *Kambujasuriya* 6, 4–6, pp. 46–80, p. 48; *Gatilok ke okhna Suttanta Prachea Ind*, in *Kambujasuriya* 7 (1927), pp. 75–93; *Gatilok ru chbpab tunmean khluon*, in *Kambujasuriya* 9 (1928), pp. 25–41 and 10 (1928), pp. 21–58. A neighbour of Ind named Chheum, a fortune-teller by profession, claimed to have written *Neang Chhantea*, but Ind's son said that his father had written it.

38 Tauch Chhong, *Battambang during the time of the lord governor*, p. 99.

39 *Chroniques 2*, pp. 99, 104, 111, 158,186, 214–215; *Chroniques royales du Cambodge*, Paris: École Française d'Extrême-Orient, 1988, vol. 3: *De 1594 à 1677*, trans. and ed. Mak Phoeun [hereafter *Chroniques 3*], pp. 79, 122, 127, 168, 171, 175–177, 423–424; Khing Hoc Dy, *Contribution*, p. 68.

40 *Chroniques 3*, pp. 79, 122, 127, 168, 171, 176–177, 423–424.

41 Perhaps this is understandable, as the king is said to have ordered all male members of the court to undergo circumcision. See Trudy Jacobsen, 'The temple of the thousand foreskins', *Phnom Penh Post*, 16–29 December 2005, p. 7. *Cbpab tumnam pi boran* [Customs of the past], composed at the end of the seventeenth century from the memoires of Princess Ang Li, does not mention any marriage between Ramadhipati and a Cham or Malay girl. It does, however, relate that 'the Muslim king' accused his principal wife, Ang Srey, of infidelity when she offered fruits to the *oknha chakvey*, demanding 'How can I practice the Malay religion when you are off speaking with other men?' and then challenging the *oknha* to a duel with swords 'according to Malay custom'. Ang Srey became enraged and demanded whether all the ministers thought she had been unfaithful as they were taking the king's side in the matter (*Cbpab tumam pi boran* [Customs of the past] [1693], in *Codes cambodgiens*, t. 1, p. 127). Dutch merchants' records may shed more light on this incident, stating that in April 1642 King Ramadhipati I accused his queen of adultery with his own elder brother. The prince's house was set on fire and he was executed; the queen was stripped of her rank, possessions, and servants, tortured or mutilated, and

either was executed or committed suicide by taking poison some weeks later. See Carool Kersten, 'Cambodia's Muslim king: Khmer and Dutch sources on the conversion of Reameathipadei I, 1642–1658', *Journal of Southeast Asian Studies* 37, 1 (February 2006), pp. 16–17. *Kambujasuriya* published a version of this tale in 1933 in which the king was referred to as 'Mao'. See *Kambujasuriya* 6, 7–9 (1933), pp. 155–163.

42 'Coffee-table' books and travel guides are particularly prone to this perspective. See for example Jeldres, *Royal house of Cambodia*, p. 20.

CHAPTER SIX

'Traditional' Cambodia

*T*he customs and beliefs prevalent in Cambodia in the late nineteenth and early twentieth centuries are today believed to reflect 'traditional' Cambodian society.[1] These traditions were based upon past practice; their retransmission and repetition in successive generations was believed to ensure orderliness and stability.[2] If the late nineteenth century represents 'traditional' Cambodia then surely it is necessary to look beyond the literature of the conservative elite for sources. The *rieong breng*, folktales written down for the first time at the end of the nineteenth century, are replete with tales of powerful women. The observations of French explorers and administrators contain details of daily life in which egalitarianism and respect for women are clearly discernable. The records of the early colonial government attest to the agency of Cambodian women in seeking justice for themselves and their families. The significance of 'female power' is also evident from legends and stories of women in the supernatural realm.

Whatever their husbands and fathers may have been reading (or writing) at the time, the available evidence shows no lessening in agency and resources for elite women in the nineteenth century. Even in the midst of civil war, the Cambodian queens and ladies of the court found time and money to establish *wats* and commission pieces of art and literature. Queen Ut, first wife of King Ang Eng, founded Wat Dhann Te after his death. Lady Prak, whose husband and son had died, commissioned a detailed chronicle in their memory and contributed funds for a new *wat* in 1856. The lady governors of Battambang, Uch and Tim, built Wat Pothiveal and Wat Komphaeng respectively. Lady Mom, known as *Neak M'cas* Khlib, eldest daughter of Governor Nhonh, seems to have been her father's most trusted official. It was her responsibility to take the annual tribute to the Thai court in addition to fulfilling her father's other duties. According to Tauch Chhong, the Thai king was so pleased with Mom that he had intended to appoint her husband the next governor of Battambang, but Mom's half-brother Chhum had him murdered to prevent this from taking place. Mom was so angry at this that she refused to go with the rest of the family to Prachinburi when Battambang was returned to Cambodia in 1907.[3]

During the reign of King Norodom (r. 1860–1904), the queen mother continued to maintain her own court at Udong after the king had relocated to Phnom Penh. Her court seems to have been a sizeable entity with its own judicial and financial processes. All *oknha* in Cambodia were divided into four classes, *sakh ek, sakh tou, sakh trey,* and *sakh chetr,* belonging respectively to the reigning king, the uncle of the king, the heir apparent, and the queen mother. She was also entitled to own elephants. Court ladies were afforded privileges denied their less elite counterparts. In Battambang, the ladies of the palace had a private floating dock in the river opposite Wat Sangkhe where they came to bathe in the evening and their own ricefields at the rear of the fort. There was also a rice-polishing factory within the fort that they were entitled to use. Ladies of the court who were 'married out' to *oknha* were protected by law from ill-treatment by their husbands. They were, however, forbidden to marry below their own status. According to the revised *Kram Sanghrey* of Ang Duong, 'free women cannot marry slaves; if they do they must be chained and promenaded in public for three days so that other women do not follow their example'. The preservation of class difference was important so as to maintain *khsae* networks and thus retain an available body of people upon whom to call for labour-intensive and military endeavours. Everyone was obligated to 'choose a noble as a patron and serve him as required'.[4]

Love and marriage

This did not mean – at least in theory – that the elite were permitted to mistreat their more humble neighbours. A law devised for palace officials when Ang Duong came to power stated that anyone among the nobility who, having an evil heart, takes or arrests the wives or daughters of another, or the slaves or another, and abuses them, without their leave, will be considered an oppressor of the people and condemned.[5]

It was also an offence 'to click the tongue when looking at the wife or daughters of another who may be passing'. Adhémard Leclère was surprised to discover that his entourage of young Cambodian men 'never boasted of their good luck' in their year of travelling the countryside together in the early 1880s, despite the presence of brothels in the larger towns. Indeed, in Battambang a brothel was conveniently located near a laneway along which farmers drove their buffalo. Nevertheless, sexual activity outside a recognised relationship such as engagement or marriage was frowned upon. Those violating very young girls who had not yet reached puberty or were yet to have undergone the ceremony of *joal m'lap* (about which more will be said shortly) were seen as depraved. Girls were also warned against going to the river in the dark, as, 'according to mortal and divine legislators, in the twilight the thief is king'. If illicit relations did take place, the man responsible had certain obligations. As in the preceding period, it was necessary to appease the *meba* lest sickness befall a near relation of the girl concerned. King Norodom issued a decree setting out the exact procedure. It was better, however, for a marriage to take place even when the woman involved had been coerced or raped. In *Rieong tambek buon neak*, 'The tale of the four bald men', the protagonists are asked to judge a matter wherein a girl caught with a man; she protests that he was a thief who had broken into the house, but the judges determined that she had to marry him anyway. If a man refused to marry a girl he had impregnated and she died in pregnancy or childbirth her seducer was obliged to pay the worth of her life to her parents plus a fine.[6]

Marriages seem to have been subject to local variation. Matchmakers were common in Battambang and elsewhere but some young women exercised more control over their choice than others. In *Dum Deav*, one of the best known of the *rieong breng*, a young man and woman fall in love but are kept apart through the interference of others. Eventually the male protagonist, Dum, is killed. Deav, when she learns what has happened, goes to the spot where her lover died and commits suicide rather than marry the man that her mother has chosen for her. In Kampot, two young women wished to marry a man they had saved from drowning. They consulted a judge as to who had more right to him: the girl who had seen that he was in trouble, or the girl who had pulled him to safety. The judge awarded the young man to a third girl, who had taken off her *kramar* and given it to the young man to hide his nakedness, as this act had 'established a relationship' befitting that between a man and his fiancée.[7]

The relatives of the prospective groom would visit the girl's family three times, bringing gifts; after the third visit the girl's parents or guardians would have to give their assent or refusal. The groom would then be required to live and work with the bride's family for at least one rice-growing season, sometimes up to twenty months; 'in so doing, the parents of the future bride were asked to evaluate the personality and quality of the man'. Grooms had to show respect and obedience to his future in-laws to the extent that they were often 'treated like slaves by the bride's family'. Although it was common for the young couple to sleep separately, there seems to have been no prohibition upon sexual relations occurring, as children born to affianced persons were not considered illegitimate. It may have been in the interests of a young man to impregnate his fiancée as quickly as possible, as unscrupulous fathers-in-law could use the slightest hint of insolence or disrespect to 'fire' him despite months of labour. One of these situations could arise when a man appeared before his father-in-law incorrectly attired, when 'his cloth, unknotted behind, fell like a skirt'.[8]

The three 'ranks' of wife – *prapuon thom, prapuon kandal* and *prapuon jerng* – continued to exist, although most ordinary Cambodians could afford only one marriage ceremony and maintain only one wife. The *rieng breng* often tell of a male protagonist who leaves one wife behind when travelling to another place on business and takes another there or one who marries another, richer wife in order to increase his status. Thus *a Lev*, although he had obtained one wife by tricking her grandmother, did not hesitate to marry the daughter of a rich man when the opportunity offered. *Chao* Kambit Pandoh, 'Mr Whittling Knife', married the daughter of a rich man, the daughter of a king, and then returned to his own home and married the daughter of the king there as well. Auguste Pavie recalled that a Chinese trader had come to Kampot with the intention of marrying a rich widow.

> 'I have all the qualities that are necessary to suit her', he told me. 'I speak French quite well, I am a trader, very numerate, I would be able to preserve and increase her fortune, but all the Chinese here try to damage me in her eyes, because they want to see her property in the hands of somebody of the

134

country... . Well, by applying this powder under my nose I force the woman I want to marry to think about me constantly. I have paid sixty piastres for this concoction and it will be given back if it does not work.' When asked whether the prospective bride knew about the powder, he replied 'But of course and she knows it works. I informed her about it during my first visit.'... The use of this powder must be an excellent suggestive means because the marriage took place some time thereafter![9]

Those who took multiple wives were forbidden to marry two sisters, the elder sister of one's father's wife, an aunt and niece, a mother and daughter, or a grandmother and grand-daughter. Men with attractive mothers-in-law were advised to 'consider her as a star in the sky', that is, to leave her alone. The practice of *koan kroach,* which, as related in Chapter 4, involved the forcible removal of the fetus from a wife in her first pregnancy, endured. Thus Leclère wrote in 1883 that 'in the good country of Cambodia, the in-laws, in the first pregnancy, are wary and prevent the young couple from isolating themselves far away'.[10] During the reign of King Norodom, the head of a provincial military force obtained a *koan kroach* from his wife.

> His father-in-law, having tried in vain to apprehend him, begged for justice from the king, who gave orders that fifty men should be brought to the exasperated old man and placed at his disposition. The *sena thong,* counseled by his *koan krak,* thwarted all traps and took refuge near the border, with the Cambodians of Chaudoc, where, they say, he inspired a real fear, so when he appeared in a village, young girls came to the house where he stopped and washed his feet in a sign of extreme respect.[11]

Less malevolent husbands, on the other hand, were required to tend to their wives' needs around the time of delivery, particularly in the procurement of wood for the ritual fire lit under the bed in order to purify the new mother and baby and in chasing away evil spirits that might take advantage of her altered state between the mundane and celestial worlds at that time to take possession of her body or kill her baby.[12]

The marriages described in the *rieong breng* often depict wives as powerful and capable women who outwit men (usually their husbands) time and again. Judith Jacob has commented that the husband 'is often less clever than the wife' in the *rioeng breng. In Rioeng Maya Srei,* a wife cuckolds her spouse, outwits four thieves, and brings a large sum of money home to her original husband, who forgives her and they go on to share a long and happy life. Men are also shown to be more scared and less capable of dealing with crisis situations. The male protagonist in *Rioeng Kang Han* becomes famous throughout the land for his bravery in killing tigers; in actual fact he hid in a tree while his wives dealt with the beast. In Auguste Pavie's village, a local man's wife and his mother organised an elaborate charade, involving the village chiefs, monks, and the district executioner, in order to save him from a perceived threat of supernatural origin. The resourcefulness and efficiency of women translated into proverbs such as 'the hearts of women are decisive and resolute', 'seeds enrich the earth; women enrich men', and 'heed not the advice of women, lose your rice seedlings'.[13]

Although women were advised to be mindful of the opinion of others – another proverb warned 'woe betide the woman who serves betel with a knife the handle of which is broken; woe betide her reputation' – if their husbands were unable or refused to satisfy them they were permitted to take a lover. Despite Ang Duong's tightening of the laws on divorce for women, observers commented that it was common and based upon mutual agreement. In fact, couples who quarrelled were believed to have bad *karma* from previous lifetimes so it was in their best interests to divorce: 'Their fate is not to be with each other, so it is better that they are separated'. *Rioeng breng samlanh pir neak jong bongring dteuk samud'*, 'Two friends who tried to empty the sea', compared a successful couple who worked together in harmony and were successful and a couple who constantly fought who were left naked and ashamed. Divorced women were free to remarry, after which their original husbands could not reclaim them. In 1853 a Chinese merchant, Khvar, attempted to reclaim his wife, who had remarried, stating that he had never repudiated her and so her new 'husband' owed him compensation for stealing his wife. The matter was brought before the king, who determined, as Khvar could produce no witnesses, that he was in contempt. Widows also remarried; a proverb demanded 'Is raw rice not rice? Is a widow any less a woman?' It was, however, preferable that a widow have only one child. 'A widow with one child is like a young girl; a widow with three children is like an old woman'.[14]

Women in public and private

Women were not afraid to assert their legal rights. As discussed above, two young women brought their quarrel over a young man to the district judge. Around the same time, a 15-year-old girl whose father had been murdered travelled to the provincial court in Battambang in order to seek justice. The judge felt that leniency was required (the killers had thought that the victim was a sorcerer who had killed their own father) and ordered the payment of a hefty fine to the girl in compensation. She did not accept the money and went to the governor of Battambang in order to demand that the murderers be sentenced to death. 'Her forehead against the ground, calm, without hearing anything, she repeated her demand with fiery insistence. The Governor had the men executed under her very eyes'.[15] Matters concerning inheritance were particularly likely to result in lawsuits and in this women were also self-confident of their rights; estates were divided not along gender lines but according to which wife the children had been born to. The children of *prapuon thom* received the lion's share, followed by those of the *prapuon kandal* and *prapuon jerng*, should they exist. *Neang* Sang, daughter of a military official, lodged a complaint in 1902 on behalf of herself and four brothers. Their father had married a woman named Tuch two years before his death. *Neang* Sang stated that 'after the cremation ceremony, we gave *neac* [*sic*] Tuch a list of goods and asked her to make over to the children, in accordance with the law, those goods that she wished us to have' but she refused. The subsequent tribunal determined that a portion of the inheritance should be given to the king and the remainder divided equally between the widow and the five children. The king determined that the widow should also receive the land and buildings, even though the two youngest sons had no other place to live.[16]

Punishments for women were virtually the same as those for men. If one spouse injured the other, the penalty was the same regardless of gender. Similarly, if 'a man beats a slave to death and his wife does not try to stop him, she must be punished as her husband, and vice versa'. Some laws entertained a slightly less severe sliding scale of punishments for women, such as *Kram Jao*, 'Law concerning thieves', revised in 1897: 'If the accused is of female sex, the number of blows will be reduced by five, and the fine also reduced by five *damlong*'.[17] Still other laws were designed for the protection of women. Men who 'injure beyond repair a woman's reputation by advertising the fact that he has fornicated with her or that she used to be his slave' were bound to pay a quarter of the price of her life; if, upon investigation, his words were found to be true, he nonetheless had to pay a reduced fine in compensation.[18] The 1897 revised *Kram tralakar* stipulated that a woman, be she the wife of an official or of a man of the people, having a matter with someone, asks to appear before a tribunal, they must, in keeping with custom, write to the husband of the woman so that he may accompany her and give advice.[19]

The ceremonies marking life stages occurred at the same time for girls and boys. Elite children could expect to undergo the tonsure ceremony around the age of thirteen. Girls would usually have their ears pierced at this time; if they did not, they would have to 'submit to this operation in a most barbaric manner' at the onset of puberty, at the time of their period of *joal m'lap*, 'entering the shade'. This corresponded roughly with the time that their brothers would enter the *sangha* for an extended period, after which they would emerge as men able to undertake adult responsibilities such as marriage and fatherhood. The *joal m'lap* had a similar effect for girls. From their first menstrual period they were known as *kramom*, 'virgins', and remained so until the birth of their first child. The first day that the signs of puberty manifested themselves, the girl's parents tied *khsae* (cotton threads) around her wrists and prepared a feast for the *meba*, solemnly informing them of the event and asking that they protect their descendant during her *joal m'lap*. A special banana tree was planted to the north-west of the house and only the girl and monks who called on almsrounds were allowed to consume its fruit. The parents of the girl gave her a number of guidelines to follow while in *joal m'lap*. She was not to be seen by any unfamiliar man; she was not to look at men, even furtively; she was to eat only between sunrise and midday; she was forbidden to eat meat and fish, consuming only rice, salt, coconuts, peas, sesame, and fruit; she could only bathe in the company of her sisters or parents, never after dark; and she was restricted to work in the house, forbidden even to visit the *wat*. Wealthy families could afford to have their daughters observe the *joal m'lap* for months or even years; girls from very poor families, whose livelihoods depended upon the contribution of all able-bodied members, could retreat for only a few days. Often daughters in their early teens or younger were required to look after their younger siblings.[20]

People usually waited for a favourable time for the ceremony of *jenh m'lap*, 'leaving the shade', particularly the months before and after the hot season. Monks came and chanted in the family home while the girl prostrated herself before them. Family and friends were invited to a feast during which the girl would have her teeth filed. If she did not have this procedure following her *joal m'lap*, she would be required to do this the night before her wedding, as it was an outward sign of that she had passed through the ceremony marking puberty. Young men would also have their teeth filed before entering the *sangha*. Once the *joal m'lap* had been completed, the girl was considered ready for marriage and suitors could begin soliciting her hand. Another transformation awaited her after her marriage: Her hair would be cut *en brosse* to signify her married state (see Fig. 6.1). Unmarried girls did not cut their hair. Regardless of their marital status, women who had successfully completed their *joal m'lap* had to purify themselves each month, seven days following their menstrual period, by washing themselves at the well or river and 'massaging their heads with soda or the soapy fruit *sampuor*, or with a small lemon.'[21]

Female power in the spiritual realm

Blood of any sort was considered potentially dangerous as it could attract malevolent supernatural forces. This was particularly true of post-partum blood;

Fig. 6.1: Photograph of Mhek Noun, c.1910. National Archives of Cambodia.

if a woman miscarried or delivered within the palace, a *sampuor polikar* ceremony involving special sacrifices for *neak ta* of the cardinal directions, the marking of a *sima* boundary, and chickens, was required before the area could be considered purified. Midwives were especially respected because they exposed themselves to the potential dangers of the delivery area as a matter of course. It was necessary to 'fire' the bed of women who had just delivered. A special fire was built under the raised bed and she and her infant were 'smoked', thus protecting them from evil spirits in the form of *brai krala plerng*, 'ghost of the fire-chamber', a woman who had died in childbirth herself and if measures were not taken would attempt to kill the new mother and take her baby. Women who died in the third trimester of pregnancy or in labour without having given birth were said to have been killed by *brai* and could become *brai* themselves if, three days following the burial, 'a man, sufficiently audacious and resolved' carried out a certain ceremony. After establishing a *sima* around the corpse, he was to place an image of an eight-headed *brai* in the centre of the room and recite magical incantations. The woman would rise from the dead as a *brai* after the third repetition and attempt to frighten him to death by making horrible faces, lolling an enormous tongue, rolling her eyes, and taking on the forms of a serpent, tiger and elephant. If the man showed any fear he would be consumed, but if he showed resolve eventually the *brai* would relinquish the body of her unborn child to him so that he might make it into a *koan kroach*.[22]

There was a still more formidable *brai:* the *brai kramom*. These were the ghosts of young women who were virgins at the time of their death. At first the *brai kramom* was indistinguishable from the living, appearing very beautiful, with long, flowing hair. Her victim was usually a young man who had been responsible for her death or the death of another young woman through infidelity or unkindness. Sometimes, like the *brai krala plerng*, the *brai kramom* targeted her living virginal counterparts. Once the victim had been lured to a remote place, the *brai kramom* changed into a terrifying hag with protruding eyes, long, lolling tongue, and wild locks of hair. The untapped sexual energy of young women was a powerful force. Around 1905 a group of virgins participated in a ceremony in which the sexual act was simulated in connection with *neak ta*, ancestor spirits, in order to bring rain. According to popular legend, the monastery of Vihear Thom in Kratie province was built on the bodies of one hundred virgins who were crushed to death in the foundations to accompany the spirit of Princess Krapum Chhouk, who was killed by a crocodile nearby. The resulting *brai kramom* protected the monastery.[23]

Sacred places were often inhabited by female spirits. Some, like the *kramom*, had been killed in ritual sacrifice. Pregnant women were also sacrificed in the foundations of important edifices, such as a dike in the Sanghke River, Battambang province. In this instance, as in Kratie, a powerful *neak ta* had to be appeased by the sacrifice before building work could proceed. The legend of the dike says that when *oknha* Baen fled to Thailand at the end of the eighteenth century, his principal wife, *Neang* Teav, was homesick for Cambodia and begged to be allowed to return home. Baen refused.

> [Teav] fled by boat down the Sanghke River back to her country. When Chaufea Baen learned of her flight, he ordered his servants to chase her and kill her immediately on her capture. The servants caught up with Neang Teav, killed her, and buried her at present-day Cape Daunteav. Neang Teav's ghost became an evil spirit who accepted any offering from passengers travelling up and down the waterway.[24]

Sima stones were placed in the water to contain the *neak ta* but such was her power that pregnant women were warned against passing in front of the dike lest they miscarry. There seems to have been an association between female *neak ta* and water; according to Ang Chouléan, in *wats* with a *srah*, or artificial lake, the *neak ta* dwelling next to the access stairs was 'almost always female'. Again, pregnant women were forbidden to walk in front of this *neak ta* for fear of premature labour. A certain canoe at Wat Kantoeng in Battambang was to be avoided for the same reason.[25]

Statues dating from much earlier periods were popular dwelling-places for female *neak ta*, according to the folk legends of the late nineteenth and early twentieth centuries. In Kien Svay, Kandal, the *chao adthika* (head monk) of Wat Prek Aing had a dream that a *koki* tree floated ashore near his *wat*. The spirit of a young girl was living in the tree and called out to him, 'I have come from a land upriver, now I have come here to your *wat*. Please, kind *loak kru*, rescue me.' The next day the *chao adthika* sent novices to search the riverbank and they found a statue. Yet they could not move it. The *chao adthika* had another dream in which the spirit of the young woman said that she did not wish to be touched by men: 'I am very shy, I will only permit women to touch me'. The *chao adthika* organised this and they were surprised to find that the statue moved easily. People came from all around to make merit in front of the statue and their wishes were fulfilled. They called her Yeay Bos, 'Grandmother of the Reeds', as she was found amongst the reeds of the riverbank. Later, worried that Yeay Bos might be lonely so far away from her own country, a 'marriage' was engineered between Yeay Bos and another *neak ta* (ancestor spirit), Ta Srei, 'Grandfather Woman', the spirit of a monk, after which they both inhabited Yeay Bos's statue. Not all ancestor spirits lived in statues, however; *neak ta* Yeay Nguon, at Wat Kbal Damrei in Kompong Thom, sometimes dwelt in mounds of earth.[26]

A particularly powerful kind of *neak ta*, a *me sa* (literally, 'white lady'), was residing in an image of Durga Mahishasuramardani at Ba Phnom in the 1880s. The statue itself had probably been there for centuries. Hundreds of *me sa* were listed in two documents of the late nineteenth century, one detailing a ceremony carried out in 1859, at the request of Ang Duong, to increase the merit and good fortune of the kingdom, and the other the text of a pledge of good faith, dating from later in the same century. The purpose of invoking their names in texts was to demonstrate an association between the king and their supernatural powers – namely, that he, and he alone, was in a position to access them.[27]

The female inhabitants of the supernatural world were often perceived as being violent and bloodthirsty. The *me sa* of Ba Phnom was ritually offered human sacrifices; the last appears to have taken place in 1877. Sacrifices were associated with an annual ritual called 'raising the ancestors'. People present at the sacrificial ceremony would ask the *me sa* 'to help them to be healthy and fortunate, to help the governing officials and all their assistants, and also the ordinary people'. David Chandler suggested that causing a sacrifice to be performed at the site may have imbued the organiser with legitimisation. The 1877 sacrifices were carried out after King Norodom's army had routed Prince Sivotha at Ba Phnom; Norodom then immediately sent a new official to rule the area. The commissioning of sacrifices to the *me sa* of Ba Phnom may have been an attempt on Norodom's part to establish an association with the supernatural power of the region as well.[28] *Neak ta* Jamdev Mau, in Kampot province, was believed by the local people to have the highest *adthipul*, a supernatural energy, of all *neak ta* in the area.

> From 1866 until 1944 this *neak ta* was very wild, very noisy; if people walked along the road toward Kampot in front of her place they would be prevented. She could not be pleased with offerings of this or that.[29]

In Battambang, the governor's sword was named *Srei Khmau,* 'Black Woman', and once unsheathed had to kill twice before being put away. Legends such as *Rieong Neang Ramsey Sok* and *Neang Kangrei* tell of *yaksini* (demons) leading their armies into battle and fighting to the death.[30]

The significance and agency of these legendary women was mirrored in their more mundane counterparts who regularly crossed the boundary between the seen and unseen worlds: the *ap,* witches, and *rup araks,* mediums. *Ap* could either inherit their powers or be schooled in the black arts from a master *thmup,* sorcerer. The *ap* were recognised 'by their bloodshot and haggard eyes' by day; after dark, they removed their heads from their shoulders and went about 'spreading foul illnesses in the entrails of sleepers'. They were considered extremely dangerous; laws setting out punishments for people accused of being *ap* or *thmup,* causing bad dreams, casting spells, reciting incantations, causing abortions, and making potions of invisibility (all of which an *ap* or *thmup* could be called upon to do) were retained into the twentieth century. The governor of Battambang, after hearing a case brought by a girl whose father was thought to be a *thmup,* 'thinking that the young girl might have inherited the occult powers attributed to her father', had her removed from his province 'and prohibited her ever to cross its borders again'.[31] On the other hand, Auguste Pavie witnessed a woman conjure supernatural forces for her fiancé when he was about to fight a Cham sailor:

> While he bowed to listen, she recited a formula or a prayer and placed a green leaf in his mouth, picked at night, they told me, from the Sangké tree, which had to bring him luck. Then, recommending him to remain cold-blooded no doubt, she returned to her companions, laughing despite herself with the approving comments they cast at her from the distance.[32]

There was a fine line between 'good' and 'bad' supernatural powers where women were concerned. *Kru,* healers, could be either men or women, and were considered positive forces. A monk had a dream in which the Queen Mother commanded him to drink from a pond inside the grounds of her palace at Udong in order to cure illness; once he publicised this, people began flocking to the site in droves. By contrast, *smir,* creatures created when women anointed themselves with *khuoc* oil over which magical incantations had been spoken, were wicked, senseless beings who 'run into the forest followed by tigers and, after seven days, their skin will be covered by fur, and they will become like tigers themselves'.[33]

Rup araks, 'mediums', had a similarly ambiguous status. Although men could be *rup*, it seems to have been more common for women to have been the vessels through which *neak ta* chose to communicate. This was particularly true when possessions were instigated by the *neak ta* through illness. An old woman named Yeay Khmau, 'Black Grandmother', living near Wat Sangkey in Takeo province, became ill with a swelling sickness and went into trances. The *chao adthika* of the *wat*, a renowned healer, was consulted. The *neak ta* who had possessed her body wished to stay as the people of the area were of good character. After her death, the *neak ta* remained in a statue and brought peace and prosperity to the *srok*. *Neak ta* could also be summoned through ritual but it was likely that they would be *araks brai*, 'wild spirits', which seem to have been more inclined toward evil deeds. They were known by their forms – *tambang taek*, 'flaming club', *rambat meas*, 'golden wand', or *srei khmau*, 'black lady'. In such rituals the *rup* was assisted by a *snang*, a female assistant, who spoke to the *rup* while possessed.[34]

∿

Notwithstanding the undeniable privileges of elite women over their less elevated counterparts, there were more differences between women of different classes than between men and women within those classes in Cambodia before the modernisation efforts of the colonial administration began to impact on Cambodian society. Girls and young women were protected in law; the importance of women as partners in the home and in business was recognised; and they were, theoretically at least, entitled to take new husbands should divorce or death leave them unexpectedly solitary. Although men were allowed greater access to the formal religious institution of the *sangha*, women seem to have enjoyed just as prominent, if not superior, a position in the supernatural realm, inhabited by a myriad of female spirits, and accessed by a host of women in their capacities as *ap, rup*, and *snang*. The equality of men and women can be seen in complementary ceremonies marking life stages; when boys were serving as novices, girls were in their *joal m'lap* period. Women, in fact, had more contact with the spiritual world than men as their biology dictated a constant affiliation with blood and the access that it afforded for potentially malevolent spirits. The late nineteenth and early twentieth centuries provide a snapshot of Cambodia as, in all likelihood, it had been for hundreds of years; but the true picture, gleaned from legends, law codes, and local practices rather than the literature of the elite, is of a society in which women were respected rather than constrained.

Notes to Chapter 6

1   See for example Saveros Pou, 'Avertissement', in Étienne Aymonier, *Notes sur les coutumes et croyances supersititeuses des cambodgiens, commenté et présenté par Saveros Pou*, Paris: Centre de Documentation et de Recherche sur la Civilisation Khmere [Cedorek], 1984, p. 3.

2   David Chandler, 'Songs at the edge of the forest: Perceptions of order in three Cambodian texts [1978]', in David P. Chandler, *Facing the Cambodian past: Selected essays 1971–1994*, St Leonards, New South Wales: Allen & Unwin, 1996, pp. 78–79.

3   Justin J. Corfield, *The royal family of Cambodia*, Melbourne: The Khmer Language & Culture Centre, 1993, p.16; Chandler, 'Songs at the edge of the forest', pp.76–99; Tauch Chhong, *Battambang during the time of the lord governor*, 2nd ed., trans. Hin Sithan, Carol Mortland and Judy Ledgerwood, Phnom Penh: Cedorek, 1994, pp. 10–11, 112, 131.

4   *Kram Sanghkrey*, in Adhémard Leclère, *Les codes cambodgiens*, Paris: Ernest Leroux, 1898, t. 1, p. 303; Leclère, *Codes cambodgiens*, t. 1, p. 5; *Kram montiro bal*, in *Codes cambodgiens*, t. 1, p. 192; *Kram tortuol bandoeng*, in *Codes cambodgiens*, t. 2, p. 135, f.n.; Tauch Chhong, *Battambang during the time of the lord governor*, pp. 32–33, 38, 61, 121.

5   *Kram Achnha luong*, in *Codes cambodgiens*, t. 2, p. 266.

6   Ang Chouléan, *Les êtres surnaturels dans la religion populaire khmère*, Paris: Cedorek, 1986, pp. 235, 238; *Kram Sanghkrey*, in *Codes cambodgiens*, t. 1, p. 326; *Rieong tambek buon neak*, in *Prachum rieong breng khmei 4*, Phnom Penh: Buddhist Institute, 1962; Aymonier, *Notes sur les coutumes et croyances*, pp. 44, 47, 72–76; Tauch Chhong, *Battambang during the time of the lord governor*, p. 39; *Kram tous piriyea*, in *Codes cambodgiens*, t. 1, pp. 280, 287.

7   A. Cabaton, 'La vie domestique au Cambodge', *Revue Indo-Chinoise* 2 (1910), p. 106; *Dum Deav*, Phnom Penh: Buddhist Institute, 1971; Auguste Pavie, *The Pavie Mission Indochina Papers 1879–1895*, vol. 1: *Pavie Mission Exploration Work: Laos, Cambodia, Siam, Yunnan, and Vietnam* [1901], trans. Walter E. J. Tips, Bangkok: White Lotus, pp. 47–48.

8   Cabaton, 'La vie domestique au Cambodge', pp. 105–107; Aymonier, *Notes sur les coutumes et croyances*, pp. 80, 81–82; Tauch Chhong, *Battambang during the time of the lord governor*, pp. 76, 80; *Rieong A Lev*, in Franklin E. Huffman, *Intermediate Cambodian reader*, New Haven: Yale University Press, 1972, pp. 141–163; *Chao Kambit Pandoh*, in *Prachum rieong breng khmei 2*, Phnom Penh: Buddhist Institute, 1960.

9   Pavie, *Pavie Mission*, vol. 1, pp. 56–57.

10 *Kram Sanghkrey*, in *Codes cambodgiens*, t. 1, p. 290; Aymonier, *Notes sur les coutumes et croyances*, pp. 68, 83.

11 Aymonier, *Notes sur les coutumes et croyances*, pp. 68–69.

12 Aymonier, *Notes sur les coutumes et croyances*, p. 43.

13 Judith Jacob, *The traditional literature of Cambodia: A preliminary guide*, Oxford: Oxford University Press, 1996, p. 15; *Rieong maya srei*, in *Kambujasuriya* 7–9 (1938), pp. 327–337; *Rieong Kang Han*, in *Kambujasuriya* 8, 4–6 (1938), pp. 45–53; Pavie, *Pavie Mission*, vol. 1, pp. 64–65; A. Pannetier, 'Sentences et proverbes cambodgiens', *BEFEO* 15 (1915), pp. 69–70.

14 Aymonier, *Notes sur les coutumes et croyances*, p. 39; Cabaton, 'La vie domestique au Cambodge', p. 110; translation of *Cbpab Cosphiriyea*, National Archives of Cambodia, *Fonds du Resident Superieure au Cambodge* [hereafter RSC] 14876; *Rieong breng pir neak jong bongring dteuk samudr'* [Two friends who tried to empty the sea], *Kambujasuriya* 12, 6 (1958), pp. 541–550; Pannetier, 'Sentences et proverbes cambodgiens', pp. 60, 70; *Kram Preas Reachea khant*, in *Codes cambodgiens*, t. 2, p. 620.

15 Pavie, *Pavie Mission*, vol. 1, p. 118.

16 Complaint of *Neang* Sang, dated 17 July 1902; *Rapport de Tribunal Supérieur*, letter No. 25/1, 26 July 1902. Both in RSC 10047.

17 *Kram Viveat*, in *Codes cambodgiens*, t. 2, pp. 455–456; *Kram tortuol bandoeng*, in *Codes cambodgiens*, t. 2, pp. 153–154; *Kram Chor*, in *Codes cambodgiens*, t. 2, p. 301.

18 *Kram Viveat*, in *Codes cambodgiens*, t. 2, p. 460. The value of a woman's life was calculated at 25 *damlong*, men were worth 30 *damlong* (*Kram Chor*, in *Codes cambodgiens*, t. 2, p. 310). This should not be taken as an indication that men were more intrinsically valued in contemporaneous Cambodian society but a calculation based upon the physical work that a healthy adult was likely to perform. Women would lose some work years due to pregnancy and primary care of young children.

19 *Kram Tralakar*, in *Codes cambodgiens*, t. 2, pp. 88–89.

20 Pavie, *Pavie Mission*, vol. 1, p. 77; Tauch Chhong, *Battambang during the time of the lord governor*, p. 36; Aymonier, *Notes sur les coutumes et croyances*, pp. 72–76, 78; 'How the koan lok bird got its feathers', in David Chandler (trans.), *The friends who tried to empty the sea: Eleven Cambodian folk stories*, Clayton, Victoria: Monash University Centre of Southeast Asian Studies, 1977.

21 Aymonier, *Notes sur les coutumes et croyances*, pp. 44, 72–76; Cabaton, 'La vie domestique au Cambodge', p. 112; *Henri Mouhot's Diary: Travels in the central parts of Siam, Cambodia and Laos during the years 1858–61* [1864], Kuala Lumpur: Oxford University Press, n.d., p. 35.

22 *Kram montiro bal*, in *Codes cambodgiens*, t. 1, pp. 191–192; Ang Chouléan, *Les êtres surnaturels dans la religion populaire khmère*, p. 105; Ang Chouléan, 'Grossesse et accouchement au Cambodge: Aspects rituels', ASEMI : Asie du Sud-Est et du Monde Insulindien, 13, 1–4, p. 100; Aymonier, *Notes sur les coutumes et croyances*, p. 69.

23 Ang Chouléan, *Les êtres surnaturels dans la religion populaire khmère*, pp. 132; 213, note 503.

24 Tauch Chhong, *Battambang during the time of the lord governor*, pp. 27–28.

25 Ang Chouléan, *Les êtres surnaturels dans la religion populaire khmère*, p. 219; Tauch Chhong, *Battambang during the time of the lord governor*, p. 82.

26 *Neak ta Ta Srei neung Yeay Bos*, in *Prajum rieong bring khmei: Krom jomnuon tomniem tomleap khmei*, vol. 8, Phnom Penh: Buddhist Institute, 2001, pp. 107–113; *Neak ta Yeay Nguon*, in *Prajum rieong bring khmei*, vol. 8, pp. 155–175.

27 For more detailed information on this goddess see David Chandler, 'Royally sponsored human sacrifices in nineteenth century Cambodia: The cult of *nak ta* me sa (mahisasura-mardani) at Ba Phnom' [1974], in Chandler, *Facing the Cambodian past*, pp. 119–135; David Chandler, 'Maps for the ancestors: Sacralized topography and echoes of Angkor in two Cambodian texts', in Chandler, *Facing the Cambodian past*, p. 42.

28 'Nak ta me sa (Ba Phnom), Chandler's translation of Khmer original in *Prajum rieong bpren* (Phnom Penh: Institute Bouddhique, 1971), vol. 8, 81–88, in 'Royally sponsored human sacrifices in nineteenth century Cambodia', p. 134; Chandler, 'Maps for the ancestors', pp. 39–40.

29 *Neak ta Jamdev Mau*, in *Prajum rieong breng khmei*, vol. 8, pp. 123–133.

30 Tauch Chhong, *Battambang during the time of the lord governor*, p. 50; Jacob, *Traditional literature of Cambodia*, pp. 139,142; *Kambujasuriya* vols 7–9 (1937), pp. 327–337.

31 Aymonier, *Notes sur les coutumes et croyances*, p. 62; *Kram Lakkhana uttar*, in *Codes cambodgiens*, t. 2, pp. 113–114; Pavie, *Pavie Mission*, vol. 1, p. 118.

32 Pavie, *Pavie Mission*, vol. 1, p. 61.

33 Aymonier, *Notes sur les coutumes et croyances*, pp. 57, 65; Jean Moura, *Le royaume de Cambodge*, Paris: Ernest Leroux, 1883, vol. 2, p. 153.

34 *Neak ta Yeay Khmau*, in *Prajum rieong bring khmei*, vol. 8, pp. 51–56; Aymonier, *Notes sur les coutumes et croyances*, pp. 58–59, 77. *Snang* was also the word for a category of royal wives. The *snang* in both roles acted as facilitators between persons who were simultaneously of the human and supernatural worlds – kings and mediums – and the mundane world itself.

CHAPTER SEVEN

Cherchez la femme

*T*he colonial period, officially established on 11 August 1863, has shaped modern Cambodian identity.[1] The tension between development and subjugation had particular ramifications for women in Cambodia. The French saw Cambodian women as simultaneously naïve and corrupting, powerless yet capable of (negative) influence. Few reforms of the colonial period were specifically directed toward the improvement of Cambodian women's lives and those that were contributed to their disempowerment by removing them from areas in which they had previously been significant. Under the French, women were forced to take their husband's surnames in interactions with the state. A rule of succession was introduced stipulating that only male descendants of Ang Duong should inherit the throne.[2] French scholars dismissed evidence that some women in the Cambodian past could have been more important than men.[3] At the same time, the French did little to eliminate practices that were discriminatory to women from a European point of few, such as polygamy and limited access to educational opportunities. These, rather than the significance and importance of women in Cambodia of the late nineteenth century discussed in Chapter 6, were enshrined as 'traditional' Cambodian practices.

Exoticism and 'encongayment'

The earliest French accounts reveal conflicting images of Cambodian women. One impression was of a demure *bonne femme*.

Those who know the Cambodian woman, have observed her within her family, at the temple, at the great religious and family celebrations, always devout, always attentive, obliging without ever losing an ounce of her dignity, busy, watching everything, placing offerings in front of the Buddha, giving alms to the monks, preparing the flowers for offering, or placing them for all ancestors, for all the village invited to the marriage of a daughter, at the hair-cutting ceremony of the children.[4]

Others described Cambodian women as 'pious Buddhists' and 'devout'. An elderly Cambodian woman in a French novel 'lived the life of a nun, distributing alms to all'. Some saw them as childish, though well-intentioned: 'She is more of a child than a woman and has a passion for jewels above all else. She is capable of most profound sentiments and delicate attentions. Her heart brims

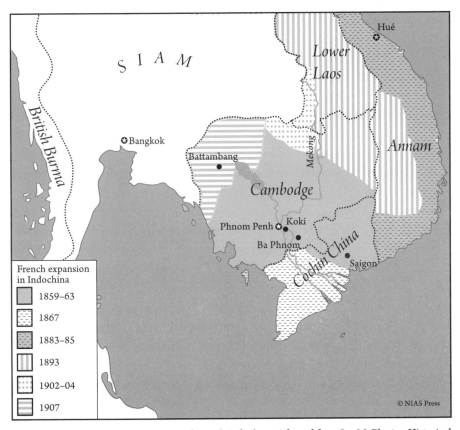

Fig. 7.1: Cambodia and the expansion of French Indochina. Adapted from Jan M. Pluvier, *Historical Atlas of South-East Asia* and other written sources.

with tenderness, often of a charming sensibility.' Such descriptions prolifer-
ate in the novels and diaries of French colonialists, although, according to
Étienne Aymonier, they did not have much opportunity to see Cambodian
women very often unless glimpsed drawing water from the well or participating in ceremonies at the *wat*. Upon seeing Europeans, 'these brown and
timid Rebeccas' would 'slip in all haste towards home, grab feverishly the
window-shutters and disappear inside, where for nothing will they leave as
long as the stranger is in sight'. Europeans fortunate enough to approach were
favourably impressed, at least with young women. Henri Mouhot described a
new addition to King Norodom's court as 'one, whose features were delicate
and pretty, dressed in the European style, and wearing long hair. She would
have been reckoned a pretty girl anywhere'.[5]

Many men seem to have detected an underlying promise of sensuality in
the appearance of Cambodian women: 'Lips partly opened to smile, with one
hand holding her dress … . [H]er sturdy but supple body undulated under
her tunic-sheath which tightly held her shoulders and her chest and displayed
her bosom'. The perceived exoticism of their appearance contributed to the
construction of Cambodian women as sexually licentious, but the casual
sexual encounters between enslaved women and their masters, observed
by Europeans for centuries before the colonial period in Cambodia, led to
a widespread belief that Southeast Asian women were inherently sexually
available and indiscriminate in their choice of partners. In the eighteenth and
nineteenth centuries, the association between slavery, perceived as a dishon-
ourable or degrading state, and the confusion of temporary marriages with
prostitution, devalued the status of the temporary wife in Southeast Asian societies. The 'exotic East' was perceived as a place of sexual freedom, free from
the guilt and responsibilities that came with metropolitan sexual activity. This
comes across in many nineteenth- and twentieth-century French novels. As
Penny Edwards has remarked, these novels 'conjured up an inverted dream-
world … . In this colonial utopia all the heroes were portrayed as French
men, the colonized were Cambodian women hungry for male domination'.
The sexual conquest of indigenous women is a metaphor for the violent
acquisitions of early colonialism. Indigenous women, because they were 'different', were thought likely to be 'more compliant' and 'less discerning' than
Europeans, 'more interested in the financial rewards of being associated with
a metropolitan male than with questions of love'.[6]

150

The commoditisation of sex was of great concern to some senior French administrators. As early as 1885 an *arrête* was promulgated giving the colonial police the power to close brothels and arrest sex workers. In a letter to the *Résident Supérieur du Cambodge*, dated 20 May 1901, Leclère drew attention to the 'houses of iniquity and the prostitutes who carry on, in Phnom Penh, their degrading profession.' He then listed a number of problems with the existing situation and called for redresses that would regularise brothels and discourage men from visiting them, including locating brothels at a distance from the town. These suggestions were not adopted in the 1901 *Code Pénal cambodgien*. Instead, 'those who run houses of prostitution that have not been authorised by the government' would be fined between 30 and 100 piastres and face imprisonment of three months. The following year, Leclère lamented that the number of sex workers in Phnom Penh had increased from five in 1892 to fifty. A later *arrête* stated that sex workers known to have transmitted diseases to clients would be imprisoned for a minimum of one month if they continued working. Numbers of sex workers increased throughout the twentieth century; Geoffrey Gorer commented in 1935 that 'every rickshaw boy, and there must be thousands of them, is a pimp'. Leclère blamed the increase in sex workers and a general decline in female morality on the French, but he was in the minority. Most colonialists believed that Cambodian women were naturally inclined toward debauchery.[7]

Temporary marriage acquired a new name during the colonial period: *encongayment*. As we have seen in earlier chapters, Cambodian women had been taking foreign husbands for centuries.[8] Large numbers of French colonial officials had the inevitable result of temporary marriages with local women who benefited materially from such unions. Léon Fonfrère, a military official, received a letter from Ang Lava (known as Marie Thérèse Fonfrère) stating that she was leaving him to live with a civil servant in Cochinchina and taking her trousseau with her.[9] Despite the prevalence of unions between French colonial men and Cambodian women, the French metropole warned against *encongayment* in the strongest possible terms:

> It must not be forgotten that in most cases, the indigenous woman who consents to live with a European is a veritable prostitute and that she will never reform. When, after several years of free union with Frenchmen, the latter disappear or abandon her, she fatally returns to the vice from which she came and she nearly always sets an example of debauchery, sloth, and immorality

for her children. She takes care of them with the sole purpose of later profiting from their labor and especially from their vices.[10]

The French feared that the influence of indigenous women would lead the colonial administrators to see things from the colonial, rather than metropolitan, point of view. These fears were realised in the Yukanthor affair, when Albert Huynh de Vernéville, *Résident Supérieur du Cambodge*, was accused of being under the influence of his native mistress Mi Ruong. Thus, whilst indigenous women were perceived as submissive and exotic, they were also seen as potential destroyers of the boundary between metropole and colony, through the children they produced.[11] According to the 1899 statute of the *Société de protection et d'éducation des Jeunes Métis Français de la Cochinchine et du Cambodge, métis* sons were destined for lives of crime and sloth, girls for prostitution, as

from the cradle, their mothers adorn them with bracelets and necklaces and maintain in them a love of luxury … . Arriving at the age of puberty, deprived of any skills which would help them survive, and pushed into a life by their mothers that they have a natural tendency to imitate, they will take to prostitution in its diverse forms.[12]

Emancipation and exploitation

The sexualised image of Cambodian women held by many French officials met its zenith with regard to the women of the palace, believing the institution to be a Cambodian version of the Middle Eastern 'harem' in which women had no function other than to provide sexual services.[13]

[The palace] is dressed in a thousand different fabrics, bare shoulders and arms, heads of black, short hair. There are old, wrinkled women, shaven-headed, collarbones like ropes, spines hard and curved under their white robes. There are opulent matrons with tight jackets who eat betel like ruminating cattle; women of round and soft figures, holding naked children, squatting on their haunches; girls dressed in *sampot* shining and brittle as stars; servants carrying boxes of betel … . One sees also some Annamite women with their black clothing, beads of gold at their necks; and Malays of opulent hairstyles. They are seated on mats, squatting, lying down, leaning on their elbows.[14]

Leclère referred to the female 'slaves' of the palace as *sauchey*, synonymous with 'prostitute', and the women whose duty it was to carry ritual objects into the king's chamber 'femme du lit (du harem)'. French writers had few opportunities for close observation but this did not prevent them from writing sensational descriptions of the lives of the women inside the palace walls, beginning with the bewilderment of the young girls who cried 'in seeing their mother disappear', but quickly finding consolation in 'the beautiful gardens, the flowers, the pretty houses, the shops selling fried cakes' inside the palace.[15] The remainder of their girlhood, according to such descriptions, was spent in learning the difficult art of Cambodian dance so that they might perform for the king and attract his favour, in avoiding the inevitable petty jealousies that exist between women, and wrestling with sexual desires that might never be fulfilled as the women of the palace were forbidden to leave the palace grounds.[16] Secret lesbian trysts abound in *Saramani, danseuse khmère*, a story largely sympathetic to women of the palace. In old age, the women of the palace have no option but to remain in their 'prison': 'Her parents are dead and her friends divided by intrigues ... . And so she becomes one of the ghastly old women with which the palace is peopled'.[17]

The French had strong objections to the number of women in King Norodom's palace. *Gouverneur Général* Jean Le Myre de Vilers wrote at the end of his posting that Norodom had, 'to crown everything, a harem, made up of four hundred women, which becomes larger each year through the recruitment of young girls carried on in Siam'.[18] Norodom was extremely reluctant to reduce the numbers of women maintained in his palace. The French thought this was because Norodom wished to avail himself of their services, and no doubt this was to some extent true; but what the French did not understand was that the presence of large numbers of women in a man's entourage represented the extent of his support base, his masculinity, and his charisma, all of which were important requirements for kings.[19] Norodom was particularly sensitive to his image as a legitimate king in possession of the necessary attributes of sovereignty, as his reign was not universally endorsed by the Cambodian *oknha* and he experienced considerable opposition during his reign. He responded to Cambodian criticism by reinforcing his image as a Cambodian king in traditional ways. One of these was to appease the *me sa* of Ba Phnom through human sacrifice, as discussed in Chapter 6.

Another was to demonstrate the fealty of his *oknha* and other subjects by taking into his palace (sometimes by force) their daughters as living symbols of their acknowledgement of his right to rule. Although his official wives were eventually downsized to five, this number retained the symbolism of the *cakravartin* king whose power extended in all four cardinal directions, with one principal queen at the heart of the kingdom. Norodom, like earlier kings, saw infidelity on the part of the women of the palace as treason, as it compromised the relationship established between the family and thus the geographic area they represented. Punishment for sexual transgressions was harsh. In 1875 an official, Kuy, was found to have slept with one of the *neak moneang,* Chhay. Kuy was condemned to death along with the two women who had acted as intermediaries for the couple. After being shot, their heads were cut off and displayed on bamboo stakes as a deterrent for others. Chhay could not be shot as her rank as a woman by whom the king had had children entitled her to mitigated punishment; thus she was beheaded with a sword.[20]

Ostensibly, the emancipation of the women of the palace was part of the process of modernisation that the French were bestowing so benevolently upon their colonial subjects. The treatment meted out to women of the palace by Norodom and the conditions in which they believed they were forced to live provided the impetus to dissolve what they considered a barbaric form of institutionalised slavery. Although the French acknowledged that the people themselves usually offered their daughters to the king, they dismissed the practice as a superstition rather than an integral part of Cambodian political culture: '[Their] fathers are persuaded that their daughters offered to the king will bring to them and their families the favour of the spirits and great protection'. There were other considerations, however, that led to the dissolution of the women of the palace. The French objected to the largesse that the king would freely distribute amongst his favourites and the control that the women of the palace had over the treasury. Norodom entrusted his finances to his favourite consorts in the latter part of his life. The women of the palace were also considered an expensive luxury. Paul Doumer described the women of the palace as wearing 'silk clothing ... [and] masses of jewels on their persons ... . His dancers possessed costumes, golden, peaked crowns, each covered in stones of an incalculable value'. In a country desperately in need of 'civilising' and 'modernisation', the women of the palace were a drain on resources. The most threatening aspect of the women of the palace, however, was the influence that they wielded over the king.[21]

The death of Norodom in April 1904 gave the French the opportunity to implement a host of reforms to the running of the palace. All members of the court, including princes and princesses, were reviewed and their salaries

brought into line with French civil service salaries. Control of the royal treas-
uries passed into the hands of the French. Roland Meyer gave a very vivid,
if fictitious, account of how the reorganisation must have appeared to the
inhabitants of the palace: 'The mayor of the palace, accompanied by a bald
Frenchman with big fish-eyes, went into the throne hall, opened the royal
treasure-coffers, and for several days appeared to be the true masters of the
house'. The number of women that the king could support was thereby reduced and many left the palace for marriages beyond its walls. King Sisowath
(r. 1904–1927), although less prolific than his father, had been an adult during
the heydey of Norodom's excesses, and following this example had established
his retinue of women of the palace. No *kang chao* (the title given to women of
the palace with close relationships to the king) were added during his reign.
Girls continued to be absorbed into the palace, but in fewer numbers; by
1913 the custom was on the wane. Those that did enter the palace after 1904
were destined for the palace troupes of singers and dancers rather than the
administrative and ritual functions of the past, and they were paid a salary
from the budget of the royal treasury. Some women managed to negotiate
important positions despite the reduced opportunities for advancement. Sou
Seth (1881–1963), the daughter of a palace official, began her palace career
as a chanter in the palace chorus, becoming secretary of the royal ballet (at
which time she held literacy classes for the dancers), the head of the women's
chorus, and the manager of the orchestra.[22] The reign of Sisowath can be seen
as a compromise between traditional Cambodian kingship and French efforts
at modernisation (see Fig. 7.2); although described as 'more easy-going' with
regard to the women of the palace, he maintained the tight control over their
sexual activities of yesteryear, as they continued to represent his potency as a
man and legitimacy as a sovereign.

> The gossips wait and follow them, so that they cannot explain away a half-
> hour. In this little world of grace and charm, a denunciation is rewarded with
> the protection of an official or a favourite. They are spied upon and watched.
> Emissaries are sent out to the town while the dancers stay in the palace, to
> find out what she, with authority, did! Who approached her? Who spoke to
> her? Who is that man? Is that really her brother?[23]

Forced to accept the continuation of an institution they regarded as de-
bauched, the French strove to find some redemption in its existence. Happily,
the 'royal ballet' – originally comprised of women of the palace gifted in dance

Fig. 7.2: Monument at Wat Phnom depicting the return of Battambang, Siem Reap and Sisophon provinces, represented as submissive women, to the Cambodian king in 1907.

but by no means their sole occupation – fulfilled the colonial agenda of *mission civilisatrice,* the perceived responsibility of the French in modernising the countries and peoples it colonised, and *mise en valeur,* the manifestation of the supposed benefits colonialism brought, 'a means through which to measure and display the beneficial impact of the French enterprise abroad'. The French had been exposed to the spectacle of the royal ballet from the beginning of their involvement with Cambodia. It was the custom for guests to the court to be honoured with a banquet and entertainment provide by the palace dancers 'in accordance with the custom of past entertainments at the court of the great king'. George Bois, a French representative at the Cambodian court in the early twentieth century, determined that the Cambodian royal ballet would make an admirable addition to the *Exposition colonial* in Marseilles in 1906. Although Paul Doumer said that the Cambodian king was 'happy to offer them to Europeans as an entertainment', Sisowath refused to allow the royal ballet dancers to travel to France without him, setting forth with a sizeable entourage that included cooks, valets, doctors, monks, a number of princes and princesses, forty-two dancers, eight rhythm-keepers, eight dressers, twelve musicians, eight narrators, and two jewellers. It is possible that the dancers themselves thought that they were accompanying their king on a period of house arrest in France,[24] as had been the custom at the Thai court.

The French modified the choreography of the Cambodian ballet in keeping with metropolitan tastes. It was feared that too accurate a representation of indigenous artistry would not enthral onlookers. This was a sentiment that had been voiced by Paul Doumer in 1903: 'The events, borrowed from scenes of the *Ramayana*, seductions, battles, battles between men and monkeys, are for us a little more incomprehensible. The Cambodians find such mimicry an extreme pleasure and the king more so than his subjects'. These augmentations were favourably received by the viewing public; after seeing the *Exhibition coloniale* in 1922, Geoffrey Gorer commented that he was 'very impressed with them' and that 'their white makeup, their expensive and peculiar costumes, and their stylised movements, is [*sic*] far pleasanter when seen in a European theatre'. Roland Meyer has his heroine, a Cambodian dancer who accompanied the troupe to Marseilles, comment upon the superficiality of Europeans, that they can conceive only of the present world, through visual means; they know nothing of spirituality. Later, two dancers discuss leaving the royal ballet, as their position has been devalued from attendants to the power of sovereignty to performing animals. When one girl worries that the art of dance will degenerate without skilled dancers, another says that 'new dancers recruited from amongst clumsy peasants will suffice to amuse the French'.[25]

When Sisowath died in April 1927, the French took control of the royal ballet corps. A royal ordinance promulgated on 14 June 1927 placed the royal ballet corps under the direct control of the *Directeur des Arts cambodgiens*. Reforms were made to the manner in which members of the troupe were chosen, conditions of training and employment, and remuneration. Previously, these had been at the discretion of the king. Some aspects of the traditional were retained in the reformed admission requirements, for example that girls under eighteen must be presented for admission by their parents. The majority of traditional elements were removed, however. Advancement and distribution of roles were no longer left to the king; according to the ordinance, henceforth promotion would be decided by an agreement between the *Ministre du Palais Royal*, the *Directeur de Arts cambodgiens*, two princes of the royal family, one princess of the royal family, two ballet mistresses, one Cambodian professor at the *École des Arts*, and one female instructor.[26] The king no longer had one of the rewards with which he used to remunerate his favourites.

The royal ballet corps was recreated according to French aesthetic principles. This meant that older women who had once been dancers could form no part of the new troupe. 'All dancers decommissioned or excluded from Our personnel troupe in the past cannot, under any circumstances, form part of that presently undergoing re-organisation', wrote King Monivong in 1927. The conditions of employment within the reformed troupe were arduous. Members were expected to practise five days a week and be ready to perform any one of six pieces. The *Directeur des Arts cambodgiens* was required to give only eight hours' notice before the troupe was needed for a performance. Other changes were proposed but not implemented. These included the requirement for adult dancers, aged between sixteen and twenty, to be presented to the ballet corps with a *Certificat de Moralité* if she was unmarried, and a *Certificat de mariage* and a letter of authorisation from her husband if married. The original Article 17 in the draft ordinance provided married dancers with legitimate children an allowance, provided that the father of the offspring did not support the child. In order to claim this allowance, dancers had to supply the *Direction des Arts cambodgiens* with a marriage certificate, the birth certificate of the child or children, and the profession of her husband. The final version of the *Ordonnance royale* makes no mention of members of the troupe entering the service already married, or marrying once admitted, or having children. Article 14 of the final version, however, addresses the matter of 'dancers wishing to leave the ballet for reasons of personal convenience'. Usually, dancers were required to inform the *Directeur des Arts cambodgiens* a minimum of six months in advance of retirement. If her health was the reason for retirement, a medical certificate signed by a French doctor, attesting that it was impossible for the girl concerned to continue dancing, was required before the pension could be claimed.[27]

Alternatives to the official, state-administered ballet corps existed, but do not appear to have been financially successful, at least in Phnom Penh. This was probably due to a degree of persecution by the French administration. Soy Sang Vann, *Directrice* of a private troupe of Cambodian dancers in Phnom Penh and wife of a lesser prince, applied for a passport in both 1931 and 1932 in order to facilitate travel to Bangkok. It is not clear why the 1931 application was rejected. Documents filed with the 1932 application, however, are informative. A note from the *Sûreté du Cambodge* was sent to the *Commissaire Central de Police* recommending that the applicant be subjected to 'the usual inquiries' before proceeding with the application. The police report stated that 'her conduct, her morals and her loyalty are good and she has never been the object of a complaint'. Five days later, however, a very different report was sent to the *Résident Supérieur au Cambodge*, recommending that Soy Sang Vann be refused a passport. Due to inquiries 'into the real purpose of this journey, it appears, from the information gathered, that the party concerned finds herself presently in a financially precarious situation and that her dance enterprise is on the point of failure.' The reason for travel given by Soy Sang Vann herself was 'tourism'. The report of the agent who conducted the inquiry was attached. He related that they had found that the princess 'wished to go to Siam to collect a dancer named Yeun, sent to Siam to learn to dance in the Siamese manner.' The report also contained the information that Soy Song Vann quarrelled with her husband each week, due to his having become romantically involved with her sister, who lived with the couple, that Soy Sang Vann owed a significant amount of money to an Indian banker, and that her dancing troupe was on the verge of collapse.[28]

Whatever the marital problems existing between Soy Song Vann and her husband, there are other interpretations of her application for a passport than a possible escape from her debts and her marriage. Struggling to turn her private ballet corps into a successful financial venture, she would have had recourse to a moneylender in order to pay salaries and rent practice rooms and costumes. In an effort to inject new techniques into the repertoire of the ballet, she sent one of the dancers abroad to acquire new methods. Wishing to escape her unhappy domestic situation and business worries for a time, she may have decided to travel to Siam in order to distract herself and check on the progress of her dancer. The French, however, did not subscribe to any possible view other than that Soy Sang Vann was a cantankerous harpy determined to evade her debts and the (deserved) failure of her private dancing troupe.

The women of the palace recruited during the reign of King Sisowath Monivong were of distinctly humbler backgrounds than their predecessors. There was no longer any political merit in *oknha* seeking to establish an alliance with the king, as he was no longer in control of the bestowal of titles, honours and wealth. As a result, there were only a few dozen women of the palace by the time of his death in 1941. Those that remained were involved in the royal ballet; Long Meak, the daughter of the private secretary to Chhim Long, private secretary of the *Résident Supérieur*, had been a dancer during the reign of King Sisowath and bore a son to the then Prince Monivong. When he acceded, she was appointed *khun preah moneang*, 'lady in charge of the ladies' and on his death a senior instructor of dance. Her cousin, Saloth Sareoun, was also a dancer in Monivong's court, attending him on his deathbed. When King Monivong died in 1941, all women of the palace below the third tier of wives were removed from the list of palace employees and their already meagre civil servants' salaries reduced to nothing.[29] In 1943 only eleven *kang chao*, very elderly women, remained at court; they had nowhere else to go and no provision had been made for them by the foreign presence that had condemned their once honourable role.

The (failed) institutionalisation of midwifery

Another colonial policy that removed women from positions of significance, but with much less success, was the institutionalisation of midwifery. As discussed in earlier chapters, midwives were accorded special status in pre-colonial Cambodia, as they habitually exposed themselves to the dangers of the delivery room and the supernatural forces that could manifest around the mother and her newborn child. Midwifery had been a profession requiring no formal education in Cambodia, merely instruction from older midwives and assisting at births. Until World War I, the only admonition made by the French in this area was that Cambodian midwives not assist women in pro-curing abortions.[30] A decree promulgated on 16 April 1924 stated that hence-forth all midwives practising in Cambodia would be required to obtain the *Diplôme de l'Infirmière Accoucheuse* from a recognised school of midwifery.[31]

Midwives who did not obtain the required qualification were prohib-ited from practising and persecuted. This is clearly illustrated in the 1925 closure of a private maternity hospital in Phnom Penh, directed by the wife of a Vietnamese official employed in the Phnom Penh mayoral residence. A woman who had spent ten days at the private clinic was admitted to the French-run *Clinique Roume* on 13 March 1925 with a puerperal infection. She died within a few hours. The local director of the *Service de la Santé* advised the *Résident Supérieur* in Phnom Penh that the private clinic should be closed pending investigation of the personnel, whom he suspected were not licensed under the provisions of the 1924 decree. The investigation revealed that the director of the clinic held a certificate in midwifery, obtained from the Cholon school in 1913, but the other two women had no formal qualifications. None had received authorisation to operate a maternity clinic by the *Direction local de la Santé*. The report of the investigation concluded by drawing attention to an attached list of other non-French midwives 'still practising in Phnom Penh without authorisation' and asking that measures be employed to prevent this state of affairs from continuing. The result was an *arrête* issued by the *Gouverneur Général en Indochine* to the effect that all midwives practising in Cambodia should belong to the state health concern, the *Assistance Médicale au Cambodge*.[32]

The French administration believed that the recruitment of young girls, educated in *écoles franco-cambodgiennes*, would result in a more obedient corps of midwives. On 17 September 1924 the *Gouverneur Général en Indochine* recommended that an *École Pratique des Sages-Femmes Ingigènes*, along the same lines as that of Cholon, be established in Phnom Penh.[33] The school opened in October 1924. The administration does not seem to have publicised the imminent opening of the *École Pratique des Sage-Femmes* as applications received for the 1924–1925 school year from inhabitants of Cambodia all sought admission to the school at Cholon. The application process was haphazard and overly bureaucratic. Madeleine Ba, a half-French, half-Vietnamese girl born in Phnom Penh, wrote to the *Résident Supérieur au Cambodge* stating her intention of enrolling in midwifery at the maternity hospital in Cholon and asking for his help, as the *Directeur Local de la Santé* had lost the results of her physical examination and the two photographs she had sent with her application.

> I am an orphan and without resources … . I appeal to your kindness in helping me go to Cholon in order to study a subject that will allow me to find work. After my two years of study, I pledge to serve in Cambodia where you will establish many maternity hospitals.[34]

An official in the police department, M. Rozier, assisted Madeleine Ba in her application. The administrative officer who handled Madeleine Ba's application spoke to him regarding his *protégée*. In the margin of the letter, beside M. Rozier's name, a handwritten comment appears: 'He suggests the *École* in Phnom Penh, which opens soon'. The application process required candidates to submit to a physical examination, during which they were required to fill out a form detailing their name, age, place of birth, nationality, race, height, weight, general state of health, and any medical problems. A photograph, expensive to obtain, was to be affixed to the bottom left-hand corner of the page. Copies of the applicant's *Certificat d'Études Primaires franco-indigènes* and *Certificat de le bonnes vie et mœurs*, literally 'good life and sound morals', were to be provided. Once admitted to the school, the applicants were expected to abide by the terms and conditions of the *Assistance Médicale au Cambodge*, which included six years of state service.[35]

The terms of employment for state midwives were complicated and did not entertain much scope for promotion. Advancement was entirely at the discretion of the *Résident Supérieur au Cambodge*, acting on the recommendations of local officials, administrators and 'interested parties'.[36] The conditions by which midwives were expected to abide must have been more than most women were prepared to adopt, as enrolments declined over the next two years. In 1927 the situation was so precarious that the *Résident Supérieur au Cambodge* wrote to the *Directeur Local de la Santé* in favour of admitting an applicant who was underage:

> I … propose that we dispense with the age requirement, if such a thing is possible, for this candidate, for three reasons. 1) The lack of midwifery personnel and the difficulties of recruitment. There are not more than two students in the first year at present. 2) This candidate is the only one who has been awarded the *Certificat d'Études Primaires*. 3) If her application is rejected and if the candidate must wait a year before reapplying, it is likely that in the interval she would find another use for her abilities, and the service has the chance of losing her altogether.[37]

There was no attempt by the French to improve the situation of student midwives in order to attract more applicants. In 1931, Justine Poggi, a half-French, half-Vietnamese girl who had been adopted by a French official, wrote that she would pledge herself 'to the service in the same terms as the other student-midwives, without board, lodging nor remuneration'.[38] These are hardly attractive terms. The unnecessarily complicated, intrusive and often expensive application process, the terms of service, and the conditions of advancement had little attraction for those who were qualified for admittance to the *École des Sages-Femmes* in Phnom Penh, and overall the institutionalisation of midwifery, one of the few colonial policies specifically directed toward the improvement of conditions for women, failed.

Education and exhibition

No comprehensive plan of reform was devised for the Cambodian education system until quite late in the colonial period, although it constituted a cornerstone of French modernisation efforts. In 1867 King Norodom established a secular school for the children of the royal family, under French patronage. The first French-administered school in Cambodia, the *École de Protectorat*, opened in 1873 under the direction of a navy corporal, Ferryrolles, but its purpose was to train indigenous men (usually Vietnamese) who could serve as intermediaries between the palace and the French. A French-administered school for indigenous children in Phnom Penh opened in 1884, but such was the local antipathy towards the largely Chinese and Vietnamese ethnicity of the students that few Cambodians attended. Those that did were the children of the royal family and wealthy local elite. In 1890 a committee was organised in order to oversee the establishment of *Instruction Publique en Indochine*. In April 1893 the *Collège du Protectorat* was created in Phnom Penh. The best students were sent to the secondary schools in Saigon, or went to France on scholarships to study in a special division of the *École Coloniale*.[39]

The lack of educational initiatives and reforms during the early phase of French intervention in Cambodia stunted Cambodia's development for decades and reflected the insouciance with which the French viewed Cambodia as a colony. Following the death of King Norodom in 1904, educational reform took on a new impetus. King Norodom made provision in his will that funds from his personal fortune be allocated for the establishment of a school for princes and princesses. King Sisowath donated the buildings he had lived in prior to his accession to the *Instruction Publique en Indochine* for use as schools in 1906. The following year 750 pupils were recorded as attending schools in Phnom Penh, of which 54 were children of the royal family, while 400 attended state schools in rural areas. These *Écoles primaires franco-cambodgiennes* were split into two categories in 1908 – *résidentielles*, primary schools in each provincial capital and Phnom Penh, and *khet*, district schools that provided a preparation for *résidentielles*.[40]

Elite girls could access primary education in Phnom Penh at the private schools and at the *École du Protectorat*. Girls enrolled at the latter institution were required to prepare work for the 1906 Marseilles *Exhibition*. Nicola Cooper has suggested that the purpose of the *Expositions coloniales* was to provide legitimacy for French imperialism through recognition of successful efforts at modernisation whilst ensuring that the 'backwardness' of the colonies was emphasised, in order to necessitate a continued presence. 'Celebrating' the arts of the indigenous peoples of the colonies was a means of including the colonised within the greater French collective. Auguste Pavie remarked that the 'silk cloths woven by the women of Cambodia, using a method preserved from the oldest civilisations, are particularly rich and remarkable'. Girls at the *Écoles Yukanthor, Norodom* and *Sutharot* were required to send their work to the *Exposition Coloniale* in 1922. Items ranged from ladies bags to plates to head-dresses. Significantly, the exhibition organisers 'eliminated all ordinary garments … obviously inspired by French fashion magazines'. Students' exercise books and examinations were shown in Vicennes. These exhibitions of people and culture served to reinforce the attitude of the metropolitan towards the colonies, propagated through adventurers' accounts, popular novels, and schoolbooks legitimising French imperialism.[41]

In 1907 an administrative division of the *Instruction Publique en Indochine* called the *Direction de l'École des Filles du Protectorat* was established,[42] but the first French-administered school for girls was not established until 1911. On 16 September 1911 Ernest Outrey, *Résident Supérieur au Cambodge* issued a circular to his administrators asking them to identify non-French officials employed by the government who had daughters and direct them to send the girls to the proposed *École des filles*, due to open on 1 October 1911. The language of the directive was menacing:

> I recommend to you that it would be good, in advising your native assistants of this measure, to make them aware that the government would look upon them with pleasure should they send their daughters to this school, and thus give the native population of the town of Phnom Penh an example that could not have a more beneficial effect.[43]

The possible benefits of education for girls were not mentioned in the circular, although Outrey commented that 'the dissemination of instruction to girls is a question of very capital importance'. The assumption was that the 'natives' would do as they were told. In order to ensure capitulation, Outrey instructed the French bureaucrats to send lists of all indigenous employees' children's names and ages and whether or not they would be attending the *École des filles*. Reactions varied. The *Hôpital mixte de Phnom Penh* acquiesced readily, sending a neatly typed table of personnel with the names of their daughters and which ones would be sent to the new school. Only five of the seventeen girls listed were not to be sent to the school and these seem to be for reasons other than parental recalcitrance, as in some cases siblings were marked down as future students. Some responses were polite yet firm. The *Tresorièr* replied that of his employees, 'the majority ... have girls too young to go often to the new school; that of secretary Binh, aged six, he will send next October'. A veterinary assistant, Thong, was the sole Cambodian member of the *Service Vétérinaire* who 'would be happy to send [his daughter] to the school, if her young age permitted him'.[44]

Others were less diplomatic. The chief of the *Services Agricoles et Communaux locaux* wrote that 'the principal native officer, Kett, has a daughter aged seven years, but he does not consent to her taking courses at the new school'.[45] The head of the *Service du Cadastre et de la Topographie* was overtly critical of the short notice given and hardly bothered to conceal his dismissiveness of the entire exercise:

> I have the honour to inform you that it is difficult for me to furnish the list of native married officials or employees before the beginning of October, as many of these agents are presently in the jungle in the course of their duties, where the means of correspondence are fairly primitive and certainly not quick. I have in vain attempted to make recruits out of my sedentary personnel; the first of these who lives in the north of the city has placed his girls in the school of the nuns who are much closer, the second has children who each day sell in the market in order to augment their resources, the third has a daughter too young (7 years), a fourth lives south of the palace ... .[46]

He concluded his letter by saying that he hoped to have more success at the end of the month, but commented that the 'eccentric situation' of the school did not lead him to think that it would be a successful experiment. Despite reservations, the *École des filles* opened under the name *École Norodom*. Enrolments increased in the next two years, a fact that the *Résident Supérieur* attributed to the teaching, 'above all professional and tactful', thus assuaging 'the obstructive instincts of the natives against the education of girls, which they have long considered a dangerous novelty'. Princess Malika, daughter of King Norodom and his 26th wife *neak moneang* Phayu, founded a private girls' school on 11 December 1911, at which both her daughters later taught.[47] Around the same time another private girls' school, *École Sutharot*, was established by another princess.[48]

A 'traditional' opposition towards educating daughters is often cited in studies of Cambodia. Virginia Thompson wrote in 1937 that 'it has been

impossible to make much headway with women's education – a development of which the bonzes are very chary. Discreet efforts have resulted in
some Franco-Cambodian schools for girls, which are, in this as well as in
other respects, more liberal than the pagoda education'. The French had little
regard for 'traditional' education across the board. Auguste Pavie was astonished to discover that the local *wat* possessed a library: 'I had not thought
that, above all, the Cambodians could have a truly deep education within
reach; I had expected to hear them say that this knowledge was transferred
from father to son'. The low regard in which the pagoda schools were held
was reflected in the endemic attempts that the French made to discourage
pupils from attending them. Royal ordinances issued in 1911 and 1916 ordered all Cambodians aged ten or more who lived less than two kilometres
from an *école franco-cambodgienne* to enrol or face a fine. Ultimately this was
not an effective threat, as an employee of the *Service de l'Instruction publique*
in Kampot lamented that 'one must literally pay our students' to attend the
écoles franco-cambodgiennes.[49]

After the promulgation of Albert Sarrault's 1918 educational reforms,
the administration set about reforming the pagoda schools in Cambodia.
Although the official reason for the campaign was that the pagoda schools
lacked practical curricula, formal examinations, and trained teachers, the
pagoda schools were far more popular. In 1925 there were 2,402 schools in
Cambodia, 105 of them *écoles franco-cambodgiennes*, the remainder pagoda
or private schools. 8,367 of the estimated 38,000 pupils in Cambodia at the
time attended the *écoles franco-cambodgiennes*. 78 per cent of children, therefore, were beyond the reach of the *Service de l'Instruction publique*. This was
unsettling for the French: 'The intellectual and moral formation of young
male Cambodians ... is, almost entirely, in the hands of the monks'. The
lack of standardisation, in terms of materials and other resources, was also
of concern. Course materials varied considerably according to the wealth of
the district. Most pagoda schools used the traditional codes of conduct, the
cbpab, in order to instruct pupils.[50]

The pagoda school system was never designed to facilitate social mobility. The concept of studying in order to 'better oneself' did not enter into the
equation for the vast majority of Cambodians. The pagoda education provided patterns of interaction between members of society, male and female,
older and younger, patron and client. Girls were also instructed in the tenets

of the *cbpab* by the monks, although it is not clear where this instruction took place. According to Adhémard Leclère, they were taught 'the discourse of the Buddha … the different types of husband … the laws concerning wives and daughters, the respect that is due to them, the duties of husbands and fiancés'.[51] Boys were educated at the pagodas because it was necessary for them to learn to read Buddhist texts, as they were all destined for a period of novicehood. Girls were not taught in the pagoda schools because their adult lives would be spent in the home, in the market, in child-rearing, in the fields, or engaged in cottage industries. The Cambodians themselves perceived these activities as necessary and valuable. The French, unable to disengage from the belief that public space was more important than private space, and, therefore, that the value of activities conducted in the former was greater than those carried out in the latter, assumed, because girls did not attend the pagoda schools, that education *per se* was denied them, and the *joal m'lap* dismissed as a mechanism for restraining the sexuality of girls of marriageable age rather than a celebration of their reaching a new life stage and an opportunity for them to be instructed in the things they would need to know in their lives.

The popularity of girls' schools did not extend beyond the municipal boundaries of Phnom Penh. In 1927 the *École primaire élémentaire de filles* in Koki, Kandal province, was shut down. The school was described as 'very irregularly frequented by a restrained number of students' and the failure of the school was put down to the Cambodian headmistress, 'only slightly educated and of fragile health'. It may not be coincidental that 1927 was the first year that the administration of the protectorate implemented financial incentives to encourage girls to stay in primary schools. Two girls attending the *École Norodom* 'whose family situation [was] really pitiable' and who lived more than two kilometres from the school were awarded a bursary in 1927 on the grounds that they were good students.[52] The problem of secondary education for girls in the provinces was addressed in 1929, when the *Résident Supérieur au Cambodge* issued a circular to all provincial *résidents* on the subject:

> To remedy, within the confines of the possible, the feebleness of the instruction given to young Cambodian girls and to facilitate the recruitment of indigenous teachers … a boarding-house for Cambodian girls will be opened on 15 September 1929 in Phnom Penh.[53]

The boarding-house was to have twenty places, to be allocated in the first instance to girls who had obtained the *Certificat d'Études primaires franco-indigènes* and who wished to further their studies in order to become midwives or teachers. The language of this circular was a far cry from its 1911 counterpart; the 1929 version politely suggested that the provincial administration 'inform the population of the opening of this boarding-house for girls and give it all desirable publicity so that the families who would most benefit from it are made aware.'[54]

Cambodian girls interested in progressing to secondary education had no choice but to relocate to Vietnam. The best schools in French Indochina were in Hanoi or Saigon.[55] Gaining admission to one of these schools was an overly complicated process, made more difficult by the necessity of sitting entrance exams in Vietnam before admission was granted and finding means of financial support once there. It is hardly surprising that the Cambodians, already disinclined to send their daughters to French-administered schools in their own country, were even more reluctant to send them to another country. Incentive was provided in the form of a number of bursaries and scholarships for girls who had graduated from primary school in Cambodia. One of these bursaries enabled a girl to attend 'an academic establishment frequented by young French girls' in Saigon for further study in French language and literature. Another allowed the daughter of a Cambodian school principal bowed down by the financial obligations of supporting an extensive family to attend the *Collège de Jeunes Filles Indigènes* in Saigon for four academic years. This girl, Tong Siv Eng, was to become intimately connected with the family of King Norodom Sihanouk for nearly half a century. Her father, Tong Keam, was very supportive of his daughter's education. In a letter to the head of the local *Service de l'Enseignement* dated 13 July 1934, he said that it was his wish that his daughter 'still young and little educated', despite having obtained her *Certificat d'Études Primaires franco-indigènes*, continue her education in a girls' school. As there was no *Collège de Filles* in Cambodia, the *Collège des filles indigènes* in Saigon would ensure Siv Eng 'a more solid education that will permit, later, the acquisition of a situation in line with her tastes and aptitudes.'[56]

Facilities for vocational training and higher education were similarly geographically remote for Cambodian women. The *École pratique d'industrie*, opened in Phnom Penh in 1903, was reserved for men, as was the *Collège du Protectorat*, which offered training in the French civil service. The one early vocational school that did allow women was the *Manufacture Royale au Palais*. It opened in Phnom Penh in 1907 and was responsible for manufacturing replicas of Cambodian art and antiques. The French established similar *manufactures* elsewhere in their colonies, ostensibly in order to ensure that indigenous artistic traditions were retained. An *École des Beaux-Arts* was added in 1912 and the entire complex renamed *École des arts Cambodgiens*, with Georges Groslier as its director, in 1918. A visitor to the *École des arts* in 1929 was full of praise for Groslier – 'a Cambodian-born French artist, archaeologist and novelist' who 'freed it at the outset from political and commercial pressure, kept its ideals pure and true to native tradition and even provided for the midday meal and the living of the accepted pupils, so that any and every promising boy or girl, whatever his or her economic status, may take advantage of the instruction'. He warned, however, that the success of the enterprise 'is a question depending upon the capacity of the Cambodians themselves … . It is too early to say what the modern Cambodians will make of their French-given opportunity'.[57]

The education offered by the *écoles franco-cambodgiennes* was designed to prepare indigenous adolescents for lives in industry or domestic service, not for higher education. The *Université Indochinoise* in Hanoi was too far for most Cambodians to reach and in most cases their secondary education was not of a high enough standard to merit entrance. The schools of Buddhism, opened in Phnom Penh and Siem Reap in 1909, and the *École de Pâli*, established in Phnom Penh in 1915, were also off-limits for women, for obvious reasons. Women were encouraged to train as teachers as a result of the reforms implemented in the 1920s. Publications for indigenous teachers were produced in order to provide teaching materials, update pedagogical methodology, and standardise curricula across the country. Although the post-1918 reforms of Albert Sarrault recognised that it was necessary 'in each colony, to adapt to particular characteristics, to local needs as to the mentalities of very different races', teachers were expected to uphold and disseminate French ideals. *Collège Sisowath*, given full *lycée* status in 1935, became a production line for bright Cambodians of both sexes who rose through the education system, departing from there to further training (usually as teachers) in Saigon, Hanoi or Paris.[58] Several future political leaders received their upper secondary education at the *Lycée Sisowath*, including the first Cambodian woman to receive a *baccalaureat*, Khieu Ponnary.[59]

Constructing a 'traditional' Cambodian identity

Increased emphasis on formal education – whether in a pagoda school, a private institution or a French *école normale* – led to a greater number of educated people. In the past, people who were 'educated' – that is, with the ability to read texts, especially those in Pali, and to write discourses and commentaries upon them – were considered to be socially superior, as they were usually members of the *sangha* or the royal family, if not both. Their elite status earned privileges and opportunities. In the colonial period, a new group of educated people emerged: the *neak che deung*,[60] 'people knowing knowledge', who had attained their status through the patronage and administrative mechanisms of the French rather than through royal favour. Despite their origin, political culture remained unchanged, and the elite, including the *neak che deung*, continued to see themselves as naturally entitled to certain perquisites. As increasing numbers of people became 'educated', and therefore, 'elite', they sought to demonstrate their right to be perceived as such by embracing 'traditional' customs such as polygamy and the values of 'traditional' literature. It became increasingly important for families seeking to ally themselves with important men to prove their own elite status through the tighter sexual control of daughters.[61]

The people responsible for determining what constituted 'tradition' were the *neak che deung*, the *sangha,* the royal family, and French officials. Printing and mass distribution of material was unknown in the Cambodian language until 1908, although printing had been available in neighbouring Vietnam since 1862. Permission from both *mahasangharaja,* the Mohanikay and Dhammayut, in addition to the Council of Ministers, was required before a text could be published. It was not until the 1920s that strict religious scrutiny of published material was relaxed, and then only after lobbying by Louis Finot, then director of the *École Française d'Extrême-Orient.* Manuscripts that had reposed forgotten in pagodas and storerooms for decades were rediscovered and rewritten with introductions commemorating their place in Cambodian literature. Many folktales and *cbpab* (codes of conduct) were incorporated into the state educational syllabus.[62]

The journal *Kambojasuriya* played a major role in shaping the notion of Cambodian 'traditional' society through the inclusion of stories and commentaries by authors who were perceived, by the *neak che deung*, as significant, such as the palace *oknha* and people who reflected 'traditional' Cambodian beliefs. The work of *oknha suttanta prachea* Ind was a popular subject, including his *Subhasit Cbpab Srei.* The *Cbpab Kram Thmei* and *Cbpab Kerti Kal Thmei* written and performed by Phiroum Ngoy were recorded and transcribed for publication in *Kambujasuriya* in the early 1930s as well. According to Ngoy, these *cbpab thmei* were necessary as 'people nowadays are of poor quality, they do foolish things, bad deeds, their speech is confused; insolence is met at every turn'; yet they are very similar to earlier versions, outlining correct behaviour and good moral conduct.[63]

It was texts such as these to which Cambodians turned in their search for a national identity separate from that of the 'Cambodge' constructed by the French.[64] Critical thinking was never inculcated in the Cambodian education system, whether religious or secular; the Buddhist tradition taught unquestioning acceptance of one's *dharma* and the French did not wish their colonial subjects to question the legitimacy of their presence. Cambodians searching 'traditional' literature for evidence of a society free of foreign influence believed that the *cbpab* reflected true patterns of behaviour rather than guidelines for them. This meant that people perceived gender roles in 'traditional' Cambodian society to reflect those outlined in *Cbpab Srei,* without reflecting upon the possible biases and motivations of its authors, and dismissing other evidence of egalitarianism or status for women in Cambodian rural traditions, because they were those of socially insignificant people rather than the elite.

The Japanese presence in Indochina in the early 1940s furthered nationalistic stirrings in Cambodia. In an attempt to negate Japanese anti-imperialist propaganda, the French (now under the Vichy administration) sought to channel the nationalist spirit (both male and female) into controllable outlets, such as patriotic youth organisations. The umbrella organisation was the *Jeunes du Cambodge* or *Yuvan Kampuchearath,* administered by the *Commisariat à la jeunesse et aux sports,* established in 1941. Other organisations existed, including the *Mouvement de rassemblement,* members of which included students, teachers and civil servants, and in which members were trained in military activities. In June 1943, there were approximately 15,500 members of youth organisations. The early 1940s were the first time that many young Cambodians – male and female – had experienced a feeling of collective solidarity beyond the traditional realms of the family and the *sangha*. This experience contributed to the nationalist movements established and joined by many young Cambodians in early 1950. Ultimately, it was the popularity and success of the nationalist movements that prompted King Norodom Sihanouk to begin his 'Royal Crusade for Independence' in June 1953. Peers, rather than family or religious leaders, were determining behaviour. Freedom of choice and liberation, not so much sexual as romantic, were popular themes in novels written by Cambodians at the time. According to Nguyen Sy Tuan, this new literature sought to re-orient the position of the individual in a society that was undergoing a series of changes, wrought by improved literacy, increasing population, and nationalism.[65]

Yet the Cambodian nationalist movement, although advocating an active role for women, did not seek to empower them beyond the limits indicated by the *Cbpab Srei*. The Cambodian-language newspaper *Kampuchea* recruited a group of female writers in 1945 in order to prepare articles concerned with moral instruction. These harked back to the *Cbpab Srei*:

> Glorious and prosperous countries are not only composed of men but also of women who help out in all fields. Indeed, the most important field is the home … . So please fulfil your duties as good housewives … . The wife holds the wealth of the family and she should have good conduct, work industriously, keep the house clean and neat, and think only of her family's well-being … . A woman is not considered civilized if she does not follow customs, and does not contribute to the development of the motherland. Khmer daughters – your nation is waiting for you to apply your collective strengths![66]

Revolutionary and nationalist movements worldwide have sought to mobilise women by blending women's liberation with emancipation from the colonial presence. In Cambodia, however, women complained that 'men tried all the means to obstruct the positive progress of women'.[67]

Cambodian women received little assistance from their French counterparts, despite some well-intentioned (if insensitive) attempts to improve the situation. Some took up the cause of *métis* children abandoned by their fathers, denouncing French men and their lax morality. Andrée Viollis, who travelled through Indochina at the end of 1931, published an account of her observations entitled *SOS Indochine*. She advocated that French women act as role models and moral instructors for indigenous women. Virginia Thompson, although not French, also conveyed an imperial feminist sentiment in 1937: 'Like so many Oriental women, they only begin to live when they become mothers'. The only signs of a genuine Cambodian women's movement were to be found amongst the educated bourgeoisie in Phnom Penh. The Cambodian Women's Association was established in 1949. Its scope, however, was limited. Some have suggested that although in the best position to resist the changes wrought by colonialism, elite women – those related to the

royal family or prominent members of the government – accepted French
policies in return for the legitimation of their social status. Kate Frieson cites
a story by a woman writer, published in 1949, which 'suggests a natural order
of hierarchy in the home that women should respect and maintain, regardless
of their personal yearnings'.[68]

∿

The French contributed to the disempowerment of women in Cambodia
through their colonial policies by effectively devaluing some areas wherein
women had enjoyed power and placing controls over others. Efforts at modernisation did little to improve the lives of Cambodian women; in at least
two ways French policies and attitudes destroyed avenues for social mobility
in which women had been able to increase their wealth and prestige – by becoming women of the palace and through temporary marriages with foreign
men. The French were simultaneously intrigued and repelled by Cambodian
women, yet displayed them as Oriental treasures of the French Empire. In
areas beyond the concern of colonial policy, in marriage, ritual practice and
spiritual status, women continued to be perceived as powerful. But the status
of women declined overall. The literature produced before the imposition of
colonial rule was taken to represent 'traditional' gender roles and maintained
as a form of resistance to French influence. It is therefore not surprising that
the nationalist movement saw a return to these values as opposition to imperialism. Once independence was achieved, however, the perpetuation of
these mores continued to disadvantage Cambodian women.

Notes to Chapter 7

1   David Chandler, *The tragedy of Cambodian history: Politics, war and revolution since 1945*,
New Haven: Yale University Press, 1991, pp. 12–13; Penny Edwards, 'Cambodge: The
cultivation of a nation, 1860–1945', PhD thesis, Monash University, 1999, p. 6.

2   Attachment to *Service de la Sûreté*, envoi No. 1381/IP, 16 September 1935, National
Archives of Cambodia, Material of the Résident Superièure du Cambodge [hereafter
RSC], file no. 12906; Hann So, *The Khmer kings*, San Jose, California, n.p., 1988, p. 35.

3   For example, in translating a passage from *Kram Srok* (1693) that lists the most important people in the land as the king, the king's father, queen mother, and *uparaj*, Leclère
says in a footnote 'I believe one must here place the *uparaja* before the queen mother'
(*Kram Srok,* in Adhémard Leclère, *Les codes cambodgiens*, Paris: Ernest Leroux, 1898, t.
1, p. 120, f.n. 2).

4   Adhémard Leclère, *Le buddhisme au Cambodge*, Paris: Leroux, 1899, p. 503.

5   Auguste Pavie, *The Pavie Mission Indochina Papers 1879–1895*, vol. 1: *Pavie Mission Exploration Work: Laos, Cambodia, Siam, Yunnan, and Vietnam* [1901], trans. Walter E. J. Tips, Bangkok: White Lotus, 1999, pp. 55, 61; Francis Garnier, *Voyage d'exploration en Indo-Chine, éfféctué par une Commission française présidée par M. le Capitaine de Frégate Doudart de Lagrée*, Paris: Hachette, 1885, p. 48; *Henri Mouhot's Diary: Travels in the central parts of Siam, Cambodia and Laos during the years 1858–61* [1864], Kuala Lumpur: Oxford University Press, n.d., p. 35; Roland Meyer, *Saramani, danseuse khmêr*, Saigon: A. Portail, 1919, p. 13; George Groslier, *Danseuses cambodgiennes: Anciennes et modernes*, Paris: Augustin Challamel, 1913, pp. 113–114; Étienne Aymonier, *Notes sur les coutumes et croyances supstititeuses des cambodgiens, commenté et présenté par Saveros Pou*, Paris: Centre de Documentation et de Recherche sur la Civilisation Khmere [Cedorek], 1984, p. 73.

6   Pavie, *Pavie Mission*, vol. 1, p. 61; Barbara Watson Andaya, 'From temporary wife to prostitute: Sexuality and economic change in early modern Southeast Asia', *Journal of Women's History* 9, 4 (1998), pp. 14, 19; Nicola Cooper, *France in Indochina: Colonial encounters*, Oxford; New York: Berg, 2001, pp. 135, 157; Penny Edwards, 'Womanizing Indochina: Fiction, nation, and cohabitation in colonial Cambodia, 1890–1930', in Julia Clancy Smith and Frances Gouda (eds), *Domesticating the empire: Race, gender, and family life in French and Dutch colonialism*, Charlottesville, Virginia: University Press of Virginia, 1998, pp. 109–110; Louis Malleret, *L'Exotisme Indochinoise dans la littérature française depuis 1860*, Paris: Larose Éditeurs, 1934, pp. 219–220; Edward W. Said, *Orientalism*, New York: Random House, 1979, p. 190.

7   *Résident de France à Phnom Penh*, letter No. 322, 20 May 1901, RSC 12858; *Code Pénal Cambodgien*, article 229, p. 208, RSC 30548; Thompson, *French Indo-China*, p. 361; Draft *arrête*, undated, article 6, RSC 12858; Geoffrey Gorer, *Bali and Angkor: A 1930s pleasure trip looking at life and death* [1936], Oxford: Oxford University Press, 1986, p. 151; Virginia Thompson, *French Indo-China*, London: Allen & Unwin, 1937, p. 361.

8   Pavie, *Pavie Mission*, vol. 1, p. 55. A popular Cambodian saying of the nineteenth century reflects the acceptance of foreign men as husbands and fathers: 'A varied diet is tasty, a varied ancestry gives good results' (A. Pannetier, 'Sentences et proverbes cambodgiens', *BEFEO* 15, 3 (1915), p. 19).

9   *Rapport*, 12 August 1912, RSC 15226.

10 Statute of the *Société de protection et d'éducation des Jeunes Métis Français de la Cochinchine et du Cambodge*, trans. Ann Laura Stoler in 'Sexual affronts and racial frontiers', in Frederick Cooper and Laura Ann Stoler (eds), *Tensions of empire: Colonial cultures in a bourgeois world*, Berkeley, California: University of California Press, 1997, p. 207; Edwards, 'Womanizing Indochina', p. 112.

11 Emmanuelle Saada, 'The empire of law: Dignity, prestige, and domination in the "colonial situation"', *French Politics, Culture & Society* 20, 2 (Summer 2002), p.99. Pierre L. Lamant, *L'Affaire Yukanthor: Autopsie d'un scandale colonial* (Paris: Société Française d'Histoire d'Outre-mer, 1989), p. 141. Cooper, *France in Indochina*, pp. 158–159; Stoler,

'Sexual affronts and racial frontiers', p. 206; Jean Leuba, *L'Aile de feu*, Paris: [n.p.], 1920, p. 115; M. Harry, *Les petites épouses*, Paris: [n.p.], [n.d.], cited in Malleret, *L'Exotisme Indochinoises*, p. 221; Cooper, *France in Indochina*, p. 102. The wives and daughters of the colonial administrators and settlers, for the most part, did not look kindly upon their indigenous counterparts. The French attempted to prevent *encongayment* by encouraging men to bring their wives and families to the colonies. The French women who settled in Indochina have been blamed for the proliferation of patronising colonialism, revelling in their social superiority, their servants, and their proximity to the Cambodian court. In most French literature dealing with colonial Cambodia, French wives cannot compete with Cambodian women. In George Groslier's *Le Retour à l'argile*, a French woman loses her husband to a Cambodian woman and, knowing that she had no chance of reclaiming his affection, leaves the colony (*Le Retour à l'argile* [1928], Paris: Kailash, 1994, p. 154).

12 Statute of the *Société de protection et d'éducation des Jeunes Métis Français de la Cochinchine et du Cambodge*, trans. Stoler in 'Sexual affronts and racial frontiers', p. 207.

13 Criticism of polygamy also became more overt in Siam as increasing numbers of foreigners began frequenting the Thai court from the 1850s. See Tamara Loos, 'Sex in the Inner City: The fidelity between sex and politics in Siam', *Journal of Asian Studies* 64, 4 (November 2005), p. 898.

14 Groslier, *Danseuses cambodgiennes*, p. 17.

15 Leclère, *Codes cambodgiens*, p. 122, f.n.; *Preas Reachea Kroet Prapdaphisek du Preas Sauriyobarn*, in *Codes cambodgiens*, p. 45; Groslier, *Danseuses cambodgiennes*, p. 28.

16 'If she goes beyond this limit, she will be punished with fifteen lashes and a month in prison. If she goes outside the palace by day, she will receive 30 lashes and three months in prison. If by night she leaves through a hole or underneath a wall, she will receive 60 lashes and six months in prison. If she goes out to find a lover or if she is trying to run away, she will be condemned to death' (*Kram montiro bal*, in *Codes cambodgiens*, t. 1, p. 181).

17 Meyer, *Saramani*, pp. 161-162; Groslier, *Danseuses cambodgiennes*, pp. 117–118.

18 Cited in Milton E. Osborne, *The French presence in Cochinchina and Cambodia: Rule and response (1859–1905)*, Ithaca, New York; London: Cornell University Press, 1969, p. 202.

19 This perspective has been retained by later historians. See for example John Tully, *France on the Mekong: A history of the Protectorate in Cambodia, 1863–1953*, Lanham, Maryland; New York; Oxford: 2002, p. 67.

20 *Kram montiro bal*, in *Codes cambodgiens*, t. 1, p. 176.

21 Groslier, *Danseuses cambodgiennes*, p. 27; Meyer, *Saramani*, p. 105; Osborne, *Rule and response*, pp.181–182; Paul Doumer, *L'Indo-Chine française*, 2nd ed., Paris: Vuibert & Nony, p. 248; King Norodom, having grown up in the Thai court, had a large number of Thai or half-Thai women in his retinue, including one of his father's consorts, *khun* Sancheat Bopha, a supporter of Thai interests. Her son, Duong Chakr, was a strong contender for the throne, but the French forced Norodom to exile him to Algeria. See Osborne, *Rule*

and response, p. 181; Justin Corfield, *The royal family of Cambodia*, Melbourne: Khmer Language & Culture Centre, 1993, p. 47.

22 Osborne, *Rule and response*, p. 255; Meyer, *Saramani*, p. 111; Groslier, *Danseuses cambodgiennes*, p. 27; Thiounn, *Danses cambodgiennes*, trans. Jeanne Cuisinier, Phnom Penh: Bibliothéque Royal du Cambodge, [1930], p. 36; Judith M. Jacob, *The traditional literature of Cambodia: A preliminary guide*, Oxford: Oxford University Press, 1996, p. 82.

23 Groslier, *Danseuses cambodgiennes*, pp. 29–30.

24 Mathew Burrows, ''Mission civilisatrice': French cultural policy in the Middle East, 1860–1914', *The Historical Journal* 29, 1 (1986), p. 109; David Chandler, *A history of Cambodia*, 3rd ed., Boulder, Colorado: Westview Press, 2000, p. 126; Cooper, *France in Indochina*, pp. 29, 84; Garnier, *Travels in Cambodia and part of Laos*, p. 49; Christopher Pym, *Mistapim in Cambodia*, London: Hodder & Stoughton, 1960, pp. 47–49; Doumer, *L'Indo-Chine*, p. 248; Thompson, *French Indo-China*, p. 359; Tully, *Cambodia under the Tricolour*, pp. 8–9; Meyer, *Saramani*, p. 126.

25 Cooper, *France in Indochina*, p. 85; Doumer, *L'Indo-Chine*, p. 248; Gorer, *Bali and Angkor*, p. 155; Groslier, *Danseuses cambodgiennes*, pp. 29–30; Meyer, *Saramani*, pp. 134, 177.

26 Ordonnance royale No. 40, 14 June 1927, RSC 9093. An earlier draft of this ordinance contends that the parents must also present a *Certificat de Moralité*. Ordonnance royale (No. 40, section 3, article 7).

27 Ordonnance royale No. 40, section 3, article 19, RSC 9093; Ordonnance royale No. 40, section 5, articles 20 & 22, RSC 9093; Ordonnance royale No. 40, section 7, article 33, RSC 9093; Draft ordonnance royale No. 40, article 3/b, RSC 9093; Ordonnance royale No. 40, section 4, articles 14 and 15, RSC 9093; Ordonnance royale No. 40, section 4, article 16, RSC 9093.

28 Passports Nos. 167 and 337, RSC 24963; *Sûreté du Cambodge*, note No. 4044, 18 June 1932, RSC 24963; *Commissaire Central de Police*, letter No. 285/5, 18 June 1932, RSC 24963; *Chef des Services Police et Sûreté*, note postale No. 4152, 23 June 1932, RSC 24963; Rapport d'agent à Monsieur le Commissaire Spécial, Chef de la Première Section, dated 22 June 1932, RSC 24963.

29 Chhim Long was the brother of Phen Saloth, father of Saloth Sar (Pol Pot). Justin Corfield does not include Sareoun in his list of Monivong's consorts. Tully, *France on the Melong*, p. 200; Corfield, *Royal house of Cambodia*, p. 92; David Chandler, *Brother number one: A political biography of Pol Pot*, rev. ed., Boulder, Colorado: Westview Press, 1999, p. 8; *Tableu de reclassement des fonctionnaires et agents en service palais royal*, 1943, RSC 29012.

30 A. Cabaton, 'La vie domestique au Cambodge', *Revue Indochinoise* 2 (fevrier 1910), p. 111; *Code penal cambodgien – exemplaire revue et corrigé*, 30 December 1908, book 3, chapter 5, article 222, RSC 30548. In 1901 the French mayor of Cholon, in Cochinchina, appalled at the high rate of infant mortality (65 per cent in 1900), attributed to 'the slovenly practices of midwives and maternal ignorance', canvassed his French and non-French constituents for donations for the improvement of maternal and child health. Having raised 30,000 piastres, he founded the *Association Maternelle de Cholon*, with

the intention of establishing maternity wards in hospitals and schools for the training of midwives. By 1904 the infant mortality rate in Cholon had fallen to 35.3 per cent. The *Association Maternelle de Cholon* became the model for other maternal and child health societies in Indochina. See Ennis, *French policy and developments in Indochina*, p. 150.

31 RSC 1094.

32 *Directeur local de la Santé au Cambodge*, letter dated 25 March 1925, RSC 1094; *Administrateur des Services Civils*, letter No. 235, 29 April 1925, RSC 1094. Unsigned *arrête*, article 1, 1925, RSC 14640.

33 *Service local de la Santé au Cambodge*, letter No. 702, 24 October 1924, RSC 14640.

34 Madeleine Ba, letter dated 30 August 1924, RSC 32287.

35 Dossiers of Néang Saroun, Pham-thi Kim, and Madeleine Ba, RSC 32287; Madeleine Ba, letter dated 30 August 1924, RSC 32287; unsigned *arrête*, article 4, 1925, RSC 14640.

36 Unsigned *arrête*, article 6, 1925, RSC 14640.

37 *Bulletin de soit communiqué* No. 639P, 7 December 1927, RSC 1151.

38 Justine Poggi, letter dated 28 September 1931, RSC 6183.

39 David M. Ayres, *Anatomy of a crisis: Education, development, and the state in Cambodia, 1953–1998*, Honolulu: University of Hawai'i Press, 2000, pp. 23–25; Osborne, *Rule and response*, p. 203; Pascale Benzançon, 'l'Impact de la colonisation française sur l'emergence d'un système éducatif moderne au Cambodge (1863–1945)', in *Proceedings of International Conference on Khmer Studies*, ed. Sorn Samnang, Phnom Penh: Sorn Samnang, 1996, vol. 2, pp. 895–897.

40 Ayres, *Anatomy of a crisis*, p. 23; Benzançon, 'L'Impact de la colonisation française', pp. 897, 899; Osborne, *Rule and response*, pp. 253, 255–156.

41 *École du Protectorat* letter No. 43, 22 November 1905, RSC 1211; Pavie, *Pavie Mission*, vol. 1, p. 114; Lists, RSC 2022. *Résident Supérieur au Cambodge*, undated letter, RSC 2022; Cooper, *France in Indochina*, pp. 79, 83, 87.

42 *Administration des Services Civils* letter No. 608, 4 June 1907, RSC 1581.

43 *Résidence Supérieur du Cambodge*, circular No. 100, 16 September 1911, RSC 1214.

44 *Résidence Supérieur du Cambodge*, circular No. 100, 16 September 1911, RSC 1214; Liste des employés indigènes mariés en service à *l'Hôpital Mixte de Phnom Penh*, attachment to *Hôpital mixte de Phnom Penh* letter No. 335, 22 September 1911, RSC 1214; *Trésorier particulier du Cambodge*, letter No. 69, 22 September 1911, RSC 1214; *Chef de Service Vétérinaire*, letter No. 330, 22 September 1911, RSC 1214.

45 *Services Agricoles et Communicaux locaux au Cambodge*, letter No. 346, 26 September 1911, RSC 1214.

46 *Service du Cadastre et de la Topographie*, letter No. 188, 18 September 1911, RSC 1214.

47 *Service du Cadastre et de la Topographie*, letter No. 188, 18 September 1911, RSC 1214; *Résident Supérieur du Cambodge*, undated letter, 1913, RSC 2022; Corfield, *Royal family of Cambodia*, pp. 36–37.

48 The princess called 'Princesse Sutharot' in the documents was Princess Norodom Phangangam (1874–1944), married to Prince Norodom Sutharot, her half-brother (Corfield, *Royal house of Cambodia*, p. 45).

49 Benzançon, 'L'Impact de la colonisation française', p. 899; Cabaton, 'La vie domestique au Cambodge', p. 112; Thompson, *French Indo-China*, p. 353; Pavie, *Pavie Mission*, p. 45; *Rapport de mission sur les écoles de pagodas au Cambodge*, Phnom Penh: Direction de l'Inspection Publique de Cambodge, 1925, p. 2, RSC 30895; *Organisation et fonctionnement des écoles de pagodas rénovées dans la province Kampot, 1931*, p. 3, RSC 26013.

50 Inspecteur d'Academie, *Rapport de mission sur les écoles de pagodas au Cambodge*, hnom Penh: Direction de l'Inspection Publique de Cambodge, 1925, pp. 1–3, RSC 30895; Ayres, *Anatomy of a crisis*, p. 24.

51 Leclère, *Buddhisme au Cambodge*, p. 504; Ayres, *Anatomy of a crisis*, p. 28.

52 *Administrateur des Services civiles*, letter No. 971, 24 June 1927, RSC 31308; *Service de l'Enseignement local*, letter No. 192c, 28 December 1927, RSC 31313.

53 *Résident Supérieur du Cambodge*, circular No. 156b, 31 July 1929, RSC 26632.

54 *Résident Supérieur du Cambodge*, circular No. 156b, 31 July 1929, RSC 26632.

55 All French policy in Cambodia was tempered by the perceived superiority of the Vietnamese. They saw the Cambodians as lazy and unorganised, although good-natured, and the Vietnamese as energetic and rational. The French accepted the geo-political makeup of mainland Indochina as it appeared in the middle of the nineteenth century, maintaining Vietnamese hegemony over Laos and Cambodia within French Indochina. Finding that Cambodia and Laos had no universal law code, the French placed all of Indochina under 'Annamite Law' as of 25 July 1864. The peoples affected included 'the Chinese, the Cambodians, the Minh Huongs, the Siamese, the Mons, the Chams, the Stiengs, the half-breeds (Malays from Chaudoc)'. School curricula also reflected the perceived predominance of the Vietnamese in Indochina. The educational reforms of 1924, which replaced francocentric subjects with *Humanités extrêmes-orientales*, did not take into account the cultural diversity of the region. Instead, Confucianism and history that depicted the Vietnamese as conquerors were taught to the Theravada Buddhist Cambodians. A greater number of schools were established in Vietnam, as the administration implemented preventative educational measures in areas where anti-imperialist sentiments were strongest. Vietnamese immigration into Cambodia was encouraged as the French found the Vietnamese better civil servants than the Cambodians. The persons included in the 1943 *Souverains et notabilités d'Indochine*, a French publication designed to show the high regard that the French had for their indigenous subjects in the face of Japanese invasion and nationalistic movements, were predominantly Vietnamese. Cambodian women, therefore, had to compete for educational, employment, and *encongayment* opportunities with Vietnamese women who had greater access to education and were perceived as culturally superior in French eyes.

56 Letter from 'Madame Mau', dated 20 March 1920, RSC 8518; diverse letters and papers concerning Tong Siv Eng, 1934–1939, RSC 25294; Tong Keam, letter dated 13

July 1934, RSC 25294. Tong Siv Eng taught some of the royal children, married a court *oknha*, held several ministerial portfolios during the 1950s and 1960s, and was a prominent behind-the-scenes figure in brokering the meetings between the king and Hun Sen in the 1980s.

57 Benzançon, 'L'Impact de la colonisation française', pp. 898, 901;Cooper, *France in Indochina*, pp. 35, 83; Thompson, *French Indo-China*, p. 354; Willowdean C. Handy, 'Renaissance in Indo-China: A French experiment in reviving Cambodian art', *Pacific Affairs* 2, 2 (February 1929), p. 72.

58 The Buddhist Institute in Siem Reap was forced to close in 1911due to lack of local interest. Benzançon, 'L'Impact de la colonisation française', p. 900. Cooper, *France in Indochina*, p. 39; Albert Sarrault, *Grandeur et servitude colonials*, Paris: Sagittaire, 1931, p. 97; Ayres, *Anatomy of a crisis*, p. 25. According to Hann So, the first female students to attend were Phana Douc, Tramouch Yen, Thouch Yen, Huon Hen, Ven Tep, Vansy Sim, Chon Pol and Ponnary Khieu (*Khmer kings*, p. 35).

59 Chandler, *Brother number one*, p. 17.

60 Edwards, 'Cambodge', p. 136.

61 This was the case throughout Southeast Asia. See Barbara Watson Andaya, *The flaming womb: Repositioning women in early modern Southeast Asia*, Honolulu: University of Hawai'i Press, 2006, p. 225.

62 Edwards, Cambodge, p. 136; Leclère, *Buddhisme au Cambodge*, p. 402; Jacob, *Traditional literature of Cambodia*, p. 5; Jacques Nepote and Khing Hoc Dy, 'Literature and society in modern Cambodia', in Tham Seung Chee (ed.), *Literature and society in Southeast Asia*, Singapore: National University of Singapore Press, 1981, p. 57; fieldnotes, 2003.

63 *Kambujasuriya* 6, 7–9, pp. 176–179; *Gatilok ke oknha Suttanta Prachea Ind*, *Kambujasuriya* 7 (1927), pp. 75–93; *Kambujasuriya* 9 (1928), pp. 25–41 and 10 (1928), pp. 21–58; *Kambujasuriya* 4, 7–12 (1932), pp. 149–180; *Kambujasuriya* 4, 7–12 (1932), pp. 181; Ngoy, 'Cpbap kram thmei', *Kambujasuriya* 4, 7–12 (1932), p. 149.

64 Penny Edwards has used the term 'Cambodge' to 'denote the political life-span and geographic domain of the Protectorate, and to denote the conceptual rubric of nation structured within this temporal and territorial frame'. See Edwards, Cambodge, p. 3.

65 Anne Raffin, 'Easternization meets westernisation: Patriotic youth organizations in French Indochina during World War II', *French Politics, Culture & Society*, 20, 2 (Summer 2002), pp. 121, 127, 130; Michael Vickery, *Kampuchea: Politics, economics and society*, Sydney; London; Boston: Allen & Unwin, 1986, pp. 11–13; Raoul M. Jennar (comp. and ed.), *The Cambodian constitutions, 1953–1993*, Bangkok: White Lotus, 1995, p. 36; Nguyen Sy Tuan, 'Khmer novel and the struggle for democracy: National independence in Cambodia during the period of 1940–1960', in *Khmer Studies*, vol. 2, p. 636.

66 'Khmer daughters', *Kampuchea* 190 (1945), p. 2, cited in and translated by Kate Frieson in 'Sentimental education: *Les sages femmes* and colonial Cambodia', *Journal of Colonialism and Colonial History* 1, 1 (2000), online print version, pp. 11–12.

67 Maria Mies, Patriarchy and accumulation on a world scale: Women in the international division of labour, London and Atlantic Highlands, New Jersey: Zed Books, 1986, p. 175; Frieson, 'Sentimental education', p. 13.

68 Stoler, 'Sexual affronts and racial frontiers', p. 206; Andrée Viollis, *SOS Indochine*, Paris: Gallimard, 1935, p. 35; Thompson, *French Indo-China*, p. 326; Vickery, *Kampuchea: Politics, economics and society*, p. 5; 'l'Association des femmes Cambodgiennes', *Cambodge Nouveau* 7 (November 1970), p. 52; Frieson, 'Sentimental education', p. 15.

CHAPTER EIGHT

'Liberation'

*I*n the years between official independence in 1953 and
the fall of Phnom Penh to the Khmer Rouge on 17 April
1975, Cambodia appeared to be a newly independent
nation embracing modernisation, led (some might say dominat-
ed) by Norodom Sihanouk. The years between 1953 and 1970
are known as the *Sangkum Reastr Niyum* period or 'Sihanouk'
era. Yet underneath this calm surface, a growing number of
Cambodians were becoming dissatisfied with the status quo.
The nearby war in Vietnam led inexorably to the bombing of
Cambodian territory in order to drive out Vietnamese insurgents
sheltering on the Cambodian side of the border. Corruption
and anti-monarchism increased in tandem as the 1960s drew
to a close, leading finally to the removal of Sihanouk as head of
state on 18 March 1970 and the establishment of the Khmer
Republic (1970–1975). The ensuing civil war pitted the stand-
ing army, loyal to General Lon Nol and backed by the United
States, Thailand and South Vietnam against the *Front National
Uni du Kampuchea* (FUNK), representing the *Gouvernement
Royal d'Union Nationale du Kampuchea* (GRUNK), comprising
Prince Sihanouk, his supporters and the communist resistance,
supported by North Vietnam and the National Liberation
Front. By 1973, the Khmer Republic controlled only the capital,
Phnom Penh, some provincial capitals, and most of Battambang
province, while the rest of Cambodia was under the control of
the Khmer Rouge.

The 1950s and 1960s are crucial for understanding the relationship of women to power today as the post-liberation nation-state was responsible for the way that subjects come to be identified.[1] The government promised, but did not deliver, gender equality. Constructs of gender roles that permitted the mobilisation and participation of women within strict parameters of support and domesticity, and in which women were entrusted with the guardianship of Cambodian traditions in the post-colonial world, persisted in the minds of the elite. This construct was disseminated to new generations of Cambodians through the entrenchment of the *Cbpab Srei* in the educational system and a confused sense that it was written by Ang Duong, hailed as the restorer of Cambodian culture and identity. Simultaneously, people who sought social mobility did so through an emulation of the values of the elite, which had changed little since the nineteenth century. When, in the 1960s, Cambodians began to be dissatisfied – education no longer resulted in lucrative government positions but unemployment; the elite were not unquestioningly obeyed; the promised democratic government was still presided over by a wilful ex-king beloved by people in the countryside – a deviation from so-called 'traditional' ways was identified as the explanation. The fact that women were no longer content to remain constrained by the boundaries of the past figured prominently in this rationale. In some ways, women achieved a greater level of equality than ever before at the end of the 1960s and early 1970s, as they were mobilised on both sides of the civil war. Yet even here attitudes toward the participation of women were tempered by a belief that 'correct' Cambodian women complied with the teachings of the *Cbpab Srei* and other 'traditional' literature, even though, as discussed in Chapter 7, these values had been absorbed uncritically. Equality was never intended to be any more than a temporary measure brought about by extraordinary times. At the same time, the significance and authority of female figures in the supernatural arena belies the construction of women as passive and powerless prior to 1975.

Sex in the Sangkum

The newly independent government of the Kingdom of Cambodia officially endorsed the participation of all its citizens in political life. The National Congress declared on 25 September 1955 that women had the right to participate in the electoral process. The 1964 Constitution stipulated that men and women were entitled both to vote and to membership of the Popular

Assemblies, and were equally eligible for office. Citizens of either sex were invited to take part in the National Congresses, in which any person might air their views regarding a matter of personal or national significance.[2] Yet these principles did not translate into practice. This is evident from the fact that the Head of State consistently addressed his speeches to a male audience: 'It is convenient that we men of politics realise ....'.[3]

A woman occupied the throne of Cambodia from 1960 but her political power was virtually non-existent. Queen Kossamak (see Fig. 8.1), born

Fig. 8.1: Queen Kossamak. Pamphlet, National Archives of Cambodia.

Sisowath Kossamak Nearireath, daughter of King Sisowath Monivong and Queen Norodom Kanviman Norleak Thevi, continued to rule after the death of her husband King Suramarit (r. 1955–1960). Her son Prince Sihanouk had sworn in 1955 that he would never ascend the throne and he had forbidden his own children from assuming sovereignty during his lifetime. A demonstration took place in Battambang soon after the death of King Suramarit in 1960 in which the protestors called for Queen Kossamak to take the throne. Article 25 of the Constitution, however, stipulated that 'the Throne of Cambodia is the heritage of the male descendants of King Ang Duong'. Prince Monireth, the Queen's brother, was in favour of amending the Constitution to allow the Queen to be instated as sovereign in her own right. In his memoirs, Prince Monireth wrote that it was 'a shame' that Kossamak had not been born male. 'What a King we would have in Her! Certainly with Her, a great many disagreements, and a great deal of foolishness could have been avoided'. The Council of Regency did propose this as a solution, only to have the idea rejected by Prince Sihanouk because of his own uneasy relationship with his mother and the perceived threat of someone other than himself as head of state. Prince Sihanouk was more enigmatic as to his motives: 'Only God understands the reasons why I do not want my mother to ascend the throne.' The relationship between mother and son certainly appears to have been problematic; Sihanouk reorganised the royal palace, in which his mother lived, once he had been made Head of State on 20 June 1960.[4] Although not wielding any political power, the Queen was nonetheless described as highly significant in newly independent Cambodia:

> Today, Her Majesty Queen Kossamak who neither reigns nor governs, exercises considerable moral authority over all Khmers and sits well in the line of past queens, compassionate towards the poor and busies herself in fulfilling her duties with regard to the Nation and the people.[5]

Queen Kossamak's duties included hosting state functions, which almost always included performances of the royal ballet corps. These occasions afforded opportunities to establish and consolidate links with potential allies, such as Chen Yi, who led a women's delegation from the People's Republic of China in November 1958.[6]

The reluctance to accord women political power was also reflected in their low numbers in government positions. In the 1958 elections the only candidates not to receive wholehearted support, as David Chandler commented, were 'women, recalcitrant Democrats, and members of the outgoing assembly'.[7] Only one woman was elected to Parliament in these elections: Tong Siv Eng. The first female member of the Cambodian parliament, she was Secretary of State for Labour and Social Action between 1958 and 1959, Minister of Social Action from 1959 to 1961, and Minister of Health between 1963 and 1968. She and her husband, Pung Peng Cheng, were amongst Sihanouk's most trusted political advisors. Khieu Thirith was offered a position in the National Assembly of 1962 but declined as the communist party advised against it.[8] Only three other women held senior political positions in the 1960s: Tip Man (1962–1966), Diep Dinar (1966–1970), and Nou Neou (1966–1970). Towards the end of the Sangkum period, more women were entering into and promoted within the government.[9] They were not permitted to retain their own names within the political arena, however. Female civil servants were legally required to take their husbands' names, whereas 'according to custom' other married women were to keep their name and add 'wife of ...'.[10] In other words, women would only be 'allowed' into politics if they were chaperoned by their husbands.

The 1959 Cambodian civil code underscored the reliance of women upon their husbands and the family as the basic social unit. According to the code, the keystone of society was marriage, 'the union of a man and a woman in order to create a cohesive unit, the dedication of their lives to that unit, and the raising and education of children'. Yet women were not legally recognised as heads of households, although they could substitute under certain conditions. The civil code considered married women as extensions of their husbands, 'bound to obey' them. Husbands had the power over all aspects of the household, including the conduct of their wives. They represented their wives in contracts and other legal undertakings. A married woman could not sign a contract without the authorisation of her husband, although he could give her permission to act on her own behalf.[11]

The civil code privileged the interests of men over those of women. Polygamy continued to be recognised, although only two levels of wife were permitted, the *prapuon jerng* having been abolished. The *prapuon thom* enjoyed 'a dominant place in the marital home' with power over the lesser wife stipulated in law. Should a man die or disappear, the *prapuon thom* had the right not only to assume command of the household finances and enterprises but make decisions regarding the children of both wives. Lesser wives did not have the right to inherit any of their husbands' property and could claim only those costs associated with accommodation, food, and basic living costs. If the *prapuon thom* did not object, both wives and their children could live in the same household, but this does not seem to have been popular: 'The rapid changes to the condition of women has made these duties more theoretical than practical. For them, life in the marital home is not appropriate, and usually, they have a separate abode'. Sarayeth remembered that her uncle, a mid-level civil servant in Kompong Thom, had maintained two establishments with four children by his first wife and two by his second. When his wife of the first rank died in 1964, he married again, installing the new wife in the house of the one who had died. This was apparently regarded as entirely appropriate because the new wife was a young girl from a good family, and the second wife had been a widow upon whom her uncle had taken pity. Women were not prohibited from re-marrying, although they had to observe a period of ten months after their divorce or the death of their husband to ensure that they were not carrying his child.[12]

Only the elite could afford to have more than one wife. Monogamy was the norm, although a man seeking to elevate his status might take a lesser wife as a social statement as to his power and wealth. Marriage customs that had prevailed in the late nineteenth and early twentieth centuries were incorporated into the 1959 civil code, for example where marriages were to be celebrated (at the bride's home) and where the couple was to live afterward (a marital home apart from either set of parents, after an initial period in which the groom lived with the bride's family). The state thus provided a template for regulation of the basic social unit in Cambodia. This was bolstered by publications outlining the history and customs of Cambodian marriage, in which references were made to the unions upon which Cambodia itself had been founded, such as that of 'Preah Thong' and the Nagini.[13]

Legally, men could not prevent their wives from working. Article 7 of the Code of Commerce entitled women to participate in commercial enterprises without requiring the consent of their husband; if he opposed her participation, a woman had the right to be heard before a tribunal on the matter.[14] It was in the interests of the newly independent state to appear to be modern and progressive, including universal access to education and employment opportunities for all, particularly women. The pages of *Femmes du Cambodge* (Cambodian Women), a 1963 government publication showcasing the progressive policies of the Sangkum, abound with photographs of women participating in all occupations. Some women were successful in pursuing a career in the civil service; towards the end of the Sangkum period an increasing number of women were being entered into or promoted within the government infrastructure and working as local staff in international organisations, radio announcers, writers, photographers, painters, musicians, and members of the police and armed forces.[15]

Women were also entering medical training programmes, although their numbers were few compared to men.[16] Midwifery, a privately practised profession despite attempts to regularise it by the colonial government, was beset by further onslaughts during the Sangkum period. The government's rural midwives' training scheme prevented women from practising midwifery without a state certificate, for which they had to pay to attend a course; in return they received free bicycles. In 1957 there were sixty state and eighteen private midwives registered in Cambodia. The royal ballet was similarly brought under state control. In 1961 the Ministry of National Education and Fine Arts announced a project that would accredit the dance instructors of the royal ballet with pedagogical qualifications. So, they too had to attend a course and pay the fees.[17]

Education policies pursued by the Cambodian government in the 1950s and 1960s should have resulted in greater employment opportunities for women. Improvement of female attendance and literacy were objectives of particular concern to the Sangkum government. On paper, these rates improved during the early 1960s. The number of girls in primary schools rose from 25.4 per cent in 1957 to 32.8 per cent in 1964. Secondary enrolments rose from 16.1 per cent to 21.7 per cent and enrolments in tertiary degrees increased from 7 per cent to 10.8 per cent over the same period, from a base figure in 1958 of only 29 women. Technical and vocational training saw the greatest increase, from 2.4 per cent in 1957 to 21.1 per cent in 1964. Yet girls were constrained from accessing education to the same degree as boys because of an ingrained perception of schools as potentially dangerous places where girls could dishonour the family. In March 1961 the government announced plans for the *Lycée Sangkum Reastr Niyum*, to open the following year. The *lycée* would be of benefit to girls in particular, as 'secondary education is usually co-educational and in all of these places girls are in the minority'. The sentence concluded by remarking that in that in co-educational schools girls were simultaneously 'cherished and wooed by the boys', thereby hindering 'the spirit of [good] behaviour and total concentration towards their studies'. Education for girls was seen as a double-edged sword. On one hand, some education was seen as positive as literate and numerate daughters could assist their families in business and household management. Two to three years of education was usually enough to ensure a basic standard of literacy and numeracy. Girls, even in some elite families, were then kept at home in order to manage the household, including participation in the family business, or the care of younger siblings. After puberty, parents exercised more control over their daughters.[18]

Control over female sexuality increased as more families sought to elevate themselves socially. Marriage alliances remained a key component in social mobility. Thus socially aspirant families believed that a good match could be achieved through an emulation of the same values that the elite appeared to embrace, such as an emphasis on virginity. The inculcation of these values occurred largely through the educational syllabus, which departed very little from the colonial model in incorporating the uncritical study of literature such as the *cbpab* and folktales.[19] The *Cbpab Srei* of Minh Mai was one of the most popular set texts, although most people were under the impression that Ang Duong was the author. As the role of education was not to encourage critical inquiry but to reinforce the status quo, students understood that these were the values that Cambodian society not only espoused during the 'golden age' before colonisation, but also was expected to adhere to in the present. Texts authored by Ang Duong were particularly revered, as he was celebrated as the liberator of Cambodia from Vietnamese imperialism.[20]

Other works published during the Sangkum period emphasised the necessity of chastity and fidelity for women, the importance of obedience to one's husband, and that social harmony and cultural heritage were the responsibility of women. In 1957 Sakhan Samon published *Kpuon Apram Chariya Satrei* (Manual for raising good women), which advised readers on how to be a good daughter, wife, and mother, and suggested good recipes; others extended this theme further, explaining how selected excerpts from the *Cbpab Srei* of Ang Duong might be observed, and the correct manner in which women should sit, stand, recline, and so forth. Some such commentaries were published in French although clearly directed toward a Cambodian audience, such as Son Siv's *Le savoir-vivre: à la famille sociale* which explained how people might observe the tenets of the *cbpab* while enjoying the benefits of affluence; it also listed the signs by which one might recognise *srei krup leakkhana* and *broh krup leakkhana*, women and men who were perfect in every way. *Morale aux jeunes filles* by Luong Vichetr Vohar was another of these. The Buddhist Institute re-issued Ang Duong's *Cbpab Srei* in French as well.[21]

A form of inductive reasoning was at work in post-colonial Cambodian society. Education was a characteristic of a socially superior person in the Cambodian past. Elite persons enjoyed privileges. Therefore, education – of any sort, pursued with no deliberation as to temperament or availability of jobs – would result in similar lifestyles for anyone who took the trouble to acquire it.[22] Most graduates expected to enter the civil service or private corporations and avail themselves of the perquisites that the elite possessed, and were upset when there were simply not enough jobs in the government or in private enterprise to meet the demand. This is a common occurrence in modernising societies. In the Cambodian context the education system, in the words of Michael Vickery, 'was thus producing an increasingly numerous class of useless people'.[23] The fact that they had degrees should have entitled them to western-style lifestyles; instead, they were stranded between the lives that they aspired to in Phnom Penh and the rice paddies to which they would not return.

The new class of recently educated people who had managed to acquire positions in the government or private enterprises required new models for correct behaviour. Popular literature provided ways in which the demands of modern life could be faced and dealt with. Women were not overlooked in this new genre. The female protagonist in *La destinée de Mademoiselle Nakri*, by Souy Nyheng, convinces her fiancé that he must go into business and defeat the Chinese and Vietnamese merchants who are trying to take over Cambodia's economy. *Socheavatadar samrap broh neung srei* (harmonious living for men and women) instructed Cambodians on how to behave in a changing social and economic milieu, including how to speak on the telephone and what was the correct attire for a cocktail party. Those who achieved their objective of upward movement along the social trajectory often rejected the mores and traditions of their origins. Some began seeing Buddhism and its teachings as quaint attributes of yesterday rather than an integral part of modern life. Ratha, daughter of an ex-Minister of Culture, recalled: 'My parents each had their own ideas, and in our house my mother's room was furnished with modern imported furniture, whereas my father's room was furnished with traditional handmade Cambodian furniture. My father observed the Buddhist precepts so rigidly that my mother said he should become a monk.'[24]

In 1963 the Sangkum announced that it had 'effectively liberated Cambodian women.'[25] Whilst it was true that women were entering more diverse fields of work outside the home than ever before, the 'liberation' of the 1950s and 1960s did not include equal representation in politics, rates of education, or participation in civil society, due to a continued perception of women's issues to focus solely upon domestic concerns.[26] The Cambodian Women's Association, originally established in 1949, lapsed in the 1960s.[27] Only one of the ten founding members of the Association of Cambodian Writers in 1956 was a woman, Suy Hieng. Although the literary prize presented every two or four years was called the 'Indradevi' after the late twelfth-century queen who had excelled in Sanskrit composition, only 'well-known literary men such as Rim Kin, Sam Thang, Hell Sumphea, and Trinh Hoanh' were elected as presidents of the association.[28] Some women, however, were more successful in individual pursuits. In 1960 Khieu Thirith was working in an English-language high school; the following year Khieu Ponnary established an underground association for women, the Women's Organisation of Democratic Kampuchea, and began working at Prince Sihanouk's official magazine, *Kambuja*, where she stayed on for two years after her husband, Pol Pot, took to the *maquis*. Tong Siv Eng was the editor-in-chief of *Samlanh Neary* (Women's Voice) newspaper for a time in the 1960s. *Daun chi* Aun built two wats, one in Phnom Penh and one in Sihanoukville, in the early 1970s. On the other hand, there is evidence that life for women was not easy. *Cheat Satrei*, written in the late 1950s, apparently recorded 'a woman's struggle for existence'. According to statistics from the late 1960s, women were marrying later. This may have been due, as Jacques Migozzi suggested, to the exodus of males to the cities in search of employment; or it may have been because when looking for potential mates, 'often, one only finds alcoholics and smokers of hashish.'[29]

Women's so-called liberation did not extend to sexual freedom. A double standard was alive and well in the 1950s and 1960s. Prostitution was widely perceived as a legitimate business and as an acceptable recreational activity for men. Haing Ngor candidly admitted that his 'previous relationships with girls were the kind best not described in public'.[30] Romanticised descriptions of visiting a brothel were included in official publications aimed at showcasing Cambodia to the world:

One gets out of the *cyclo*, and directs oneself to 'Flower Alley'. At their windows, the pretty girls look at you, smiling … . A door opens, you enter. A dozen of young women are there, kneeling on mats, naked and brown, pert breasts, white teeth, mouths lipsticked and luscious.[31]

Maslyn Williams was told that the best-looking girls rounded up in the periodic crackdowns were sent to the seaside resort of Sihanoukville, the only place in Cambodia where prostitution was legal, and where the elite congregated on weekends and for public holidays. One madam took advantage of the public forum offered by the National Congresses to bitterly protest the closure of her premises. The government displayed an ambivalent attitude towards prostitution. Every edition of the *Cahiers du Sangkum* recorded how many people had been arrested for 'clandestine prostitution' and measures taken to prevent them re-offending. Although civil servants were advised not to 'frequent places of pleasure, exercise restraint', short-term sexual liaisons in the company of one's relatives, friends and colleagues was considered to be a normal method of relaxation, male bonding, and even hospitality. An Australian journalist visiting Phnom Penh in the late 1960s was invited to the home of a young Cambodian friend. After an afternoon chatting, eating and drinking, he was invited to stay the night. Just before he turned out the light, there was a knock at his bedroom door. He opened it to find a young Cambodian girl of around twenty standing there with his host. His friend explained that she was a distant relative, and would be his companion for the night should he be so inclined.[32] Temporary sexual encounters, therefore, were considered to be a normal part of social life and hospitality for the men who had the resources to purchase them.

Although some elite women may have taken advantage of their husbands' preoccupations with lesser wives and mistresses to indulge their own proclivities, there was no tacit approval of such activities. Similarly, although men were expected to have had sexual experience before marriage, virginity became mandatory in brides. Prince Sihanouk, for example, told his sons that he would not take responsibility for their 'mistakes' and that he had no sympathy for the girls who put themselves at risk by associating with the princes. Love letters were seen as a landmine in the field of arranged marriages as they could be used to prove that the girl concerned was not a virgin, and therefore it would not be necessary to go through the full marriage ceremony in order to marry her (if at all). In effect, this meant that the bride's family would receive fewer gifts, less social prestige, and they could not demand that the groom perform a period of service in their home after the engagement, as was usual in marriages of the first rank. *Sambat Neary* of 4 August 1968 contained an article that stressed the importance of maintaining and preserving one's beauty, unquestionable conduct, and virginity for one's husband. Beauty pageants were well patronised in the 1950s and 1960s. Youth, beauty, obedience, and purity were considered to be the necessary qualities in a woman before marriage and the *meba* (ancestral spirits) still required appeasement after transgressions of a sexual nature on the part of their female descendants.[33]

There was an underlying assumption that Cambodian women must simultaneously *appear* modernised yet retain the essence of traditional Cambodian femininity. A visitor to Cambodia in 1957 wrote that the Cambodian woman 'occupies a key position' in the family and was 'a carrier of the basic social and moral values of Cambodian culture'. In this way Cambodia would remain uniquely Cambodian whilst having 'caught up' with the rest of the world. Female chastity began to be identified with the purity of Cambodian culture. Modernisation threatened the integrity of both. Some found it impossible to reconcile the construct of the chaste Cambodian woman as guardian of culture with the freedoms that Cambodian society was beginning to exhibit and sought to reorient women back toward their 'proper' roles. Although women were legally entitled to remarry, one author warned that 'married two or three times, one becomes less pure'. Another wrote of a young woman who wore modern clothes and makeup, drove her own car, and habitually went out unaccompanied. A friend drugged her and facilitated her rape by a male acquaintance. This was her own fault, he asserted, as she did not act in accordance with correct behaviour. Similarly, sex workers were regarded as being morally corrupt influences from which 'nice' girls should preserve a distance, as even being seen in the same area could blemish their reputations.[34]

Women who exerted themselves in public life or appeared superior to their husbands were seen as threatening to the preservation of Cambodian cultural identity. Men seemed to have been slightly alarmed at the achievements of the 'weaker' sex, although the government painted their bemusement in a generally positive light:

> The last ten years have been marked by profound transformations of social comportment of Cambodian women, mainly in the urban regions … . But young girls and young women are quickly seeking and finding a compromise,

sacrificing a bare minimum of customs and adapting them to the necessities of modern life. The young Khmer woman today is by the side of her husband at receptions, informs herself of all aspects of national life and international events before expressing her point of view, interests herself in literature and music, goes often to cinemas, learns western dances and follows fashion. And men, dumbfounded, face a metamorphosis wherein they must be at the same time proud and worried at the extent to which women assert prerogatives![35]

There was a definite sense that women should not outshine or dominate men. Inverting the 'traditional' domestic hierarchy and placing men in subservient positions would have disastrous consequences. In 1967 Sam Neang, a woman, wrote *Socheavatadar samrap broh neung srei* (harmonious living for men and women), which gently suggested that some women were 'forgetting the *Cbpab Srei*' and thinking they were 'bigger' (i.e., more important) than their husbands, which did not contribute to a harmonious home and therefore endangered society as a whole. She also stated that although women should work outside the home in order to contribute to the family finances, they should not neglect their domestic responsibilities.[36] Women who sought to deviate from these social norms were not exhibiting correct behaviour. This was reinforced in the social handbooks of the 1960s. In a cartoon illustrating what *not* to do, the husband sits calmly, in control of himself and his emotions, whereas the wife is belligerent and accusing (see Fig. 8.2).

The perceived failure of some Sangkum initiatives was attributed to inherently 'female' characteristics that could not cope with the demands of the new, modern Cambodia. The government was sensitive to criticisms that there were too few women in political office; a Ministry of Information publication of 1963 said that although there were only two women in the 73-member National Assembly, 'one might remark that this proportion of women in the Assembly is equal or greater to that elected to parliaments in western democracies'. Another explained that the absence of women in politics was due to the natural 'timidity' of women:

In Cambodia today, as in most democratic countries, it is necessary to remember that women only very rarely and timidly use the means that they have been given in order to effect their complete emancipation. One may note in particular that although they come in large numbers to electoral meetings and to the National Congresses it is still exceptional that they have the courage to find the words to bare their troubles there ... . It is this timidity that results in their reduced numbers in elections to the National Assembly, and the absence of female representation in the Council.[37]

The dearth of women in politics was a problem facing most modernising nations in Southeast Asia in the immediate post-colonial period. Far from being due to any biological inclination toward shyness, however, this was directly related to education. Admission to the Royal School of Administration, necessary for a career in the civil service (and, therefore, a career in politics), was contingent upon a candidate obtaining the full *baccalaureat* upon leaving secondary school and passing a complicated entrance examination. The Cambodian government acknowledged that this requirement posed a problem for women, but blamed the 'tradition' of families being reluctant to send

Fig. 8.2: Cartoon depicting a woman who is 'bigger' than her husband. San Neang, *Socheavatadar samrap broh neung srei* [Harmonious living for men and women], Phnom Penh: n.p, 1967.

their daughters to school after a certain age.[38] The unspoken implication was that this was an aspect of life over which the government had no control.

The presence of a pervasive sex industry was also perceived as being a result of female immorality, vanity, and lack of willingness to engage in 'real work'. In 1964 the government launched a series of crackdowns on the sex industry in which unlicensed brothels were closed and sex workers arrested. The women were ostensibly sent for re-training and employment elsewhere, although the Minister of Social Action did not have much faith in the efficacy of the programme.[39] Sihanouk described the attempted implementation of the government's retraining programme as follows:

> One day, Her Excellency *luok jamdev* Pung Peng Cheng [Tong Siv Eng], Minister of Social Action within the Royal Sangkum Reastr Niyum government, went to the prostitutes in order to tell them this: 'Ladies, the profession that you follow, although officially recognised by the Sangkum Reastr Niyum national administration, is not at all honourable. It is time that you change your profession. With your agreement, I will contact the directors of our factories, textile factories in particular. Ladies, you will become honourable and respectable workers in our lovely factories.' The prostitutes contacted, in all good faith, by Her Excellency Minister Pung Peng Cheng, responded: '*Luok jamdev*, look at our long nails, shaped, filed, and their beautiful varnishes of red, pink, and purple! Is it that our hands and our fingers, destined for a sensual profession, can reasonably be used for a profession as primitive, as strenuous as that of a worker in a textile factory, or any other?' A little later … my very respectable Minister for Social Action, came to see me at my residence, at Chamcar Mon, in order to tell me and my wife the previous misadventure. My wife Monique, *luok jamdev* Pung Peng Cheng and myself had lots of laughs.[40]

In other words, the government had offered the women a way out of their allegedly immoral lives through respectable employment in the factories that were contributing to the national economy. The women refused because they preferred the less strenuous work of the brothel, which would not damage their nails. In the face of such vanity and obstinacy, a progressive government's hands were tied.[41]

Private spaces, sacred places

The role of women in public life was constrained by elite perspective that women did not belong there. Private space was considered to be appropriate for women. Yet in Cambodia the private sphere extended beyond the household and family to include the realm of the supernatural, which was an integral part of daily life. People in the modern Cambodia of the 1950s and 1960s were as likely to see a *kru khmei*, practitioner of traditional healing, as they would a doctor of western medicine, if not both. Every house, government compound, and business had an area in which *moneang pdteah*, 'household spirits', were said to dwell and which were venerated through offerings of incense, fruit, cakes, rice, and, as consumption of Western products grew, cans of soft drink. Some *neak ta* lived in statues or rocks. *K'mouch* (ghosts) and malevolent spirits such as *brai* were well-known to congregate near stagnant water and women in childbirth. Spirit mediums and fortune-tellers plied a brisk trade as people consulted their ancestors on business decisions, potential spouses or a likely exam results.[42] In other words, the unseen world had resonance. Female power permeated the supernatural realm and women of the mundane world participated in it.

Women were not permitted to ordain as *bhikkhuni* but they constituted an active presence in Buddhism. When boys became *samre* (novices) for a short time at the age of twelve, it was said to be in honour of their mothers; when they ordained as *bhikku* at age twenty they did so in honour of their fathers. The women who became *daun chi* were not precluded from studying Buddhist texts and meditation. Many travelled, alone, to remote wats and mountains in order to fulfil their spiritual quest. Pao Chin became a *daun chi* in 1960 rather than marry again after the death of her husband. She studied *dhamma* and *vipassana* with a learned teacher and learned Pali to the highest level. Not all *daun chi* actively practised meditation or participated in formal education, however. Some women maintained the wat grounds or cooked, washed and cleaned for the monks in return for food and shelter. The *daun chi* seem to have transcended space beyond the parameters of formal Buddhism.[43]

Images of Preah Dharani maintained a presence in wats and new images were commissioned during the Sangkum period. Anthropologist Milada Kalab observed a meditation ceremony in the 1960s in which participants first paid their respects to a statue of the Buddha, then to an image of Preah Dharani on the other side of the altar. Preah Dharani was depicted vanquishing Vietnamese forces in anti-communist propaganda of the early 1970s. Possibly the best-known statue of Preah Dharani in Cambodia was erected in 1966 as part of a general beautification of Phnom Penh. The mayor of the city, Tep Phon, specifically commissioned the statue, which rests in the centre of a roundabout near Psar Orussei. Traffic islands seem to have been popular places for statues imbued with female spirits in the years after 1954. A statue of the god Yama, identical to that known as the 'Leper King' except that it had no 'fangs' protruding from its mouth, was unearthed at Wat Khnat Rangsei in Siem Reap and relocated to a traffic island northwest of the royal residence in the provincial capital. Although male, it was worshipped as a female deity called *Yeay Deb*, 'Grandmother Goddess'. Another statue, a modern cement replica of the 'Leper King' statue housed in the National Museum in Phnom Penh, was placed outside the museum site in 1970 in order to confuse would-be thieves; this too was worshipped as Yeay Deb. Kong Sovonn recounted that in her village monastery there was a hut of a *yeay deb* in front of which pregnant women could not pass or they would give birth prematurely. Two gilded wooden statues of the Buddha from Siem Reap were also feminised as *Preah Neang Chek* and *Preah Neang Cham* and used in a procession involving Queen Kossamak.[44]

Many beliefs of 'traditional' Cambodia described in Chapter 6 endured despite policies of modernisation after indepedence. The practice of the *koan kroach* was one of these; Aing Chum Sarun recounted that while chief of district in Kompong Staung in the early 1970s 'some people came to complain to me against a man who had eviscerated his pregnant wife in order to extract the foetus'. Taking some soldiers with him, he went to the house of the man's father-in-law, where they found him near the body of his wife, covered with blood and holding the foetus as a talisman. Sites that had been significant due to the presence of *brai* and female *neak ta* continued to be significant places for most Cambodians. In 1968 six girls were alleged to have died because of a *brai* near a river in Sisophon. François Bizot described a journey to Wat Phnom Sampou, in Battambang province, in which people descended to the 'womb' of the earth mother (*m'dey doeum*), in a cave beneath the wat complex, and were reborn by cleansing themselves in the 'amniotic fluid' of a pool of water.[45] Buddhist and local beliefs fused to provide significant space for women in terms of ideological power.

The tradition of *rup*, 'mediums', also continued in the postcolonial period. The statue of Preah Dharani near the Olympic Stadium was the scene of a possession in 1972, when a woman climbed onto the roundabout and went into a trance. Ang Chouléan has published the testimonies of several Cambodians who had female relatives or neighbours who were *rup* during this period. The Cambodian grandmother of Kong Sovonn communicated through the (Vietnamese) maid of Kong Sovonn, for example. Prince Sihanouk was well known to consult his dead female relatives. A nineteenth-century princess, Nojeat Khsatri Varpheyak, regularly advised Prince Sihanouk in the Sangkum period. He also brought the ashes of his four-year-old daughter, Princess Kantha Bopha, on overseas trips. In Kratie province, the stupas of Wat Vihear Thom were inhabited by the spirit of a princess, Krapum Chhuk, who had been eaten by a crocodile in the sixteenth century. She often communicated through a medium who then transmitted her messages to the government. In 1969 she interpreted a message to the effect that Prince Sihanouk would no longer lead the country and was never seen again.[46] Less than a year later, Prince Sihanouk was overthrown in a coup d'etat.

The Khmer Republic

The short-lived Khmer Republic also guaranteed equal rights to participation and representation for women. Yet there were fewer women in the upper echelons of the Khmer Republic than there had been in the Sangkum period. Indeed, Nou Neou, who had been Undersecretary of State for Tourism in 1969, was removed from her position in 1970 when the government was reorganised 'in order to assure the best efficiency possible in government activity, in a time when Cambodia is mobilising'. Clearly, having women in high political office was not in the interests of efficiency according to the new government. Nou Neou then channelled her energies into resuscitating the Cambodian Women's Association. By 1972 she was once again in office. The same year Pheng Santhan was appointed Under-Secretary of State for Finances in the Son Ngoc Thanh government and the first unmarried woman to serve in a Cambodian government, Plech Phirun, was made Under-Secretary of State for Labour and Social Welfare. With the exception of Plech Phirum, these women were referred to in official publications by their husbands' names, for example 'Mrs Ung Mung' for Nou Neou, and it is debatable whether they would have been appointed had their husbands not been involved in the management of the country. It is fairly unlikely that 'Mrs In Tim' would have been appointed one of the eight deputies in the Cambodian delegation to the Eighth Conference of Asiatic Congressmen in July 1970 had her husband, Chairman of the National Assembly, not headed the mission.[47] Women's activities in the public sphere, therefore, continued to be mediated by their relationships to men.

This did not mean that the contributions of women in the political arena were unimportant, although they were largely unrecognised. The governments of the Khmer Republic frequently turned to women as intermediaries and envoys in times of political crisis. In the aftermath of the coup that deposed Sihanouk, Queen Kossamak communicated between her son and the National Assembly 'in a last-ditch attempt to turn the people's anger and save her son'.[48] As we have seen, Cambodia had precedents for women diplomats dating back to the classical period. During the Khmer Republic, the Cambodian Deputy Permanent Representative to the United Nations was a woman, 'Mrs Nhoung Peng':

> Being highly dynamic, she speaks incessantly, without discrimination, with all delegations accredited to the UN, even with those countries who have recognised the GRUNK. In an easy, moderate way, she explains, refutes, decries, confirms, reaffirms the permanent position of the Khmer Republic.[49]

Nou Neou claimed to have been ordered by Lon Nol to broker an agreement with Khmer Rouge forces with a view to integration of resistance fighters into the standing army. She stated that she had reconciled a local resistance commander to the idea, but the plan was rejected because all members of the standing army had to have passed through the Cambodian Military Academy – a requirement that all military leaders in the resistance could not meet.[50] Yet women seem to have been considered appropriate mediums for diplomacy in the Khmer Republic.

Female metaphor was often invoked in relation to the civil war. Cambodia was spoken of as a woman 'with the crushing weight of her remote and recent past, with her naked and sometimes revolting realities, her first own experiences made up of trials and errors, sparks of hopes and disappointments, but also her firm will to succeed'. Slogans such as 'Defend the motherland against invasion' began appearing on classroom walls as the civil war intensified. Government publications such as *New Cambodge* depicted the fledgling FUNK forces as a baby being nursed by China, anthropomorphised as a large, middle-aged woman with drooping breasts, dressed as a Chinese peasant. Cartoons represented Cambodia as a young, innocent woman, frequently 'molested' by drooling male representations of Vietnam, China, and GRUNK. Chhang Song entitled his 1971 interview with Henry Kamm

'The rape of Cambodia'. The 'purity' of Cambodia was further symbolised in the first flag-raising ceremony of the Khmer Republic. General Lon Nol is purported to have ordered that young, unmarried – and therefore morally 'pure' girls – be involved with the manufacture and consecration of the flag. In a ceremony reminiscent of Shaivite *puja* ceremonies, the girls were made to 'kneel around the flag holding lotus blossoms. Then he ordered the girls to wrap the flag about a tall gold-and-silver candlestick, then to unfurl it again. The monks showered jasmine blossoms over the girls and the flag'. Even military operations were named after women who had resonance in the minds of Cambodians, such as 'Operation Kangrey', which was named after 'a woman of dazzling beauty who held everyone under her spell'.[51] The success of the mission, therefore, was inevitable.

Not all imagery associated with women was positive. As had occurred in the nineteenth century (see Chapter 5), women of earlier periods were held responsible for mistakes made by Cambodian kings in the past, such as the 'fall' of Angkor, the 'occupation' of Cambodia by the Vietnamese in the nineteenth century, and the imposition of colonialism.[52] The propaganda machine of the Khmer Republic laid the blame for the corruption and excesses of the Sangkum era at the feet of Princess Monique.[53] Although some censured Prince Sihanouk for interfering in processes that were supposed to be democratic, or allowing himself to be distracted by frivolous pursuits such as film-making while the country slid toward chaos,[54] he was represented even by the Khmer Republic has having been led astray by his favourite consort.[55] Sihanouk 'passed his time making films and spending money while his wife lined her pockets'; the state casino, seen by many as the symbol of the depths of depravity to which Cambodian society had sunk by the end of the 1960s, was 'the private creation of Sihanouk-Monique-Pomme and their associates'.[56] Monique, with the collaboration of her brother Oum Manorine, and her mother, Madame Pomme, was implicated in every corrupt practice, including the selling of government positions:

> Instead of seeking means to halt this development, the Prince's entourage, directing the State in his name, was in favour of corruption, offered lucrative positions to the highest bidders ... the position of Director of Customs was priced at a million riels to be paid monthly, clandestinely and in the sewers of Chamcar Mon, to the Goddess of the South ... . This practice became so usual and so frequent that even the man in the street knew by heart the adage:

'Everything goes to Chamcar Mon, and everything comes from Chamcar Mon'.[57]

The name 'Goddess of the South' associated Princess Monique with Vietnam, Cambodia's aggressor. Female power, therefore, became connected with corruption, social ills, and the loss of Cambodian sovereignty to 'hereditary enemies'. She was even accused of supplying the Viet Cong.[58]

Princess Monique was also held responsible for Prince Sihanouk's strained relationship with his mother, Queen Kossamak. Sihanouk's reluctance to allow his mother to become Head of State in 1960 was explained by some members of the Khmer Republic literati as due to his being 'blinded by his passion for his wife Monique'. Queen Kossamak made no secret of the fact that she disliked Princess Monique, however, and any strain between mother and son could have resulted from his irritation with anyone who showed their disapproval toward his behaviour. Some have suggested that Queen Kossamak also exercised the prerogative of the elite in making appointments to civil service positions and investment in enterprises that were less than transparent.[59] Neither woman fared well under the Khmer Republic; Queen Kossamak was placed under virtual house arrest in one wing of Khemarin Palace in order to prevent her involvement in a royalist uprising against the new government. Princess Monique was burned in effigy in public condemnation of her alleged involvement in corruption.[60] The message was clear: Women had to be constrained from wielding too much power. If they overstepped these boundaries, society would suffer. Yet this did not prevent the Khmer Republic from mobilising hundreds of thousands of women into action in the civil war.

Fine lines: Mobilisation and morality

The image of Cambodia as a peaceful, idyllic island in a sea of regional conflict in the 1960s hid the existence of a resistance movement that increased in membership as the decade wore on. After independence in 1954, communists were able to participate as leftist activists in the political life of the country, although they continued to operate as a clandestine organisation. The Samlaut uprising of 1967 prompted the government to target officials whose sympathies lay with the far left. Those purged joined an increasing number of Cambodians, disillusioned with the limited employment opportunities and corruption of mainstream society, who took to the *maquis*. The following year guerrilla warfare broke out. In 1970 the communist resistance joined the *Front uni national du Kampuchea* (FUNK), led by the ousted Prince Sihanouk. The participation of the one politician whom every Cambodian could identify, and who continued to be perceived as a semi-divine being in the countryside, guaranteed the co-operation of much of the rural population. By 1973 the revolutionaries held most of the country with the exception of Phnom Penh, some provincial capitals, and most of Battambang province. Refugees, escaping the encroachment of communist power and the bombing campaigns of the Vietnam War, flocked to the cities, overloading an infrastructure already compromised by increased corruption and reduced American aid. The mobilisation of young Cambodians occurred on all sides of the political landscape, and in some ways resulted in the highest level of gender egalitarianism the country had ever seen. François Ponchaud saw the militarisation of women during this period as a natural consequence of the equality between men and women in Cambodian society.[61] Yet ingrained attitudes as to the correct place of women endured. There was a distinct sense that the mobilisation of women, and the freedoms that they began to enjoy as a result, were temporary measures for both sides of the civil war.

The mobilisation of Cambodian youth had begun in the colonial period. In 1957 the *Jeunesse Socialiste Royale Khmère* (JSRK) was established to continue to channel the energies and aspirations of Cambodian young people into 'safe' areas that posed no threat to the government. The aims of the JSRK were to 'inculcate to the young the ideals of National Socialism devised by Prince Sihanouk and the Sangkum Reastr Niyum'. Students enrolled in primary and secondary schools were thereby politicised (see Fig. 8.3). Prince Sihanouk was attended by boy and girl JSRK members, one on each side, at official functions; when foreign visitors of state arrived, schoolchildren were given flags and taught to pronounce their names for days beforehand before being assembled, in a special uniform that included 'closed-in' shoes, on the footpaths to cheer the visitors into town. Members of the JSRK functioned as diplomats and exemplars of Cambodia's progressive policies, participating in regional and international youth sports and artistic competitions. Their activities and devotion to Prince Sihanouk were widely publicised. By the middle of the 1960s, however, groups of young people were collectivising in the pursuit of other objectives, such as the trashing of the offices of the rightist newspaper *Khmei Ekareach* in June 1967, and many were choosing to join the communist resistance.[62]

The government of the Khmer Republic was similarly concerned at the potentially disruptive force represented by Cambodian youth. A few days after the coup of 18 March 1970, all secondary-school students were gathered at the National Assembly, where government representatives explained why Prince Sihanouk had been deposed. The following week students were given four days of holiday so that they could return to their villages and relay the explanation to their relatives. The following month, a larger plan of mobilisation was announced that required all public servants and students, irrespective of age or gender, were to wear military uniforms. As Khmer Republic uniforms quickly outsold demand, people incorporated any combination of uniform into their daily attire, including South Vietnamese, American, and even old French uniforms. Adults

Fig. 8.3: Girls and young women in the *Jeunesse Socialiste Royale Khmère. Femmes du Cambodge*, Phnom Penh: Ministère de l'Information du Gouvernment Royal du Cambodge, 1963.

of both sexes began receiving basic paramilitary training. Students were drilled in marching, combat and weapons and were made responsible for the defence of their schools. Some proposed that 'youth colonies' be established during the school holidays so that young people could remain useful. Government publications constantly emphasised that women were willing and active participants in all mobilisation activities, including photographs of female students affixing propaganda signage to walls, being drilled in formation, and going out to the countryside to 'rally' the rural population to the Khmer Republic. On 11 April 1970, '100,000 young men and girls, representing the Life-Forces of the nation' participated in a 'March of National Concord' to symbolise the commitment of Cambodian youth to the new regime.[63]

Female mobilisation was not restricted to schoolgirls. Large numbers of women joined the armed forces and their photographs were published with captions such as 'she also participates in the defense of national territory against the Communist aggressors' and 'François Sully of *Newsweek* presents his press card to a charming Cambodian female soldier'. Cambodian women could also 'mobilise' from home, depending upon the individual's 'intellectual and physical capabilities'. The Cambodian Women's Association joined the Writer's Association and the Committee of Cambodian Patriots in Europe in an open letter asking that the temples of Angkor be spared in the bombing, for example; but its leader, Nou Neou, was also the head of the Patriotic Women's Youth Commandos.[64]

The resistance provided many Cambodian women with their first taste of public power. The anti-Republic activities of 'liberated' women were applauded by the movement:

> Just like the men, Cambodian women, yesterday and today, have contributed greatly to the struggle against foreign aggression in defense … . At the front, women take part in combat, in medical teams, in destroying communications, in voluntary work teams. Behind the lines, women play a top-level role. Numerous guerrilla units have been formed entirely of women. Women take charge of various tasks, replacing men who have left for the front; village defense, making booby-traps, agricultural production, planing, medical work, etc … . Many other such examples demonstrate the political responsibility of women in Cambodia.[65]

Some of the *mit neary*, 'female comrades', were very young. In Kompong Chhnang province Yen Savannary encountered a group of Communist soldiers that included 12-year-old girls who forced him into the jungle at gun-point. Life in the *maquis* offered girls an alternative to marriage and provided opportunities for an equal standing with men that they found hard to achieve in mainstream Cambodian society. Numbers increased after the deposition of Sihanouk in 1970. Bun Rany, wife of current Prime Minister Hun Sen, joined the *maquis* after the coup, opting for medical training. Five years later she was director of the Kroch Chhmar district hospital. Male and female recruits were trained as soldiers, cooks, and manufacturers among others. They were also put to work disseminating anti-government propaganda and promulgat-ing the equitable vision of the resistance movement, as their counterparts in the Khmer Republic were doing in the 'unliberated' zones. Interviews and publications produced by FUNK included photographs of girls putting up banners in preparation for International Labour Day, women in fields with hoes, and constant emphasis that the contribution of women was valued in the movement. The best known of the women in the resistance were Khieu Thirith and Khieu Ponnary. The former was a vice-minister in the GRUNK and with her husband, Ieng Sary, acknowledged to be the leading political authority amongst the Cambodian communist community in Hanoi in the early 1970s.[66]

The achievements of women mobilised in the cause were extolled as ex-emplars for other women to follow on both sides of the conflict. One woman, whose husband had been killed in a FUNK attack on her village, 'wiped away the tears on her cheeks with her hand and solemnly swore to avenge her hus-band. How? To become a soldier'. Her responsibilities as a mother were not forgotten, however, and luckily an 'old woman of the village took charge of her daughter'.[67] Those who died as a result of enemy fire received widespread coverage in the news. Diep Vandar, a 19-year-old from Siem Reap, was killed in a bazooka attack on the high school that she was defending on 5 June 1970. Her father was reported in *New Cambodge* as saying

> I mourn the loss of my daughter without however receiving a severe emo-tional shock. Dying on active service, she truly fulfilled her duty as a citizen, as a true patriot who sacrificed her herself for the defence of her country in grave danger. My daughter was extremely courageous.[68]

The courage of women in the resistance was also acclaimed. A FUNK propa-ganda pamphlet of 1973 told the story of a poor woman, Oeurn, who cou-rageously stood up to government agents and accused them of cowardice in not doing more to halt corruption and exploitation of the working masses. Another document told the story of four girls who had outwitted a group of armed Khmer Republic soldiers in 'Village T'.[69]

Yet despite the emphasis placed upon the participation and contribution of women, there persisted a conviction that women were mentally and physically 'weaker' than men and that equality with men was defeminising. In describing a poster used in a youth demonstration of 3 September 1970, San Sarin wrote that the female fighter 'has for a moment abandoned her natural gentleness. But she still keeps, however, her gracious features, nevertheless being also firmly resolved to oppose the aggressors'. The new emblem of general mobilisation adopted in 1971 included the image of a woman, who signified that 'even the weaker sex is mobilised'. This was echoed by the resistance. One of the revolutionary songs, *The beauty of Kampuchea,* ran as follows: 'O beautiful, beloved Kampuchea, our destiny has joined us together, uniting our forces so as not to disagree. *Even* [emphasis added] young girls get up and join in the struggle.'

Moreover, although their participation at all levels of the civil war was encouraged, women were expected to also fulfil their 'traditional' roles of nurturers and domesticity. Kate Frieson suggested that these 'traditional restrictions placed on women's activities outside the home, duties to take care of their children and parents, and a general disinterest in male-dominated political affairs' was the reason that more women did not defect to the *maquis*. Those that did were expected to conform to many of the same mores to which they had always lived, such as cooking for their work units. *Democratic Kampuchea is Moving Forward* published photographs of women with guns juxtaposed against photographs of women in the ricefields.[70] This was the same on the other side of the conflict. Thea Voss, a Dutch freelance journalist, accompanied government forces on a series of reconnaissance missions in Siem Reap, and observed that the female soldiers

> were fighting in the front line like men do, and they were very brave. Some went back with the ambulance to take care of the wounded. Many of them were students from the Lycée. When the battles were over, they put on the sarongs and started cooking.[71]

The courage of Cambodian women in the field was also attested by Yos, who at age 22 had been trained in basic combat in Battambang: 'Let me tell you, when we were waiting to be attacked, we were glad we had been handling choppers in the kitchen since we were small – we knew how to use them, the boys vomited with fear'.[72]

Many women became unwillingly 'mobilised' as the conflict intensified. On 18 March 1969, the United States began its bombing campaign to rout out Viet Cong sheltering within Cambodian borders. After three-year respite, the bombing restarted in 1973. Over the next year approximately two million refugees sought shelter in Phnom Penh and 250,000 in Battambang. Those who could afford it left the country, seeking refuge in France or the United States. Food, already in short supply due to the disruption of the civil war, became scarce and the infrastructures of the provincial and municipal capitals were stretched to their utmost. The Women's Association distributed aid to refugees in Phnom Penh and the nearby provinces. Centres offering vocational training and machinery for small business enterprises were provided by the Ministry of Community Development, assisted by private donors. One of these was the Butterflies Center, along the north side of the Boeung Kak lake. Traditional mechanisms that would usually have provided alternatives for women in dire circumstances were not available because of the disruption of the conflict. Families had fewer resources to extend to distant relatives. Some women sought refuge as *daun chi* in local wats when their husbands died.[73] Mom, originally from Prey Veng, said that when her mother's aunt's husband died in 1972, the family was placed in a quandary:

> Food was getting difficult. We already had a house full of family members whose husbands and fathers were away being soldiers or had been killed. She had no children so she had nowhere that they had to take her. So she went to the wat and asked to become a daun chi; but ten days later she came back, saying that the pagoda was not a calm place, and there was no food.[74]

It was inevitable that the conflict would impact upon urban Cambodian society in negative ways. Western journalists, diplomats and advisors and the Cambodian elite continued to enjoy the same luxuries as they had in the 1960s. Corruption reached its heights in the last years of the Khmer Republic, with Ministry of Education employees selling exam questions to students, army officers refusing to pay bills in restaurants, and the siphoning of government supplies of food and other goods, destined for the army, hospitals and refugees, disappearing into the black market. The increased wealth and prestige of the military forces led to an increased demand for sex workers, which in turn led to an apparent trend for the kidnapping and sex slavery of young women. Serey

Phal's parents 'carefully watched over us, especially me, because bad people kidnapped girls and sold them to brothels'. People in the villages were afraid that Lon Nol soldiers would kidnap their girls and take them to Phnom Penh to be sold. The unprecedented freedoms of the mobilised society afforded women more control over their lives than ever before, but this does not seem to have resulted in wholesale permissiveness toward premarital sex. The men and women who married during the early 1970s, for the most part, observed the regulations surrounding chastity as laid down in the past. Sovanna, who married her husband Sa in 1974, said that they 'followed Khmer tradition and never met privately or spoke together alone before our wedding'. The integrity of the movement, on both sides of the conflict, seemed to be directly related to the moral purity of its young women. As a concession to 'tradition', girls were not required to staff the night shifts in the youth commandos of the Khmer Republic; and in the FUNK Liberated Zones 'the morality of the troops is such that families are easily convinced to allow their young girls to join the cultural groups or production units in the countryside'.[75]

Young women enjoyed their new-found freedoms. Some seemed to see mobilisation as an opportunity to explore new fashions – especially the 'tight khaki pants' they could now legitimately wear as a symbol of their commitment to the cause – and to spend time with their friends, although this was couched in more patriotic terms in the press. Diep Vandar's father said that his daughter had approached him for permission to join the commando unit at her high school.

> I tried to restrain her but in vain. As an answer, she said to me, 'Papa, why be afraid, we must not wait for the North Vietnamese and Viet Cong to come and swallow us up. The daughters of our officers are already serving in the commando.' Finally she joined the commando and underwent military training with her friends.[76]

Henry Kamm recounted that students appeared to have no real conviction regarding the new regime. He asked two 'sweetly smiling girls' for their opinions. They told him that they hated Sihanouk. 'But a couple of weeks ago you loved him, didn't you? They agreed, and one added quickly, "But now I don't dare." "I waver between the two," said her friend. The first giggled. "But if Sihanouk comes back, I'll shout 'Bravo, Sihanouk!'"'[77]

Elite Cambodian society responded to the rapid changes with which it was faced by retreating into the 'traditional'. A survey of popular literature produced at this time reveals a preoccupation with the timeless and far-off Cambodia of legend and romance, not to mention 'traditional' models of Cambodian femininity, as opposed to the growing harshness of real life. The Buddhist Institute published *Chansons populaires* in 1970, remarking that 'although our poets exalt the enviable qualities of young girls, they do not forget to remark upon the importance of older women who, best of all, often prepare for their husband an appetising dish or a nice chew of betel'. Semi-official government magazines and the Buddhist Institute continued to publish Cambodian folktales and *cbpab*. The Women's Association also colluded in ensuring that despite their participation in the militarisation of Cambodia, women knew that their true place was in the home, having as its aim 'to acquaint women of their responsibilities as young women, mothers and citizens, to make women understand the importance of their place in the family as well as in society'.[78] Once the civil war was over, women would no longer be needed in the public realm; they should therefore be prepared to return to their natural sphere of domestic concerns and acceptance of male privilege.

∿

The policies implemented by the Cambodian governments following independence should have enhanced women's access to power. Women were entitled to the same civil and legal status as men. Policies for increased literacy and education were implemented. Yet women were impeded from exercising greater social and political power due to deeply ingrained male attitudes and 'traditional' social constructs that maintained the idea that men were superior to women. These constructs were assimilated through the non-critical study of 'traditional' Cambodian literature dating, in most cases, only from the nineteenth century, and embodied the conservative morality of elite men. For the people that led Cambodia to independence, a Cambodia free of external interference meant a return to the values that were believed to have been in place the last time Cambodia had been unfettered – in other words, during the reign of Ang Duong. Cambodian women had to remain as 'traditional' as possible so that Cambodian culture was not lost in the face of rapid modernisation. Thus women were constrained from accessing positions in the political realm, although they maintained their significance in the domestic and supernatural realms. As in other countries at war, the politicisation and militarisation of men and women on both sides of the conflict – the defense of the nation and the realisation of the revolutionary objective – went a long way towards recognising the value of gender equality and offset the (temporary) loss of 'traditional' culture. Yet women continued to be seen as the custodians of Cambodian cultural identity, and too great a deviation from models of correct Cambodian womanhood brought censure. It is very unlikely that had the Lon Nol government prevailed, Cambodian women would have rebelled against their relegation to domesticity when the war was over; but many of them never had the chance.

Notes to Chapter 8

1   Maria Mies, *Patriarchy and accumulation on a world scale: Women in the international division of labour*, London and Atlantic Highlands, New Jersey: Zed Books, 1986, p. 177.

2   *Femmes du Cambodge*, Phnom Penh: Le Ministère de l'Information du Gouvernment Royal du Cambodge, 1963, p. 5; Articles 49, 50, 85, and 92 of the 1964 Constitution, in Raoul M. Jennar, *The constitutions of Cambodia*, Bangkok: White Lotus, 1995, pp. 44, 50, 51; speech given by Prince Sihanouk on the tenth anniversary of the Constitution, 6 May 1957, National Archives of Cambodia, material of the Sangkum Reastr Niyum period (hereafter SRN), Box 340. The national congresses were biennial affairs held outside the royal palace, with Prince Sihanouk presiding, commentating, and interjecting. Later, they became a forum for the prince to defend himself and his actions and vilify his enemies.

3   Speech commemorating the tenth anniversary of the promulgation of the constitution, 6 May 1957, SRN Box 340.

4   Article 25 of the 1964 Constitution, in Jennar, *Constitutions of Cambodia*, p. 40. Milton E. Osborne, *Sihanouk: Prince of light, prince of darkness*, St. Leonards, New South Wales: Allen & Unwin, 1994, p. 116; memoirs of Prince Monireth, cited in David Chandler, *The tragedy of Cambodian history: Politics, war and revolution since 1945*, New Haven: Yale University Press, 1991, p. 115; Milton E. Osbourne, *Politics and power in Cambodia: The Sihanouk years*, Camberwell, Victoria: Longman, 1973, pp. 65–66; Kret No. 30, *Réorganisation des services du palais royal*, 31 December 1960, SRN Box 108. Sihanouk seems to have been jealous of the Queen's popularity even after stripping her of all real power. The *Cahiers du Sangkum* recorded that the January 1961 production of posters bearing the photograph of the queen was 4,000. Posters of Prince Sihanouk totalled 3,000. The following edition of the *Cahiers du Sangkum* stated that 3,000 posters of Queen Kossamak and 4,500 of Prince Sihanouk had been produced. See *Cahiers du Sangkum* 9 (Avril 1961), p. 55.

5   *New Cambodge* 5 (September 1970), p. 4; *Femmes du Cambodge*, p. 2.

6   Osbourne, *Politics and power in Cambodia*, p. 84; Osborne, *Prince of light, prince of darkness*, pp. 140–142; speech of Queen Kossamak, delivered at Khemarin Palace, 24 November 1958, SRN Box 343.

7   Chandler, *Tragedy of Cambodian history*, p. 95.

8   Ben Kiernan, *How Pol Pot came to power: A history of communism in Kampuchea, 1930–1975*, London: Verso, 1985, p. 176.

9   Kret 36/70 CE *Journal Officiel du Cambodge* [hereafter *JOC*] 7-1-70. The Sangkum government felt that the natural concerns of women would continue to revolve around the household and family, as is evident from the portfolios managed by women (Social Action, Health, National Education, and Tourism).

10   *Droit civil khmèr*, comp. Marcel Clairon, Phnom Penh: Faculté du Droit, 1959, t. 1, p. 23.

11   In 1956, Prince Sihanouk established a commission to carry out reforms to the existing 1920 civil code, itself largely based upon colonial-era customs and the *cbpab* (see Chapter 7). Articles 194–203, 804, *Droit civil khmèr*, t. 1, pp. 49, 66–67.

12   Articles 114-148, 245, *Droit civil khmèr*, t. 1, pp. 51, 58; fieldnotes, 2006.

13   Articles 74 and 138, *Droit civil khmèr*, t. 1, pp. 45–46; Chau Seng and Charles Meyer, *Le mariage cambodgien*, Phnom Penh: Université Buddhique Preah Raj Sihanouk, [1962?], p. 1.

14   Article 7 of the Cambodian Code of Commerce, cited in *Droit civil khmèr*, t. 1, p. 66.

15   Roles included, for example, Secretary in the Ministry of Foreign Affairs (*Kret 36/70 CE, JOC* 7-1-70) and Chief Doctor (*Kret 67/70, JoC* 8-1-70). See also Cambodian Genocide Database records (hereafter CGD) Y06010, Y06414, Y06016, Y06409, Y06160, Y06456 Y06440, Y06455; *Femmes du Cambodge*, pp. 27, 36.

16   When Lieng started medical school in 1969, there were four other women in her class of fifty. See Lieng's story, in *Soul survivors*, p. 94; CGBY06131, Y06042.

17   These were midwives registered by the state; there were, of course, many more who were unregistered. *Cambodian statistical yearbook 1958* data, cited in David J. Steinberg, *Cambodia: Its people – its society – its culture*, New Haven, Hraf Press, 1959, p. 248; *Cahiers du Sangkum: Revue mestrièlle des realisations du Sangkum* (Communauté Socialiste Populaire) 8 (Mars 1961), p. 44.

18   *Cahiers du Sangkum* 2 (October – Novembre – Decembre 1958), p. 40; *Cahiers du Sangkum* 8 (Mars 1961), p. 33; *Femmes du Cambodge*, pp. 8, 39; fieldnotes, 2001, 2002, 2006. For ethnographic data on school attendance see the holdings of the Buddhist Institute archives Project 4: Gender & Buddhism, 2005–2006.

19   Published works of literary criticism did appear during the 1950s and 1960s. See George Chigas, 'The emergence of twentieth century Cambodian literary institutions: the case of *Kambujasuriya*', in David Smyth (ed.), *The canon in Southeast Asian literatures: Literatures of Burma, Cambodia, Indonesia, Laos, Malaysia, the Philippines,Thailand and Vietnam*, Richmond, Surrey: Curzon, 2000, p. 144.

20   Ang Duong, *Cbpab srei*, Phnom Penh: Buddhist Institute, 1962, p. k.

21   Sakhan Samon, *Kpuon Apram Chariya Satrei* [Manual for raising good women], Phnom Penh: n.p., 1965; Aing Sokroeun, 'A comparative analysis of traditional and contemporary roles of Khmer women in the household: A case study in Leap Tong village', MA thesis, Royal University of Phnom Penh, 2004, pp. 15, 46; Luong Vichetr Vohar, *Morale aux jeunes filles*, Phnom Penh, [n.p.]; fieldnotes, 2006.

22 Some, however, saw reincarnation, not education, as their path to a better life; in the mid-1960s May Ebihara encountered an eighteen-year-old girl who had decided to participate in as many *kathin* festivals as possible that year in the hopes of improving her *karma* enough to be reborn as a rich American. May Ebihara, 'Svay, a Kmer village in Cambodia', PhD thesis, Columbia University, 1968 [Ann Arbor, Michigan: University Microfilms, 1971], p. 383.

23 S.N. Eisenstadt, 'Post-traditional societies and the continuity and reconstruction of tradition', *Daedalus* 102, 1 (Winter 1973), p. 4; Peter Poole, *Cambodia's quest for survival*, New York: American-Asian Educational Exchange, 1969, p. 21; Steinberg, *Cambodia: Its people – its society – its culture*, p. 93; Michael Vickery, *Cambodia: 1975–1982*, North Sydney, New South Wales: Allen & Unwin, 1984, pp. 19–21, 24.

24 Steinberg, *Cambodia: Its people – its society – its culture*, p. 266; San Neang, *Socheavatadar samrap broh neung srei* [Harmonious living for men and women], Phnom Penh: n.p, 1967, pp. 54, 36; Vickery, *Cambodia 1975–1982*, p. 10; Ratha, in *Soul survivors*, p. 34.

25 *Femmes du Cambodge*, p. 39.

26 This is, of course, a global phenomenon, not something peculiar to Cambodia.

27 'l'Association des femmes Cambodgiennes', *Cambodge Nouveau* 7 (November 1970), p. 52.

28 Other members were Nhok Them, Hell Sumphea, Ma Lai Khem, Thack Thuon, Ly Theam Teng, Leang Hap An, Sien Khandy, Biv Chhay Leang, and Ung Saron. *New Cambodge* 4 (August 1970), p. 53.

29 *New Cambodge* 4 (August 1970), p. 53; Kiernan, *How Pol Pot came to power*, p. 185; Communist Party of Kampuchea, 'Decisions of the Central Committee on a variety of questions', 30 March 1976, trans. Ben Kiernan, in *Pol Pot plans the future: Confidential leadership documents from Democratic Kampuchea, 1976–1977*, trans. and ed. David P. Chandler, Ben Kiernan and Chanthou Boua, New Haven, Connecticut: Yale University Southeast Asia Studies, 1988, p. 5; Chandler, *Tragedy of Cambodian history*, p. 127; Kiernan, *How Pol Pot came to power*, pp. 193, 204; Aing Sokroeun, personal communication; Aun, in *Soul survivors*, pp. 124–127. Ma Lai Khem, 'Khmer literature', *New Cambodge* 2 (June 1970), p. 70. Jacques Migozzi, 'Population, economic development, land planning in Cambodia', *New Cambodge* 2 (June 1970), pp. 45–50, at pp. 45–46; Luong Vichetr Vohar, *Morale aux jeunes filles*, Phnom Penh: Université Bouddhique Preah Sihanouk Raj, [n.d.], pp. 5–6.

30 Vickery, *Cambodia: 1975–1982*, p. 176; Haing S. Ngor, *A Cambodian odyssey*, New York: Macmillan, 1987, p. 33.

31 *Cambodge: Revue illustrée khmère*, 1 janvièr 1953, pp. 48–49.

32 Williams, *Cambodian dilemma*, pp. 97, 102; *Cahiers du Sangkum*, 6 (Janvièr 1961), pp. 18, 45; fieldnotes, 2002.

33 Fieldnotes, 2003, 2005. Milton Osborne, *Before Kampuchea: Preludes to tragedy*, Sydney: George Allen & Unwin, 1979, p. 46; Aing Sokroeun, 'A comparative analysis of traditional and contemporary roles of Khmer women in the household', p. 61; fieldnotes,

2001, 2003, 2006; Ang Chouléan, *Les êtres surnaturels dans la religion populaire khmère*, Paris: Cedorek, 1986, p. 234.

34 Steinberg, *Cambodia: Its people – its society – its culture*, p. 79; Luong Vichetr Vohar, *Morale aux jeunes filles*, pp. 8, 14; Judy L. Ledgerwood, 'Changing Khmer conceptions of gender: Women, stories, and the social order', PhD thesis, Cornell University, 1990, p. 114.

35 *Femmes du Cambodge*, p. 37.

36 San Neang, *Socheavatadar samrap broh neung srei*; Ledgerwood, 'Changing Khmer conceptions of gender', p. 26.

37 *Femmes du Cambodge*, p. 5; *Cambodge*, Phnom Penh: Le Ministre de l'Information du Gouvernment Royal du Cambodge, 1962, p. 5.

38 Grégoire Kherian, 'Instruction de la femme, condition de l'évolution et de la croissance', in *Éducation et développement dans le Sud-Est de l'Asie: Colloque tenu à Bruxelles les 19, 29, et 21 avril 1966*, Brussles: Éditions de l'Institut de Sociologie, Université Libre de Bruxelles, 1967, p. 55; loose leaf of *Cambodia Today*, p. 18, SRN Box 341.

39 Williams, *Cambodian dilemma*, p. 102.

40 Excerpt from King Sihanouk's website.

41 Prostitution probably allowed some women earn money, although perhaps the institution did not have the wide-sweeping liberalising effect that Michael Vickery claims (*Cambodia: 1975–1982*, p. 330, note 371).

42 Fieldnotes, 2005, 2006.

43 Ebihara, Svay, note 2 at p. 385; Bizot, *Le chemin de Langka*, Paris: EFEO, 1992, pp. 35–36; interviews compiled as part of the Buddhist Institute Project 4: Gender & Buddhism, 2005–2006. Transcripts are archived at the Buddhist Institute in Phnom Penh under the code BTB–DC20, BTB–DC31 and BTB–DC32.

44 Milada Kalab, 'Buddhism and emotional support for elderly people', *Journal of Cross-Cultural Gerontology* 5 (1990), pp. 12–13; Elizabeth Guthrie, 'Outside the sima', *Udaya: Journal of Khmer Studies* 2 (2001), p. 13; Hang Chan Sophea, 'Stec Gamlan and Yāy Deb: Worshipping kings and queens in Cambodia today', in John Marston and Elizabeth Guthrie (eds), *History, Buddhism and new religious movements in Cambodia*, Hawai'i: University of Hawai'i Press, 2004, pp. 113–126. Ang Chouléan, *Les êtres surnaturels*, pp. 134, 219. See Ian Harris, *Cambodian Buddhisim: History and practice*, Honolulu: University of Hawai'i Press, 2005, p. 57.

45 Ang Chouléan, *Les êtres surnaturels*, pp. 150, 162–163; Vickery, *Cambodia 1975–1982*, p. 4; François Bizot, 'La grotte de la naissance', *BEFEO* 67 (1980), pp. 221–273; fieldnotes, 2005, 2006.

46 Ang Chouléan, *Les êtres surnaturels*, pp. 40–41, 222; Guthrie, 'Outside the sima', p. 13; fieldnotes 2001, 2005; Harris, *Cambodian Buddhism*, note 72, page 282; Osborne, *Before Kampuchea*, pp. 46–47; Osborne, *Prince of light, prince of darkness*, p. 70.

47 Articles 2, 10 and 25 of the 1972 Constitution, in Jennar, *Constitutions of Cambodia*, pp. 59–60, 62.*New Cambodge* 3 (July 1970), p. 4; 'l'Association des femmes Cambodgiennes',

Cambodge Nouveau 7 (November 1970), pp. 52–55; *New Cambodge*, 1 (May 1970), p. 2; *New Cambodge* 17 (Jan–Feb 1972), p. 3; Justin J. Corfield, *Khmers stand up! A history of the Cambodian government 1970–1975*, Clayton, Victoria: Monash Papers on Southeast Asia No. 32, 1994, pp. 132, 175.*New Cambodge* 4 (August 1970), p. 15.

48 *New Cambodge*, 1 (May 1970), p. 9.

49 *New Cambodge* 28 (February 1973), p. 29.

50 American intelligence did not believe that Nou Neou had been entrusted with such a mission, claiming that she was an unimportant political figure with a lively imagination. Corfield, *Khmers stand up!*, p. 190.

51 Nuon Khoeun, 'She has survived', *New Cambodge* 3 (July 1970), p. 40; Geoffrey Coyne, 'Schools in crisis: Phnom Penh high schools and their reaction to the war in Cambodia, March-December 1970', *Malaysian Journal of Education* 9, 2 (1972), p. 140. *New Cambodge* 3 (July 1970), p. 15; Henry Kamm, *Cambodia: Report from a stricken land*, New York: Arcade Publications, 1998, pp. 85–86; *New Cambodge* 6 (October 1970), p. 28; Chhang Song, 'The rape of Cambodia: A chat with Henry Kamm of the *New York Times*', *New Cambodge* 10 (February 1971), pp. 9–21; .*New Cambodge* 13 (August 1971), p. 26. This is not a typical description of *Neang Kangrey*, who was a *yaks* from the underworld; perhaps the author confused *Neang Kangrey* with *Neang Kaki*. Then again, *Neang Kangrey* led her forces on an expedition to reclaim her husband, so the name may not be entirely inapposite.

52 'The kings and us', *New Cambodge* 4 (August 1970), pp. 38–41, at pp. 40–41.

53 Monique Izzi was the daughter of a Frenchman and the stepdaughter of an Italian.

54 See for example Soth Polin, *L'Anarchiste*, Paris: La Table Ronde, 1980; Ros Chantrabot, *La République khmère (1970–1975)*, Paris: L'Harmattan, 1993, p. 13; Eng Hun, 'Norodom Sihanouk and the national economy: A catastrophic balance', *New Cambodge*, 1 (May 1970), p. 49.

55 Sihanouk was fond of female company and his numerous liaisons resulted in a large number of potential claimants to the throne. Prince Sihanouk's first wife was *neak m'neang* Phat Kanhol, mother of Princess Norodom Bopha Devi and Prince Norodom Ranariddh. They divorced and Phat Kanhol married again. Prince Sihanouk also married Princess Sisowath Monivong Pongsanmoni, mother of Prince Norodom Yuvaneath, Prince Norodom Ravivong, Prince Norodom Chakrapong, Princess Norodom Soriya Roeunsey, Princess Kantha Bopha, Prince Norodom Khemanourak, and Princess Botum Bopha. Princess Pongsanmoni also remarried. Princess Thavet Norleak, who had divorced her husband, Prince Norodom Vakrivan, in order to join then King Sihanouk's household in 1946, was officially married to him on 4 March 1955; she left him the next day, when he married Monique Izzi. The fourth wife, Princess Sisowath Monikessan, had one child with Prince Sihanouk, Prince Norodom Naradipo, and died giving birth to another. Prince Sihanouk had two daughters with his Lao wife, Mam Monivann, Princess Norodom Suchata and Princess Arun Rasmei. See Justin Corfield, *The royal family of Cambodia*, Melbourne: Khmer Language & Culture Centre, 1993, pp. 99–100, 102–106.

56 Op Kim Ang, 'The state casino in Phnom Penh', *New Cambodge* 2, (June 1970), p. 35; Prom Thos, 'Margain's affair', *New Cambodge* 2 (June 1970), pp. 36–37.

57 Phouk Chhay, 'The social and economic heritage of the old regime', *New Cambodge*, 1 (May 1970), p. 52.

58 San Sarin, 'For Victory', *New Cambodge* 5 (September 1970), p. 68.

59 Chandler, *Tragedy of Cambodian history*, pp. 116, 146; Osborne, *Prince of light, prince of darkness*, pp. 69–70; Osbourne, *Politics and power in Cambodia*, p. 84; Osborne, *Before Kampuchea*, p. 20; Williams, *Cambodian dilemma*, pp. 68–69.

60 *New Cambodge* 5 (September 1970), p. 4; *New Cambodge* 6 (October 1970), p. 31.

61 François Ponchaud, 'Social change in the vortex of revolution', in *Cambodia 1975–1978: Rendezvous with death*, ed. Karl D. Jackson, Princeton, New Jersey: Princeton University Press, 1989, pp. 151–177, at p 163.

62 *Cambodge*, p. 67; Williams, *Cambodian dilemma*, p. 22; Someth May, *Cambodian witness*, London; Boston: Faber and Faber, 1986, p. 87; Osbourne, *Politics and power in Cambodia*, p. 71; *Cahiers du Sangkum*, 5 (mai – decembre 1959), p. 19; Ben Kiernan, *The Samlaut rebellion and its aftermath, 1967–70: The origins of Cambodia's liberation movement*, Part 2, Clayton, Victoria: Monash University Centre of Southeast Asian Studies Working Paper 5, [1975], p. 1.

63 Coyne, 'Schools in crisis', p. 138; Osbourne, *Politics and power in Cambodia*, pp. 9, 61; David Chandler, 'Changing Cambodia', *Current History* 59, 352 (1970), pp. 333–338 at p. 337; Coyne, 'Schools in crisis', p. 138; Nuon Khoeun, 'She has survived', *New Cambodge* 3 (July 1970), p. 40; Seua Tiansath, 'Battambang: Granary of Cambodia', *New Cambodge* 5 (September 1970), pp. 76–77; San Sarathsy, 'The activity of our Youth' *New Cambodge* 13 (August 1971), pp. 35–41; *New Cambodge*, 1 (May 1970), pp. 22–25, 34; *New Cambodge* 6 (October 1970), p. 50; *New Cambodge* 29 (March 1973), p. 38; *New Cambodge* 27 (December 1973), p. 32; *New Cambodge*, 1 (May 1970), p. 11.

64 *New Cambodge* 4 (August 1970), pp. 23, 48; *New Cambodge* 11 (June 1971), p. 38; *New Cambodge* 3 (July 1970), p. 27; *New Cambodge*, 1 (May 1970), p. 27.

65 'Cambodian women in the revolutionary war for the people's national liberation (1973)', *Cambodian Genocide Program Resources*, www.yale.edu/cgp/kwomen.html, retrieved 24 June 2003.

66 John Barron and Anthony Paul, *Peace with horror: The untold story of communist genocide in Cambodia*, London: Hodder and Stoughton, 1977, pp. 55, 126; Harish C. Mehta and Julie B. Mehta, *Hun Sen: Strongman of Cambodia*, Singapore: Graham Brash, 1999, p. 29; David Chandler, *Voices from S–21: Terror and history in Pol Pot's secret prison*, St Leonards, New South Wales: 2000, p. 33; Ponchaud, 'Social change in the vortex of revolution', p. 163; Vickery, *Cambodia: 1975–1982*, p. 100; Kiernan, *How Pol Pot came to power*, pp. 321, 359, 371; *La classe ouvrière et les travailleurs du Kampuchea dans la guerre révolutionaire de liberation nationale et populaire*, distributed by the Gouvernement Royal d'Union Nationale (GRUNK) in 1973, p. 23; *Cambodge: Textes et documents*, [Cambodia?]: Mouvement national de soutien aux peuples d'Indochine, février 1973;

Ieng Sary, *Cambodge 1972*, booklet distributed by GRUNK in 1972 in *Cambodge: Textes et documents*, [Cambodia?]: Mouvement national de soutien aux peuples d'Indochine, février 1973.

67   Bonghom Devi, 'A prison with invisible walls', *New Cambodge* 13 (August 1971), pp. 32–33.

68   Seau Tiansath, 'The defence of the Lycée at Siem Reap by the school battalion', *New Cambodge* 3 (July 1970), p. 35.

69   *La classe ouvrière et les travailleurs du Kampuchea dans la guerre révolutionaire de liberation nationale et populaire*, p. 53; 'Cambodian women in the revolutionary war for the people's national liberation (1973)', *Cambodian Genocide Program Resources*, www.yale.edu/cgp/kwomen.html, retrieved 24 June 2003.

70   San Sarin, 'For Victory', *New Cambodge* 5 (September 1970), p. 67. *New Cambodge* 11 (June 1971), p. 38; translation of *The beauty of Kampuchea*, one of 'Six revolutionary songs', in Ben Kiernan and Chanthou Boua (eds), *Peasants and politics in Kampuchea, 1942–1981*, London: Zed Press; New York: M.E. Sharpe, 1982, p. 327; Kate G. Frieson, The impact of revolution on Cambodian peasants, 1970–1975, PhD thesis, Monash University, 1991, p. 42; *Democratic Kampuchea is moving forward*, [Cambodia?], [n.p.], August 1977, p. 11.

71   *New Cambodge* 4 (August 1970), p. 50.

72   Fieldnotes, 2006.

73   Chandler, *Tragedy of Cambodian history*, pp. 184, 207, 230, 235; Chandler, 'Changing Cambodia', p. 338, note 19; *New Cambodge* 12 (July 1971), p. 20; *New Cambodge* 25 (October 1973), 12; *New Cambodge* 29 (March 1973), pp. 24–27; Sovanna, in *Soul survivors*, p. 180; Chantrabot, *La République khmère (1970–1975)*, p. 98; interviews compiled as part of the Buddhist Institute Project 4: Gender & Buddhism, 2005–2006.

74   Fieldnotes, 2005.

75   Walter J. Burgess, 'The role of the foreign media in Cambodia 1970-75', in *Khmer studies: Knowledge of the past, and its contributions to the rehabilitation and reconstruction of Cambodia*, proceedings of the International Conference on Khmer Studies, Phnom Penh, 26–30 August 1996, ed. Sorn Samnang, Phnom Penh: Toyota Foundation, French Embassy, British Embassy, 1998, vol. 2, p. 941; Chantrabot, *La République khmère*, p. 93; Osbourne, *Politics and power in Cambodia*, p. 89; Chantrabot, *La République khmère*, pp. 101–105, 107; Vickery, *Cambodia: 1975–1982*, p. 25; Serey Phal, in *Soul survivors*, pp. 138–139; Vickery, *Cambodia: 1975–1982*, p. 177, and *Kampuchea: Politics, economics and society*, London: Frances Pinter; Boulder, Colorado: Lynne Rienner Publishers, 1986, p. 57; Sovanna, in *Soul survivors*, p. 180; fieldnotes, 2003, 2005, 2006; Coyne, 'Schools in crisis', p. 139.

76   Seau Tiansath, 'The defence of the Lycée at Siem Reap by the school battalion', *New Cambodge* 3 (July 1970), p. 35.

77   Kamm, *Report from a stricken land*, p. 51

78 The first three traditional Cambodian stories in the English-language publications series of the Buddhist Institute were about women: *Neang Kangrey, Neang Roumsey Sok*, and *Neang Kaki*. See advertisement in *New Cambodge* 4 (August 1970), p. 71; l'Association des femmes Cambodgiennes', *Cambodge Nouveau* 7 (November 1970), pp. 52–55; *Chansons populaires*, Phnom Penh: Institut Bouddhique, 1970, p. 4; 'Une femme cupide', trans. Tvear (René LaPorte), *Realités Cambodgiennes* 719 (October 1970), p. 27.

CHAPTER NINE

Into the fields

O n 17 April 1975, a new era unfolded with the fall of Phnom Penh to the Khmer Rouge. The policies of Democratic Kampuchea endorsed gender equality, both in official instruments and in the codes of conduct laid down by 'Angkar', the organisation comprising the Khmer Rouge leadership. Women were mobilised into public works, agriculture, and military activities wherein they could technically attain high positions. Yet political power remained the perquisite of those connected to men. The legacy of earlier periods was still apparent in the attitudes of men in power. Thus, emulation of past models of elite male behaviour and therefore male privilege continued, to the detriment of women. It could be argued that rural women now had more opportunities in terms of diversification of tasks and control over others than ever before, but women who had been living middle-class or elite lives were totally bereft of choice or personal freedoms. The sufferings of women during this period are markedly different to those of men. Dysmenorrhoea, miscarriage, and death in childbirth were widespread. The punishments visited upon women often involved an element of sexual sadism or superstition surrounding 'female power'. Democratic Kampuchea was gender-equal only insofar as both men and women from non-rural backgrounds equally suffered from starvation, over-work, disease, deprivation of basic freedoms, torture, and death.

The gender-neutral state

At the outset it appeared that Democratic Kampuchea represented a new level of gender egalitarianism. Women continued to be active in the revolutionary movement throughout the final weeks of the Khmer Republic. The *mit neary* (female comrades) who participated in the liberation of Phnom Penh were witnessed administering beatings, giving orders and executing people with as much zeal as the boys and men who marched into the cities on 17 April 1975. Once the war was over, men and women were demobilised and put in charge of civilian work units or given positions within the district party administration. Many of the cadres brought in to replace the purged Eastern Zone cadres after 1977 were women. The countryside was divided into *khum*, 'districts', comprising several *phum*, 'villages', which in turn were made up of *krom*, or 'collectives', of around ten families. Several villages made a *khum*. The village was organised into work units divided according to gender, marital status, and age. Some work units, *chalat*, comprised groups of young men and women who could be dispatched over great distances to provide labour for irrigation and agricultural work, and to provide good examples of model workers to the inhabitants of the areas they visited. The leaders of these groups were entitled *me kong*, 'group mother', regardless of their gender. Some were people who had had positions of authority or some education prior to the revolution. Others earned their elevated rank through displaying skill at their allotted task; for example, Penh Lieng Aun became the *me kong* of a state weaving enterprise. Most were very young; Molyda Szymusiak recalled that the 17-year-old *me kong* in charge of her work group was replaced by one aged fifteen.[1]

Other women worked in factories. Soon after 17 April 1975, eighty Khmer Rouge men and women arrived at the textile factory where Peang Sophi worked in order to learn industrial techniques. Women worked on construction projects (such as on the railway), in state enterprises (doing sewing or weaving, for instance), and in fishing and agriculture. Yet the Vietnamese delegation invited to Cambodia by the Women's Association found the factories and other enterprises initiated by the government to be sub-standard. One factory was completely deserted, its workers having been sent *en masse* for 're-education'. A Cambodian textile worker, described as being incredibly proficient with the machines she learned to use only a few months before, was discovered to be absent with a cold when a member of the Vietnamese delegation asked for a demonstration. The 17-year-old director of a pharma-

ceutical manufacturing concern claimed that her premises produced tetracy-
cline, aspirin, and anti-diarrhoeal tablets. There were no ingredients in sight
and the mixing was carried out by hand. She explained that machinery was
not necessary as the Cambodian communists had invented a special recipe
during the civil war.[2]

It was Khmer Rouge policy to applaud the efforts of those whom they
considered model workers. Often, these were young girls. A teenage girl
named Phali from Kandal lost first her father, then her mother, leaving her to
care for her three young brothers. Her dedication to the revolution in the face
of this adversity was celebrated, even more so when her brothers died after
eating something they had foraged in the jungle. The emulation campaign
ended when Phali died of malaria. Similarly, a cadre at the district hospital
ensured that girls renowned for being hard workers received medical attention: 'These girls need to be looked after. You can let old women die, that's
not important, but these girls have been promoted. I've come to tell you that
they are now Daughters of Pol Pot, because of the exemplary work they accomplished up on the mountain.'[3]

The Constitution of Democratic Kampuchea supported gender equality,
referring to 'men and women fighters and cadres'.[4] 'Arts teams', comprising
singers, musicians, and dancers of both genders,[5] would travel from region
to region performing new material written specifically for purposes of disseminating Democratic Kampuchea values, or pre-revolutionary material
that had been suitably modified. Songs that were broadcast over the radio
while people worked in the fields or attended political education sessions
took gender equality for granted. Titles of these songs included: 'Boys and
girls flourish under the light of the revolution', 'Men and women soldiers are
stirred like boiling water to build a new country', 'Young men and women
resolve to make restitution for the blood of the people', 'The women of the
solidarity teams increase production', 'Mothers advise their children to strive
to build a new Kampuchea', 'We, the newly liberated young men and women,
resolve ourselves', 'The troops – men and women – repair train tracks', and
'We young men and women, fighters and factory workers, resolve to fight to
increase production'.[6]

Songs addressed both men and women listeners. Speeches were addressed
to 'all cadres, male and female combatants, and the people in the Zone'.[7]
Perpetuating the traditions of the colonial and both post-independence

governments, a youth association comprising young men and women, the *Yuveajun neung yuvea neary padevat* ('Revolutionary male and female youth'), was established whose members, though they lived apart, often worked together (see Fig. 9.1). Gender relations as prescribed by 'Angkar', the name under which the government of Democratic Kampuchea issued its orders, were enforced by the *me kong*. Men and women were segregated in village gatherings for political education and self-criticism sessions. Even husbands and wives were forced to live apart in some places. In fact, as John Marston has pointed out, 'instead of an emphasis on individual women and men in interaction with each other we have the image of women as a class interacting with men as a class'.[8]

Obedience and obfuscation

The purity of the young men and women of Democratic Kampuchea reflected the purity of the revolution itself. This integrity was manifested in the voluntary

Fig. 9.1: *Yuvea jun neung yuvea neary* [Revolutionary male and female youth].

sacrifice of individuality to the collective revolutionary ideal and in sexual restraint. 'Everyone was proper and well aware of the correct simplicity. Everyone lived in a happy state. They worked conscientiously and studied hard. They devoted themselves towards the service of their people, their country and the revolution. They asked nothing in exchange'.[9] Haircuts were to be uniform – a neat bob below the ears for women and short back and sides for men. Men and women were to wear loose-fitting shirts and pants or skirts. Women were to button their shirts to the neck. No jewellery was permitted. The reasoning behind the adoption of uniform hairstyles and clothing was that 'Western' influence, as identified with long hair and fashions such as flared trousers and mini-skirts, was equated with the lax morality and corruption of the Khmer Republic and Sangkum periods.[10] A radio broadcast of 14 May 1975 announced that when the revolutionary army marched into the cities

> they were very astonished at what they saw. Boys and girls were mixed up, with their strange clothes and hair styles. Customarily, we used to wear simple pants and shirts, but our youth, under the rule of the US and the Lon Nol clique, liked the opposite. Their pants were all different, and had big sleeves [flares].[11]

The loss of female identity took its toll on young women. Chea, sister of Chanrithy Him, composed a poem in which she says:

> I pity myself
> Though a virgin, I am called an old man
> In the previous society, how furious I would have been
> But now it's normal for a woman.[12]

Kunthea, fourteen in 1975, felt that the loss of her hair jeopardised her future happiness:

> The wife of the village chief asked me if I was a prostitute. I said no. She asked me why I had such long hair. I said it was the fashion. She said that there were no fashions any more, and cut my hair off to my ears with a knife. I cried for days because I thought that nobody would think I was beautiful, and I would never get married.[13]

The 'unfeminine' behaviour of the *mit neary* shocked some observers more than the summary executions. A Khmer Republic officer recalled three Khmer Rouge soldiers whom he described as 'black-clad country girls no older than seventeen, armed as heavily as their male colleagues and totally unsmiling'.

Another female cadre forced members of the defeated government army to disarm and strip off their uniforms at the Olympic market. Yet some *mit neary* appropriated western clothes and makeup from 'new' people and experimented with them.[14]

The purity of the revolution extended to intimacy. Democratic Kampuchea, as Michael Vickery commented, monitored 'much more strictly than in prewar society, the official morality of ordinary Cambodian culture'.[15] The sixth of the twelve rules for correct behaviour, according to Angkar, was 'Do not behave inappropriately towards women'.[16] People were left in no doubt as to what was meant by this: a total ban on interaction with the opposite sex. Even holding hands, according to one source, could result in death.[17] Restrictions also applied to married couples although this was subject to local variation. Someth May recounted that even married men and women were expected to live apart in many villages, men in one hut and women in another. In Phnom Penh, a set of office buildings were transformed into living quarters, with one section for men, another for mothers with infants, and one for women who had no young children. This segregation of husbands and wives is peculiar considering that the DK government had set a population target of 20 million by 1990. Peang Sophi stated, however, that this was an unrealistic expectation, as everyone was too tired by the end of the day to take any steps toward increasing the population.[18] A member of the Vietnamese delegation to Cambodia in 1977, reasonably enough, asked Khieu Thirith how women could expect to become pregnant if husbands and wives did not live together. She retorted, 'You do not understand the problem of women at all.'[19] The official rationale behind the separation of husbands and wives was that personal happiness could not be indulged as long as 'the people' suffered: there was too much work to be done in reconstructing the nation. So that the people would not be distracted, songs that spoke of romantic love were banned. Husbands and wives were forbidden to call each other by pet names; instead, the correct way was to call each other *mit p'dai* ('comrade husband') and *mit prapuan* ('comrade wife').[20]

The marriages that took place during Democratic Kampuchea have been described by some scholars as 'forced' and the relationships between men and women therein constructed as sexual violence;[21] but as others have commented, it would be hard to describe any marriage in Cambodia prior to 1975 (or, indeed, since then) as the result of individual choice by the parties involved.[22] Marriages were 'suggested' with varying degrees of force by local cadres on behalf of Angkar. Revolutionary heroes sometimes were rewarded for their efforts through marriage to a 'new' girl who took their fancy. Some areas allowed for a higher degree of personal choice than others, although at times the choice lay between marrying or working in the harshest conditions in an 'unmarried' labour brigade. Women agreed to arranged marriages in order to remain where they were, near family members, rather than have to travel in work units.[23] The important issue was that Angkar was kept appraised of every circumstance: 'If someone falls in love in Unlong Run and fails to inform *Angkar*, the penalty is death. If you talk to your fiancée's parents ahead of *Angkar*, you're killed.'[24] Once Angkar had been informed of a couple's desire to marry, they would have to wait until a certain number of couples in the village were ready to be married, then all would be married *en masse* (see Fig. 9.2).[25] Regardless of how these mass marriages deviated from usual practice, once they had taken place, men and women considered themselves legitimately married, with all the obligations that this had entailed in the past.[26]

State regulation of behaviour that in the past had been considered 'private' was perhaps the most disorienting factor of day-to-day life in Democratic Kampuchea. Discontinuation of traditional practices associated with pregnancy and childbirth, such as the 'firing' of the new mother and the burial of the placenta, were common grievances. Some women could choose whether to have their babies at home or in a hospital; others recounted that no official medical personnel were available to act as midwives, but they survived nevertheless. In the event of complications, however, there was no help to be had. Bun Rany and Hun Sen lost their first child through the ineptitude of an untrained midwife. Haing Ngor lost his wife Huoy in childbirth, whereas had there been the equipment for a caesarean section (which he could have performed himself), she would almost certainly have lived. Poet U Sam Oeur lost his twin daughters in a barbaric display of ignorant midwifery. Lack of food and the physical toll of agricultural labour resulted in dysmenorrhoea and a high rate of miscarriage. The lack of adequate medical facilities further increased the risk of maternal and neonatal mortality. So many wives in one area died that there was a special collective made up of widowers.[27]

The 'Four-Year Plan', tabled by the Standing Committee in July and August 1976, stipulated that women be allowed 'two months' rest for pregnancy and confinement' and that child-care be provided.[28] This was not implemented across the board, however, and most areas discouraged bonding between mothers and children. In 1977, all young children no longer breastfeeding were taken from their mothers and cared for permanently by female members of the Khmer Rouge. This was supposed to free the mothers for more productive work. Sokha complained of local cadres' interference when she was trying to nurse her youngest son in late 1976. She was prevented from foraging for ingredients to make medicines and when she was unwilling to take the baby to the hospital (she was afraid that he would die due to the slap-dash treatments meted out there) she was accused of not trusting Angkar.[29]

Defiance of the models of correct behaviour as outlined by Angkar was perceived as subversion. The penalty for establishing connections that could

Fig. 9.2: Mass wedding organised by 'Angkar'. Martin Stuart-Fox and Bunheang Ung, *The murderous revolution: Life and death in Pol Pot's Kampuchea*, Bangkok: Orchid Press, 1999.

225

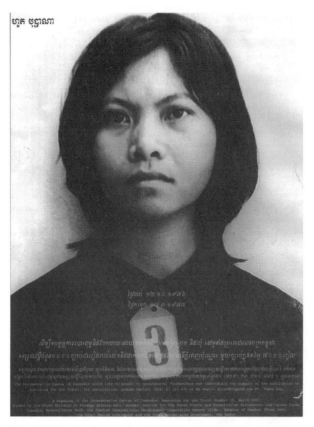

Fig. 9.3: Huot Bophana, taken before her execution. Documentation Center of Cambodia.

potentially outweigh obedience to Angkar was imprisonment with torture, hard labour, or death, depending on the area. Insubordinate members of society, therefore, could be dealt with by allegations that they had behaved with impropriety, as in the case of Siet Chhe, who was accused of incest with his own daughter.[30] It was far more usual for women to be accused of 'prostitution', however. Men Pich, executed at S-21, was arrested for suspected 'illicit liaisons'. Her 'rank' during Democratic Kampuchea was given as 'prostitute'. At Chamcar Khnor temple in Sisophon province, a truck driver saw the bodies of twenty young women, executed by a blow to the back of the head; he was told that they were suspected prostitutes. The elimination of prostitutes, as symbols of the decadence of the prewar society, was often referred to as a goal immediately after the communist victory. A cadre commented to Haing Ngor: 'Life is much better now. There is no more corruption. No more

gambling or prostitution.' If they were not killed outright, women were also
sent to provincial prisons for punishment and 're-education'. Huot Bophana
(see Fig. 9.3) was one of these. The wife of her *krom* leader began spreading
rumours that Bophana had been a prostitute during the civil war. She and her
lover, Ly Deth, with whom she had had a relationship since 1965, were caught
exchanging love letters. Bophana was imprisoned in S-21 and tortured before
being executed on 18 March 1977. In the final 'confessions' she was forced
to write, Bophana eventually broke down, writing that she had never loved
Ly Deth and that professions of affection were part of a CIA plot to corrupt
high-ranking Khmer Rouge cadres.[31]

Fig. 9.4: Chan Khem-Saroeun and infant, Tuol Sleng. Documentation Center of Cambodia.

Gendered punishment

Women sent for re-education and punishment faced a humiliating and usually fatal ordeal. Those who were not model workers, or had connections, however tenuous, to members of the Lon Nol army or the urban elite, faced harsh treatment. Moreover, if Angkar decided that someone was contaminated with pre-revolutionary ideology, it might decide that their spouse and children, including infants, had been 'infected' and eliminate them as well (see Fig. 9.4). The wife of a Lon Nol general whose true identity was revealed never spoke a word to anyone after her husband 'disappeared'. Many of the tortures devised for women in during Democratic Kampuchea were more sadistic than any account of nasal amputation or vice-squeezing from the tenth century. Haing Ngor recounted seeing a woman tied spread-eagled to a bench, covered with red ants, and the sexual mutilation of another woman, who was pregnant. The *koan kroach* custom, in which pregnant women would have their stomachs ripped open and the foetus removed, was carried out by Khmer Rouge cadres. The foetus would then be hung up to dry for some weeks before being used as a talisman against evil spirits, worn around the neck. There were special tortures for women – genitals burned with hot pokers, breasts slashed, and poisonous reptiles placed all over them. Mothers were forced to watch their children be tortured.[32]

Sexual violence assists in constructing the victim as the 'other' through intimidation and dehumanisation, after which it should theoretically be easier to kill them.[33] This was mitigated somewhat by the interdict on sexual activity of any sort. Documented cases of rape were rare in Democratic Kampuchea.[34] People were constantly told not to 'do anything improper respecting women'. Haing Ngor knew that his nurses would be safe on their way to their home villages as 'Khmer Rouge didn't rape or rob'. The brand of morality promulgated by Angkar prohibited sexual activity, even in torture. An interrogator at S-21 recorded in his notebook that 'When questioning females, there must always be two people asking the questions. Don't lie down, and don't pinch their hair or their cheeks.'[35] The penalty for transgressing this tenet was death for the cadre concerned. Even the hint of impropriety would result in an investigation.

Punishments were especially harsh for cadres and those in positions of power were warned against transgressing. The chief of Phum Andong was purged for allowing and then attempting to conceal a rape perpetrated by two of his underlings. Personnel at S-21 were arrested for the sexual mistreatment of female prisoners.[36] One woman used the strict morality of the Khmer Rouge to take revenge on unpopular cadres. Caught having sex with the vice-chairman of the locale, she claimed that she had also had had liaisons with a *cholop* ('spy') and the secretary of the local committee. The two other men were executed on her word alone; the vice-chairman and the woman herself were also killed. The 'new' people, who had suffered at the hands of all three men, regarded the woman as a heroine: 'She had had her revenge, and had struck back for all of us.'[37] Perhaps in order to protect cadres from temptation, several female interrogators were on the staff at S-21. One of these was Prak Khoeun, the wife of another member of the S-21 staff. Another was Cheng Sron, a 'group worker leader'. Ung Pech, one of the few to survive incarceration and torture at Tuol Sleng, remembered one female interrogator whom he nicknamed *a-yaks*, 'demon'. Others also existed, although some who had been imprisoned in S-21, and a guard at the prison, could not remember any women being employed in such a capacity.[38]

Widespread massacres of women occurred during the evacuation of the cities and the elimination of those whom Angkar considered to pose a threat to the establishment of Democratic Kampuchea. The wives and daughters of 200 Lon Nol soldiers were led away from their menfolk and massacred by *mit neary* outside Sisophon. In Siem Reap, 'frenzied troops' murdered over a hundred men, women and children in the civilian and military hospitals. The purge of the Eastern Zone in 1978 was particularly horrific. All cadres were called to attend a meeting, ostensibly to discuss new policies, before being seized and tied up. They were forced to dig their own graves and the women were raped before they were killed. One female cadre named Pheng, a leader of a woman's mobile work group, shouted 'Long live the Communist Party of Kampuchea' before she died. Those killed included the chiefs and party committee members of each *phum* and *khum*, the leader of the village mobile group, *cholop*, down to medical personnel from the district hospital. Soon afterwards, another massacre took place in the district, at Svay Chrum hospital, in which men, women and children were led naked to their deaths, tortured, raped, and humiliated in droves.[39]

The triumph of 'tradition'

In many ways the elitism of previous periods continued in Democratic Kampuchea, only now the 'elite' were Cambodians who had fought in the resistance or had acquiesced to the communists early in the piece – and, of course, those in the core leadership group. As kings had done in the past, the DK elite treated people as 'objects rather than subjects'.[40] Their individual lives did not matter as long as the revolutionary objective was achieved. 'Base' or 'old' people who had lived in the liberated zones before 17 April 1975 were accorded greater status than those who had been evacuated from the cities. The rural population had been won over to the communist cause by the claim that the towns were parasitic on the countryside. 'Base' people seized the opportunity to get their own back on the urban elite who had corrupted Cambodian society and engineered the deposition of Prince Sihanouk, whom many people still believed to possess the power of sovereignty despite his abdication. Thus the evacuees were usually given the hardest and most physically demanding tasks to perform, such as digging irrigation ditches and transporting tons of soil with nothing more than baskets and rudimentary tools, while the 'base' women and ex-Khmer Rouge soldiers supervised and carried out less rigorous activities. The available evidence indicates that 'base' people were entitled to more food in some areas and would exchange their surplus for luxury items. They would also accord the 'new' people special favours in exchange for additional chores.[41] Patronage thus continued, albeit in a reverse form.

Some men sought to demonstrate their new-found status through the same mechanisms that had always operated in elite society, namely establishing alliances through marriage and maintaining more than one wife, or having a sexual relationship, themselves. As Margaret Slocomb has commented, the 'sudden rise to power of poor, uneducated, and, for the most part, male adolescents of peasant stock ... resulted in an easy return to traditional interpretations of power relations'.[42] Women sometimes traded their bodies for food.[43] Ta Mok's daughters were married to ascending political and military cadres in order to expand their father's influence.[44] Disabled soldiers and war heroes were gifted with marriages to young, urban women as a reward for their efforts during the revolution: 'Just think, these guys have not had a woman in five years!' one village chief was alleged to have said. 'They paid for victory with their blood, and the weddings will be their reward.' The conversation then continued about the 'decadent city girls who had lived in luxury throughout the war' and how they deserved whatever their husbands felt like doing to them.[45] According to Henri Locard, the elite (men) in the DK apparatus 'retained all the feudal privileges of deflowering virgins'.[46] Several seem to have maintained two households of women, in separate villages, despite the official prohibition of polygamy.[47]

Women continued to be associated with nurturing, domestic roles despite their activities in the fields and factories. Even though young children were removed from their mothers and placed in the care of the state, the cadres who replaced their parents were female. Similarly, in the areas where schools operated, teachers were women. So were nurses. When women occupied ministerial positions, they were associated with issues that were thought to be appropriate for women – such as Social Action, Education, and Culture. Although Alex Hinton suggests that the estimation of a woman in terms of a *srei krup leakkhana* ('woman of virtue') was replaced by her performance of 'revolutionary zeal',[48] it appears that women had to continue to act 'traditionally'– that is, according to the *Cbpab Srei – as well as* cheerfully comply with the new social regime that removed them from any of the pleasures associated with being wives or mothers whilst preventing all but a select few from exercising any freedom of choice or authority.

There were few women in the senior leadership of Democratic Kampuchea. Those that did appear did so because of their relationship to politically powerful men. Khieu Thirith stands out as the most powerful woman in Democratic Kampuchea. In April 1976 she was appointed minister for Social Action and vice-minister for Education, Culture, and Propaganda.[49] One of her first ministerial duties was to carry out an evaluation of conditions in the Northwest Zone at the request of Pol Pot. Although she found conditions inadequate, people ill and overworked, and generally 'very queer', she took no steps to redress the situation. Instead, she concluded that 'Agents had got into our ranks' and blamed the Northwest Zone cadres for not carrying out their duties correctly.[50] Described as 'even more of a zealot than her husband', Ieng Sary, Khieu Thirith seems to have been universally regarded as someone to be reckoned with. She instigated an inquiry into the death of the third Khieu sister, Thirath, in 1977, and weathered allegations of CIA involvement that would have resulted for most Khmer Rouge cadres in being taken to S-21. She was not afraid to air her views. Annoyed at the 'slavish devotion' with which Khieu Samphan regarded Pol Pot, she allegedly told the former: 'You should talk back to him. You act like the head of his office, not like the head of state.'[51] Yun Yat, married to Son Sen, also served as Minister of Education,

Culture and Propaganda, and seems to have been as outspoken as Khieu Thirith. On the flight out of Cambodia in January 1979, she had no hesitation in interrupting and correcting Ieng Sary.[52]

Khieu Ponnary, 'Mrs Pol Pot', was allotted various posts in the government of Democratic Kampuchea that do not seem to have had much impact upon government policy, including Vice-President of the FUNK Committee for the Capital and the presidency of the Women's Association of Democratic Kampuchea. She became ill with what appears to have been either depression or dementia before 1975 and spent most of her time living apart from her husband, under the care of her sister. Although still the president of the Women's Association in name, Khieu Ponnary was not on hand to greet the Vietnamese delegation in February 1977. The explanation given was that she was unwell. One member of the Vietnamese delegation left Cambodia with the impression that the Women's Association existed in name only. Nevertheless, Khieu Ponnary was hailed as *me padevat* ('Mother of the revolution') at a party meeting in 1978.[53] It is extremely unlikely that she would have been accorded any of these honours had she not been married to Pol Pot.

Other women formed part of the party leadership at the district and provincial levels. Some *me kong* had administrative positions in the party leadership. A woman named Roeun was described as the 'right arm' of Ieng Sary. Moc Men was an executive member of the party in Region 31. The Vietnamese delegation, however, encountered no women among the provincial welcoming committees in February 1977. The women who were employed in various ministries in Phnom Penh seem to have been related to men who were also employed in the capital. Lawrence Picq, a French woman married to a Cambodian national, worked at the Ministry of Foreign Affairs. Similarly, the few women who were appointed village chiefs were older and usually married to men who were themselves locally significant. They also exercised the prerogatives of the elite of earlier periods in having more freedoms than their counterparts at lower levels of society. Women in positions of power conducted their own marriage negotiations. Hun Sen received a proposal from a woman who was 'a professor' twelve years his senior. She had been told, by Angkar, 'to marry a man with the rank of commander' and had chosen him. He had difficulty extricating himself from the proposal. Elsewhere, the daughter of a local leader attempted to seduce a handsome man so that she would become pregnant and her father would then force the man to marry her.[54] Even the strict sexual mores of Democratic Kampuchea, it seems, were not expected to apply to the new elite.

∿

Democratic Kampuchea, as was the case for the postcolonial governments preceding it, promised but did not deliver gender equality because there was no attempt to change the ingrained assumptions surrounding (male) political culture at the grassroots level. People in the countryside, for the most part, had been coopted to the revolutionary cause because compliance allowed them to live in relative safety and may have brought enhanced prestige in the area; after the revolutionary objective was realised these people constituted a new elite, but an elite nonetheless, with the privileges of rank that had always applied in Cambodian society. True, DK society reinforced the notion that men and women were capable of performing the same tasks. However, women did not comprise a strong presence at the highest levels of the Democratic Kampuchea government. Those with high office seem to have been 'allowed' to participate, awarded token portfolios that do not seem to have accomplished much, on the basis of their connection to men at the top of the regime. This is not to say that Khieu Ponnary, Khieu Thirith, and Yun Yat were not committed to the Party cause; rather, once the legitimising and mobilising power of women had been utilised in the accomplishment of the revolutionary political goal, they were expected to go back to their supporting, nurturing, domestic roles, and the rest of Cambodian womanhood was to follow.

Notes to Chapter 9

1   Tuol Sleng Prison Records [TSPR] B15412, B15370, B15897, B15368, B16026; Ben Kiernan, 'Social cohesion in revolutionary Cambodia', *Australian Outlook* 30, 3 (1976), p. 377; Ly Y, *Heaven becomes hell: A survivor's story of life under the Khmer Rouge*, New Haven: Yale University Press, 2000, pp. 15, 49; Jean Morice, *Cambodge, du sourire à l'horreur*, Paris: Éditions France-Empire, 1977, p. 291; Michael Vickery, *Cambodia: 1975–1982* [1984], Chiang Mai: Silkworm Books, 1999, pp. 102, 106, 109; Chanrithy Him, *When broken glass floats: Growing up under the Khmer Rouge – A memoir*, New York; London: W.W. Norton & Company, 2000, p. 130; Kenneth M. Quinn, 'The pattern and scope of violence', in Karl D. Jackson (ed.), *Cambodia, 1975–1978: Rendezvous with death*, Princeton, New Jersey: Princeton University Press, 1989, p. 199; John Barron and Anthony Paul, *Peace with horror: The untold story of communist genocide in Cambodia*, London: Hodder and Stoughton, 1977, p. 132; David Chandler, *The tragedy of Cambodian history: Politics,*

war and revolution since 1945, New Haven: Yale University Press, 1991, p. 259; Molyda Szymusiak, *The stones cry out*, New York: Hill and Wang, 1986, p. 174. It should be noted that the Barron and Paul text is regarded with reservation by some historians citing Cold War geopolitical bias.

2   Peang Sophi, cited in David Chandler with Ben Kiernan and Muy Hong Lim, *The early phases of liberation in northwestern Cambodia: Conversations with Peang Sophi*, Clayton, Victoria: Monash University, Centre of Southeast Asian Studies, 1976, p. 3;TSPR B15875,B15702,B15687,Y05030,Y05018,B16067,B16007,B16006,Y05018,B16040, B16030, B16025, Y05028, B15896, B15508; *Democratic Kampuchea is moving forward*, [Cambodia?], August 1977, pp. 30–33, 55; Lawrence Picq, *Au-delà du ciel: Cinq ans chez les Khmers rouges*, Paris: Éditions Bernard Barrault, 1984, p. 72; Ben Kiernan, *The Pol Pot regime: Race, power, and genocide in Cambodia under the Khmer Rouge, 1975–79*, New Haven: Yale University Press, 1996, p. 161.

3   Barron and Paul, *Peace with horror*, pp. 197–198; Szymusiak, *Stones cry out*, p. 80.

4   Article 19 of the DK Constitution, in Raoul M. Jennar (comp. and ed.), *The Cambodian constitutions, 1953–1993*, Bangkok: White Lotus, 1995, p. 87.

5   Including some who had been popular before 17 April 1975 and who were later executed in S-21 (TSPR Y06414).

6   Haing S. Ngor, *A Cambodian odyssey*, New York: Macmillan, 1987, p. 140; John Marston, 'Khmer Rouge songs', *Crossroads* 16, 1 (2002), pp. 100–127, at pp. 104, 120–122; Morice, *Cambodge, du sourire à l'horreur*, p. 380.

7   'Speech at the Opening of the Assembly', 3 June 1976, in David Chandler, Ben Kiernan and Chanthou Boua (eds), *Pol Pot plans the future: Confidential leadership documents from Democratic Kampuchea, 1976–1977*, New Haven: Yale University, 1988, p. 13.

8   Marston, 'Khmer Rouge songs', p. 109.

9   Picq, *Au delà du ciel*, pp. 54–55.

10 Peang Sophi, in Ben Kiernan and Chanthou Boua (eds), *Peasants and politics in Kampuchea, 1942–1981*, London: Zed Press; Armonk, New York: M.E. Sharpe, 1982, p. 325; Chanrithy Him, *When broken glass floats,*p. 99; Chandler, *Conversations with Peang Sophi*, p. 12; Chandler, *Tragedy of Cambodian history*, pp. 244, 259; Ben Kiernan, 'The Genocide in Cambodia, 1975-79', *Bulletin of Concerned Asian Scholars* 22, 2 (April–June 1990), p. 38.

11 Cited in Kiernan, 'Social cohesion in revolutionary Cambodia', p. 378.

12 Chanrithy Him, *When broken glass floats*, p. 232.

13 Fieldnotes, 2005.

14 Haing Ngor, *Cambodian odyssey*, pp. 133, 208; Barron and Paul, *Peace with horror*, p. 69; Kiernan, *Pol Pot regime*, p. 35.

15 Vickery, *Cambodia 1975–1982*, p. 187.

16 Morice, *Cambodge, du sourire à l'horreur*, p. 383. Peang Sophi (Chandler, *Conversations with Peang Sophi*, p. 8) did not list the directive to respect women amongst the rules of Angkar that he remembered.

17 This must have been a deeply ingrained threat; Hun Sen recounted 'somewhat defensively' in his biography that although he was often lonely as a resistance fighter in the *maquis*, 'When I say that I was popular with any girl I do not mean that I had a love affair with her.' (Harish C. Mehta and Julie B. Mehta, *Hun Sen: Strongman of Cambodia*, Singapore: Graham Brash, 1999, p. 31).

18 Someth May, *Cambodian witness*, p. 233; Picq, *Au delà du ciel*, p. 22; Chandler, *Conversations with Peang Sophi*, pp. 9–10.

19 Kiernan, *Pol Pot regime*, p. 162.

20 Picq, *Au delà du ciel*, p. 54; Marston, 'Khmer Rouge songs', p. 106; Haing Ngor, *Cambodian odyssey*, p. 221; Barron and Paul, *Peace with horror*, p. 136.

21 See for example Elizabeth Becker, *When the war was over*, New York: Simon & Schuster, 1986, p. 257.

22 See for example Patrick Heuveline and Bunnak Poch, 'Do marriages forget their past? Marital stability in post-Khmer Rouge Cambodia', *Demography* 43, 1 (February 2006), p. 110; Peg LeVine, 'A contextual study into marriages under the Khmer Rouge: The ritual revolution', PhD thesis, Monash University, 2006, p. 11.

23 Vickery, *Cambodia: 1975–1982*, p. 187; Chanrithy Him, *When broken glass floats*, p. 243; Martin Stuart-Fox and Bunheang Ung, *The murderous revolution: Life and death in Pol Pot's Kampuchea*, Bangkok: Orchid Press, 1999, p. 104; François Ponchaud, 'Social change in the vortex of revolution', in *Cambodia 1975–1978: Rendezvous with death*, pp. 166–167; Thoun Cheng, in *Peasants and politics in Kampuchea*, p. 292; Heuveline and Bunnak, 'Do marriages forget their past?', p. 109.

24 Barron and Paul, *Peace with horror*, p. 200.

25 Stuart-Fox and Ung, *Murderous revolution*, p. 102; Morrice, *Cambodge, du sourire à l'horreur*, p. 393; Mehta and Mehta, *Hun Sen*, p. 38; fieldnotes, 2001, 2004, 2005.

26 Peg LeVine found that over 80 per cent of respondents thought that their DK-era marriages were legitimate arrangements ('A contextual study into marriages under the Khmer Rouge', p. 10). However, some women no doubt took advantage of the general atmosphere of paranoia and suspicion and invented false backgrounds for their husbands in the hope that they would be killed, leaving them free to take another husband (Judy Ledgerwood, 'Changing Khmer conceptions of gender: Women, stories, and the social order', PhD thesis, Cornell University, 1990, pp. 201–202).

27 Someth May, *Cambodian witness*, pp. 132, 155, 176; Tae Hui Lang, in *Peasants and politics in Kampuchea*, p. 360; Mehta and Mehta, *Hun Sen*, p. 40; U Sam Oeur, 'The Loss of My Twins', in Thomas Beller, 'A reluctant prophet', *Cambodia Daily*, Saturday and Sunday, April 28–29, 2001, p. 12; Haing Ngor, *Cambodian odyssey*, p. 293; Chanrithy Him, *When broken glass floats*, p. 174; Chandler, *Tragedy of Cambodian history*, p. 278; Ledgerwood, Changing Khmer conceptions of gender, p. 202; Ida Simon-Barouh, *Le Cambodge des Khmers Rouges: Chronique de la vie quotidienne, recit de Yi Tan Kim Pho*, Paris: L'Harmattan, 1990, p. 117; Maureen H. Fitzgerald, et al., *Hear our voices: Trauma, birthing and mental*

health among Cambodian women, Paramatta, New South Wales: Transcultural Mental Health Centre, 1998, p. 44.

28 'The Party's Four-Year Plan to Build Socialism in All Fields', in *Pol Pot plans the future*, p. 112.

29 Sat, in *Peasants and politics in Kampuchea*, p. 335; fieldnotes, 2005.

30 Vickery, *Cambodia: 1975–1982*, p. 9; Ponchaud, 'Social change in the vortex of revolution', p. 167; memorandum of Siet Chhe (alias Tum), 5 June 1977, in David Chandler, *Voices from S-21: Terror and history in Pol Pot's secret prison*, St Leonards, New South Wales: Allen & Unwin, 2000, pp. 158–159.

31 TSPR B16134, Y06455; Barron and Paul, *Peace with horror*, p. 77; Haing Ngor, *Cambodian odyssey*, p. 199, 244; Becker, *When the war was over*, p. 225.

32 Chandler, *Tragedy of Cambodian history*, p. 254; Simon-Barouh, *Le Cambodge des Khmers Rouges*, p. 49; Becker, *When the war was over*, p. 235; Haing Ngor, *Cambodian odyssey*, pp. 223, 245–246; fieldnotes, 2004, 2005. Of the six people I interviewed who recounted incidences such as these, only one actually witnessed the event; the others had heard about it from others. They were, however, adamant that these events had occurred.

33 Christoph Schiessl, 'An element of genocide: Rape, total war, and international law in the twentieth century', *Journal of Genocide Research* 4, 2 (2002), p. 208.

34 Ledgerwood, 'Changing Khmer conceptions of gender'. As Ledgerwood states, however, the prevalence of rape is difficult to determine given the shame attached to rape in Cambodian society, in which the woman is always perceived as at fault.

35 Haing Ngor, *Cambodian odyssey*, pp. 113, 124; Chandler, *Voices from S-21*, p. 131.

36 Stuart-Fox and Ung, *Murderous revolution*, p. 129; Chandler, *Voices from S-21*, p. 131; Vickery, *Cambodia: 1975–1982*, p. 151.

37 Pin Yathay, *Stay alive, my son*, pp. 172-173.

38 TSPR B15847; Chandler, *Voices from S-21*, p. 26; Vickery, *Cambodia: 1975–1982*, p. 97.

39 Barron and Paul, *Peace with horror*, pp. 37, 85; Fitzgerald *et al.*, *Hear our voices*, p. 43; Stuart-Fox and Ung, *Murderous revolution*, pp. 139, 142.

40 David Chandler, 'A revolution in full spate: Communist party policy in Demo-cratic Kampuchea, December 1976' [1987], in *Facing the Cambodian past*, p. 265.

41 Barron and Paul, *Peace with horror*, pp. 93–94, 154; Becker, *When the war was over*, p. 228; fieldnotes, 2005.

42 Margaret Slocomb, *The People's Republic of Kampuchea, 1979–1989: The revolution after Pol Pot*, Chiang Mai: Silkworm Books, 2003, p. 256.

43 Kate Frieson, *In the shadows; Women, power and politics in Cambodia*, Victoria, British Columbia: University of Victoria Centre for Asia-Pacific Initiatives Occasional Paper 26, 2001, p. 11.

44 Vickery, *Cambodia: 1975–1982*, p. 99.

45 Barron and Paul, *Peace with horror,* p. 96.

46 Henri Locard, *Pol Pot's Little Red Book: The sayings of Angkar,* Chiang Mai: Silkworm Books, 2004, p. 257.

47 Article 13 of the DK Constitution, in Jennar, *Cambodian constitutions,* p. 86; fieldnotes, 2003, 2005.

48 Alexander Laban Hinton, *Why did they kill? Cambodia in the shadow of genocide,* Berkeley; Los Angeles; London: University of California Press, 2005, p. 193.

49 Becker, *When the war was over,* p. 247; Chandler, *Brother number one,* p. 113; Craig Etcheson, *The Rise and demise of Democratic Kampuchea,* Boulder, Colorado: Westview Press; London: Frances Pinter, 1984, pp. 166–167.

50 Becker, *When the war was over,* p. 247.

51 Barron and Paul, *Peace with horror,* p. 44; Chandler, *Voices from S-21,* p. 93; Kamm, *Cambodia: Report from a stricken land,* p. 139.

52 Chandler, *Brother number one,* p. 113; Kamm, *Cambodia: Report from a stricken land,* p. 155.

53 Etcheson, *Rise and demise of Democratic Kampuchea,* pp. 166–167; Vickery, *Cambodia: 1975–1982* [1984 version], p. 145; Chandler, *Brother number one,* pp. 137, 172; Kiernan, *Pol Pot regime,* pp. 160, 162. She was hospitalised with a nervous complaint in Beijing in the early 1980s and in 1987 she is purported to have given Pol Pot permission to take another wife, with whom he had a daughter.

54 TSPR-Y05199, B16191, Y05035; Picq, *Au delà du ciel,* pp. 31, 73; Ly Y, *Heaven becomes hell,* p. 151; Kiernan, *Pol Pot regime,* p. 161; Barron and Paul, *Peace with horror,* p. 103; Ledgerwood, Changing Khmer conceptions of gender, p. 194; Mehta and Mehta, *Hun Sen,* p. 36.

CHAPTER TEN

Picking Up the Pieces

*V*ietnamese forces entered Cambodia on 25 December 1978 with members of the National United Front for the Salvation of Kampuchea, their joint purpose to overthrow Democratic Kampuchea. The Khmer Rouge forces were no match for the comprehensively trained and equipped Vietnamese; moreover, the civilian population made no attempt to prevent the takeover. On 7 January 1979 Phnom Penh fell and the Khmer Rouge leadership fled to the most remote provinces, where it continued to wage war for over a decade. The Kampuchean People's Revolutionary Council was officially proclaimed, composed of Cambodians who had been in exile in Vietnam, some since the 1950s, others having defected from Democratic Kampuchea. The country was renamed the People's Republic of Kampuchea (PRK). The Vietnamese remained intimately connected with post-revolutionary Cambodia until September 1989, when the last Vietnamese forces withdrew from Cambodian territory. The same year, the country changed its name to the State of Cambodia. Democratic elections, monitored by the United Nations, were held on 23 May 1993. No women feature in the 'who's who' of post-revolutionary Cambodia as established by political scientists.[1] Yet the role that women played in the reconstruction of Cambodia and Cambodian society cannot be overemphasised. This contribution, and the particular burdens faced by women in the 1980s and early 1990s, was diminished

Fig. 10.1: Villagers, Kompong Speu, 1989.

by the return of Cambodians from refugee camps and from overseas who had conflicting notions as to what constituted appropriate space and agency for women. Constructs of 'traditional' Cambodia were resurrected, but once again, the tradition invoked was sourced from the conservative literature such as the Cbpap Srei; once again, women were co-opted into the symbolism of the purity and unassailability of Cambodian culture.

The People's Republic of Kampuchea, January 1979–April 1989

Cambodians who had managed to escape death through starvation, illness, or the purges of an increasingly paranoid and brutal regime faced the reconstruction of their country. Tragically, those who were most necessary in this process – that is, people who had received some education and experienced members of pre-revolutionary public and private sectors – had been targeted for execution and ill-treatment between 1975 and 1979. More than a million people died during those years – some estimates put the number as high as three million – and hundreds of thousands more had fled. Over half, and perhaps as many as 65 per cent of the survivors were women (see Fig. 10.1). Reconstruction was carried out with the direct involvement of the Vietnamese, an involvement that some have chosen to call an occupation. Each Cambodian minister was shadowed by a Vietnamese counterpart; government documents had to be approved by the Vietnamese before promulgation. 180,000 Vietnamese soldiers ensured the protection of Cambodia between 1979 and 1989, although they sometimes compromised the personal safety of Cambodian women in so doing.[2]

One of the first state initiatives implemented by the PRK government was the creation of *krom samaki bongko bongkoeun phol*, 'production solidarity groups' or 'co-operatives', at the commune and village level. Each *krom samaki*, comprising between five and twenty families, was allocated an equal amount of good and bad land for cultivation, owned in common.[3] Equipment and animals were owned by individuals, according to their means, but other members of the same *krom samaki* were entitled to their use. In return, owners received an extra portion of the harvest. Women participated in leadership roles in the *krom samaki*, although some have commented that this probably reflected the high ratio of female to male survivors. According to the Secretariat of State for Women's Affairs, one of the main purposes of the *krom*

Fig. 10.2: Rural women selling food by the roadside, Kompong Speu, 1989.

samaki system was to enable widows, and other women without 'manpower' and means of agricultural production, to support themselves.[4]

The fact that the majority of able-bodied survivors of the Democratic Kampuchea regime were women meant that responsibility for providing for the family fell on their shoulders. In 1986, a survey revealed that women headed a quarter of all households in Phnom Penh and that 91 per cent of these were widows. Faced with having to support their families with no help from an extended family, women eked out a living through a range of activities. Some sold fried bananas from baskets in the streets or set up food stalls selling rice porridge and noodles on the pavements. Some 85 per cent of market vendors were women, selling fruit, vegetables, fish or groceries. The profits from these enterprises were small or non-existent. Many women would have preferred to undertake other work but were not given any opportunity to do so. Others wanted to expanded their businesses, but were unable to obtain any capital for expansion, though some did borrow money to establish restaurants. In addition to vending and market enterprises, women were employed in the industrial sector. According to data presented at the Women's Congress in 1988, women constituted 65 per cent of textile workers, 70 per cent of salt factory employees and 50 per cent of those engaged in rubber production.[5]

Rural women were more directly involved in the physical reconstruction of Cambodia. Although men and women had both participated in the physically demanding agricultural work of rural communities, men had assumed the most laborious of tasks such as ploughing and irrigation. Many women were now required to shoulder these tasks. Loung Ung's sister Chou took cooking, fishing, cleaning, tending to the young children of the family, nursing, and chopping wood in her stride and still attempted to go to school when the opportunity offered. When the cycle of harvesting permitted, rural women would travel to provincial capitals or Phnom Penh in search of other work or bring 'luxury' goods home for re-sale. Older women, precluded from physically taxing work, ran roadside food stalls (see Fig. 10.2). Large numbers of rural women were engaged in military activities, some in direct combat, but most in logistical support. Women transported supplies of food, arms and ammunition and made uniforms. The PRK's appreciation of women's contribution was expressed in the following slogan: 'Her fingers move from morning until night … and the fact that their husbands become cadres is due to their wives' contributions to the cause of the nation.'[6]

The post-revolutionary government installed in January 1979 searched survivors camping outside Phnom Penh for educated and experienced people whom they could employ in the civil service and vocational professions. Reflecting the urgency with which the process of rehabilitation was regarded, people with hardly any formal education were sent on training courses lasting from one month to one year in duration, and sent to the provinces for 'fieldwork'. The School of Pedagogy offered a one-month training course before dispatching graduates to schools. Some of the training conducted by government officials was by women such as Chhouk Chhim, vice-president of the Women's Association, who lectured on 'Qualities of a cadre trained in the mores of a revolutionary'. Women were enthusiastic about their contribution to national reconstruction through these training programmes. A nursing student finishing her course in 1981 said: 'When we finish the course we shall serve the people well – and just as competently as the men do!' Graduates of civil service courses worked in municipal offices in a variety of capacities, including legal advisory and clerical work.[7]

Official state initiatives and policies of the PRK espoused gender equality. The constitution of the People's Republic of Kampuchea, based on that of Vietnam and adopted on 27 June 1981, endorsed 'equal rights in marriage' for men and women, 'measures to alleviate the burden of housewives and ensure them the conditions necessary to participate like men in social activities', equality in law, universal suffrage, and equal pay. Article 27 provided for the particular needs of women:

> The State cares for mothers and children. The State and society organise maternity hospitals, crêches and kindergartens … . Working women or women employed by the State enjoy a ninety-day maternity leave with pay. Nursing mothers enjoy a reduction of daily work hours while receiving the public welfare fixed by the State. The State shall take concrete measures concerning women working outside the State sector.

A visitor to Cambodia in 1981 recorded that female government officials were entitled to two months' paid maternity leave and access to a special maternity hospital. Some ministries organised day care for their employees' young children, as did factories. Women were employed as heads of departments in health and industry and throughout the public sector. Women themselves did not feel that they were discriminated against. One woman said, 'I think I am treated equally to my male colleague; I have enough knowledge to perform the task and so does he.'[8]

Women and men were encouraged to join associations as a means of contributing to the restructuring of the country, as directed by Article 38 of the PRK constitution: 'All citizens may join mass organizations to protect revolutionary gains and the social order, to build and defend the country and to develop national and international solidarity'. In reality, all associations were organs of the state. The Women's Association was one of the most important of these. The official date of its establishment is given as 2 December 1978, three weeks before the official liberation of Cambodia by the Vietnamese. Representatives of the Women's Association were present at central, provincial, district, commune and village level, and one woman in each *krom samaki* would also act as the representative of the Women's Association. The Women's Association maintained a presence throughout Cambodia. At times this presence put representatives at risk. In 1981, Khmer Rouge soldiers arrested a sub-district president of the Women's Association in Stung Treng. She was held captive for two months, during which time she was tortured and sexually assaulted.[9]

The Women's Association implemented programmes aimed at redressing poor literacy, improving education, and offering vocational training for women.[10] Material assistance was also provided in the form of capital for the establishment of small enterprises or in cases of severe hardship. Urban women and, to a lesser extent, rural women, received advice, informal marriage counselling, and help in emergencies. They were also 'reminded' of the correct behaviour that a model citizen should exhibit and government policies and initiatives expounded. Representatives of the Women's Association made recommendations to the Council of Ministers regarding issues of concern to women and commented on draft legislation directly impacting upon women, such as the marriage code and family planning policy.[11] The Women's Association held National Women's Congresses in 1983 and 1988, published a magazine for women from 1984 onwards, and organised yearly events to celebrate International Women's Day every 8 March.[12]

Women aged between 16 and 28 were also encouraged to join the Youth Association, described in 1981 as having 'more drive and impact that the Women's Association'. Perhaps this was due to the comparative youth and energy of its constituents. The Youth Association expounded political propa-

243

ganda; its official publication, *Yuvajun-yuvaneary Kampuchea*, provided pages of information about governmental ideology and initiatives in a 'frequently asked questions' format. The backs of the booklets were printed with inspirational songs, complete with musical score, or photographs of men and women working industriously in rice paddies. Men and women aged between 17 and 25 also served in the armed forces. Women's Livelihood Groups were established in 1980 at village level. They convened each month to discuss problems facing local women and convey matters of concern to the Women's Association for representation to government policy-makers. Women's Associations were also active in the refugee camps along the Thai-Cambodian border. Representatives, usually young women, determined entitlement to supplementary food and organised the distribution of additional goods for births, deaths and marriages. In 1985 Princess Norodom Marie Ranariddh established the Khmer Women's Association, later the Samdech Rasmi Sobhana Women's Foundation, which provided materials and training in education and health services in the refugee camps.[13]

There were some active and influential female commune leaders in rural areas. Ya Soeun, appointed acting chief of Krala commune, Kompong Cham in 1981 and then permanent chief in 1984, regularly accompanied the district militia on military offensives against Democratic Kampuchea soldiers. Thlang Yam, deputy leader of Tang Krang commune, Kompong Cham, conducted regular sorties into DK areas in order to persuade 'misled people' to defect to the PRK. After some success persuading men to integrate into the PRK – once by snatching two live grenades from the hands of a DK soldier – she recounted that she was approached by other several other women wanting to leave the DK-controlled areas. Life for women in these remote areas under control of Democratic Kampuchea was especially difficult. They assumed the preponderance of labour roles, working in the fields and transporting goods in addition to food preparation and other household work. They also retrieved food from relief trucks, in line with aid agencies' policies of distributing food to women only, and carried ammunition for the DK military forces.[14]

More women were elected to leadership positions at the municipality and provincial commune level. A study conducted in early 2000 reported that there were four women commune leaders in Phnom Penh. The Chief of Boeung Keng Kang I quarter had held the position since 1985; the Chief of the Olympic quarter had been elected in 1981, downgraded to Deputy in

1985, then appointed Chief again in 1987; and the Chief of Psar Kandal II quarter came to office in 1985 after working at a series of low-ranking authority positions since late 1979. In the 1981 commune elections, 21 out of the 24 provincial female candidates won their seats and the other three were elected deputy leaders. These elections are particularly significant, as prior to 1985 candidacy was not based on central party nominations. After the introduction of this requirement, fewer women were nominated, resulting in fewer women in leadership roles.[15]

Officially, there were no impediments to the empowerment of women in the PRK. Yet there were few women in high-profile roles. Writing in 1982, Chanthou Boua remarked: 'The accelerated short-term training has already produced numerous, surprisingly forceful and capable cadres. Among them, there are many women, but, as yet, very few occupy important positions.' Although the government espoused equal access to education for boys and girls, the latter comprised only one-third of children enrolled in the last year of primary school. The Women's Association was criticised for not doing much to change the situation of Cambodian women. An observer remarked in 1981 that the Women's Association was not addressing women's issues: 'It does not yet seem to exert much influence on vital decisions concerning women's economic and social well-being.' This included a glossing over of questions such as divorce, a phenomenon that did not fit the desired image of a functional society of happy workers. Many visitors to Cambodia in the early 1980s commented that the main activity of the Women's Association appeared to be propounding the policies and programmes of the new government rather than promulgating a developmental agenda. The accessibility of training programmes for rural women was also an area of contention. Critics of the Women's Association acknowledged, however, that its activities were constrained by the government policies and budgetary priorities.[16] As Viviane Frings has remarked, there was a 'persistent gap between theory and practice' in the PRK.[17]

They were also constrained by 'tradition'. In 1995, the Secretariat of State for Women's Affairs estimated that the average number of female parliamentary numbers until the signing of the Paris Peace Accords was 18 per cent. Only eight of the 162 full members of the Communist Party of Kampuchea (CPK) attending the Fourth Congress in May 1981 were women, and only one woman, Men San An, was appointed to the 22-member CPK Central Committee for Organisation. Three years later the Central Committee for Organisation admitted its second female member, Mean Saman. The following year saw more women in key party positions. Men San An was appointed President of the Central Committee for Organisation as well as the Central Committee for Propaganda and Education. Other women occupying key political positions included Ho Non (Deputy Council Minister), Som Kim Suor (editor of the state newspaper); and Lak On (Party Secretary, Ratanakiri province).[18]

Why was the PRK government so reluctant to do more to empower women and why were women amenable to this state of affairs? Chantou Boua has suggested that the lack of Cambodian women within the government hierarchy was the result of ingrained modesty, 'the widespread chauvinism of Khmer men', and a lack of self-esteem and self-confidence due to trauma suffered during Democratic Kampuchea. Many women had lost their husbands and faced raising their children without any emotional or financial support from the extended family typical of Cambodian kinship.[19] This identity crisis was compounded by the presence of the Vietnamese and the state-driven reconstruction of Cambodian culture to reflect a 'tradition' that included friendship toward Vietnam and omitted any references to a monarchy.[20] Many Cambodians wished for a return to the 1950s and 1960s, having forgotten the chaos hidden beneath its peaceful exterior; those in the refugee camps, politicised toward either the anti-Vietnamese Khmer People's National Liberation Front or the royalist FUNCINPEC, were more vocal about how this could be achieved politically, but all had very definite ideas about the role of women in maintaining social harmony. Thus a journey by a group of Cambodians living in diaspora to Cambodia in the late 1980s included a picture montage of women in *sampot* engaged in 'traditional' practices of dancing and weaving with the caption 'keeping the traditions alive'.[21]

Margaret Slocomb has argued that, despite the inability of the PRK to sustain socialism, 'it ended the terror and gave the people the means with which to restore their lives'.[22] For many, restoration meant a return to values perceived as 'traditional' pi doeum, 'the time before' the upheaval of the Khmer Rouge period – in other words, those espoused in *Cbpab srei*. As Judy Ledgerwood has explained, the socially acceptable Cambodian woman of these texts 'is not discussed as being "strong" or "powerful", but as "virtuous"'.[23] Although some commentators warned that Cambodian women should not be so weak as to lead to the troubles of the past, it also conflated notions of Cambodia's past glory during the Angkorian age, the family as the building block upon which social harmony rests, and the role of women in ensuring this accord through the observance of correct behaviour (see Fig. 10.3).[24] Chou, faced with the prospect of an arranged marriage in the 1980s, remembered her mother's words: 'A proper woman is neutral, doesn't gossip, never screams, complains, or throws tantrums, and blends in with the crowd. A proper woman is like warm water, not shocking like cold or burning like hot.'[25] Soeur remembered her mother telling her and her sisters that it was very important not to act like boys 'all loud and crazy', but to sit quietly, lest people not realise they were girls, or think that they were Vietnamese.[26]

This notion of correct action for women restricted their choices in the PRK period. Women who did not marry were perceived as being peculiar, as

Fig. 10.3: Cover of Meun Thalla, *Vijjea apram satrei khmei* [Manual on raising Cambodian women], Koh-I-Dang: 1981.

247

if their unmarried state resulted from their own determination to defy social conventions rather than the lack of available men. Chantou Boua recounted that a young Cambodian woman complained to a foreign aid worker, 'I wish you would bring a shipload of men instead of food!' Polygamy, despite its prohibition by Article 7 of the Constitution, became socially acceptable. In 1981, a senior (female) member of the Women's Association suggested that polygamy be legalised in order to ease the economic burden and loneliness of women. Although Chantou Boua believed that the situation in the provinces was better for women as there was 'more solidarity between women', there is evidence that some male commune leaders undermined the ability of women to act autonomously.[27] As early as 1980, a PRK document related concern over some cadres who were 'getting excited by females and materialism ... some other cadres think only of themselves, living every day to gather lovely girls to come and serve them and forgetting about their revolutionary stance'.[28] Some women overcame issues of isolation and hardship by amalgamating with other women and their children, thus creating a combined household financial and support unit. Others took the only socially sanctioned route available to women (aside from marriage) and became daun chi (Buddhist nuns).[29] Yet this was not met with approval by the government; in 1982 a memo was circulated stating that 'old women seeking the shelter of wats should be sent back home if any family exists to provide for them'.[30]

Women were therefore constrained on all fronts. A shortage of men meant that 'untraditional' characteristics had to be repressed or 'un-Khmer' women could not fulfil their 'destinies' as wives and mothers. This meant not complaining at the scarcity of women in high political office or when practices that had been the privilege of elite men in the past were resumed, such as polygamy, or the education of boys instead of girls, who, given their 'natural' association with domesticity, were kept home when circumstances dictated. Even those that retreated to the spiritual world were subject to the directives of the government. Although women did assume a more varied range of tasks and were more directly associated with the reconstruction of Cambodia than men were, particularly in rural areas, this did not translate into gender equality.

The State of Cambodia, May 1989–September 1993

In April 1989, the National Assembly of the PRK adopted a number of amendments to the constitution as part of a general policy of liberalisation.

The name of the country was changed to State of Cambodia; the flag and national anthem were altered; state policies such as the *krom samaki* were abolished; Buddhism was reinstated as the state religion; private ownership of land was introduced; price controls were instated; and many state-owned enterprises were partially or completely privatised.[31] The last Vietnamese troops withdrew in September 1989, setting the scene for political reconciliation, and leading to the signing of the Paris Peace Accords in 1991. This resulted in the mobilisation of the United Nations, first as the United Nations Advanced Mission in Cambodia (UNAMIC) and then as the United Nations Transitional Authority in Cambodia (UNTAC), consisting of over 20,000 people from all over the world.

The official statistics of women's participation in the political realm in the 1980s and early 1990s do not take into consideration the behind-the-scenes roles played by many women in brokering the agreements between the factions in exile and in Cambodia, thereby bringing about the Paris Peace Accords in 1991. Tong Siv Eng is credited by some as having been responsible for the first meetings between Norodom Sihanouk and Hun Sen in 1987 and 1988. As Evan Gottesman has pointed out, the importance of Queen Monineath (Monique) has also gone unnoticed by most observers, yet she was present at almost all of the reconciliation meetings. She was not always successful in preventing Prince Sihanouk from perpetrating a diplomatic debacle, however: 'As delegates to the month-long international conference on Cambodia, held in Paris last August [1989], stared at the speaker [who had just announced "I support genocide!"], his wife vainly tried to restrain him. "Don't breathe a word," he hissed at her'. Staff witnessed letters, telephone calls, and meetings between the Queen and members of political factions before the first recorded meetings between the latter and the King. Princess Royal Norodom Arunrasmy, the youngest surviving daughter of the King, was a member of his cabinet between 1982 and 1985.[32] Yet their presence would not have been tolerated had they not been near relations or established members of the inner circle.

The liberalisation policies implemented by the Cambodian government had significant social and economic consequences for women. In order to conform to the standard *modus operandi* of market economies, the government had to cut the number of staff employed in the public sector. Women, who staffed many of the lower- and mid-level positions of the ministries, were the

249

most affected by this. Public expenditure was reduced across the board. The Women's Association was one of the first casualties. Lack of staff and funding undermined the organisation from within and by January 1992 the government cut off all financial support. Many of its representatives, however, continued to work in development initiatives for women with local and international non-governmental organisations. Others began seeking employment in the more lucrative private or mixed sectors. Some found employment in UNTAC. Rural women were affected by the abolition of the *krom samaki* in that they lost authority and decision-making opportunities. The loss of the *krom samaki* also placed more demands upon rural households, which were still predominantly headed by women, as resources that had been shared became precluded from collective use. Another result was that farmers were compelled to sell a portion of their rice produce to the government at state prices.[33]

Only 5 per cent of the candidates put forward by over twenty political parties for the May 1993 elections were women, and only five were amongst the 120 members elected to the National Assembly. Although the percentage of women candidates on the ballot for the 1993 elections was small, women were indispensable at the grassroots political level. The contribution of non-governmental organisations in educating women about the electoral process cannot be over-emphasised. Khemara, established in 1990 by Mu Sochua (Minister for Women's and Veteran's Affairs, 1998–2003), was the first non-governmental organization dedicated to advancing women's leadership. The stability of the UNTAC era and the subsequent influx of donor funding saw the creation of many interest groups in addition to political parties. Many had women's issues as core objectives.[34]

Human rights groups in particular advocated women's rights. One group, LICHADO, was founded by Kek Galabru, who returned to Cambodia after decades in exile in France. Her mother was Tong Siv Eng, who was, as we have seen in the preceding chapter, closely connected to Prince Sihanouk. Women were enthusiastic patrons and members of these organisations, which extended their agendas to development, HIV/AIDS, and health. Although most were initially based in Phnom Penh, some maintained a presence in the provinces. They organised debates and provided forums for women to question the various candidates as to their parties' policies towards women and women's concerns. The Women's Association organised the celebration of International Women's Day on 5–8 March 1993 at which a national summit on women's affairs was held, a five-stage proposal specifying recognition, participation, equal rights, development, and solidarity as aims for the post-election government to work towards. [35]

The official reasons, put forward by the Secretariat of State for Women's Affairs in 1995, that so few women ran in the May 1993 elections, were political harassment, lack of true democracy, and 'the lack of political will of the parties' leaders, who were predominantly men'.[36] Some have also pointed out that UNTAC did not set a good example in this regard; there were no female heads of components and few provincial heads.[37] Male politicians were not adverse to using women in order to confer legitimacy upon themselves, however. Judy Ledgerwood attended a political rally in Kompong Cham province in April 1993 in which a khmei khieu (diaspora) politician drew upon the presence of two women imbued with the power of tradition in order to establish himself as man who deserved election to a position of power. One of the women was his wife, dressed and styled in a traditional Cambodian silk sampot with expensive jewellery identifying her as a wealthy (and therefore influential) woman. She did not address the crowd but remained attentive and approving in the background. The other woman was older, dressed as a secular nun. She was the leader of a local militia in the province. The politician said that she was 'too strong' to address the crowd but referred to her and her loyalty to him frequently. Conversely, the politician verbally castigated another woman, the wife of the chief provincial official of the politician's party, for daring to take the microphone and make a statement that supported a point that the politician had just made; he delivered a harangue against American women and their freedom, and said that 'Khmer women would never reach this stage'.[38] As Kate Frieson has remarked, when women do appear in the public, political sphere, it must be in a (preferably silent) supporting role rather than as an agent.[39] Deviation from 'tradition' meant the further obfuscation of Cambodian culture.

Sex work, sexual permissiveness, and sexual depravity were categorised as resulting from foreign influences. A negative consequence, and one that tends to be dwelt upon in histories of the period, is that liberalisation, the sudden appearance of wealth, and foreigners led to inflation, corruption, nepotism, widespread prostitution, and the spread of HIV/AIDS.[40] There were, however, some 6,000 prostitutes in Cambodia before UNTAC arrived. Some Cambodians assert that these were Vietnamese, brought in by the

Vietnamese tandem government of 1979–1989 and who chose to remain in order to 'corrupt' Cambodian men.[41] The number jumped to 20,000 in Phnom Penh by the end of 1992. This seems abnormally high even for a military mission that had only a few hundred women in its numbers, but it must be said that the behaviour of certain of the UNTAC forces seemed to indicate that there could not be enough women to satisfy the appetites of the peace-keepers. In the early days of the UN operation, it was possible to identify the location of particular people from their vehicle's UN numberplate. One of the most popular past-times for some (female) expatriates was to cruise up and down the street in Tuol Kork, the 'red-light district', in order to spot who was patronising the brothels. Mocking and derisory comments would ensue in the office the next day. During the election itself, in May 1993, an Australian electoral process observer was supposed to be billeted in the house rented by the Bulgarian contingent. As she and her fellow observer approached the house, they realised that what they had initially taken to be a moat was in fact a metre-wide perimeter of used condoms that had been flung out of the nearest window or door.

The idea that paid sex was a perfectly natural recreation for military men was, alarmingly, initially reinforced by the head of UNTAC, Yasushi Akashi. This tacit approval from the 'man in charge', the perceived exoticism of Asian women and their favourable comparison to aggressive, demand-ing, possibly critical Western women (whose numbers were too few in any case for a balanced ratio of 'peacekeeper' liaisons),[42] and an environment in which 'emergency sex' was condoned as a release for the pressures that UN personnel found themselves under,[43] all contributed to the rise of sex work in 1992–1993. The name 'UNTAC' is synonymous with an explosion of sex work in Cambodia; the tableau representing the UNTAC period in the tourism museum in Siem Reap comprises a blue-beret-wearing soldier with his arm draped around a vaguely Vietnamese-looking young woman. Both look sad and resigned at their imminent parting. Unexpectedly, a number of reports of sexual assaults began to occur during the UNTAC period. At the Human Rights Component, a number of women or their families came to report assaults carried out on them by foreign men. Unfortunately, as they had sometimes waited days or even weeks before coming in, there was little that the HRC could do. The men concerned, however, almost universally de-clared that sexual relations had been taking place for some time and reporting the 'rape' was retribution for a failure on the man's part to give the woman money, or agree to marry her. Some Cambodian men associated the presence of UNTAC with the rise in prostitution and the rape of Cambodian women. Both activities resulted in the 'contamination' of Cambodian society, whether the prostitutes were Vietnamese or not. If they were, then Cambodia was being invaded by a 'fifth column' aimed at sedition when Cambodia's men were off their guard; if they were Cambodian, the presence of the UN was forcing Cambodian women to act in a most un-Cambodian way.

In her PhD thesis Judy Ledgerwood identified two social absolutes that showed no sign of changing in Cambodian societies whether in Cambodia or in diaspora: sexual control and the ordering of society, wherein virginity and sexual fidelity within marriage and the dominance of husbands over wives were of prime importance.[44] The maintenance of social harmony devolved upon women acting 'correctly', that is in accordance with the social mores espoused in Cbpab Srei and other contemporaneous literature. This has occurred elsewhere in Southeast Asia: '[Men] may enjoy new freedoms and opportunities because women have been given the task of preserving traditional values … . Women are to be responsible for filtering out negative influences from abroad'.[45] This results in a disassociation of women and political power. As the modernising policies of post-conflict governments impact upon even private space, however, the household gradually grows to replicate the gender hierarchy of the public arena, however significant women initially may have been in other areas.[46]

∿

Women contributed directly and materially to the reconstruction of Cambodia and Cambodian society. Although the number of women was greater than that of men in the aftermath of Democratic Kampuchea, the number of *educated* men was greater than that of educated women. The legacy of colonial- and Sangkum-period educational trends weighed heavily against women in being selected for public service positions in reconstruction. Fewer women than men went on to secondary education in the 1950s and 1960s and fewer still to tertiary institutions (see Chapter 8). There were more women than men left alive after the fall of Democratic Kampuchea, but hardly any had completed secondary school. The disparity of the male-to-female ratio meant that the burden of women in post-revolutionary Cambodia was greater than that of men because they were often the only members of a family able to work. Women whose husbands had died or were in the refugee camps, or who had been conscripted into an army were forced to provide subsistence for their children and their husbands' relatives who were unable to fend for themselves. In many cases, there was neither the time nor support for the upgrading of skills that would enable women to take white-collar positions. This also contributed to the lack of women in post-revolutionary political positions between January 1979 and April 1989.

The policies of liberalisation and reconciliation that heralded the second phase of post-revolutionary Cambodia resulted in an influx of returning Cambodians and a large-scale international peacekeeping mission. This impacted on the empowerment of women in two ways. Men assumed many roles within the industrial and public service sectors that had hitherto been taken by women. Returning Cambodians brought with them their own ideas of a 'correct' Cambodian society that did not take into consideration changes to gender roles that had occurred in the intervening 25 years. Those who had left before 1975 were, for the most part, members of the educated elite. The majority were men, reflecting pre-revolutionary educational trends. These returnees were seen as integral to the reconstruction of Cambodia. High-profile public and mixed sector opportunities were made available to them to ensure their continued participation. They also brought with them their own nostalgia for pre-revolutionary Cambodia. The tendency of Cambodians to remember the time prior to the civil war as a 'golden age' is common.[47] Whereas the PRK had precluded a return to practices deemed 'royalist' rather than populist – such as patronage, nepotism, and, to some extent, chauvinism – they formed an integral part of the memories of many returnees. This underlying perception of women sat uneasily with official policies of gender equity and has resulted in the multiple and conflicting identities imposed upon – and in some cases assumed by – women since the re-establishment of the Kingdom of Cambodia in September 1993.

Notes to Chapter 10

1   See for example Evan Gottesman, *Cambodia after the Khmer Rouge: Inside the politics of nation building*, New Haven; London: Yale University Press, 2003, pp. xxi–xxv.

2   Grant Curtis, *Cambodia reborn? The transition to democracy and development*, Washington, DC; Geneva: Brookings Institution Press and the United Nations Research Institute for Social Development, 1998, p. 4; Eva Mysliviec, *Punishing the poor: The international*

isolation of Kampuchea: Oxford: Oxfam, 1984, pp. ix, 30; William Shawcross, *The quality of mercy: Holocaust and modern Cambodia*, Bangkok: DD Books, 1985, p. 37. See also Viviane Frings, 'The failure of agricultural collectivization in the People's Republic of Kampuchea (1979–1989)', Clayton, Victoria: Monash University Centre of Southeast Asian Studies Working Paper 80, 1993. Michael Vickery, *Kampuchea: Politics, economics and society*, Sydney; London; Boston: Allen & Unwin, 1986, p. 3; David Chandler, *A history of Cambodia*, 3rd ed., Boulder, Colorado: Westview Press, 2000, p. 229. Some Cambodians relate stories of rape perpetrated by the Vietnamese during the 1980s; others allege that the Khmer Rouge were responsible for all sexual violence. It is probably fair to say that some such acts occurred on all sides – by the Vietnamese and PRK troops in addition to Khmer Rouge forces. In the refugee camps women were also vulnerable to sexual attacks by Thai authorities and Cambodian men.

3   Chanthou Boua, 'Women in today's Cambodia', *New Left Review* 131 (1982), p. 49; Gottesman, *Cambodia after the Khmer Rouge*, p. 91.

4   Chanthou Boua, 'Observations of the Heng Samrin government, 1980–1982', in David P. Chandler and Ben Kiernan (eds), *Revolution and its aftermath in Kampuchea: Eights essays*, New Haven: Yale University Southeast Asia Studies Monograph Series No. 25, 1983, p. 261; Mysliwiec, *Punishing the poor*, p. 30; *Women: Key to national reconstruction*, Phnom Penh: Secretariat of State for Women's Affairs, Kingdom of Cambodia, 1995, p. 10.

5   Boua, 'Women in today's Cambodia', p. 49; *Women: Key to national reconstruction*, pp. 10–12; Shawcross, *Quality of mercy*, p. 203.

6   Boua, ' Women in today's Cambodia', pp. 47, 49; Mysliwiec, *Punishing the poor*, p. 58; Loung Ung, *Lucky child: A daughter of Cambodia reunited with the sister she left behind*, London; New York; Sydney; Auckland: Fourth Estate, 2005, p. 40; *Gender in election and female leadership at the communal level*, Phnom Penh: Women's Media Centre of Cambodia and the Royal Embassy of the Netherlands, 2000, p. 16.

7   David M. Ayres, *Anatomy of a crisis: Education, development, and the state in Cambodia, 1953–1998*, Honolulu: University of Hawai'i Press, 2000, p. 129; Boua, 'Women in today's Cambodia', pp. 51, 56; Gottesman, *Cambodia after the Khmer Rouge*, pp. 39, 75; *Gender in election*, p. 22; Boua, 'Observations of the Heng Samrin government', p. 287.

8   Articles 7, 27, 31, 33 and 81 of the Constitution of the People's Republic of Kampuchea, in Raoul M. Jennar, *The Cambodian constitutions (1953–1993)*, Bangkok: White Lotus, 1995, pp. 94, 97–99; Boua, 'Women in today's Cambodia', pp. 52, 58; Boua, 'Observations of the Heng Samrin government', pp. 260, 266.

9   Article 38, Constitution of the People's Republic of Kampuchea, in *Cambodian constitutions*, p. 100; *Women: Key to national reconstruction*, p. 26; *Gender in election*, p. 5; Judy L. Ledgerwood, Changing Khmer conceptions of gender: Women, stories, and the social order', PhD thesis, Cornell University, 1990, p. 225; Boua, 'Observations of the Heng Samrin government', p. 264.

10 Article 22, Constitution of the People's Republic of Kampuchea, in *Constitutions of Cambodia*, p. 97; *Women: Key to national reconstruction*, p. 15.

11   Jacqueline Desbarats, *Prolific survivors: Population change in Cambodia, 1975–1993*, Tempe, Arizona: Program for Southeast Asian Studies, Arizona State University, 1995, p. 59; *Women: Key to national reconstruction*, p. 27.

12   Mysliwiec, *Punishing the poor*, p. 61; *Women: Key to national reconstruction*, pp. 5, 26–27, 34–35; Boua, 'Women in today's Cambodia', p. 59; Jacqueline Desbarats, *Prolific survivors: Population change in Cambodia, 1975–1993*, Tempe, Arizona: Program for Southeast Asian Studies, Arizona State University, 1995, p. 59.

13   Boua, 'Women in today's Cambodia', p. 59; *Yuvajun-yuvaneary Kampuchea*, 3 (1981) and 6 (1982); *Women: Key to national reconstruction*, p. 26; Ledgerwood, 'Changing Khmer conceptions of gender', p. 225; Julio A. Jeldres, *The royal house of Cambodia*, Phnom Penh: Monument Books, 2003, p. 76.

14   *Gender in election*, pp. 24–25; Shawcross, *Quality of mercy*, pp. 350, 352; Mysliwiec, *Punishing the poor*, p. 100.

15   *Gender in election*, pp. 16, 22.

16   Boua, 'Women in today's Cambodia', pp. 52, 55, 59; Boua, 'Observations of the Heng Samrin government', p. 260; Shawcross, *Quality of mercy*, p. 266; *Women: Key to national reconstruction*, pp. 34–35, 58; Mysliwiec, *Punishing the poor*, p. 61; *Gender in election*, p. 16.

17   Frings, 'The failure of agricultural collectivization in the People's Republic of Kampuchea', p. 1.

18   *Women: Key to national reconstruction* (Phnom Penh: Secretariat of State for Women's Affairs, Kingdom of Cambodia, 1995), p. 26; Vickery, *Kampuchea*, pp. 74, 80–81. Vickery, *Kampuchea*, pp. 80–81.

19   Boua 1982, 'Women in today's Cambodia', p. 52; *Women: Key to national reconstruction*, p. 7.

20   Gottesman, *Cambodia after the Khmer* Rouge, p. 218. The PRK altered the lyrics of traditional songs and re-named traditional dances to reflect contemporary events and the relationship between Cambodian and Vietnam, such as the *robam joon bper kang taib* ('wishing the army well dance') and the *robam mittapheap aindoa-chun* ('Indochina friendship dance'). Names that referred to the glory of Cambodia's distant past, however, were retained, such as the *robam apsara*, 'apsara dance'. See Sam-Ang Sam, 'Role of Khmer culture in social development within the global context of the new millennium', in *Khmer studies: Knowledge of the past, and its contributions to the rehabilitation and reconstruction of Cambodia*, proceedings of the International Conference on Khmer Studies, Phnom Penh, 26–30 August 1996, ed. Sorn Samnang, Phnom Penh: Toyota Foundation, French Embassy, British Embassy, 1998, vol. 1, p. 86.

21   Hann So, *The Khmer kings*, San Jose, California, n.p., 1988.

22   Margaret Slocomb, *The People's Republic of Kampuchea, 1979–1989: The revolution after Pol Pot*, Chiang Mai: Silkworm Books, 2003, p. 268.

23   Ledgerwood, Changing Khmer conceptions of gender, p. 24.

24 Meung Talla, *Vijjea apram satrei kh'mei* [Manual for raising Cambodian women], Khao-I-Dang, Thailand: International Rescue Committee, 1981.

25 Ung, *Lucky child*, p. 184.

26 Fieldnotes, 2006. Soeur was, in fact, one-quarter Vietnamese; her father was born in Kampuchea Krom to a Cambodian mother and Vietnamese father.

27 *Gender in election*, p. 18.

28 'Decisions of the Third Party Plenum, 1980', cited in Slocomb, *People's Republic of Kampuchea*, p. 136.

29 Mysliwiec, *Punishing the poor*, p. 60. In some cases the elaborate *puos* ceremony was dispensed with given the exigent circumstances. See Trudy Jacobsen et al., *The situation of daun chi in Cambodia*, Phnom Penh: Buddhist Institute/HBF-Asia, 2006, pp. 6, 15, 26.

30 Heike Löschmann, 'The revival of the *don chee* movement in Cambodia', in Karma Lekshe Tsomo (ed.), *Innovative Buddhist women: Swimming against the stream*, London: Curzon, 2000, pp. 91–95, at p. 92–93.

31 For a detailed treatment of the failure of collectivisation in the PRK and policy changes under the State of Cambodia, see Vivianne Frings, *Le socialisme et le paysan Cambodgien: La politique agricole de la République Populaire du Kampuchea et de l'Etat du Cambodge*, Paris: l'Harmattan, 1997.

32 Minh Sucheata, pers. comm., 30 March 2001; T.D. Allman, 'Sihanouk's sideshow', *Vanity Fair*, April 1990, p. 152; Jeldres, *Royal house of Cambodia*, p. 83.

33 *Women: Key to national reconstruction*, pp. 10, 28–29; Gottesman, *Cambodia after the Khmer Rouge*, p. 329; Curtis, *Cambodia reborn?*, p. 124; Judy Ledgerwood, *An analysis of the situation of women in Cambodia*, Phnom Penh: UNICEF, 1992, p. 14.

34 *Women: Key to national reconstruction*, p. 17; Chanthou Boua, *Cambodia's country report: Women in development*, prepared for the Second Asia-Pacific Ministerial Conference, Jakarta, 7–14 June 1994 (Phnom Penh: Secretariat of State for Women's Affairs, 1994), p. 14; Curtis, *Cambodia reborn?*, p. 119; Shawcross, *Cambodia's new deal*, p. 59.

35 *Women: Key to national reconstruction*, pp. 31–32. The creation of these groups during the UNTAC era belies Robert Muscat's assertion that Cambodian society has shown little tendency towards, or tolerance for, interest groups or other extra-familial associations (Curtis, *Cambodia reborn?*, p. 124).

36 *Women: Key to national reconstruction*, p. 18.

37 Sandra Whitworth, *Men, militarism, and UN peacekeeping: A gendered analysis*, London: Boulder, 2004, p. 71.

38 Judy L. Ledgerwood, 'Politics and gender: Negotiating changing Cambodian ideas of the proper woman', *Asia Pacific Viewpoint* 37, 2 (1996), pp. 141–142.

39 Kate Frieson, *Women in the shadows: Power and politics in Cambodia*, Victoria, British Columbia: University of Victoria Centre for Asia-Pacific Initiatives Occasional Paper 26, 2001, p. 3.

40 *Women: Key to national reconstruction*, p. 20; Shawcross, *Cambodia's new deal*, p. 15. A typical description of these influences can be found in Chou Meng Tarr and Peter Aggleton, '"Sexualising" the culture(s) of young Cambodians: Dominant discourses and social reality', in *Khmer Studies*, vol. 2, p. 1034: The 'young and glamorous appearance' of *srei beer* 'symbolised what the consumption of alcohol could do for young males. Before the appearance of UNTAC in 1992 alcohol was not marketed in this fashion'. At the same time, some authors laud the UN's achievements in Cambodia. Usually, however, their analysis does not have a gender dimension. See Roland Paris, *At war's end: Building peace after conflict*, Boulder, Colorado: Cambridge University Press, 2004, p. 89; Leviseda Douglas, *Sex trafficking in Cambodia*, Clayton, Victoria: Monash Unviersity Centre of Southeast Asian Studies Working Paper 122, 2003, p. 1.

41 Fieldnotes, 2004, 2006. Interestingly, one of the people who shared this view was himself an advocate for sex workers' rights.

42 Some contingents saw any woman as a potential sex partner, whether expatriate or local. One evening in the Rock Hard Café, my friend and I were repeatedly harassed by a group of soldiers. They kept asking what it would take for us to agree to speak to them. Sarcastically, I eventually said that they couldn't afford us – we were USD1,000 per hour. The spokesman returned to the group but came back five minutes later saying 'We can get together USD600 – what would that buy?'

43 For a realistic account of the lives of UN peacekeepers, see Andrew Thomson, Ken Cain and Heidi Postlewait, *Emergency sex (and other desperate measures)*, London: Ebury Press, 2004.

44 Ledgerwood, 'Changing Khmer conceptions of gender', p. 243.

45 Elizabeth Fuller Collins, '(Re)negotiating gender hierarchy in the New Order: A South Sumatran field study', *Asia Pacific Viewpoint*, 37, 2 (1996), p. 136.

46 Linda K. Richter, 'Exploring theories of female leadership in South and Southeast Asia', *Pacific Affairs* 4 (Winter 1990–1991), p. 526; Frieson, *Women in the shadows*, p. 15.

47 See for example Chandler, *History of Cambodia*, p. 190; Ledgerwood, Changing Khmer conceptions of gender, p. 126.

CHAPTER ELEVEN

Contemporary Conspiracies

*T*he new Constitution of the Kingdom of Cambodia, promulgated on 21 September 1993, promised an unprecedented age of gender egalitarianism. Special protections and services for women were included; issues such as trafficking, exploitation, workplace discrimination, maternity leave, and rural needs were addressed. One of the first international instruments signed by the newly-formed government was the *Convention on the Elimination of All Forms of Discrimination Against Women* (CEDAW). Two months later, the Secretariat of State for Women's Affairs was established. Its mandate was to become the focal point and platform for the advancement of Cambodian women through advocacy and the improvement of living conditions. This was to be effected by increasing women's participation in the economy and in health, education and social services.[1] Despite these assurances, however, most women in Cambodia continue to be discriminated against and prevented from realising their potential. Their contribution to Cambodian society is considered one of guardianship and heritage; any divergence from the comportment of a *srei krup leakkhana* (virtuous woman) is considered threatening to the stability of Cambodian culture.

Locating women in contemporary Cambodia

Two underlying tenets in Cambodian society preclude the realisation of gender equality, despite state policy to the contrary.

259

Not all Cambodians subscribe to these generalisations, but they are pervasive at all levels of society, and are often used to rationalise a host of activities that are detrimental to women. The first principle is that the world outside the household is the realm of men. In this Cambodia follows the global paradigm wherein men 'dominate the public space and the field of power ... whereas women remain (predominantly) assigned to the private space'.[2] Article 16 of the Constitution prohibits the queen from exercising political power.[3]

No women were appointed to ministerial positions after the 1993 elections, although they constituted a large percentage of the civil service. There were five female Under-Secretaries of State in the Secretariat of State for Women's Affairs, the Ministry of Social Action, the Ministry of Justice and the Ministry of Foreign Affairs. Most women who had run for election or campaigned for political parties found low-ranking jobs in government ministries after the elections. Subsequent administrative reshuffles increased the number of women parliamentarians to seven in 1995. No women were elected to governorships at the provincial level, although there was one female deputy governor in Stung Treng province. In the 1998 parliamentary elections, 16.47 per cent of candidates were women but only 9.1 per cent were successful in the final analysis. Princess Bopha Devi was appointed Minister of Culture and Fine Arts, having held the positions of Deputy Minister and Advisor to the Royal Government regarding the portfolio since 1991. Mu Sochua replaced Keat Sukhun as Minister for Women's and Veteran's Affairs. There were also four female Secretaries of State and four Under-Secretaries of State during this period and Kit Kimhourne was appointed the director-general of AKP, the official Cambodian press agency, on 6 September 2000. After the results of the 2003 elections were finally ratified, the number of female members of parliament increased from 12 in 1999 to 22 in 2006 (out of a total of 122 seats); there are currently two female ministers, Men Sam An, Minister of Parliamentary Affairs and Inspection, and Ing Kantha Phavi, Minister of Women's Affairs. There are also three female Secretaries of State.[4] Although there has been improvement over time (see Fig. 11.1), these figures are low considering that the total number of ministerial portfolios is 31.

Even this slight female presence has been mediated, for the most part, by relationships to powerful men. Princess Vacheahra, half-sister to King Sihanouk, has been a Member of Parliament for Siem Reap (1998) and Phnom Penh (2003) and Chair of the Parliamentary Committee for Foreign Affairs,

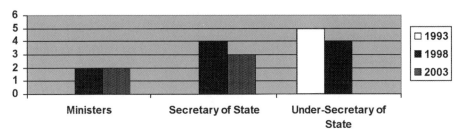

Fig. 11.1: Number of women in high political office, 1993–2001.

International Cooperation, Press and Information. A major focus of her portfolio has been border demarcation. Princess Sisowath Santa, daughter of Prince Sisowath Sirik Matak and Princess Norodom Kethneary (a grand-daughter of King Norodom), was elected to the National Assembly as representative for Prey Veng in 1998 and 2003. She also participated in the Commission on Public Health, Social and Women's Affairs. Princess Norodom Rattanadevi is a Member of Parliament for Kratie. Tioulong Saumura, daughter of Nhiek Tioulong and wife of Sam Rainsy (himself son of Sam Sary, confidant of the young King Sihanouk and later Deputy Prime Minister and Minister of Finance), has been elected twice as Member of Parliament for Phnom Penh.[5]

This does not mean that these women are not committed to the interests of the people they represent; most fulfil their functions admirably and some Cambodians see them as less corrupt than their male counterparts. Yet it is unlikely that they would have been admitted to the political sphere had they not had connections to male politicians. This phenomenon is not, of course, restricted to Cambodia. All female heads of state in Southeast Asia have been the daughters and/or widows of charismatic male political leaders. In the aftermath of the 1998 elections Mona Lilja and Tevy Prom found that many female politicians had one or more family members engaged in politics and that this made their own presence more acceptable. The women themselves believed that khsae (connections) 'had contributed in some way to their power in politics' and that their husbands were encouraging of their political aspirations.[6] This may be so, but there are obvious benefits for male politicians in having wives – who are socially constrained to agree with them – in politics. The khsae that the women establish in their positions can then be co-opted by their husbands in requiring support for a proposed development, constitutional amendment, or candidate.

Another means by which women have been successful in negotiating a presence in public space is to negate their gender through modification of their appearance. Women who assume the clothes and ascetic habits of daun chi (Buddhist nuns) carry far greater legitimacy than other women. The activities of the Me Daw Karuna organisation, for example, have been successful in community engagement, including conflict resolution. Whereas a group of normally attired women would be seen as 'busybodies', the daun chi were 'not women, but come from Buddhism'. Some commune-level female leaders adopted the appearance of daun chi during election campaigns as they found that people paid more attention to them. Significantly, one of these was praised not for her political leadership but as 'a woman full of great sacrifice'.[7] Other women disguise their feminine characteristics by wearing loose shirts, buttoned to the neck, with trousers or long skirts, cut their hair short, and eschew jewellery. Still others opt for a very traditional appearance, wearing sampot and modest tops that cover their arms and décolletage. These strategies are most common in the civil service, state educational institutions, and Cambodian non-government organisations – in other words, where male Cambodian perspectives on what constitutes appropriate activities for women predominate. This reassures men that the women concerned are not moving too far from the Cambodian standard of 'correct' female behaviour.

The second general belief is that women are either 'good' or 'bad' with no area for negotiation.[8] 'Good' women are dutiful and obedient daughters, faithful wives, and nurturing mothers who devote themselves to their families. Daughters are expected to abide by their parents' decisions, contribute to the family economy, and not behave in a manner that would attract social censure. In practical terms, this means that girls are expected to agree to whichever marriage partner is selected for them, drop out of school in order to assume responsibilities in the household (rice planting, the care of younger siblings or farm animals, domestic tasks, weaving, marketing) or take whatever cash jobs are available, and not put themselves in positions wherein the honour of the family could be compromised – in other words, wherein they could lose their virginity, and therefore their value as prospective marriage partners. These requirements pose a dichotomy for many young Cambodian women. Obedience to parental demands and the necessity of providing for the family means that the young women who are put up as surety for loans cannot resist. For the term of the loan, they are then considered the property of the money-lender and bound to obey them. It is no coincidence that many money-lenders are also me bon (brothel manager).

Other girls are sold outright to distant relatives or people who are no relation at all, who come to rural areas offering lucrative jobs elsewhere; whether or not parents believe that their daughters will really work as housekeepers or seamstresses is debatable, but the outcome is the same. The girls have a duty to contribute to the family and respect their parents' wishes. Therefore, they have no choice but to accept and poverty constrains the parents from refusing such offers. Some parents worry that their daughters, far from home, will meet 'bad people' who will lead them astray; but this is almost always articulated in terms of daughters being 'tricked' into illicit behaviour, not violence being perpetrated against them unwillingly. There is growing concern of women being 'kidnapped' and sold into sex trafficking in some places but the link between parental culpability in selling their daughters into 'service' in distant places and the sex industry is not well articulated. On the other hand, parents continue to construe a girl's ability to send and receive love letters as potentially destructive to their marriage prospects as they are evidence of premarital 'contact' with a man. This results in their removal from the education system, often before completing primary school, which limits their employment options and awareness of their rights.[9]

A 'good' daughter will evolve into a 'good' wife who obeys her husband, supports him in his endeavours, manages the household, and does not shame the family name by revealing any inadequacies her husband may have. This translates into a scenario wherein women are expected to fulfil domestic obligations of shopping, cooking, cleaning, laundry, and child-rearing, whilst participating in the family business or working outside the home in the civil service or private organisations. They are also constrained from attaining a higher position than their husband, as this would be shaming for him, and cannot question his decisions, report domestic violence, or ask relatives for assistance, as this would be 'carrying fire outside the house' – in other words, airing publicly that which should be private. Women should not respond to their husband's anger, but go away, and come back with 'sweet words' that will make him see the error of his ways, or simply accept his viewpoint in order to maintain domestic harmony. This includes acceptance of husbands who frequent sex workers or maintain second wives. In fact, the taking of a mistress or second wife is a public statement on the man's part that his current wife is not adequate in some way.

On the other hand, sexual fidelity on the part of wives is absolute; those who transgress it bring shame upon their husband as his virility is placed in doubt, and the family unit is thus destabilised. In a 2006 survey of attitudes toward sexual activity, premarital sex for women was considered acceptable by 30 per cent of male university students and 28 per cent of male unskilled workers; yet none condoned married women having extramarital sexual partners.[10] Wives who deviate from their role are asking for trouble. Vanna, a nurse in a private hospital in Phnom Penh, often treats women after beatings from their husbands; in her opinion 'such women are not clever; they don't know when to be quiet'. Women are often blamed for causing the violence perpetrated against them, but how did the women whose husbands beat them after their preferred candidates lost in the 1998 elections cause their injuries?[11]

At the same time, men who are not married are perceived as somehow incomplete. Women's superior knowledge of household management and child-raising contribute to the reputation and well-being of the family, and thus to the image of the family carried into public space by men. Work carried out in the domestic space is valued in this regard. This is the reason that decision-making within families continues to be made by both parents. Cambodian proverbs emphasise the importance of women to men: 'Behind every husband is a clever wife' and 'The seedling supports the soil, the woman supports the man' are two such examples used today.[12] Yet as paid work becomes increasingly valued in Cambodian society for the status it can confer (in terms of consumer goods), the *significance* of work carried out by women in private space is declining, although the need for it remains.

Women who are not *srei krup leakkhana* as defined by the *Cbpab Srei* and other literature of the past are by definition *srei aht leakkhana* – women with no good qualities, 'bad' women, whose redemption is impossible and whose current situation is the result of an accumulation of bad *karma* from previous existences. Such women, it is thought, deserve any and all evils that may befall them. It thus becomes very easy to legitimise violence against them. Wives who contravene the 'traditional' mores of submission and passivity deserve to be punished by their husbands. If a woman does not observe the dictums that she should stay close to home, remain indoors after nightfall, and wear modest clothing, then she should expect to be raped or have people think she is a sex worker. The fact that woman are also expected to contribute to the family economy and so must agree to overtime or jobs long distances away from her house are immaterial. If she was a *srei krup leakkhana*, she would not have been in a position to be violated; therefore she must be a *srei aht leakkhana*, and deserves everything she gets.[13]

Should a girl's virginity be taken before marriage, under any circumstances (including rape), she immediately becomes a *srei kouch*, 'broken woman', and her value plummets to zero. Sokha, a 26-year-old administration assistant in an international NGO, said that in the event that his fiancée was sexually assaulted, 'I would feel sorry for her, but I would not want to marry her, and my family would call off the wedding'. There is a brief window of opportunity in which the situation can be redressed; if the perpetrator is made to marry the victim and/or the *meba* (ancestral spirits) of the latter placated through a special ceremony. The sexual act then becomes legitimate, not a transgression, because sex is sanctioned between married couples.[14] Many families only report rape to authorities after attempts to have the perpetrator marry the victim have failed, in the hope that the threat of prosecution will be an added incentive.[15]

As *srei kouch* have no value, their treatment is of no importance and their futures immaterial. This is why Cambodian women in the sex industry – even those who are coerced – remain there. They can never be *srei krup leakkhana* again. This view is shared by many Cambodians, even those working in advocacy and rights for victims, who refer to the futility of trying to 'convert' bad women into virtuous ones. Similarly, there is a sense that once a woman has become *srei kouch*, it should not matter who else she has sex with. In August 2005 I saw a sex worker who kept trying to elude a drunk Japanese tourist forced to leave with him by security guards. One of the guards explained to me in a fatherly manner that this man was the woman's boyfriend and the reason she was crying and begging me for help was that they had argued and she was now trying to make him embarrassed so he would give her nice presents. This was patently untrue; the tourist had been speaking loudly at the bar about his overland arrival from Bangkok that day. The security guard also advised me not to concern myself with the lives of *srei kouch*. I said that I had heard that Cambodia now had *setthi manus* (human rights). He smiled and said, 'Human rights are for people. This is a *srei luok khluen* [woman who sells herself].'[16] The same sentiment applies to the practice of *bauk*, rapes perpetrated by gangs of young men against sex workers or those believed to be sex workers because they work in hospitality or entertainment. Usually one or two men will engage the services of the woman, or offer to give her a lift somewhere, and take her to a house or hotel where a room has been reserved and where a further group of ten or more men is waiting. The fact that the number of clients has been changed or that she never agreed to the arrangement in the first place cannot matter to her, it is assumed; she is *srei kouch*.

Given the intolerance toward women who are not srei krup leakkhana, it is hardly surprising that the articulation of new female identities is met with hostility. Although daun chi are generally seen in a positive light as having a family member accruing merit is a good thing, it is only respectable for women who have fulfilled their obligations as daughters, wives, and mothers – in other words, those who no longer have a husband or family to care for and support. Many people believe that only women who have been wives and mothers themselves know how to give advice on these issues to others. Women who become daun chi following divorce or the death of their husband seem to be more acceptable. People describe daun chi as being elderly women with shaved heads.[17] Young, never-married women who declare their intentions of becoming daun chi because of a personal inclination are regarded with suspicion. Yiey Phal, 21, was drawn to the life of the daun chi; her family would prefer her to remain with them and assist with the family enterprise. She had to run away in order to take up a religious life.[18] Young daun chi pose a dichotomy for Cambodian society. They cannot be srei aht leakkhana because they are daun chi. But they cannot be srei krup leakkhana because they are not fulfilling the roles of 'good' women as set out in the Cambodian codes of correct behaviour.

A similar issue arises for the women working in garment factories. They are young women, often unmarried, living far from home, with no parents at hand to observe and correct their behaviour. This makes them srei aht leakkhana. Yet most have taken jobs in these factories in order to contribute to the family economy, thus easing the burden for their parents and perhaps facilitating the education of younger siblings. They are therefore srei krup leakkhana as well. This dual identity most often reverts to the srei aht leakkhana, however, as the women who work in factories are described as being 'loud', 'noisy', 'gossiping', and materialistic. Mom, a roasted-corn vendor at the riverside in Phnom Penh, described the women who worked in the factories as 'always thinking about clothes and furniture; they don't think about their future and don't care that their parents have nobody to look after them'. Female factory workers participating in a demonstration to protest against working conditions were told by police to return to work or to find work as srei kouch.[19] The implication was that they were srei aht leakkhana already, and thus there was no respectable option for them.

Women who work in environments such as restaurants, beer gardens, bars, and as vendors around Phnom Penh's popular evening entertainment venues are believed to be sex workers regardless of their actual functions. During the course of fieldwork in 2005, I became friendly with a group of young women who worked in Western-patronised restaurants and bars along the river and at the Boeung Kak lake. One night five of us (including the French boyfriend of one of the girls) went to Spark, a popular Cambodian dance venue. When I went to the bar, one of the waitresses asked me why I was socialising with sex workers. I said that they were my friends regardless of their jobs, but as it happened, they were waitresses. She smiled wryly and said, 'It means the same thing in my country.' I asked if she was a sex worker. She was shocked. I pointed out that she was a waitress and had just said that all waitresses were sex workers. She said that of course she was not referring to girls like herself – her brother was a bouncer at the same club and took her home every night. I said that for all she knew my friends could have similar arrangements. She admitted that this might be true. For the most part, however, old associations of entertainment with sexual activity have been retained, and women who work as waitresses, hostesses, and *srei beer* – waitresses who work for a particular beer company and continually fill patrons' glasses from large jugs of their product – are regularly propositioned by their customers. Whether they accept the offers every night, some nights, or never does not matter. They have been devalued in the eyes of society by the fact that the only employment they could find was in a less-than-respectable environment. This becomes internalised by the women themselves.[20]

Male culture and double standards

Many attribute the impact of the Khmer Rouge years to the culture of violence in contemporary Cambodia; but this has not been definitively established.[21] The violence against women in Cambodia today seems to be a product of a male culture that has its origins in earlier times and has found new expression in a society that legitimises behaviour according to past mores. Lyda was 22 years old when I met her in an internet shop near Lucky Supermarket in Phnom Penh in May 2001. Two years earlier, her stepbrother, then seventeen, had raped her in the family home in Battambang. She said that for some months she had noticed him looking at her in a strange way, and he constantly came into her room when she was in bed or might be dressing. One day, when her mother had gone to see a neighbour's new baby, he came in to her room, and proceeded to assault her so badly that she required a blood transfusion. When she was well enough to travel, her mother sent her to a distant relative in Phnom Penh, who organised a 'marriage' for her with a Taiwanese businessman living in Singapore, where he already had a Chinese wife. Lyda now runs his business in Phnom Penh and sees him once a month. She told me that she was lucky not to have been sold to a brothel. This is only one of many similar stories of violence perpetrated against women, often family members or children, by young Cambodian men.

Louise Brown has commented, in reference to the sex industry, that the clients tend to disappear from the discussion. The same can be said of men in relation to gender issues in Cambodia. Yet it is male perspectives, particularly those of the elite, that dominate the discourse on women and shape their destinies. Men are content with the status quo and so have little reason to alter trends that demean women and privilege men. While the Cbpab Srei is held up as a model for women to follow, the tenets of the Cbpab Broh – the 'Code of conduct for men' – is not. In fact, of 58 men and women aged between 18 and 35 surveyed in 2005, 38 had heard of Cbpab Broh as a piece of Cambodian literature; but only eight could recite or paraphrase any of its teachings, in contrast to over 80 per cent who could provide a detailed account of the Cbpab Srei.[22]

Men are not held to the same moral yardstick as women. This is because men are believed to have inherent inclinations and characteristics that they cannot help and from which they need to be protected. One of these characteristics is that men are sexually voracious by nature and require many female partners in order to reach a level of satiation. It is therefore only right that they patronise sex workers; if they did not, then 'good' women would be compromised as men would not be able to contain their sexual needs. A consequence of this belief is that sex workers themselves are blamed for preying on men, who are struggling on a daily basis to resist their natural urges. In early 1998, Riem Sarin, then chief of the Phnom Penh Municipal Office of Minor Offences in the Ministry of Interior, said that a crackdown on prostitution 'helps bring happiness to every household because prostitution distracts husbands from their wives. If the prostitutes are available only at rather inaccessible places, husbands will stay at home and concentrate on caring for their families'. Some women also believe that removing the temptation will re-orient men in the right direction. Acid attacks, orchestrated and perpetrated by 'first wives' against lesser wives, mistresses, and sex workers frequented by their husbands, have mutilated and killed many women.[23] The husbands themselves are not held responsible for having transgressed the tenet of marital fidelity – at least not in public.

Paid sexual encounters continue to be associated as a natural component of recreation, hospitality, and fealty for Cambodian men. Migrant workers from the provinces, such as construction workers and *moto* drivers,[24] who come to the large towns in search of short-term work during the agricultural off-season, comprise the main customers for the 'low class' brothel areas of Tuol Kork and Boulding in Phnom Penh, where women are expected to service up to twenty customers per day and encounters take place on wooden pallets separated by thin curtains. Most *moto* drivers said that they would only be able to afford a brothel visit once every five or six weeks. When asked whether they would continue to frequent sex workers when they returned home to their wives in the provinces or once they were married, fifteen of nineteen said no; one man introduced a caveat: 'Unless it was a special time, like a public holiday, or I won the lottery, when it is normal to celebrate with friends.'

End-of-year festivities for many male university students (and usual weekend activities for the sons of politicians and business people) involve an *en masse* visit to pool halls, 'dancing restaurants', and beer gardens where they will end up paying for sex to round off the night's entertainment. In many respects the group or shared experience of sex-for-cash serves to reinforce the notion of Cambodian 'maleness'; as Bourdieu described, 'manliness must be validated by other men, in its reality as actual or potential violence'. Gang rape is validation of masculinity in its most extreme form. In this context, *bauk* provides Cambodian men with an opportunity to establish themselves as powerful men, regardless of their actual social position, whilst reaffirming their 'membership of the group'. As Luke Bearup of the NGO Gender and Development for Cambodia commented in 2002, '20 people can rape a woman at the same time, and consider this a fun, bonding experience between males'. Annuska Derks has pointed out that it is also more economical and secure as personal property is guarded by the group while the individual takes his turn.[25]

It continues to be the prerogative of elite men to demonstrate their potency and superiority over other men through sexual access to large numbers of women. If these women are virgins, the higher the prowess of the man involved, because virginity is an expensive commodity. High-level business agreements are 'ratified' by deflowering virgins procured for the purpose, in order to demonstrate mutual high regard. A Western parallel might be the decanting of a 30-year-old single malt in order to toast the business agreement. Virginity carries with it the assurance that there will be no ill-effects from the encounter (for the man, at least) and some believe that taking the virginity of a girl will remove bad luck, rejuvenate a flagging libido, or cure HIV/AIDS.[26] This is why so many sex workers are young teenagers. Their value is diminished once their virginity has been sold, but they will not physically show the toll that the sex industry takes on their bodies for some years. Another attractive characteristic in young sex workers is that they are socially constrained to be obedient. Most Cambodian men expect their sexual partners, including sex workers, to be submissive and are disconcerted when their expectations are not met. It was extremely difficult to convince any Cambodian man to speak openly about why Cambodian women should not enjoy sex. Many seemed to think that it was an inherent aspect of Cambodian femininity. One *moto* driver said 'If I wanted a *srei rijoh rilenh* [wriggly woman] I would go to a Vietnamese.' Ly Ly, a sex worker, told me that she had been surprised at first when her Western clients 'told me to make noise, to move around, to sit on top … . If I did this with a Cambodian man, he would be shocked and afraid'.[27]

The majority of Cambodian men believe that Cambodian women are naturally timid, docile, and less capable than they are.[28] The fact that these same men may have wives, mothers and sisters who run businesses, work in private and government organisations, and share equally in family decision-making has nothing to do with the dominant notion of abstract Cambodian womanhood. This view permeates to the highest levels of the political apparatus. In 1995, for example, the Cambodian government was astonished that there could be any objection to the delegation to the Fourth World Conference on

Women in Beijing being headed by the incumbent (male) Secretary of State for Women's Affairs. The rationale was as follows:

> If we send [an] inferior woman, it means we don't give importance to the meeting ... . They are used to sitting in the back row. If we put them in the front row and ask them to make a speech, take notes and answer questions, I think they would be unable to manage.[29]

Sending women to lead a delegation, therefore, would be an insult to the level of importance placed upon the conference. When women do demonstrate that they are as capable as men, they are regarded with suspicion for not acting in accordance with notions of correct behaviour. Rath Yong, district governor of Ba Phnom in Prey Veng, was dismissed on charges of corruption in August 1999. Many held that, if Yong had been male, her skill in manipulating traditional Cambodian mechanisms for power and wealth would have resulted in promotion. Women as public agents are not looked upon kindly by Cambodian male politicians, even when their talent for diplomacy is well regarded. A civil servant said that 'women are more gentle and straightforward than men in communications and resolving problems for residents' but pointed out that night duty had a detrimental effect on their domestic tasks.[30]

The continued association between women and domesticity on one hand and men and public activities on the other is hardly surprising. As others have discussed in relation to global and regional instances wherein women have been mobilised in revolutionary or reconstruction efforts and then later relegated to the domestic sphere, this not only profits the state, but privileges men. The competition for positions is removed; men's wages, necessarily low as the nation seeks to reconstruct itself, are subsidised by women's private labour; women are fixed to their activities throughout the day, thus freeing men for 'nine-to-five' work in more prestigious and economically lucrative fields. Last but not least, men thereby control women's work. Some Cambodian women themselves have commented on 'the understandable lack of will from our male leaders to allow any challenge to their dominant position' whilst insisting that this cannot be permitted to endure.[31] Clearly, Cambodian men would have no interest in power-sharing, as this would put an end not only to the arrangements that have privileged them, but change what it means to be a Cambodian man. This is a serious proposition for a society that has already faced a number of violent changes in the past thirty years. The erosion of further traditional values – or values inculcated as traditional – would increase the vulnerability of Cambodian identity.

Complicity in the foreign quarter

Perhaps one of the most shocking aspects of the current situation of women in Cambodia is the level to which foreigners and Cambodians living in diaspora are complicit in perpetuating stereotypes that depict Cambodian women as passive and enabling practices that contribute to their disempowerment. The supposed submissiveness of Cambodian women makes them a valuable commodity as potential marriage partners for some overseas Cambodians, as they are likely to be more obedient than those raised in the west, described as 'too liberated' and 'ignorant of Cambodian traditions'.[32] Some Western men have also come to Cambodia on the express purpose of marrying Cambodian women for similar reasons. Some of these partnerships are the result of genuine affection and compatibility between the men and women concerned; but a far greater number are predicated on the belief that Cambodian women will 'put up and shut up' with behaviour that Western women would not accept, including patronage of sex workers or girlfriends on the side.

The perceived exoticism of Asian women has assisted Cambodia economically as thousands of men from Western countries come in search of the legendary licentiousness and permissiveness of expatriate life therein. For many Western men, Cambodia is a paradise of consequence-free sex with young, pretty, submissive women who will obey their every whim and not judge their social status, income, behaviour, and sexual prowess. Brian, a 23-year-old American teacher living in Phnom Penh explained:

> Chantha ... she's sexy, she's smart, she's happy to be with me. She doesn't hassle me to get a better job. And it's not like I'm paying her for sex. We've travelled together, seen some of the country. I buy her meals when we're together and sometimes clothes. And her mom was sick so I paid for her to go to the doctor and get medicine. I'm helping her family.

Chantha keeps a toothbrush and some clothes at Brian's apartment. Some nights, however, he takes other girls home. On those nights, Chantha has to make alternative arrangements. When I asked her how she felt about this, she said 'Of course it hurts me, but if I complain to him he will tell me to go and then take another girlfriend.' Competition between Cambodian women who frequent the Western bars is fierce, especially for the attention of young, attractive foreign men. Women often fought over Steve, a British NGO worker. One night Somaly was sitting next to him at the bar when another girl, Thida, came in. They began quarrelling. Thida explained to me that Somaly had gone home with Steve on Wednesday, so tonight it was her turn. Women who engage exclusively with Western clients are among the upper echelons of the sex industry in Cambodia and most see their position as privileged, an opportunity for freedom of expression and behaviour denied their counterparts who abide by the constraints that Cambodian society has devised for them.[33] Yet their position is hardly one of empowerment. Some will earn USD 10 per night; others USD 5; and towards dawn I have seen women agreeing to have sex with men in exchange for the price of the moto ride to her own home afterwards (around 50 US cents).

Foreign men come to Cambodia and find their every fantasy can be easily facilitated while not earning any disapproval from society at large because it is acceptable for Cambodian men to do the same. A popular 'gentleman's bar' in Phnom Penh offers a particular service combining the exoticism of the east with the pleasures of the local pub. As soon as they walk in, men are given a complimentary beer. Shortly afterward, a hostess will appear and fellate them against the wall while they wait their turn at the pool table. Disapproval of this and other exploitative practices is portrayed as jealousy on the part of Western women who secretly desire the attention lavished upon their ostensibly more attractive counterparts. A cartoon in a locally-produced English-language magazine showed a Western man dancing with four young, slim, sexily dressed Cambodian women while at a nearby table four overweight older Western ladies voiced their disapproval over their colleague's contribution to the exploitation of women. In the next frame, each woman had a thought-bubble over her head expressing sentiments such as 'I wonder how much liposuction costs' and 'Can I get out to Bangkok for a facelift before New Year?' Criticism is dismissed as jealousy and participation in an industry that subjugates and exploits hundreds of thousands of women condoned because it is part of male culture in Cambodia. Western tourists and expatriate residents constitute an elite class in Cambodian society.[34] The behaviour of the elite is emulated. Yet far from taking a stand against practices that privilege men and exploit women, outlawed or censured in their own countries, many foreign men see them as a perquisite of expatriate life.

Stereotypes of Cambodian women as passive and incapable have also been perpetuated by women in the region and the west. This attitude was expressed in an interview with an international sponsor of a beauty pageant in 2002:

> 'In Cambodia, women are traditionally not as respected as men,' she explained. 'When you get married, you stay home. But now, women are becoming freer and more confident, and this contest is a celebration of that.' In addition, [she] said the Miss Tourism contest will promote Cambodia's own tourism and will give women the opportunity to interact with the international and regional community. 'It will encourage women to look after themselves,' she said.[35]

Notwithstanding the questionable legitimacy of beauty pageants as vehicles of empowerment, the director of Lux Cosmetics echoed the sentiments of many women who encourage their Cambodian counterparts to pull themselves out of their unemancipated predicament. Appraisals of women in Cambodia almost inevitably include a warning that gender equity will only be possible when Cambodian women 'themselves organise in their mutual interest', that development initiatives will be detrimental to future generations of women until they 'themselves voice their dissatisfaction with existing gender imbalances'. The achievements and processes of women elsewhere in the world are held up as models for the mobilisation of Cambodian women. Some consultants assert that Cambodian women 'perpetuate the rules of servility and subservience from one generation to the next' and that Cambodia's social problems stem from a lack of 'gifted social leaders with the necessary skills, training, and political or social connections to allow them to be effective advocates and change agents'. Only a handful of scholars recognise that Cambodian women have been working within the constraints of their culture to effect change for the better in women's issues.[36]

Advocating women's rights (or not)

The Cambodian women's movement faces serious obstacles, not the least of which is the identification of feminism as a dangerous Western concept that would not translate well to Cambodian society. In 1994, Eva Mysliviec, then director of the Cambodian Development Resource Institute, concluded that gender awareness training had not been effective due to 'a fixation that gender is feminism (which, in their view, is bad), there is a lack of interest and a failure to see the relevance to the Cambodian development context'.[37] The often unrestrained behaviour, immodest clothing and licentiousness of female expatriates and tourists in Cambodia send the message that this is how the free, liberated women of the west act on a day-to-day basis. Western feminism has therefore become associated with unrestrained hedonism and disreputable behaviour. The extensions of these same freedoms to Cambodian women, it is felt, will result in similar behaviour; therefore, they must not be allowed if the purity of Cambodian culture is to be maintained.

Leading politicians fail to see the need for women to organise or agitate for gender equality, preferring them to bolster existing platforms along political party lines. In an interview conducted by the Women's Media Center in 2000, Men Sam An said that there was no women's movement within the structure of the CPP but there was 'a 30-per-cent principle for women', realised through the Women's Association for Development, which was 'all for women but not for the party'.[38] FUNCINPEC has been the worst of the main parties in terms of gender equality, despite Articles 1(b) and 3 of the 1999 party by-laws guaranteeing gender equality. There were no women on the Permanent Committee in February 2003 and only five on the 40-member Board of Directors. The women's movement within FUNCINPEC was described in 2000 as 'not doing much'. The Sam Rainsy Party, by contrast, has been the more active. In 1999 the SRP created the National Council of Women, comprising two women for each province and 48 for Phnom Penh, in order to monitor women's affairs. The guiding force for this initiative was Tioulong Saumura. Elected to the National Assembly in 1998, she later chaired the Electoral Reform Task Force of the Alliance for Reform and Democracy in Asia.[39] She has also been vocal in advocating the necessity of involving more women in Cambodian politics and criticising the attitude of male Cambodian politicians, including her own husband, Sam Rainsy:

> I am now fighting a double battle: one for democracy and freedom for all Cambodians against dictators, and one for better recognition of the contribution of female activists within the party, against my own colleagues and friends. I try to convince my male colleagues and party leaders, not to forget my dear husband, Madame Chair, that freeing political leadership will bring a beneficial evolution for both men and women.[40]

In the same speech she stated that she would establish her own political party for women eventually, but the first priority for all Cambodian politicians was to ensure 'the basic rights for Cambodians of both sexes'. In 1998, a woman named Noun Bunna established the Cambodian's Women's Party. Interviewed in 2002, she claimed that by 2013 the Cambodian Women's Party would 'become the leading, ruling party and I will become prime minister.'[41]

The Cambodian women's movement has devised its own strategies for 'encouraging' women to participate more in the political life of their nation. One of these is to emphasise the equality between men and women, downplaying the hostility of individual male politicians toward activities that may be construed as 'feminist' and therefore un-Cambodian:

> Weak women make the younger generation weak, thus affecting half the total population since women account for fifty percent of the country's population … . A nation or government with men who do not understand women, might have families in which spouses disagree with one another or with spouses disgracing their children … . The objective of this publication is to encourage women to be firm and to upgrade their capacities and abilities to a new status where men will understand and help promote women as their equal partners. [42]

Another strategy for augmenting the number of women in public life has been to point out past involvement of women in times of crisis and their subsequent relegation to supporting roles, citing slogans such as 'riding a buffalo to cross a muddy field' (riding a buffalo at any other time would invite ridicule) and drawing readers' attention to the fact that women 'were actively involved in wars during the times of Banteay Srei, the US imperialists and the Khmer Rouge. Why then, can women not participate in the commune election?'[43]

Cambodian non-governmental organisations (NGOs) focussing on women's issues and human rights were established in 1993 and 1994, and these were vocal in demanding the enforcement of legal protections for women. In 1995, there were sufficient local NGOs to warrant the establishment of the Amara Women's Network, an umbrella organization that oversaw dialogue and co-ordination of activities, particularly at the village and commune level. Members of Cambodian Women Against Violence founded the Women's Media Centre in 1995. The same year, Koh Kor Island, a resettlement program for abused women, was established. The women-run community supported itself through farming and sewing and elected its own leaders annually. Khemara also began running outreach workshops for sex workers at this time. In October 1996 the Khmer Women's Voice Centre conducted a grassroots national training programme in women and family law. The Khmer Women's Voice Centre began publishing an eponymous bilingual magazine each month in 1998. Articles included summaries of women's advocacy activities,

Fig. 11.2: Cartoon in *Khmer Women's Voice Center Magazine.*

training programmes, and comments by politicians and activists (see Fig. 11.2). The Women's Media Center of Cambodia established Radio WMC in 2000 in order 'to raise awareness of social issues in Cambodia and to improve the situation of women for the benefit of Cambodian society'. Young women have been a particular target for rights awareness and initiatives. The non-governmental organization Vulnerable Children Assistance Organisation initiated a project that re-trained liberated child domestic workers, the majority of whom are girls, in skills such as hairdressing.[44]

A number of NGOs with women's issues as their focus trained women candidates in topics germane to political participation, including electoral process and decentralisation, prior to the commune elections in 2003.[45] Women in Prosperity was described in 2000 as the first organisation 'committed to helping women in political positions to develop skills and gain the courage to take the candidacy and become members of the parliament and the senate', including leadership training project for women candidates in all three political parties.[46] On 25 February 2000 the gender unit of Khmer Women's Voice Center, led by Koy Veth, in cooperation with the Ministry for Women's and Veteran's Affairs, laid sixteen proposals before the Senate and the Royal Government of Cambodia concerning 'the strengthening of women's power, promoting women to assume mid-level positions and creating favourable conditions for equality and equity'. The proposals included the organisation of gender training courses in all localities to promote the understanding of the population in general, the introduction of gender issues into school curriculum, the establishment of dormitories for female students and the provision that 30 per cent of the candidacy will be women standing for the commune elections. A fortnight later, on 6 March, a rally of over 200 representatives from national and international NGOs, United Nations agencies, and government bodies marched from the Independence Monument to the National Assembly, where they presented proposals advocating women's rights to Prince Ranariddh. On 28 March 2000 Prime Minister Hun Sen granted an audience to representatives of women's non-governmental organizations and rights groups who were asking for a quota of female candidates. The Prime Minister, however, favoured the 'encouragement' of women rather than a quota system.[47]

∿

Gender identity, particularly female, is intricately bound up with ideas of culture and tradition, and resistance to change in this area is therefore connected to notions of ethnicity and nationalism. This is not, of course, a peculiarly Cambodian phenomenon; across the region, when 'women embrace alternative gender roles and openly express their sexual autonomy, existing power relations are destabilized'. Cambodians find any assault on practices or beliefs regarded as 'traditional' particularly difficult to countenance due to the reconfiguration of Cambodian society during the Khmer Rouge period. Relinquishing Cambodian customs that have been resurrected since 1979, especially those that dictate one's correct place in the complicated social hierarchy, is perceived as inviting chaos. Politicians criticise and delay the ratification of legal instruments that will afford women greater protections as 'they will be so happy with their freedom that they [will] not respect ancient Cambodian customs'. Periodic crackdowns on sex workers are carried out as too great a presence will adversely affect the good reputation of Cambodia. In any case, there is a widespread belief amongst Cambodians that all sex workers in Cambodia are Vietnamese, as 'Khmer women are thought to keep up certain moral ideals, which are different (or non-existent) for Vietnamese women'. Advertising and television programming reinforce 'traditional' stereo-

Fig. 11.3: Postcard on sale in the central post office in Phnom Penh, December 2005.

types of gender roles wherein women are relegated to the domestic sphere (see Fig. 11.3); the correct observance of their role therein ensures the harmony of Cambodian society.[48] Deviation from these 'traditional' roles, it is implied, will bring about another catastrophic inversion of Cambodian society. Yet the 'tradition' of female powerlessness is false, constructed out of bias and perpetuated by those who have dismissed the significance of women in Cambodia's past and ignored evidence for their consequence in the present.

Notes to Chapter 11

1   Articles 31, 34–36, 43, 45–46, 50, and 73 of the 1993 Constitution of the Kingdom of Cambodia, in Raoul M. Jennar, *The Cambodian constitutions (1953–1993)*, Bangkok: White Lotus, 1995, pp. 12–13, 15–16, 19; Astrid Aafjes and Bama Athreya, *Working women in Cambodia*, Phnom Penh: Asian American Free Labor Institute, 1996, p. 6; *Women: Key*

to national reconstruction, Phnom Penh: Secretariat of State for Women's Affairs, Kingdom of Cambodia, 1995, p. 3. The Secretariat admitted in 1995 that these objectives 'may be difficult to achieve given the Secretariat of State for Women's Affairs received only 0.12 per cent of the 1994 national budget' (*Women: Key to national reconstruction,* p. 29).

2   Pierre Bourdieu, *Masculine domination,* trans. Richard Nice, Stanford, California: Stanford University Press, 2001, pp. 93–94.

3   Article 16 of the 1993 Constitution of the Kingdom of Cambodia, in *Constitutions of Cambodia,* p. 10. The throne of Cambodia was once again occupied by Norodom Sihanouk when the Kingdom was officially reconstituted; his favourite consort, Princess Monique as was, took the reign-name Queen Monineath in order to eradicate her non-Cambodian background. Article 16 is interesting. Should it be read as a pre-emptive strike against the possibility of Monique reigning in the event of her husband's death, the legacy of her unsavoury reputation as the root cause of Cambodia's social ills in the late 1960s, or plain gender discrimination?

4   *Women: Key to national reconstruction,* pp. 17–19; *Gender in election and female leadership at the communal level,* Phnom Penh: Women's Media Centre, 2000, p. 7; Katarina Larsson, *Country gender profile: Cambodia,* Report for the Asia Department, Swedish International Development Agency, 1996, p. 18; Xinhua New Agency, 6 September 2000. No data was available for Under-Secretaries of State in 2006.

5   Julio A. Jeldres, *The royal house of Cambodia,* Phnom Penh: Monument Books, 2003, pp. 85–86, 94; *Gender in election,* p. 8

6   Mark R. Thompson, 'Female leadership of democratic transitions in Asia', *Pacific Affairs* 75, 4 (Winter 2002/2003), p. 538; Mona Lilja and Tevy Prom, 'Female politicians in Cambodia', in John L. Vijghen (ed.), *People and the 1998 national elections in Cambodia: Their voices, roles and impact on democracy,* Phnom Penh: Experts for Community Research, 2002, pp. 50–51.

7   *Gender in election,* p. 15.

8   This dichotomy is not, of course, limited to the Cambodian context.

9   Fieldnotes, 2003, 2005, 2006; see also Aing Sokroeun, 'A comparative analysis of traditional and contemporary roles of Khmer women in the household: A case study in Leap Tong village', MA thesis, Royal University of Phnom Penh, 2004, p. 67; Annuska Derks, 'The broken women of Cambodia', in Evelyne Micllier (ed.), *Sexual cultures in East Asia: The social construction of sexuality and sexual risk in a time of AIDS,* London: RoutledgeCurzon, 2004, pp. 127–155; Annuska Derks, 'Khmer women on the move: Migration and urban experiences in Cambodia', PhD thesis, University of Amsterdam, 2005; Mark Bray and Seng Bunly, *Balancing the books: Household financing of basic education in Cambodia,* Hong Kong: Comparative Education Research Centre, The University of Hong Kong and The World Bank, 2005, p. 55.

10   Fieldnotes, 2006. Female perspectives on this were also low; 20 per cent of university students and 9 per cent of unskilled workers thought it was acceptable for women to have affairs after they were married.

11 *Gender in election*, p. 7.

12 Field research conducted in 2006 showed 74.14 per cent of participants experienced this in their family (fieldnotes, 2005, 2006; see also Aing Sokroeun, 'A comparative analysis of traditional and contemporary roles of Khmer women in the household', p. 48; Audrey Riffaud, 'Contextual and cultural pressures in development projects implemented by GTZ in Cambodia', Masters thesis, Université La Sorbonne-Paris IV, 2006, p. 24).

13 Fieldntoes, 2005, 2006.

14 Fieldnotes, 2005, 2006; see also Rebecca Surtees, 'Rape and sexual transgression in Cambodian society', in Linda Rae Bennett and Lenore Manderson (eds), *Violence against women in Asian societies*, London: RoutledgeCurzon, 2003, p. 107.

15 In any case rape is seldom reported due to lack of trust in law and order. See Caroline Hughes, *The political economy of Cambodia's transition, 1991–2001*, London; New York: RoutledgeCurzon, 2003, p. 56.

16 Derks, 'The broken women of Cambodia', p. 137; fieldnotes, 2005.

17 This is based upon nearly 200 interviews conducted as part of the Buddhist Institute Project 4 in 2005 and 2006. See Trudy Jacobsen et al., *The situation of daun chi in Cambodia*, Phnom Penh: Buddhist Institute, 2006.

18 Interviews of the Project 4: Gender and Buddhism, 2005–2006, BTB-DC6.

19 Annuska Derks found that in 2001 garment factories in Phnom Penh employed over 200,000 people, of which between 80 and 90 per cent were women (Khmer women on the move, p. 113).

20 A *srei beer* said in 2002 'Whether I should vote is not important, because no political party is going to improve our living conditions … . We are beer girls and we will remain beer girls'. 'You can say that again – 2002's quotable quotes', *Phnom Penh Post*, 20 December 2002–2 January 2003, p. 14.

21 Helen Jenks Clarke, 'Research for empowerment in a divided Cambodia', in Marie Smyth and Gillian Robinson (eds), *Researching violently divided societies: Ethical and methodological issues*, Tokyo; New York; Paris: United nations University Press; London: Pluto Press, 2001, p. 96.

22 Louise Brown, *Sex slaves: The trafficking of women in Asia*, London: Virago, 2001, p. 126; fieldnotes, 2005.

23 Fieldnotes, 2005; *8 March*, Phnom Penh: Khmer Women's Voice Centre, 1998, p. 9. See also Brown, *Sex slaves*, p. 131; *Gender and behaviour towards love*, Phnom Penh: Women's Media Centre, 2000, p. 27. For a Thai parallel see Nerida Cook, "Dutiful daughters', estranged sisters: Women in Thailand', in Krishna Sen and Maila Stivens, *Gender and power in affluent Asia*, London: Routledge, 1998, p. 260.

24 'Moto' or 'moto-dup', are the main form of public transport in urban areas in Cambodia. Drivers convey passengers and goods on a medium-sized motorcycle for an agreed price.

25 Fieldnotes, 2001, 2006; Brown, *Sex slaves*, pp. 137, 139; Chou Meng Tarr and Peter Aggleton, "Sexualising' the culture(s) of young Cambodians: Dominant discourses and

social reality', in Sorn Samnang (ed.) *Khmer studies: Knowledge of the past and its contributions to the rehabilitation and reconstruction of Cambodia:Proceedings of International Conference on Khmer Studies, Phnom Penh, 26–30 August 1996,* Phnom Penh: Sorn Samnang, 1996, vol. 2, pp. 1031–1032, 1035; Bourdieu, *Masculine domination,* p. 52; 'You can say that again! – 2002's quotable quotes', *Phnom Penh Post,* 20 December 2002–2 January 2003, p. 14; Peter S. Hill and Heng Thay Ly, 'Women are silver, women are diamonds: Conflicting images of women in the Cambodian print media', *Reproductive Health Matters* 12, 24 (2004), p. 111.

26 In 1999 a rumour was circulated to the effect that the royal palace had become inhabited by 'an evil god demanding thousands of long-haired virgin girls'; the implication was that the 'inhabitant' (the king) was old, ailing and impotent. His political opinions, therefore, could carry no weight. It is probably no accident that this rumour was documented on the CPP website (www.cambodianpeopleparty.org/29-02-00.htm).

27 Fieldnotes, 2003, 2006; see also Brown, *Sex slaves,* pp. 118–199, 120. Lisa Law also found that 'sex workers do not conceive their encounters with foreign men in strictly oppressive terms' (Lisa Law, *Sex work in Southeast Asia: The place of desire in a time of AIDS,* Abingdon, Oxon: Routledge, 2000, p. 121).

28 This was also what Mona Lilja and Tevy Prom found in their study ('Female politicians in Cambodia', pp. 48–49.

29 Hill and Heng, 'Women are silver, women are diamonds', p. 108.

30 *Gender in election,* pp. 16–17, 24.

31 Maria Mies, *Patriarchy and accumulation on a world scale: Women in the international division of labour,* London and Atlantic Highlands, New Jersey: Zed Books, 1986, p. 193; Elizabeth Fuller Collins, '(Re)negotiating gender hierarchy in the New Order: A South Sumatran field study', *Asia Pacific Viewpoint,* 37, 2 (1996), p. 130; Tioulong Saumura, 'Gender, security and human rights: The case of Cambodia', speech presented at the *14th Asia-Pacific Roundtable,* 3–6 June 2000, Kuala Lumpur. Available at www.samrainsyparty. org/national_assembly/KL_ISIS_CONF_JUNE2000_ts_speech.html.

32 Fieldnotes, 2001; Maureen H. Fitzgerald et al., *Hear our voices: Trauma, birthing and mental health among Cambodian women,* Paramatta, NSW: Transcultural Mental Health Centre, 1998, p. 51.

33 Fieldnotes, 2003, 2005, 2006; see also Derks, 'The broken women of Cambodia', p. 151, and Leviseda Douglas, *Sex trafficking in Cambodia,* Clayton, Victoria: Monash University Centre of Southeast Asian Studies Working Paper 122, 2003, p. 6.

34 'See Audrey Riffaud: 'Foreigners have de facto a power since they are associated to people having knowledge, resources and money' (Contextual and cultural pressures in development projects implemented by GTZ in Cambodia, p. 22).

35 Flora Stubbs, 'Pageant strives to open door for all Cambodian women', *Cambodia Daily,* Wednesday, December 11, 2002, p. 20.

36 See for example Judy Ledgerwood, *Analysis of the situation of women in Cambodia: Research on women in Khmer society,* UNICEF consultancy report, Phnom Penh, February–

June 1992; Siobhan Gorman with Pon Dorina and Sok Kheng, *Gender and development in Cambodia: An overview*, Phnom Penh: Cambodia Development Resource Institute, Working Paper 10, 1999.

37 Gorman et al., *Gender and development in Cambodia*, p. 6; Larsson, *Country gender profile*, p. 25.

38 *Gender in election*, p. 20.

39 *Gender in election*, pp. 19–20. 'Women leaders', www.onlinewomeninpolitics.org/cambo/cmbdleads.html.

40 Tioulong Saumura, 'Gender, security and human rights'.

41 Tioulong Saumura, 'Gender, security and human rights'; Vanphone Phomphipak and Sun Heng, 'Women's party takes single-minded approach to winning', *Light of the voters*, www.ijf-cij.org/folder_file_for_cambodia/9.htm. This party, although still in existence, has not achieved much of a following in terms of voter turnout.

42 *Gender in election*, p. 2.

43 *Gender in election*, p. 17.

44 Fieldnotes, 2001; *Women: Key to national reconstruction*, p. 3; Kate Frieson, *In the shadows: Women, power and politics in Cambodia*, Victoria, British Columbia: Centre for Asia-Pacific Initiatives Occasional Paper No. 26, University of Victoria, 2001, p. 16; Aafjes and Athreya, *Working women in Cambodia*, p. 3; Charlotte McDonald-Gibson, 'The bleak and lonely world of child servants', *Phnom Penh Post*, 3–16 January 2003, p. 12; Larsson, *Country gender profile*, p. 25; David Kihara and Phann Ana, 'Program lets women regain control of lives', *Cambodia Daily*, Thursday, March 8, 2001, pp. 1, 9; *8 March*, p. 11; KWVC, *Women and family law: October 96–March 97 advocacy project report*, Phnom Penh: Khmer Women's Voice Center, 1997; *Women.s Media Centre of Cambodia* information leaflet, Phnom Penh, 2001.

45 Manila Vanthanouvong and Sak Linda, 'Women moving toward power', *Light of the voters*, www.ijf-cij.org/folder_file_for_cambodia/8.htm

46 The Women's Association for Peace and Development had similar proposals in process in 2000. See *Gender in election*, pp. 19–20.

47 *Gender and behaviour towards love*, pp. 35–37; *Gender in election*, p. 11.

48 Gorman et al., *Gender and development in Cambodia*, p.1; Frieson, *In the shadows*, p. 17; Bennett and Manderson, 'Introduction: Gender inequality and technologies of violence', p. 11; Hill and Heng, 'Women are silver, women are diamonds', p. 109; Derks, Khmer women on the move, pp. 122, 125; Larsson, *Country gender profile*, pp. 20–21.

CHAPTER TWELVE

Goddesses Found

*T*his book began by asking a number of questions. Who or what is responsible for the denial of female power in Cambodian history? Have Cambodian women ever been powerful? If so, when did this begin to change, and by what agency? Having examined the political, social and ideological status of different categories of women throughout Cambodian history, it is now possible to suggest some answers.

Until the middle of the nineteenth century, the women in the upper echelons of society, namely the royal families and the nobility, took an active role in court politics. The daughters of kings were believed to embody the land into which they were born; thus princes from other places would travel to their brides' kingdoms and through union with them would access the right to rule. Exigent circumstances at times led some of these women to rule alone, as we have seen in the cases of Jayadevi and the Śambhupura queens in the seventh and eighth centuries, the two 'breakaway' queens of the eighteenth centuries, and Ang Mei in the nineteenth century. Although autonomous queens were not the norm, they did receive sufficient support from the *oknha* that allowed them to reign. Similarly, other queens and princesses of the middle period, such as Devikhsatri, Ang Chuv and Ang Li, were able to draw upon the support of their clients to overthrown unpopular kings. Elite women were thus critical members of the intricate *khsae* system upon which political power in the Cambodian past rested. Wealthy women made donations and participated in ceremonies, whether Brahmanical or Buddhist; others 'entered into religion' as *kantai kloñ* and nuns; still others joined their menfolk as temple officiants responsible for the maintenance of cults and indentured servants tending the lands and enterprises associated with particular religious establishments. Women and men beyond the palace were treated equally in law, with special protections for young women in the event of seduction and ill-treatment at the hands of their masters and husbands. Although epigraphy and codes of conduct after the ninth century began to reflect a lessening of importance and agency for women, these were ideals rather than a true reflection of Cambodian society.

The nineteenth century is a pivotal one for understanding how female power came to be denied in modern Cambodia. If we are to accept the late nineteenth and early twentieth centuries as indicative of 'traditional' Cambodia, then a holistic overview, sourced from folktales and observers' accounts, is one of egalitarianism and agency for women. Yet the literature that has been taken to represent an accurate picture of Cambodian society at this time is the genre to which texts such as the *Cbpab Srei* belongs, in which female sexuality is regarded as dangerous and female autonomy anathema. These texts, authored by conservative men, at first did not permeate Cambodian society beyond a literary appreciation at court. Similarly, the court chronicles written (and those of earlier reigns revised) during this period, reflected the perspective of the king who had emerged as the victor from the civil instability of the first half of the nineteenth century: Ang Duong. As the histories of Cambodia written during the colonial period did not reflect upon possible biases in authorship, and the inculcation of critical faculties in colonial subjects was contrary to French interests, successive generations of Cambodians came to believe that female inferiority and passivity were characteristics of the Cambodian past. Ang Duong and his reign became associated with the period of Cambodian history between Vietnamese domination and the imposition of colonialism; in other words, a Cambodian society free of external interference. The texts and histories of elite authors, and thus the perspectives on correct action for men and women therein, were considered more important than folktales, and it was to the former that Cambodians turned when searching for a national cultural identity free of colonial interference.

The powerlessness and subservience taken to be 'traditional' for Cambodian women is based upon a false premise. Yet it is this role that has become identified as 'correct behaviour' in the minds of generations of Cambodians and which has constrained women from accessing a greater share of positions in public life. As modernisation began to impact upon Cambodian society in the 1950s and 1960s, women were charged with guardianship of the Cambodian past; any attempt to move beyond the parameters of a *srei krup leakkhana* was perceived as a threat to Cambodian culture. Even when mobilised in the course of patriotic and revolutionary activities, women were expected to fulfil 'traditional' roles that tied them to domestic rather than national concerns, and for many Cambodians in the 1990s the re-establishment of society after decades of civil war meant a return to the gender roles set out in *Cbpap Srei* and its ilk. Women, not men, are entrusted with the continuation of Cambodian culture. As Kate Frieson has said,

> the imprint of Khmer nationalism, with racial survival as its *leitmotif*, is embossed on all nationalist movements, in and out of power, and as such, it has placed an onerous burden on women to be the Khmer nation's reproducers, its ideological protectors, and its cultural guardians – sometimes with tragic results.[1]

Cambodians must now choose whether to continue to accept this false 'tradition' that relegates over half the population to inferior positions in society and legitimises violence and discrimination against them. There comes a time when all traditions must be reappraised. Some Cambodians are questioning the relevance of the *Cbpab Srei* to modern life, acknowledging that 'old ideas' on good conduct, written in the nineteenth century, will make it difficult to improve the status of women in the future.[2] There are other indications of a positive change in social attitude towards women. Some feel that the events of 5 and 6 July 1997 'would not have seen bloodshed if women had been the political leadership'. This attitude has been fostered by new slogans devised by people involved in women's issues advocacy, such as 'Man is one hand, woman is the other: Cambodia uses both hands to build the nation!' and 'Women in power means that the country is powerful'. Women have been described as better at conflict resolution and implementing initiatives than men; they have also been described as less corruptible.[3]

In the supernatural world, however, female power has retained its significance throughout the historical period. The legendary ruler of the earliest Cambodian kingdom was an unmarried warrior queen; her legacy is apparent in the many autonomous goddesses such as Durga Mahishasuramardani of the earliest period. Although independent representations of goddesses waned in the ensuing period, the supernatural significance of women continued in the cult of the *kanlong kamraten an* and the many *neak ta, me sa,* and *brai* who pervade the Cambodian past and remain firmly entrenched in the lives of most Cambodians today.[4] The Naga king regularly manifests himself in *kru* as Neang Nak, 'Lady Naga'; other popular spirits are Parvati, Srei Khmau, Preah Dharani and Umavati, believed to be the sister of Soma, the original ruler of Cambodia. Didier Bertrand has found that the majority of *rup* are women.[5] Perhaps, instead of looking for 'significance' of women in political office, we should be looking to the unseen world that has far more resonance for everyday life in Cambodia than the abstract decisions of an elite governing body.

Masculine domination, as Pierre Bourdieu described it, is a 'paradox of doxa' in which it is astonishing that

> the established order, with its relations of domination, its rights and prerogatives, privileges and injustices, ultimately, perpetuates itself so easily, apart from a few historical accidents, and that the most intolerable conditions of existence can so often be perceived as acceptable and even natural.[6]

The reluctance of Cambodians today to abolish customs, particularly gender roles, that they believe are cornerstones of Cambodian 'tradition' is understandable. The last time Cambodian society was radically inverted, between 1975 and 1979, roughly 2.5 million people died. 'Tradition' is also a convenient scapegoat upon which to blame poor performance in terms of human development indicators, such as low female literacy and high levels of violence against women. But traditions that are detrimental to over half the population cannot continue to be upheld. People often cite the Cambodian adage 'Men are like gold, women are like white cotton'. This is understood as saying that gold (read: men) can be dropped in mud and washed clean, whereas white cotton (read: women), once 'soiled', loses its value. This is an obvious comment upon autonomy for women and legitimises limiting opportunities for female empowerment. Yet there are alternative interpretations of the relative merits of gold and cloth. White cotton, even when it is stained, is still useful. It can tie things together, transport them, thresh grain, polish, clean, and cover people for warmth. It can keep out the rain and protect from the sun. Gold, on the other hand, is practically useless in real terms; it is put away for safekeeping and brought out to exchange for other, more useful goods.

Cambodian women in the past have been valued by their societies. Some have led rebellions and instigated revolts. There is no doubt that women were busily employed behind the scenes of palace life – whether they were machinating successions, conferring legitimacy, or involved in diplomacy – and working side-by-side with their menfolk in the less ostentatious, but equally important, surroundings of the ricefields. Women may not have been required to perform corvée labour to the same extent as men; on the other hand, we know that Cambodian women and men were required to accompany the Thai army to Burma in the eighteenth century in order to mill rice for the troops. The different roles that men and women undertook in agriculture, animal husbandry, and family life do not mean that one was valued more highly than another. The continued effort of all was necessary for the assured good fortune of the family, the village, society, and ultimately the kingdom, whether this activity took place in the economic realm, where the marketing skills of women were key, in an ideological sense, wherein the performance of certain rituals by women ensured peace and prosperity, or the political sphere, in which the association between women and the land was of paramount importance for would-be male rulers. The importance of women in the Cambodian past can be discerned from the creation mythology, the legal codes protecting women's interests and rights, and the continued presence of female power in supernatural space, unbroken for centuries.

To deny women a similar value in the Cambodian present is to perpetuate the interpretation of history by elite Cambodian men who had their own reasons for perhaps resenting and controlling women, and the mistaken assumptions of colonial-era historians as they 'discovered' the Cambodian past through the texts of these authors. In any case, assuming that a female presence (or lack thereof) in political representation is indicative of gender equality is to perpetrate Western meanings of power in a non-Western context. This is not to suggest that it is 'un-Cambodian' for women to seek to act as representatives for like-minded men and women in 21st-century Cambodia. Yet until Cambodians realise that letting go of elements of presumed 'traditional' culture will not result in cultural extermination we must look beyond political office for signs of female power in Cambodia. The supernatural world – ignored by most Western historians and political scientists – is omnipresent in Cambodian society. In every home, *meba p'dteah* are offered fruit or rice daily. *Yeay Deb* and other *neak ta* live on in *wat*s and sacred places. *Brai* and *ap* stalk the night seeking fulfilment in bloody revenge for real or imagined slights. Preah Dharani stands proudly at the gates of the Ministry of Water Resources and Meteorology (see Fig. 12.1), on her roundabout near the Olympic market, and in countless *wat* murals. The significance and relevance of the female in this sphere – arguably the one of most resonance for Cambodians – has never been diminished, despite repeated assaults on the role of women in the tangible world by imported ideologies that relegated women to inferior and dependent positions. It is here that we should look for the empowerment of women in Cambodia, in a culturally context-specific locale rather than a hybrid interpretation of misogynist perspectives foisted upon Cambodian culture by foreigners for over a millennium.

Cambodian goddesses were never lost; we simply have been looking for them in the wrong places.

Fig. 12.1: Statue of Preah Dharani, Phnom Penh.

Notes to Chapter 12

1   Kate Frieson, *In the shadows: Women, power and politics in Cambodia*, Victoria, British Columbia: University of Victoria Centre for Asia-Pacific Initiatives Occasional Paper 26, 2001, p. 17.

2   Aing Sokroeun, 'A comparative analysis of traditional and contemporary roles of Khmer women in the household: A case study in Leap Tong village', MA thesis, Royal University of Phnom Penh, 2004, p. 74; Editorial, *The Mirror* 7, 315 (2003), p. 1; Frieson, *In the shadows*, pp. 16–17; Kek Galabru, *The situation of women in Cambodia*, Phnom Penh: LICHADO (Cambodian League for the Promotion and Defense of Human Rights), July 2004, pp. 31–32.

3   *8 March*, Phnom Penh: Khmer Women's Voice Centre, 1998, p. 15; *Gender in election and female leadership at the communal level*, Phnom Penh: Women's Media Centre, 2000, pp. 10, 28, 30.

4   Ashley Thompson, 'Introductory remarks between the lines: Writing histories of Middle Cambodia', in Barbara Watson Andaya (ed), *Other past: women, gender and history in early modern Southeast Asia*, Honolulu: University of Hawai'i Press, 2001, pp. 47–68.

5   Didier Bertrand, 'A medium possession practice and its relationship with Cambodian Buddhism: The *grū pāramī*', in John Marston and Elizabeth Guthrie (eds), *History, Buddhism, and new religious movements in Cambodia*, Honolulu: University of Hawai'i Press, 2004, pp. 153, 159.

6   Pierre Bourdieu, *Masculine domination*, trans. Richard Nice, Stanford, California: Stanford University Press, 2001, p. 1.

Bibliography

AA	*Artibus Asiae*
ASEMI	*Asie du Sud-Est et le Monde Insulindien*
BEFEO	*Bulletin de l'École Française d'Extrême-Orient*
EFEO	*École Française d'Extrême-Orient*
JGIS	*Journal of the Greater India Society*
JRAS	*Journal of the Royal Asiatic Society*
JSEAS	*Journal of Southeast Asian Studies*
JSS	*Journal of the Siam Society*

PRIMARY SOURCES

Epigraphy

Bergaigne, Abel (comp. and ed.). 1891. *Inscriptions sanscrites du Cambodge*. Paris: Académie des Inscriptions et Belles-Lettres.

Chirapat Prapandvidya. 1990. 'The Sab Bak inscription: Evidence of an early vajrayana Buddhist presence in Thailand'. *JSS* 78, 2, pp. 11–14.

Cœdès, George. 1913. 'Études cambodgiennes 11: La stèle de Palhal'. *BEFEO* 13, 6, pp. 143–52.

——. 1931. 'Études cambodgiennes 25. Deux inscriptions sanskrites du Fou-nan'. *BEFEO* 31, pp. 1–12.

——. 1937. 'A new inscription from Fu-nan'. *JGIS* 4, pp. 112–121.

——. 1937–1966. *Inscriptions du Cambodge*, 8 vols. Paris and Hanoi: Imprimerie de l'EFEO and Imprimerie Nationale.

——. 1956. 'Études cambodgiennes 40: Nouvelles données sur les origines du royaume khmèr'. *BEFEO* 48, 1, pp. 209–240.

Cœdès, George and Pierre Dupont. 1942–1943. 'L'Inscription de Sdok Kak Thom'. *BEFEO* 43, pp. 57–135.

Digraphic Inscriptions. The Digraphic Inscriptions comprise twelve identical inscriptions (K. 42, K. 45, K. 47, K. 57, K. 95, K. 101, K. 110, K. 223, K. 309, K. 323, K. 346, K. 362) commissioned by Yaśovarman I (889–912) and erected in 889. The inscription referred to in this instance is K. 323. In Bergaigne, *Inscriptions sanscrites du Cambodge*. Paris: Imprimerie Nationale, 1891, pp. 391–411.

Finot, Louis. 1904. 'Les inscriptions de Mi-son'. *BEFEO* 4 (1904), pp. 897–977.

——. 1925. 'Inscription de Mebon oriental'. *BEFEO* 25 (1925), pp. 309–352.

Inscriptions modernes d'Angkor (IMA). *Textes en kmer moyen. Inscriptions modernes d'Angkor*, trans. Saveros Lewitz/Pou. In *BEFEO* 57 (1970), pp. 99–126; 58 (1971), pp. 105–123; 59 (1972), pp. 101–121, 221–249; 60 (1973), pp. 163–203, 204–242; 61 (1974), pp. 301–337; 62 (1975), pp. 283–353.

Vickery, Michael. 1977. 'The 2/k.125 fragment: A lost chronicle of Ayuthya'. *JSS* 65, 1 (1977), pp. 1–80.

——. 1982. 'L'Inscription K. 1006 du Phnom Kulen'. *BEFEO* 71 (1982), pp. 77–86.

Literary material

Ang Duong. 1962 [1837]. *Cbpab srei*. Phnom Penh: Institute Bouddhique.

——. 1997 [1813]. *Rieong Kaki*. Phnom Penh: Buddhist Institute.

Buddhist Institute. 1962. *Prachum rieong breng khmei* 4. Phnom Penh: Buddhist Institute.

——. 1971. *Dum Deav*. Phnom Penh: Buddhist Institute.

——. 2001. *Prachum rieong bring khmei* 8. Phnom Penh: Buddhist Institute.

Bühler, Georg (trans.). 1969. *Laws of Manu*. New York: Dover.

Carrison, Muriel Paksin (comp.). 1987. *Cambodian folk stories from the Gatiloke*. Rutland: C.E. Tuttle.

Chalmers, Robert (trans.). 1957. *The jataka, or stories of the Buddha's former births*, vol. 1. Cambridge: Cambridge University Press.

Dampier, William. [1697] 1968. *A new voyage around the world*. New York: Dover.

Garnier, Francis. 1885. *Voyage d'exploration en Indo-Chine, éfféctué par une Commission française présidée par M. le Capitaine de Frégate Doudart de Lagrée*. Paris: Hachette.

Groslier, George. [1928] 1994. *Le Retour à l'argile*. Paris: Kailash.

Hamilton, Alexander. [1727] 1930. *A new account of the East Indies*. London: Argonaut Press.

Harry, M. [n.d.]. *Les petites épouses*. Paris: n.p.

I-Tsing. [671–695]. 1896. *A record of the Buddhist religion as practised in India and the Malay Archipelago (671–695 AD)*, trans. J, Takakusu. Oxford: Clarendon Press.

Institute Bouddhique. 1964. *Bpram brachea brey khmei*. Phnom Penh: Institute Bouddhique.

——. 1964. *Leng bprachea prey khmei*. Phnom Penh: Institut Bouddhique.

——. 1970. *Chansons populaires.* Phnom Penh: Institut Bouddhique.

——. 1971. *Vorivong et Sarivong.* Phnom Penh: Institut Bouddhique.

Kanhya San Neang. 1967. *Socheavatame samrap broh neung srei.* Phnom Penh: n.p.

Kautilya. [c. 400 BCE]. 1961. *Arthasastra,* trans. R. Sharmasastry, 7th ed. Mysore: Mysore Publishing House.

Leonowens, Anna. [1872] 1991. *The romance of the harem,* ed. Susan Morgan. Charlottesville, Virginia: University of Virginia Press.

Leuba, Jean. 1920. *L'Aile de feu.* Paris: n.p.

Luong Vichetr Vohar. n.d. [1960s]. *Morale aux jeunes filles.* Phnom Penh: Université Bouddhique Preah Sihanouk Raj.

Ma Duanlin. [12th/13th century] 1883. *Ethnographie des peuples étrangers à la Chine, ouvrage composé à XI siècle du notre ère.* 2 vols. Geneva: Mueller.

Meyer, Roland. 1919. *Saramani, danseuse khmêr.* Saigon: A. Portail.

Minh Mai. [c.19th century] 2001. *Cbpab Srei-broh.* Phnom Penh: Phsep pseay juon koan khmei, 2001.

Ministry of Information. 1967. *Cambodge.* Phnom Penh: Le Ministre de l'Information du Gouvernment Royal du Cambodge.

Mouhot, Henri. 1864. *Travels in the central parts of Indo-China (Siam), Cambodia and Laos.* 2 vols. London.

van Neck, Jacob. [1599–1604] 1980. *De vierde schipvaart der Nederlanders naar Oost-Indïe onder Jacob van Neck (1599–1604),* ed. H.A. van Foreest and A. de Booy, vol. 1. The Hague: Linschoten-Vereeniging.

Pavie, Auguste. [1901]. *The Pavie Mission Indochina Papers 1879–1895,* vol. 1: *Pavie Mission Exploration Work: Laos, Cambodia, Siam, Yunnan, and Vietnam,* trans. Walter E. J. Tips. Bangkok: White Lotus.

Pe Maung Tin and G.H. Luce (trans.). 1923. *The Glass Palace chronicle of the kings of Burma.* London: Oxford University Press.

Quiroga de San Antonio, Gabriel. 1998. *A brief and truthful relation of events in the kingdom of Cambodia.* Bangkok: White Lotus.

Rickmans, C. Mabel (trans.). 1973. *Cūḷavamsa, being the more recent part of the Mahāvamsa.* London: Pali Text Society.

Sakhan Samon. 1965. *Kpuon Apram Chariya Satrei* [Manual for raising good women]. Phnom Penh: n.p.

San Neang. 1967. *Socheavatadar samrap broh neung srei* [Harmonious living for men and women]. Phnom Penh: n.p.

Sarrault, Albert. 1931. *Grandeur et servitude colonials,* Paris: Sagittaire.

Soth Polin. 1980. *L'Anarchiste.* Paris: La Table Ronde.

Tauch Chhong. 1994. *Battambang during the time of the lord governor,* 2nd ed., trans. Hin Sithan, Carol Mortland and Judy Ledgerwood. Phnom Penh: Cedorek

Thiounn. [1930]. *Danses cambodgiennes,* trans. Jeanne Cuisinier. Phnom Penh: Bibliothéque Royal du Cambodge.

Thiphaakoravong, Cawphraya. 1985 *The dynastic chronicles of the Bangkok era: The fourth reign; B.E. 2394–2411 (A.D. 1851–1868)*, trans. Chadin (Kanjanavanit). 2 vols. Tokyo: The Center of South East Asian Cultural Studies.

Zhou Daguan [14th century]. 1992. *The customs of Cambodia*, trans. J. Gilman d'Arcy Paul, 2nd ed. Bangkok: The Siam Society.

Archival material

Buddhist Institute Project 4: Gender and Buddhism interviews, 2005, 2006. Buddhist Institute, Phnom Penh.

Cambodia Genocide Biographic Database, Cambodian Genocide Program, Yale University. www.yale.edu/cgp

Fonds du Résidence Supérieur du Cambodge (RSC), 1863–1953. Archives National du Cambodge, Phnom Penh.

Fonds du Sangkum Reastr Niyum (SRN), 1953–1969. Archives National du Cambodge, Phnom Penh.

Journal Officiel du Cambodge. 1970. Secretariat Général du Conseil du Ministres, Phnom Penh.

Mouvement national de soutien aux peuples d'Indochine. 1973. *Cambodge: Textes et documents*, [Cambodia?]: Mouvement national de soutien aux peuples d'Indochine.

S–21 records and confessions. Documentation Centre of Cambodia, Phnom Penh.

SECONDARY SOURCES

Aafjes, Astrid and Bama Athreya. 1996. *Working women in Cambodia*. Phnom Penh: Asian American Free Labor Iinstitute.

ADHOC. 2001. *Satrei khmei neung setthi manus* [Cambodian women and human rights]. Phnom Penh: ADHOC.

Agrawala, R.C. 1958. 'The goddess Mahisasuramardini in early Indian art'. *AA* 21, pp. 123–130.

Aing Sokroeun. 2004. 'A comparative analysis of traditional and contemporary roles of Khmer women in the household: A case study in Leap Tong village'. MA thesis, Royal University of Phnom Penh.

Alangir, Jalal. 1997. 'Against the current: The survival of authoritarianism in Burma'. *Pacific Affairs* 70, 3, pp. 333–350.

Allen, Louis. 1972. 'Studies in the Japanese occupation of Southeast Asia, 1944–1945'. *Durham University Journal* 64, pp. 120–132.

Andaya, Barbara Watson. 1998. 'From temporary wife to prostitute: Sexuality and economic change in early modern Southeast Asia'. *Journal of Women's History*, 9, 4, pp. 11–35.

—— (ed.). 2000. *Other pasts: Women, gender and history in early modern Southeast Asia*. Manoa, Hawai'i: University of Hawai'i Press.

——. 2002. 'Localising the universal: Women, motherhood and the appeal of early Theravada Buddhism'. *JSEAS*, 33, 1, pp. 1–30.

——. 2006. *The flaming womb: Repositioning women in early modern Southeast Asia.* Honolulu: University of Hawai'i Press.

Andaya, Leonard Y. 1993. 'Cultural state formation in eastern Indonesia'. In Anthony Reid (ed.), *Southeast Asia in the early modern period: Trade, power, and belief.* Ithaca, New York; London, pp. 23–41.

Anderson, Benedict R. O'G. 1990. *Language and power: Exploring political cultures in Indonesia.* Ithaca, New York; London: Cornell University Press.

Ang Chouléan. 1982. 'Grossesse et accouchement au Cambodge: aspects rituals'. *ASEMI* XIII, 1–4, pp. 87–109.

——. 1986. *Les êtres surnaturels dans la religion populaire khmère.* Paris: Cedorek.

——. 1987–1990. 'Le sacré au féminin'. *Seksa Khmer* 10–13, pp. 7–9.

Angladeete, André. 1979. 'La vie quotidienne en Indochine de 1939 à 1946'. *Mondes et cultures* 30, pp. 467–498.

Anon. 1943. *Souverains et notibilités d'Indochine.* Hanoi: Éditions du Gouvernement Général de l'Indochine.

Anon. [1954]. *Mémoire du Cambodge sur ses terres au Sau-Vietnam (Cochinchine).* Phnom Penh: Imprimerie du Palais Royale.

Anon. 1998. *Love letters.* Phnom Penh: Am Ta.

Appel, Michael. 2000. 'Cultural identity in myth and ritual: A case of west Java'. In Chandra Lokesh (ed.), *Society and culture of Southeast Asia: Continuities and changes.* New Delhi: International Academy of Indian Culture; Aditya Prakashan, pp. 1–12.

Ashley, David W. 1998. 'The failure of conflict resolution in Cambodia: Causes and lessons'. In Frederick Z. Brown and David G. Timberman (eds), *Cambodia and the international community: The quest for peace, development, and democracy.* Singapore: Institute of Southeast Asian Studies, pp. 49–78.

Association Française des Amis de l'Orient. 1997. *La Musée de Sculpture Cam de Đà Năng.* Paris: Association Française des Amis de l'Orient.

Atkinson, Jane Monnig and Shelly Errington (eds). 1990. *Power and difference: Gender in island Southeast Asia.* Stanford, California: Stanford University Press.

Aymonier, Étienne. 1900–1903. *Le Cambodge.* 3 vols. Paris: E. Leroux.

——. 1903. *Le Founan.* Paris: Imprimerie Nationale.

——. 1984. *Notes sur les coutumes et croyances supersititeuses des cambodgiens, commenté et présenté par Saveros Pou.* Paris: Centre de Documentation et de Recherche sur la Civilisation Khmere [Cedorek].

Ayres, David M. 2000. *Anatomy of a crisis: Education, development, and the state in Cambodia, 1953–1998.* Honolulu: University of Hawai'i Press.

Azad, Nandini. 1994. *Sisters of hope: A monograph on women, work and entrepreneurship in Cambodia.* Report of the UNDP/ILO Small Enterprise and Informal Sector Project, Phnom Penh.

Bachhofer, Ludwig. 1935. 'The influx of Indian sculpture into Funan'. *JGIS* 2, pp. 122–127.

Barron, John and Anthony Paul. 1977. *Peace with horror: The untold story of communist genocide in Cambodia*. **London: Hodder and Stoughton.**

Becker, Elizabeth. *When the war was over.* New York: Simon & Schuster, 1986.

Benisti, M. 1974. 'Note d'iconographie khmère 10: premières représentations de Sri Laksmi'. *BEFEO* 61, 2, pp. 349–354.

Bennett, Linda Rae and Lenore Manderson (eds). 2003. *Violence against women in Asian societies.* London: RoutledgeCurzon.

Benzançon, Pascale. 1998. 'L'Impact de la colonisation française sur l'emergence d'un système éducatif moderne au Cambodge (1863–1945)'. In Sorn Samnang (ed.), *Khmer studies: Knowledge of the past, and its contributions to the rehabilitation and reconstruction of Cambodia, proceedings of the International Conference on Khmer Studies, Phnom Penh, 26–30 August 1996.* Phnom Penh: Toyota Foundation, French Embassy, British Embassy. Vol. 2, pp. 895–897.

Berger, Mark T. 2001. '(De)constructing the New Order: Capitalism and the cultural contours of the patrimonial state in Indonesia'. In Souchou Yao (ed.), *House of glass: Culture, modernity, and the state in Southeast Asia.* Singapore: Institute of Southeast Asian Studies, pp. 191–212.

Bertrand, Didier. 2004. 'A medium possession practice and its relationship with Cambodian Buddhism: The *grū pāramī*'. In John Marston and Elizabeth Guthrie (eds), *History, Buddhism, and new religious movements in Cambodia.* Honolulu: University of Hawai'i Press, 150–169.

Bhattacharya, Kamaleswar. 1961. *Les religions brahmaniques dans l'ancien Cambodge, d'après l'épigraphie et l'iconographie.* Paris: EFEO.

———. 1966. 'Notes d'iconographie khmère 12: Les images de Lakṣmī à Prasat Kravan'. *Arts Asiatiques* 13, pp. 111–113.

Bizot, François. 1980. 'La grotte de la naissance'. *BEFEO* 67, pp. 221–273.

———. 1989. Ramaker, ou, l'amour symbolique de Ram et Seta. Paris: EFEO.

———. 1992. *Le chemin de Langka.* Paris: EFEO.

——— (ed.). 1994. *Recherches nouvelles sur le Cambodge.* Paris: EFEO.

Boisselier, Jean. 1955. 'Une statue féminine inédite du style de Sambor'. *Arts Asiatiques* 2, 1, pp. 18–24.

———. 1966. *Le Cambodge.* Paris: Èditions A et E Picard & Co.

———. 1989. *Trends in Khmer Art*, trans. Natasha Eilenberg and Melvin Elliott. Ithaca, New York: Southeast Asia Program, Cornell University.

Le Bonheur, A. 1972. 'Un bronze d'époque préangkorienne représentant Maitreya'. *Arts Asiatiques* 25, pp. 129–154.

———. 1989. 'Une statue khmère célèbre entre au musée Guimet: l'Avalokiteśvara Didelot (VIIe siècle environ)'. *Arts Asiatiques* 44, pp. 123–125.

Le Bonheur, Albert and J. Poncar. 1995. *Des dieux, des rois, des hommes: Les bas reliefs d'Angkor Vat et du Bayon.* Geneva: n.p.

Bose, Mandakranta (ed.). 2000. *Faces of the feminine in ancient, medieval, and modern India*. New Delhi: Oxford University Press.

Boua, Chanthou. 1982. 'Women in today's Cambodia'. *New Left Review* 131, pp. 45–61.

——. 1994. *Cambodia's country report: Women in development, prepared for the Second Asia-Pacific Ministerial Conference, Jakarta, 7–14 June 1994*. Phnom Penh: Secretariat of State for Women's Affairs.

Boudreau, Vincent. 2002. 'State repression and democracy protests in three Southeast Asian countries'. In David S. Meyer, Nancy Whittier, and Belinda Robnett (eds), *Social movements: Identity, culture, and the state*. Oxford; New York: Oxford University Press, pp. 28–46.

Bouinais, A. and A. Paulus. 1885. *L'Indo-Chine française contemporaine, Cochinchine, Cambodge, Tonkin, Annam*, 2nd ed. 2 vols. Paris.

Boulbet, J. 1968. 'Des femmes Bu Dih à quelques apsaras originales d'Angkor Vat'. *Arts Asiatiques* 17, pp. 209–218.

Bourdieu, Pierre. 2001. *Masculine domination*, trans. Richard Nice. Stanford, California: Stanford University Press.

Bray, Mark and Seng Bunly. 2005. *Balancing the books: Household financing of basic education in Cambodia*. Hong Kong: Comparative Education Research Centre, the University of Hong Kong and World Bank.

Briggs, Lawrence Palmer. 1947. 'A sketch of Cambodian history'. *Far Eastern Quarterly* 6, 4, pp. 345–363.

——. 1950. 'The Khmer empire and the Malay peninsula'. *Far Eastern Quarterly* 9, 3, pp. 256–305.

——. 1951. *The ancient Khmer empire*. Philadelphia, PA: The American Philosophical Society.

Brown, Louise. 2001. *Sex slaves: The trafficking of women in Asia*, London: Virago.

Bun Srun Theam. 1981. 'Cambodia in the mid-nineteenth century: A quest for survival, 1840–1863'. MA thesis, Australian National University.

Burgess, Walter J. 1998. 'The role of the foreign media in Cambodia 1970–75'. In Sorn Samnang (ed.), *Khmer studies: Knowledge of the past, and its contributions to the rehabilitation and reconstruction of Cambodia, proceedings of the International Conference on Khmer Studies, Phnom Penh, 26–30 August 1996*. Phnom Penh: Toyota Foundation, French Embassy, British Embassy. Vol. 2, pp. 931–942.

Burrows, Mathew. 1986. '"Mission civilisatrice": French cultural policy in the Middle East, 1860–1914'. *The Historical Journal* 29, 1, pp. 108–115.

Cabaton, A. 1910. 'La vie domestique au Cambodge'. *Revue Indo-Chinoise* 2, pp. 103–114.

Cady, John F. 1954. *The roots of French imperialism in Eastern Asia*. Ithaca, NY: Cornell University Press.

de Casparis, J.G. and I.W. Mabbett. 1999. 'Religion and popular beliefs of Southeast Asia before c.1500'. In Nicholas Tarling (ed.), *The Cambridge history of Southeast*

Asia, vol. 1: *From early times to c. 1500.* Cambridge: Cambridge University Press, pp. 276–339.

Chakravarti, Adhir. 1970–1971. 'The caste system in ancient Cambodia'. *Journal of Ancient Indian History* 4, pp. 14–59.

——. 1978. *The Sdok Kak Thom inscription part I: A study in Indo-Khmer civilization.* Calcutta: Sanskrit College.

Chanda, Nayan. c. 1986. *Brother enemy: The war after the war.* San Diego; London: Harcourt Brace Jovanovich.

Chandler, David P. 1970. 'Changing Cambodia'. *Current History* 59, pp. 333–338, 352.

——. [1970] 1996. 'An eighteenth-century inscription from Angkor Wat'. In David P. Chandler, *Facing the Cambodian past: Selected essays 1971–1994.* St Leonards, New South Wales: Allen & Unwin, pp. 15–24.

——. 1973. 'Cambodia before the French: Politics in a tributary kingdom, 1794–1848'. PhD thesis, University of Michigan.

——. [1975] 1996. 'Maps for the ancestors: Sacralized topography and echoes of Angkor in two Cambodian texts'. In Chandler, *Facing the Cambodian past,* pp. 15–42.

——. 1977. *The friends who tried to empty the sea: Eleven Cambodian folk stories.* Clayton, Victoria: Monash University Centre of Southeast Asian Studies Working Paper.

——. [1978] 1996. 'Songs at the edge of the forest: Perceptions of order in three Cambodian texts'. In Chandler, *Facing the Cambodian past,* pp. 76–99.

——. [1979] 1996. 'Royally sponsored human sacrifices in nineteenth century Cambodia: The cult of *nak ta* Me Sa (Mahisasuramardini) at Ba Phnom'. *JSS* 67, pp. 54–62. Also in Chandler, *Facing the Cambodian past,* pp. 119–136.

——. [1982] 1996. 'Normative poems (*chbap*) and pre-colonial Cambodian society'. In Chandler, *Facing the Cambodian past,* pp. 45–60.

——. 1983. 'Strategies for survival in Kampuchea'. *Current History* 82, 483, pp. 149–153.

——. 1983. *A history of Cambodia.* Boulder, Colorado: Westview Press.

——. 1991. *The tragedy of Cambodian history: Politics, war and revolution since 1945.* New Haven: Yale University Press.

——. 1996. *Facing the Cambodian past: Selected essays 1971–1994.* St Leonards, New South Wales: Allen & Unwin.

——. 1998. *A history of Cambodia,* 2nd rev. ed. Chiang Mai, Thailand: Silkworm Books.

——. 1999. *Brother number one: A political biography of Pol Pot,* rev. ed. Boulder, Colorado: Westview Press.

——. 2000. *A history of Cambodia,* 3rd ed. Boulder, Colorado: Westview Press.

——. 2000. *Voices from S–21: Terror and history in Pol Pot's secret prison.* St Leonards, New South Wales: Allen & Unwin.

——. 2007. *A history of Cambodia*, 4th ed. Colorado: Westview Press.

Chandler, David P. and Ben Kiernan (eds). 1983. *Revolution and its aftermath in Kampuchea: Eights essays*. New Haven: Yale University Southeast Asia Studies Monograph Series No. 25.

Chandler, David P., Ben Kiernan and Chanthou Boua (eds). 1988. *Pol Pot plans the future: Confidential leadership documents from Democratic Kampuchea, 1976–1977*. New Haven: Yale University Southeast Asian Studies, Yale Center for International and Area Studies.

Chandler, David P. with Ben Kiernan and Muy Hong Lim. 1976. *The early phases of liberation in northwestern Cambodia: Conversations with Peang Sophi*. Clayton, Victoria: Monash University, Centre of Southeast Asian Studies.

Chanrithy Him. 2000. *When broken glass floats: Growing up under the Khmer Rouge – a memoir*. New York; London: W.W. Norton & Co.

Chantrabot, Ros. 1993. *La République khmère (1970–1975)*. Paris: L'Harmattan.

Chau Seng and Charles Meyer. [1962?]. *Le mariage cambodgien*. Phnom Penh: Université Buddhique Preah Raj Sihanouk.

Chhabra, B. Ch. 1935. 'Expansion of Indo-Aryan culture during Pallava rule as evidenced by the inscriptions'. *Yearbook of the Royal Asiatic Society of Bengal* 1, 1, pp. 1–44.

Chigas, George. 2000. 'The emergence of twentieth century Cambodian literary institutions: the case of *Kambujasuriya*'. In David Smyth (ed.), *The canon in Southeast Asian literatures: Literatures of Burma, Cambodia, Indonesia, Laos, Malaysia, the Philippines,Thailand and Vietnam*. Richmond, Surrey: Curzon, pp. 135–146.

Chirapat Prapandvidya. 1990. 'The Sab Bak inscription: Evidence of an early *vajrayana* Buddhist presence in Thailand'. *JSS* 78, 2, pp. 11–14.

Church, Cornelia Dimmit. 1975. 'Temptress, housewife, nun: Women's role in early Buddhism'. *Anima* 1, 2, pp. 53–58.

Claessen, Henri J.M. and Peter Skalnik (eds). 1978. *The early state*. The Hague: Mouton.

Clairon, Marcel (comp.). 1959. *Droit civil khmèr*, 2 vols. Phnom Penh: Faculté du Droit.

Clarke, Helen Jenks. 2001. 'Research for empowerment in a divided Cambodia'. In Marie Smyth and Gillian Robinson (eds), *Researching violently divided societies: Ethical and methodological issues*. Tokyo; New York; Paris: United nations University Press; London: Pluto Press, pp. 92–105.

Cœdès, George. 1904. 'Une inscription de Bhavavarman I, roi de Cambodge'. *BEFEO* 4, pp. 691–697.

——. 1911. 'Études cambodgiennes 1. La legende de la Nāgī'. *BEFEO* 11, pp. 391–393.

——. 1911. 'Études cambodgiennes 2. Une inscriptions du sixième siècle çake'. *BEFEO* 11, pp. 393–396.

——. 1913. 'La fondation du Phnom Peñ'. *BEFEO* 13, 3, pp. 6–11

———. 1913. 'Études cambodgiennes 9: Le serment des fonctionnaires de Suryavarman I'. *BEFEO* 13, 6, pp. 11–17.

———. 1918. 'Études cambodgiennes 12. Le site primitif du Tchen-la'. *BEFEO* 18, 9, pp. 1–3.

———. 1924. 'Études cambodgiennes 18. L'extension du Cambodge vers le sud-ouest au VIIe siècle (nouvelles inscriptions du Cantabouri)'. *BEFEO* 24, pp. 352–358.

———. 1928. 'Études cambodgiennnes 20. Les capitales de Jayavarman II'. *BEFEO* 28, pp. 113–23.

———. 1928. 'Études cambodgiennes 21. La tradition généalogique des premiers rois d'Angkor d'après les inscriptions de Yaçovarman et de Rājendravarman'. *BEFEO* 28, pp. 124–144.

———. 1931. 'Études cambodgiennes 25. Deux inscriptions sanskrites du Fou-nan'. *BEFEO* 31, pp. 1–12.

———. 1935. *Un grand roi du Cambodge: Jayavarman VII.* Phnom Penh: Éditions de la Bibliothèque Royale.

———. 1936. 'Études cambodgiennes 31. A propos du Tchen-la d'eau: trois inscriptions de Cochinchine'. *BEFEO* 36, pp. 1–13.

———. 1937. 'A new inscription from Fu-nan'. *JGIS* 4, pp. 112–121.

———. 1943–1946. 'Études cambodgiennes 36. Quelques précisions sur la fin de Fou-nan'. *BEFEO* 43, pp. 1–5.

———. 1944. *Histoire ancienne des états hindouisés d'Extrême-Orient.* Hanoi: Imprimerie d'Extrême-Orient.

———. 1956. 'Études cambodgiennes 40. Nouvelles données sur les origines du royaume khmèr'. *BEFEO* 48, 1, pp. 209–220.

———. 1963. *Angkor: An introduction,* trans. Emily Floyd Gardiner. Hong Kong: Oxford University Press.

———. 1968. *The Indianized states of Southeast Asia,* trans. Susan Brown Cowing. Canberra: Australian National University Press.

———. 1989–1992. *Articles sur le pays khmer par George Cœdès,* 2 vols. Paris: EFEO.

Cœdès, George and Pierre Dupont. 1942–1943. 'L'Inscription de Sdok Kak Thom'. *BEFEO* 43, pp. 57–135.

Colani, Madeleine. 1940. 'Récherches sur le préhistorique indochinois'. *BEFEO* 40, pp. 299–422.

Colless, B.E. 1973. 'The ancient Bnam empire: Fu-nan and Po-nan'. *Journal of the Oriental Society of Australia* 9, 1–2, pp. 21–31.

Collins, Elizabeth Fuller. 1996. '(Re)negotiating gender hierarchy in the New Order: A South Sumatran field study'. *Asia Pacific Viewpoint,* 37, 2, pp. 127–138.

Cook, Nerida. 1998. '"Dutiful daughters", estranged sisters: Women in Thailand'. In Krishna Sen and Maila Stivens (eds), *Gender and power in affluent Asia.* London: Routledge, pp. 250–290.

Cooler, R.M. 1978. 'Sculpture, kingship, and the triad of Phnom Da'. *AA* 40, 1, pp. 29–40.

Coomaraswamy, Ananda K. 1945. 'On the loathly bride'. *Speculum* 20, 4, pp. 391–404.

Cooper, Nicola. 2001. *France in Indochina: Colonial encounters.* Oxford; New York: Berg.

Corfield, Justin J. 1993. *The royal family of Cambodia.* Melbourne: Khmer Language & Culture Centre.

——. 1994. *Khmers stand up! A history of the Cambodian government 1970–1975.* Clayton, Victoria: Monash Papers on Southeast Asia No. 32.

Correze, Françoise. 1984. *Le Cambodge à deux voix.* Paris: Harmattan.

Cowan, C.D. and O.W. Wolters (eds). 1976. *Southeast Asian history and historiography: Essays presented to D.G.E. Hall.* Ithaca, New York: Cornell University Press.

Coyne, Geoffrey. 1972. 'Schools in crisis: Phnom Penh high schools and their reaction to the war in Cambodia, March-December 1970'. *Malaysian Journal of Education* 9, 2, pp. 137–141.

Creese, Helen. 2004. *Women of the kakawin world: Marriage and sexuality in the indic courts of Java and Bali.* New York and London: M.E. Sharpe.

Curtis, Grant. 1998. *Cambodia reborn? The transition to democracy and development.* Washington, DC; Geneva: Brookings Institution Press and the United Nations Research Institute for Social Development.

Dasgupta, Manasi and Mandakranta Bose. 2000. 'The Goddess-woman nexus in popular religious practice: The cult of Manasa'. In Mandakranta Bose (ed.), *Faces of the feminine in ancient, medieval, and modern India.* New Delhi: Oxford University Press, pp. 148–161.

Dauphin-Meunier, Achille. 1961. *Histoire du Cambodge.* Paris: Presses Universitaires de France.

Delvert, Jean. 1951. *Le paysan cambodgien.* Paris and The Hague: Mouton.

Derks, Annuska. 2004. 'The broken women of Cambodia'. In Evelyne Micllier (ed.), *Sexual cultures in East Asia: The social construction of sexuality and sexual risk in a time of AIDS.* London: RoutledgeCurzon, pp. 127–155.

——. 2005. 'Khmer women on the move: Migration and urban experiences in Cambodia'. PhD thesis, University of Amsterdam.

Desbarats, Jacqueline. 1995. *Prolific survivors: Population change in Cambodia, 1975–1993.* Tempe, Arizona: Program for Southeast Asian Studies, Arizona State University.

Đoàn Lâm. 1999. 'A brief account of the cult of female deities in Vietnam'. *Vietnamese Studies* 131, pp. 5–19.

Douglas, Leviseda. 2003. *Sex trafficking in Cambodia.* Clayton, Victoria: Monash University Centre of Southeast Asian Studies Working Paper 122.

Doumer, Paul. 1905. *L'Indo-Chine française,* 2nd ed. Paris: Vuibert & Nony.

Downie, Sue and Damien Kingsbury. 2001. 'Political development and the re-emergence of civil society in Cambodia'. *Contemporary Southeast Asia* 23, 1, pp. 43–63.

Dupont, Pierre. 1943–1946. 'La dislocation du Tchen-la et la formation du Cambodge angkorien (VIIe-IXe siècle)'. *BEFEO* 43, pp. 17–55.

———. 1952–1954. 'Études sur l'Indochine ancienne, II: Les débuts de la royauté angkorienne'. *BEFEO* 46, pp. 119–176.

———. 1955. *La statuaire préangkorienne*. Paris: Ascona.

Ea, Meng-try. 1981. 'Kampuchea: A country adrift'. *Population and Development Review* 7, 2, pp. 209–228.

Ebihara, May. 1971 [1968]. 'Svay, a Kmer village in Cambodia'. PhD thesis, Columbia University [Ann Arbor, Michigan: University Microfilms, 1971].

———. 1984. 'Societal organization in 16th and 17th century Cambodia'. *Journal of Asian Studies* 15, 2, pp. 280–295.

Edwards, Penny. 1998. 'Womanizing Indochina: Fiction, nation, and cohabitation in colonial Cambodia, 1890–1930'. In Julia Clancy Smith and Frances Gouda (eds), *Domesticating the empire: Race, gender, and family life in French and Dutch colonialism*. Charlottesville, Virginia: University Press of Virginia. 108–130.

———. 1999. 'Cambodge: The cultivation of a nation, 1860–1945'. PhD thesis, Monash University.

———. 2002. '"Propagender": Marianne, Joan of Arc, and the export of French gender ideology to colonial Cambodia (1863–1954)'. In Tony Chafer and Amanda Sackur (eds), *Promoting the colonial idea: Propaganda and visions of empire in France*. Basingstoke, Hampshire; New York: Palgrave, pp. 116–130.

———. 2007. *Cambodge: The cultivation of a nation, 1860–1945*. Honolulu: University of Hawai'i Press.

Eisenstadt, S.N. 1973. 'Post-traditional societies and the continuity and reconstruction of tradition'. *Daedalus* 102, 1, pp. 1–27.

Ennis, T.E. 1936. *French policy and development in Indochina*. Chicago: Russell and Russell.

van Esterik, Penny (ed.). 1996. *Women of Southeast Asia*, rev. ed. De Kalb, Northern Illinois: Center for Southeast Asian Studies, Northern Illinois University.

Etcheson, Craig. 1984. *The rise and demise of Democratic Kampuchea*. Boulder, Colorado: Westview Press.

Falk, Nancy Auer and Rita M. Gross (eds). 1989. *Unspoken worlds: Women's religious lives*, 2nd ed. Belmont, California: Wadsworth.

Fantham, Elaine, Helene Peet Foley, Natalie Boymel Kampen, Sarah B. Pomeroy, and H.A. Shapiro. 1994. *Women in the classical world: Image and text*. New York; Oxford: Oxford University Press.

Fergusson, Lee C. and Gildas Le Masson. 1997. 'A culture under siege: Post colonial higher education and teacher education in Cambodia from 1953 and 1979'. *History of Education* 26, 1, pp. 91–112.

Fernando, Basil. 1998. *Problems facing the Cambodian legal system*. Hong Kong: Asian Human Rights Commission.

Filliozat, Jean. 1954. 'Le symbolisme du monument de Phnom Bakheng'. *BEFEO* 44, 2, pp. 527–554.

——. 1966. 'New researches on the relations between India and Cambodia'. *Indica* 3, 2, pp. 95–106.

——. 1967. 'Les symboles d'une stèle khmère du VIIe siècle'. *Arts Asiatiques* 16, pp. 111–117.

Finot, Louis. 1911. 'Sur quelques traditions indochinoises'. *Bulletin de la Commission Archéologique Indochinoise* 11, pp. 20–37.

——. 1915. 'L'Inscription de Sdok Kak Thom'. *BEFEO* 15, pp. 275–304.

Fiske, Edward. 1995. *Using both hands: Women and education in Cambodia*. Manila: Asia Development Bank.

Fitzgerald, Maureen H., Vannak Ing, Tek Heang Ya, Sim Heang Hay, Thida Yang, Hong Ly Duong, Bryanne Barnett, Stephen Matthey, Derrick Silove, Penny Mitchell, and Justine McNamara. 1998. *Hear our voices: Trauma, birthing and mental health among Cambodian women*. Paramatta, NSW: Transcultural Mental Health Centre.

Forest, Alain. 1980. *Le Cambodge et la colonisation française: Histoire d'une colonisation sans heurts (1897–1920)*. Paris: Harmattan.

——. 1992. *Le culte des genies protecteurs au Cambodge: Analyse et traduction d'un corpus de textes sur les neak ta*. Paris: Harmattan.

Frieson, Kate G. 1991. 'The impact of revolution on Cambodian peasants, 1970–1975'. PhD thesis, Monash University.

——. 2000. 'Sentimental education: *Les sages femmes* and colonial Cambodia'. *Journal of Colonialism and Colonial History* 1, 1: [e-journal].

——. 2001. *In the shadows: Women, power and politics in Cambodia*. Victoria, British Columbia: Centre for Asia-Pacific Initiatives Occasional Paper No. 26, University of Victoria.

Frings, Viviane. 1993. *The failure of agricultural collectivization in the People's Republic of Kampuchea (1979–1989)*. Clayton, Victoria: Monash University Centre of Southeast Asian Studies Working Paper 80.

——. 1997. *Le socialisme et le paysan Cambodgien: La politique agricole de la République Populaire du Kampuchea et de l'Etat du Cambodge*. Paris: l'Harmattan.

Fukuyama, Francis. 2005. 'Re-envisioning Asia'. *Foreign Affairs* 84, 1, pp. 75–80.

Galabru, Kek. 2004. *The situation of women in Cambodia*. Phnom Penh: LICHADO.

Galland, Oliver. 2003. 'Le Cambodge de Sihanouk: De l'independence à l'Etat-Nation. Le projet existentiel de Norodom Sihanouk pour la nation khmère – Analyse de discours'. PhD thesis, Université de Paris 1.

Gaudes, Rudiger. 1993. 'Kaundinya, Preah Thaong, and the "Nagi Soma": Some aspects of a Cambodian legend'. *Asian Folklore Studies*, 52, 2, pp. 333–359.

Giteau, Madeleine. 1967. 'Note sur les frontons du sanctuaire central du Vatt Nokor'. *Arts Asiatiques* 16, pp. 136–137.

——. 1975. *Iconographie du Cambodge postangkorien*. Paris: EFEO.

——. [1976]. *Les Khmers: sculptures khmères – Reflets de la civilisation d'Angkor*. Freibourg: Office du livre.

Goloubew, Victor. 1924. 'Mélanges sue le Cambodge ancien 1. Les légendes de la nāga et de l'apsara'. *BEFEO* 24, pp. 501–510.

Gorer, Geoffrey. 1986. *Bali and Angkor: A 1930s pleasure trip looking at life and death*. Singapore; Oxford; New York: Oxford University Press.

Gorman, Siobhan with Pon Dorina and Sok Kheng. 1999. *Gender and development in Cambodia: An overview*. Phnom Penh: Cambodia Development Resource Institute, Working Paper 10.

Gottesman, Evan. 2003. *Cambodia after the Khmer Rouge: Inside the politics of nation building*. New Haven; London: Yale University Press.

Groslier, Bernard P. 1958. *Angkor et le Cambodge au XVIe siècle, d'après les sources portugaieses et espagnoles*. Paris: Presses Universitaires de France.

——. 1962. *The art of Indochina, including Thailand, Vietnam, Laos and Cambodia*, trans. George Lawrence. New York: Crown.

Groslier, George. 1913. *Danseuses cambodgiennes: Anciennes et modernes*. Paris: Augustin Challamel.

——. 1925. 'La femme dans la sculpture khmères ancienne'. *Revue des Arts Asiatiques. Annales du Musée Guimet* 2, pp. 35–40.

Gupta, Samjukta Gombrich. 2000. 'The Goddess, women, and their rituals in Hinduism'. In Mandakranta Bose (ed.), *Faces of the feminine in ancient, medieval, and modern India*. New Delhi: Oxford University Press, pp. 87–206.

Guthrie, Elizabeth. 2001. 'Outside the sima'. *Udaya: Journal of Khmer Studies* 2, pp. 7–18.

Hajesteijn, Renée. 1987. 'The Angkor state: Rise, fall and in between'. In Henri J.M. Claessen and Pieter van de Velde (eds), *Early state dynamics*. Leiden and New York: E.J. Brill.153–171.

Hall, Kari Rene. 1992. *Beyond the killing fields*. New York: Aperture in association with California State University, Long Beach and Asia 2000 Ltd., Hong Kong.

Hall, Kenneth R. 1985. *Maritime trade and state development in early Southeast Asia*. Honolulu: University of Hawai'i Press.

Hang Chan Sophea. 2004. 'Stec Gamlan and Yāy Deb: Worshipping kings and queens in Cambodia today'. In John Marston and Elizabeth Guthrie (eds), *History, Buddhism and new religious movements in Cambodia*. Hawaii: University of Hawai'i Press, pp. 113–126.

Hann So. 1988. *The Khmer kings*. San Jose, California, n.p.

Harris, Ian. 2005. *Cambodian Buddhisim: History and practice*. Honolulu: University of Hawai'i Press.

Heder, Steven. 1989. *Kampuchean occupation and resistance.* Bangkok: Chulalongkorn University Press.

Heine-Geldern, Robert. 1956. *Conceptions of state and kingship in Southeast Asia.* Ithaca, New York: Southeast Asia Program, Cornell University.

Heuveline, Patrick. 1998. '"Between one and three million": Towards the demographic reconstruction of a decade of Cambodian history (1970–79)'. *Population Studies* 52, 1, pp. 49–65.

Heuveline, Patrick and Bunnak Poch. 2006. 'Do marriages forget their past? Marital stability in post-Khmer Rouge Cambodia'. *Demography* 43, 1, pp. 99–125.

Higham, Charles F. 2001. *The civilization of Angkor.* London: Weidenfeld & Nicholson.

Higham, Charles and Rachanie Bannurag. 1990. 'The princess and the pots'. *New Scientist* (26 May 1990), pp. 50–55.

Hill, Peter S. and Heng Thay Ly. 2004. 'Women are silver, women are diamonds: Conflicting images of women in the Cambodian print media'. *Reproductive Health Matters* 12, 24, pp. 104–115.

Him, Chanrithy. 2000. *When broken glass floats: Growing up under the Khmer Rouge – a memoir.* New York; London: W.W. Norton & Co.

Hinton, Alexander Laban. 2005. *Why did they kill? Cambodia in the shadow of genocide.* Berkeley; Los Angeles; London: University of California Press.

Ho, Minfong. 1992. *The clay marble.* Singapore: Times Books International.

Hong Lysa. 1998. 'Of consorts and harlots in Thai history'. *Journal of Asian Studies* 57, 2, pp. 333–353.

Huffman, Franklin E. 1972. *Intermediate Cambodian reader.* New Haven: Yale University Press.

Hughes, Caroline. 1996. *UNTAC in Cambodia: The impact on human rights.* Singapore: Institute of Southeast Asian Studies.

——. 2003. *The political economy of Cambodia's transition, 1991–2001.* London; New York: RoutledgeCurzon.

Ibbitson Jessup, Helen and Thierry Zephir (eds). 1997. *Sculpture of Angkor and ancient Cambodia: Millennium of glory.* New York and London: Thames and Hudson.

Institute de Sociologie Libre de Bruxelles. 1967. *Éducation et développement dans le Sud-Est de l'Asie: Colloque tenu à Bruxelles les 19, 20, et 21 avril 1966.* Brussells: Éditions de l'Institute de Sociologie Libre de Bruxelles.

Jackson, Karl (ed.). c. 1989. *Cambodia 1975–1978: Rendez-vous with death.* Princeton: Princeton University Press.

Jacob, Judith. 1979. 'Pre-Angkor Cambodia: Evidence from the inscriptions in Khmer concerning the common people and their environment'. In R.B. Smith and W. Watson (eds), *Early Southeast Asia: Essays in archaeology, history, and historical geography,* Oxford University Press, New York and Kuala Lumpur, pp. 406–426.

———. 1993. *Cambodian linguistics, literature and history: Collected articles*, ed. David A. Smyth. London: School of Oriental and African Studies, University of London.

———. 1996. *The traditional literature of Cambodia: A preliminary guide*. Oxford: Oxford University Press.

Jacobsen, Trudy. 1999. 'Buddhist flesh, Hindu bones: The legitimation of Jayavarman VII'. Honours thesis, University of Queensland.

———. 2002. 'Brimming vessels, empty hands: Women and power in the age of Angkor'. *Proceedings of the History Research Group*, 13, pp. 14–16.

———. 2003. 'Autonomous queenship in Cambodia, 1st–9th centuries AD'. *JRAS* 13, 3, pp. 1–19.

Jacobsen, Trudy, Aing Sokroeun, Ham Samnom, Som Soreasey, and Lim Leum. 2006. *The situation of daun chi in Cambodia*. Phnom Penh: Buddhist Institute/HBF-Asia.

Jacques, Claude. 1972. 'Études d'épigraphie cambodgienne VII. Sur l'émplacement du royaume d'Aninditapura'. *BEFEO* 59, pp. 193–205.

———. 1972. 'Études d'épigraphie cambodgienne VIII: La carrière de Jayavarman II'. *BEFEO* 59, pp. 205–220.

———. 1973. 'A propos de l'esclavage dans l'ancien Cambodge'. *Proceedings of the Congrès International des Orientalistes, XXXIX*. Paris: n.p., pp. 71–76.

———. '"Funan", "Zhenla": The reality concealed by these Chinese views of Indochina'. In R.B. Smith and W. Watson (eds), *Early Southeast Asia: Essays in archaeology, history, and historical geography*. New York and Kuala Lumpur: Oxford University Press, pp. 371–389.

———. 1986. 'Le pays Khmer avant Angkor'. *Journal des Savants* (janvier-septembre 1986), pp. 59–94.

———. 1997. *Angkor: Cities and Temples*. London: Thames and Hudson.

Jamison, Stephanie W. 1996. *Sacrificed wife/sacrificer's wife: Women, ritual, and hospitality in ancient India*. New York and Oxford: Oxford University Press.

Jeldres, Julio A. 2003. *The royal house of Cambodia*. Phnom Penh: Monument Books.

Jeldres, Julio A. and Somkid Chaijitvanit. 1999. *The royal palace of Phnom Penh and Cambodian royal life*. Bangkok: Post Books.

Jennar, Raoul M. 1995. *Les cles du Cambodge*. Paris: Maisonnueve et Larose.

———. (comp. and ed.) 1995. *The Cambodian constitutions, 1953–1993*. Bangkok: White Lotus.

Jenner, Philip N. 1982. *A chronological inventory of the inscriptions of Cambodia*, 2nd ed., rev. Honolulu: Center for Asian and Pacific Studies, University of Hawaii.

Jenner, Philip N., Laurence C. Thompson, and Stanley Starosta (eds). 1976. *Austroasiatic Studies*. 2 vols. Honolulu: University of Hawai'i Press.

Jenner, Philip N. and Saveros Pou. 1976. 'Les *cpap* ou <codes de conduite> khmers II: *cpap prus*'. *BEFEO* 63: 313–350.

Kalab, Milada. 1990. 'Buddhism and emotional support for elderly people'. *Journal of Cross-Cultural Gerontology* 5, pp. 7–19.

Kamm, Henry. 1998. *Cambodia: Report from a stricken land.* New York: Arcade Publications.

Kampuchean Inquiry Commission. 1982. *Kampuchea in the seventies: Report of a Finnish inquiry commission.* Helsinki: Kampuchean Inquiry Commission.

Karim, Wazir Jahan. 1992. *Women and culture: Between Malay Adat and Islam.* Boulder, Colorado: Westview Press.

Kersten, Carool. 2006. 'Cambodia's Muslim king: Khmer and Dutch sources on the conversion of Reameathipadei I, 1642–1658'. *JSEAS* 37, 1, pp. 1–22.

Khanna, Madhu. 2000. 'The Goddess-women equation in *sakta* tantras'. In Mandakranta Bose (ed.), *Faces of the feminine in ancient, medieval, and modern India.* New Delhi: Oxford University Press. 109–123.

Khathirithamby-Wells, J. 1999. 'The age of transition: The mid-eighteenth to the early nineteenth centuries'. In Nicholas Tarling (ed.), *The Cambridge history of Southeast Asia,* vol. 2: *From c.1500 to c.1800.* Cambridge: Cambridge University Press, pp. 228–275.

Kherian, Grégoire. 1967. 'Instruction de la femme, condition de l'évolution et de la croissance'. In *Éducation et développement dans le Sud-Est de l'Asie: Colloque tenu à Bruxelles les 19, 29, et 21 avril 1966.* Brussles: Éditions de l'Institut de Sociologie, Université Libre de Bruxelles.

Khin Sok. 1988. *Chroniques royales du Cambodge,* vol. 2: *De Bonea Yat à la prise de Lanvaek (1417–1595).* Paris: École Française d'Extrême-Orient.

——. 1991. *Le Cambodge entre le Siam et le Vietnam (de 1775 à 1860).* Paris: EFEO.

Khing Hoc Dy. 1977. 'Note sur le thème de la femme 'marquée de signes', dans la littérature populaire khmère'. *Cahiers d'Asie Sud-Est* 2, pp. 15–43.

——. 1990. *Contribution à l'histoire de littèrature khmère.* Paris: l'Harmattan.

Khmer Women's Voice Center. 1997. *Women and family law: October 96–March 97 advocacy project report.* Phnom Penh: Khmer Women's Voice Center.

Kiernan, Ben. [1975]. *The Samlaut rebellion and its aftermath, 1967–70: The origins of Cambodia's liberation movement,* Part 2. Clayton, Victoria: Monash University Centre of Southeast Asian Studies Working Paper 5.

——. 1976. 'Social cohesion in revolutionary Cambodia'. *Australian Outlook* 30, 3, pp. 371–386.

——. 1985. *How Pol Pot came to power: A history of communism in Kampuchea, 1930–1975.* London: Verso.

——. 1990. 'The genocide in Cambodia, 1975–79'. *Bulletin of Concerned Asian Scholars* 22, 2, pp. 35–40.

—— (ed.). 1993. *Genocide and democracy in Cambodia: The Khmer Rouge, the United Nations and the international community.* New Haven, Conn.: Yale University Southeast Asia Studies.

——. 1996. *The Pol Pot regime: Race, power, and genocide in Cambodia under the Khmer Rouge, 1975–79*. New Haven: Yale University Press.

Kiernan, Ben and Chanthou Boua (eds). 1982. *Peasants and politics in Kampuchea, 1942–1981*. London; Armonk, NY: Zed Press; M.E. Sharpe.

Kiljunen, Kimmo (ed.). 1984. *Kampuchea: Decade of the genocide*. London: Zed Books.

Kirsch, A. Thomas. 1976. 'Kinship, genealogical claims and social integration in ancient Khmer society: An interpretation'. In C.D. Cowan and O.W. Wolters (eds), *Southeast Asian history and historiography: Essays presented to D.G.E. Hall*. Ithaca, New York: Cornell University Press. 190–202.

Kishore, K. 1965. 'Varṇas in early Kambuja inscriptions'. *Journal of the American Oriental Society* 85, pp. 566–569.

Kulke, Hermann. 1978. *The devaraja cult*, trans. I.W. Mabbett. Ithaca, New York: Southeast Asia Program, Cornell University.

Kumar, Ann. 2000. 'Imagining women in Javanese religion'. In Barbara Watson Andaya (ed.), *Other pasts: Women, gender and history in early modern Southeast Asia*. Honolulu: University of Hawai'i Press, pp. 87–104.

Lamant, Pierre L.1989. *L'Affaire Yukanthor: Autopsie d'un scandale colonial*. Paris: Société Française d'Histoire d'Outre-mer.

Larsson, Katarina. 1996. *Country gender profile: Cambodia*. Report for the Asia Department, Swedish International Development Agency.

Law, Lisa. 2000. *Sex work in Southeast Asia: The place of desire in a time of AIDS*. Abingdon, Oxon: Routledge.

Leclère, Adhémard. 1884. *Recherches sur le droit public des cambodgiens*. Paris: Challamel.

——. 1889. *Le Buddhisme au Cambodge*. Paris: E. Leroux.

——. 1898. *Les codes cambodgiens*. 2 vols. Paris: E. Leroux.

Ledgerwood, Judy L. 1990. 'Changing Khmer conceptions of gender: Women, stories, and the social order'. PhD thesis, Cornell University.

——. 1992. *Analysis of the situation of women in Cambodia*. Phnom Penh: UNICEF.

——. 1995. 'Khmer kinship: the matriliny/matriarchy myth'. *Journal of Anthropological Research* 51, 3, pp. 247–262.

——. 1996. 'Politics and gender: Negotiating changing Cambodian ideas of the proper woman'. *Asia Pacific Viewpoint* 37, 2, pp. 139–152.

Leslie, Julia (ed.). 1991. *Roles and rituals for Hindu women*. London: Pinter.

LeVine, Peg. 2006. 'A contextual study into marriages under the Khmer Rouge: The ritual revolution'. PhD thesis, Monash University, 2006.

Levy, Paul. 1986. 'L'étymologie de *Fan*, le titre donné par les Chinois aux souverains du Fou-nan et du Campa'. *Journal Asiatique* 274, pp. 139–143.

Lewis, M.D. 1962. 'One hundred million Frenchmen: The 'assimilation' theory in French colonial policy'. *Comparative Studies in Society and History* 4, 2, pp. 129–153.

Librairie générale de droit et de jurisprudence. 1959. *Études d'histoire du droit privé offertes à Pierre Petot.* Paris: Montchrestien.

LICHADO. 1995. *Women's rights: caricatures and cartoons,* comp. LICHADO. [Phnom Penh]: LICHADO.

Lilja, Mona and Tevy Prom. 2002. 'Female politicians in Cambodia'. In John L. Vijghen (ed.), *People and the 1998 national elections in Cambodia: Their voices, roles and impact on democracy.* Phnom Penh: Experts for Community Research, pp. 45–58.

Lingat, R. 1947–1950. 'La conception du droit dans l'Indochine hinayaniste'. *BEFEO* 44, 1, pp. 163–187.

Lobo, Wibke and Stephanie Reimann (eds). 2000. *Southeast Asian archaeology 1998: Proceedings of the 7th International Conference of the European Association of Southeast Asian Archaeologists, 1998.* Hull: Centre for Southeast Asian Studies, Hull University.

Locard, Henri. 2004. *Pol Pot's Little Red Book: The sayings of Angkar.* Chiang Mai: Silkworm Books.

Loos, Tamara. 2005. 'Sex in the Inner City: The fidelity between sex and politics in Siam'. *Journal of Asian Studies* 64, 4, pp. 881–909.

Löschmann, Heike. 2000. 'The revival of the *don chee* movement in Cambodia'. In Karma Lekshe Tsomo (ed.), *Innovative Buddhist women: Swimming against the stream.* London: Curzon, pp. 91–95.

Ly Y. 2000. *Heaven becomes hell: A survivor's story of life under the Khmer Rouge.* New Haven, Connecticut: Yale University Southeast Asia Studies.

McCoy, Alfred W (ed.). 1980. *Southeast Asia under Japanese occupation.* New Haven: Yale University Press.

Mabbett, I.W. 1969. 'Devaraja'. *Journal of South East Asian History,* 10, 2, pp. 202–223.

——. 1977. '*Varnas* in Angkor and the Indian caste system'. *Journal of Asian Studies* 36, 3, pp. 429–442.

——. 1978. 'Kingship in Angkor'. *JSS,* 66, 2, pp. 1–58.

——. 1983. 'Some remarks on the present state of knowledge about slavery in Angkor'. In Anthony Reid (ed.), *Slavery, bondage and dependency in Southeast Asia.* St Lucia, Queensland; London; New York: University of Queensland Press, pp. 44–63.

Mabbett, Ian and David Chandler. 1995. *The Khmers.* Oxford: Blackwell.

Majumdar, R.C. 1953. *Inscriptions of Kambuja.* Calcutta: Asiatic Society.

——. 1963. *Hindu colonies in the Far East,* 2nd ed. Calcutta: Mukhopadhyay.

Mak Phoeun. 1981. *Chroniques royales du Cambodige,* vol. 3: *De 1594 à 1677.* Paris: École Française d'Extrême-Orient.

——. 1984. *Chroniques royales du Cambodge,* vol. 1: *Des origines légendaires jusqu'à Paramaraja 1er.* Paris: École Française d'Extrême-Orient.

——. 1995. *Histoire du Cambodge: de la fin du XVIe siècle au début du XVIIe.* Paris: EFEO.

Malleret, Louis. 1934. *L'Exotisme Indochinoise dans la littérature française depuis 1860.* Paris: Larose Éditeurs.

——. 1948. 'L'Art et la métallurgie de l'étain dans la culture d'Oc-Eo'. *AA* 11, 4, pp. 274–284.

——. 1959–1963. *L'Archéologie du delta du Mékong,* 4 vols. Paris: EFEO.

Mann, Michael. 1986. *The sources of social power.* 2 vols. Cambridge: Cambridge University Press.

Marchal, Sappho. 1927. *Costumes et parures khmèrs d'áprès les devata d'Angkor-Vat.* Paris: Librairie Nationale d'Art et d'Histoire.

Marlin, Frédérique Apffel. 1985. *Wives of the god king: The rituals of the Devadasis of Puri.* Delhi: Oxford University Press.

Marr, D.G. and A.C. Milner (eds). 1986. *Southeast Asia in the 9th to 14th centuries.* Singapore: Institute of Southeast Asian Studies.

Marston, John. 2002. 'Khmer Rouge songs'. *Crossroads* 16, 1, pp. 100–127.

Martin, Marie Alexandrine. 1994. *Cambodia: A shattered society.* Berkeley: University of California Press.

Maspero, Georges. 1928. *Le royaume de Champa.* Paris: van Oest.

May, Someth. 1988. *Cambodian witness: The autobiography of Someth May.* London: Faber and Faber.

Meas Nee. 1995. *Towards restoring life: Cambodian villages.* [Phnom Penh]: JSRC.

Meas Yang. 1978. *Le Buddhisme au Cambodge.* Brussels: Thanh Long.

Mehta, Harish C. and Julie B. Mehta. 1999. *Hun Sen: Strongman of Cambodia.* Singapore: Graham Brash.

Menski, Werner F. 1991. 'Marital expectations as dramatized in Hindu marriage rituals'. In Julia Leslie (ed.), *Roles and rituals for Hindu women.* London: Pinter, pp. 47–68.

du Mestier du Bourg, Henri. 1969. 'Au propos du culte du dieu-roi (devaraja) au Cambodge'. *Cahiers d'histoire mondiale,* 2, 3, pp. 499–516.

Meyer, Charles. 1971. *Derrière le sourire khmer.* Paris, Hachette.

Mies, Maria. 1986. *Patriarchy and accumulation on a world scale: Women in the international division of labour.* London and Atlantic Highlands, New Jersey: Zed Books.

Ministère de l'Information du Cambodge. 1965. *Biographie de S.A.R. le prince Norodom Sihanouk, Chef d'etat du Cambodge.* [Phnom Penh]: Ministère de l'Information du Cambodge.

Ministère de l'Information du Gouvernment Royal du Cambodge. 1963. *Femmes du Cambodge.* Phnom Penh: Le Ministère de l'Information du Gouvernment Royal du Cambodge.

Ministry of Education, Youth and Sport. 1998. *Survey on girls' education in Cambodia*. [Phnom Penh]: Ministry of Education, Youth and Sport, Kingdom of Cambodia.

Morice, Jean. 1977. *Cambodge, du sourire à l'horreur*. Paris: Éditions France-Empire.

Moura, Jean. 1883. *Le royaume de Cambodge*, 2 vols. Paris: Leroux.

Mus, Paul. 1975. *India seen from the east: Indian and indigenous cults in Champa*, trans. I.W. Mabbett. Clayton, Victoria: Centre for Southeast Asian Studies, Monash University.

Myeun Thalla. 1981. *Vichea aprom satrei kh'mei*. [Khao-I-Dang, Thailand]: International Rescue Committee.

Mysliviec, Eva. 1988. *Punishing the poor: The international isolation of Kampuchea*. Oxford: Oxfam.

Nepote, Jacques and Khing Hoc Dy. 1981. 'Literature and society in modern Cambodia'. In Tham Seung Chee (ed.), *Literature and society in Southeast Asia*. Singapore: National University of Singapore Press, pp. 56–84.

Ngo Duc Thinh. 1996. 'The cult of the female spirits and the Mother Goddesses "*Mãu*"'. *Vietnamese Studies* 121, pp. 83–96.

Ngor, Haing S. 1987. *A Cambodian odyssey*. New York: Macmillan.

Nguyen Sy Tuan. 1998. 'Khmer novel and the struggle for democracy: National independence in Cambodia during the period of 1940–1960'. In Sorn Samnang (ed.), *Khmer studies: Knowledge of the past and its contributions to the rehabilitation and reconstruction of Cambodia: Proceedings of International Conference on Khmer Studies, Phnom Penh, 26–30 August 1996*. Phnom Penh: Toyota Foundation, French Embassy, British Embassy. Vol. 2, pp. 634–637.

Nguyen-vo Thu-huong. 1992. *Khmer-Viet relations and the Third Indochina conflict*. Jefferson, North Carolina and London: McFarland & Company.

Norodom Sihanouk. 1961. *La monarchie cambodgienne et la croisade royale pour l'independence*. Phnom Penh: n.p.

——. 1972. *L'Indochine vue de Pékin*. Paris: Éditions du Seuil.

——. 1974. *My war with the CIA: the memoirs of Prince Norodom Sihanouk*. London: Penguin Books.

——. 1979. *Chroniques de guerre et d'espoir*. [Paris]: Hachette/Stock,

——. c. 1980. *War and hope: The case for Cambodia*, trans. Mary Feeney. New York: Pantheon Books.

——. 1982. *Souvenirs doux et amers*. Paris: Fayard.

O'Sullivan, Kevin. 1962. 'Concentric conformity in ancient Khmer kinship organization'. *Bulletin of the Institute of Ethnology, Academia Sinica*, 13, pp. 87–95.

Osborne, Milton E. 1966. 'History and kingship in contemporary Cambodia'. *Journal of Southeast Asian History* 7, 1, pp. 1–14.

——. 1966. 'Notes on early Cambodian provincial history'. *France-Asie*, 20, 186, pp. 433–449.

———. 1969. *The French presence in Cochinchina and Cambodia: Rule and Response (1859–1905)*. Ithaca, New York; London: Cornell University Press.

———. [1973]. *Politics and power in Cambodia: The Sihanouk years.* [Camberwell, Victoria]: Longman.

———. 1973. 'Kingmaking in Cambodia, Sisowath to Sihanouk'. *Journal of South East Asian Studies*, 3, 3, pp. 169–185.

———. 1994. *Sihanouk: Prince of light, prince of darkness.* St. Leonards, New South Wales: Allen & Unwin.

Ovesen, Jan. 1996. *When every household is an island: Social organization and power structures in rural Cambodia.* Uppsala; Stockholm: Department of Cultural Anthropology, Uppsala University; Swedish International Development Agency (SIDA).

Pachow, W. 1958. 'The voyage of Buddhist missions to South-East Asia and the Far East'. *JGIS* 17, pp. 1–22.

Panivong Norindr. 1996. *Phantasmic Indochina: French colonial ideology in architecture, film, and literature.* Durham and London: Duke University Press.

Pannetier, A. 1915. 'Sentences et proverbes cambodgiens'. *BEFEO* 15, 3, pp. 15–71.

Paris, Roland. 2004. *At war's end: Building peace after conflict.* Boulder, Colorado: Cambridge University Press.

Parmentier, Henri. 1927. *L'Art khmer primitif,* 2 vols. Paris: EFEO.

Pateman, Carole. 1988. *The sexual contract.* Stanford, California: Stanford University Press.

Pateman, Carole and Elizabeth Gross (eds). 1986. *Feminist challenges: Social and political theory.* Sydney: Allen & Unwin.

Pavie, Auguste. 1988. *Contes du Cambodge.* Paris: Éditions sudestasie.

Pelliot, Paul. 1903. 'Le Fou-nan'. *BEFEO* 3, pp. 248–303.

Phim, Toni Samantha and Ashley Thompson. 1999. *Dance in Cambodia.* [Kuala Lumpur]; New York: Oxford University Press.

Pich Sal. n.d. [1960s]. *Le mariage cambodgien.* Phnom Penh: Université Buddhique Preah Sihanouk Raj.

Picq, Lawrence. 1984. *Au-delà du ciel: Cinq ans chez les Khmers rouges.* Paris: Éditions Bernard Barrault.

Pin Yathay. 1987. *Stay alive, my son.* New York: Free Press.

Pollock, Sheldon. 1996. 'The sanskrit cosmopolis, 300–1300: Transculturation, vernacularization, and the question of ideology'. In Jan E.M. Houben (ed.), *Ideology and status of sanskrit: Contributons to the history of the sanskrit language.* Leiden; New York; Köln: Brill. 197–247.

Poole, Peter. 1969. *Cambodia's quest for survival.* New York: American-Asian Educational Exchange.

Porée, Gaston and Eveline Maspero. 1938. *Moeurs et coutumes des Khmèrs: Origines, histoire, religions, croyances, rites.* Paris: EFEO.

Porée-Maspero, Éveline. 1950. Nouvelle etude sur la nāgī Somā. *Journal Asiatique* 238, pp. 237–267.

——. *Cérémonies des douze mois.* Phnom Penh: Institute Bouddhique.

——. 1969. *La vie du paysan khmer.* Phnom Penh: Éditions de l'Institut Bouddhique.

Pou, Saveros. 1970. 'Inscriptions modernes d'Angkor 2 et 3'. *BEFEO* 57, pp. 99–126.

——. 1971. 'Inscriptions modernes d'Angkor 4, 5, 6 et 7'. *BEFEO* 58, pp. 105–123.

——. 1972. 'Inscriptions modernes d'Angkor 1, 8 et 9'. *BEFEO* 59, pp. 101–121.

——. 1972. 'Inscriptions modernes d'Angkor 10, 11, 12, 13, 14, 15, 16a, 16b et 16c'. *BEFEO* 59, pp. 231–249.

——. 1973. 'Inscriptions modernes d'Angkor 17, 18, 19, 20, 21, 22, 23, 24 et 25'. *BEFEO* 60, pp. 163–203.

——. 1973. 'Inscriptions modernes d'Angkor 26, 27, 28, 29, 30, 31, 32 et 33'. *BEFEO* 60, pp. 205–243.

——. 1974. 'Inscriptions modernes d'Angkor 35, 37 et 39'. *BEFEO* 61, pp. 301–337.

——. 1975. 'Inscriptions modernes d'Angkor 34 et 38'. *BEFEO* 62, pp. 283–353.

——. 1987–1988. 'Notes on Brahmanic gods in Theravâdin Cambodia'. *Indologica Taurinensia* 14, pp. 339–351.

——. 1988. *Une guirlande de cpap*, 2 vols. Paris: Cedorek.

——. 1992. 'Indegenization of Ramayana in Cambodia'. *Asian Folklore Studies* 51, 1, pp. 89–102.

Pou, Saveros and Philip N. Jenner. 1975. 'Les *cpāp'* ou "Codes de conduite" Khmers I: Cpāp' Kerti Kāl'. *BEFEO* 62, pp. 369–394.

——. 1977. 'Les *cpap'* ou <codes de conduite> khmers III: *cpap kun cau'*. *BEFEO* 64, pp. 167–215.

——. 1978. 'Les *cpap'* ou <codes de conduite> Khmers IV: Cpap Rajaneti ou cpap' brah Rajasambhir'. *BEFEO* 65, pp. 361–402.

——. 1979. 'Les *cpap'* ou <codes de conduite> Khmers V: *Cpap' Kram*", *BEFEO* 66, pp. 129–160.

——. 1981. 'Les *cpāp'* ou "Codes de conduite" Khmers VI: Cpāp' Trineti'. *BEFEO* 70, pp. 135–193.

Pryzluski, Jean. 1925. 'La princesse à l'odeur de poisson et la nāgī dans la traditione de l'Asie Orientale'. *Études Asiatiques* 2, pp. 265–284.

Pym, Christopher. 1960. *Mistapim in Cambodia.* London: Hodder & Stoughton.

Raffin, Anne. 2002. 'Easternization meets westernisation: Patriotic youth organizations in French Indochina during World War II'. *French Politics, Culture & Society,* 20, 1, pp. 121–140.

Ramusack, Barbara N. and Sharon Sievers (eds). 1999. *Women in Asia: Restoring women to history.* Indianapolis: Indiana University Press.

Rawson, P. 1989. *The art of Southeast Asia.* London: Thames and Hudson.

Reid, Anthony (ed.). 1983. *Slavery, bondage, and dependency in Southeast Asia.* St. Lucia, Queensland; London; New York: University of Queensland Press.

———. 1988. *Southeast Asia in the Age of Commerce, 1450–1680,* vol. 1, *The lands below the winds.* New Haven and London: Yale University Press.

———. 1993. *Southeast Asia in the age of commerce, 1450–1680,* vol. 2, *Expansion and Crisis.* Chiang Mai: Silkworm Books, 1993.

———. 2000. *Charting the shape of early modern Southeast Asia.* Singapore: Institute of Southeast Asian Studies and Chiang Mai, Thailand: Silkworm Books.

Riffaud, Audrey. 2006. 'Contextual and cultural pressures in development projects implemented by GTZ in Cambodia'. Masters thesis, Université La Sorbonne-Paris IV.

Roberts, David W. 2001. *Political transition in Cambodia: Power, elitism and democracy.* Richmond, Surrey: Curzon.

Robinson, Kathy. 1988. 'What kind of freedom is cutting your hair?' In Glen Chandler, Norman Sullivan and Jan Branson (eds), *Development and displacement: Women in Southeast Asia.* Clayton, Victoria: Monash University Centre of Southeast Asian Studies, Monash Papers on Southeast Asia 18.

Rooney, Dawn. 1999. *Angkor: An introduction to the temples.* Hong Kong: Odyssey Publications.

Roveda, Vittorio. 1998. *Khmer Mythology.* London: Thames and Hudson.

Saada, Emmanuelle. 2002. 'The empire of law: Dignity, prestige, and domination in the "colonial situation"'. *French Politics, Culture & Society* 20, 2, pp. 98–181.

Sahai, S. 1970. *Les institutions politiques et l'organisation administrative du Cambodge ancien.* Paris: EFEO.

Said, Edward W. 1979. *Orientalism.* New York: Vintage Books.

Sam-Ang Sam. 1998. 'Role of Khmer culture in social development within the global context of the new millennium'. In Sorn Samnang (ed.), *Khmer studies: Knowledge of the past, and its contributions to the rehabilitation and reconstruction of Cambodia, proceedings of the International Conference on Khmer Studies, Phnom Penh, 26–30 August 1996.* Phnom Penh: Toyota Foundation, French Embassy, British Embassy, vol. 1, pp. 82–87.

Sanday, Peggy Reeves. 1981. *Female power and male dominance: On the origins of sexual inequality.* Cambridge: Cambridge University Press.

Sarrault, Albert. 1931. *Grandeur et servitude colonials.* Paris: Sagittaire.

Saunders, Kriemild (ed.). 2002. *Feminist post-development thought: Rethinking modernity, post-colonialism and representation.* London and New York: Zed Books.

Schier, Peter and Manola Schier-Oum with Waldtraut Jarke (comp. and trans.). 1980. *Prince Sihanouk on Cambodia: Interviews and talks with Prince Norodom Sihanouk.* Hamburg: Institut für Asienkunde.

Schiessl, Christoph. 2002. 'An element of genocide: Rape, total war, and international law in the twentieth century'. *Journal of Genocide Research* 4, 2, pp. 197–210.

Scott, Joan W. 1986. 'Gender: A useful category of historical analysis'. *American Historical Review* 91 (1986), pp. 1053–1075.

Secretariat of State for Women's Affairs. 1995. *Women: Key to national reconstruction.* Phnom Penh: Secretariat of State for Women's Affairs, Kingdom of Cambodia.

Sharan, Mahesh Kumar. 1986. *Political history of ancient Cambodia from 1st to 15th cent. AD.* New Delhi: Vishnavidya Publishers.

Shawcross, William. 1985. *The quality of mercy: Cambodia, holocaust and modern Cambodia.* Bangkok: DD Books.

———. 1994. *Cambodia's new deal: A report by William Shawcross.* Washington, DC: Carnegie Endowment for International Peace.

Simon-Barouh, Ida. 1990. *Le Cambodge des Khmers Rouges: Chronique de la vie quotidienne, recit de Yi Tan Kim Pho.* Paris: L'Harmattan.

Sircar, D.C. (ed.). 1971. *Social life in ancient India.* Calcutta: Centre of Advanced Studies in Ancient Indian History and Culture, Calcutta University.

Slocomb, Margaret. 2003. *The People's Republic of Kampuchea, 1979–1989: The revolution after Pol Pot.* Chiang Mai: Silkworm Books.

Smith, R.B. and W. Watson (eds). 1979. *Early South East Asia: Essays in archaeology, history, and historical geography.* New York and Kuala Lumpur: Oxford University Press.

Sok Siphana and Denora Sarin. 1998. *The legal system of Cambodia.* Phnom Penh: Cambodian Legal Resources Center.

Somboon Suksamran. 1976. *Political Buddhism in Southeast Asia: The role of the sangha in the modernization of Thailand.* New York: St Martin's Press.

Sorn Samnang (ed.). 1998. *Khmer studies: Knowledge of the past and its contributions to the rehabilitation and reconstruction of Cambodia:Proceedings of International Conference on Khmer Studies, Phnom Penh, 26–30 August 1996.* 2 vols. Phnom Penh: Toyota Foundation, French Embassy, British Embassy.

Sponberg, Alan. 1986. 'Attitudes toward women and the feminine in early Buddhism'. In J.I. Cabeson (ed.), *Buddhism, sexuality and gender.* Albany, New York: State University of New York Press, pp. 3–36.

Stark, Miriam T. 1998. 'The transition to history in the Mekong Delta: A view from Cambodia'. *International Journal of Historical Archaeology* 2, 3, pp. 175–203.

Stark, Miriam T., P. Bion Griffin, Chuch Phoeun, Judy Ledgerwood, Michael Dega, Carol Mortland, Nancy Dowling, James M. Bayman, Bong Sovath, Tea Van, Chhan Chamroeun, and Kyle Latinis. 1999. 'Results of the 1995–1996 archaeological field investigations at Angkor Borei, Cambodia'. *Asian Perspectives* 38, 1, pp. 7–36.

Steinberg, David J. 1959. *Cambodia: Its people – its society – its culture.* New Haven: Hraf Press.

Stern, Philippe. 1954. 'Diversité et rhythme des fondations royales khmeres'. *BEFEO* 44, 2, pp. 649–685.

Stoler, Ann Laura. 1997. 'Sexual affronts and racial frontiers'. In Frederick Cooper and Ann Laura Stoler (eds), *Tensions of empire: Colonial cultures in a bourgeois world.* Berkeley, California: University of California Press. 198–237.

Stuart-Fox, Martin. 1993. 'Who was Maha Thevi?' *JSS* 81, 1, pp. 103–108.

Stuart-Fox, Martin and Bunheang Ung. 1998. *The murderous revolution: Life and death in Pol Pot's Kampuchea.* Bangkok: Orchid Press.

Surtees, Rebecca. 2003. 'Rape and sexual transgression in Cambodian society'. In Linda Rae Bennett and Lenore Manderson (eds), *Violence against women in Asian societies.* London: RoutledgeCurzon, pp. 93–113.

Szymusiak, Molyda. 1986. *The stones cry out.* New York: Hill and Wang.

Tarling, Nicholas (ed.). 1999. *The Cambridge history of Southeast Asia,* vol. 1: *From early times to c.1500.* Cambridge: Cambridge University Press.

—— (ed.). 1999. *The Cambridge history of Southeast Asia,* vol. 2: *From c.1500 to c.1800.* Cambridge: Cambridge University Press.

Tarr, Chou Meng and Peter Aggleton. 1998. '"Sexualising" the culture(s) of young Cambodians: Dominant discourses and social reality'. In Sorn Samnang (ed.), *Khmer studies: Knowledge of the past and its contributions to the rehabilitation and reconstruction of Cambodia: Proceedings of International Conference on Khmer Studies, Phnom Penh, 26–30 August 1996.* Phnom Penh: Toyota Foundation, French Embassy, British Embassy. Vol. 2. 1029–1038.

Tham Seung Chee (ed.). 1981. *Literature and society in Southeast Asia.* Singapore: National University of Singapore Press.

Thion, Serge. 1981. *Khmers Rouges! Materiaux pour l'histoire du communisme au Cambodge.* Paris: J.E. Hallier-Albin Michel.

Thompson, Ashley. 2000. 'Introductory remarks between the lines: Writing histories of middle Cambodia'. In Barbara Watson Andaya (ed.), *Other pasts: Women, gender and history in early modern Southeast Asia.* Manoa, Hawaii: University of Hawai'i Press, pp. 47–68.

——. 2000. 'Lost and found: The stupa, the four-faced Buddha, and the seat of royal power in Middle Cambodia'. In Wibke Lobo and Stephanie Reimann (eds), *Southeast Asian Archaeology 1998: Proceedings of the 7th International Conference of the European Association of Southeast Asian Archaeologists, 1998.* Hull: Centre for Southeast Asian Studies, Hull University, pp. 245–264.

Thompson, Mark R. 2002/2003. 'Female leadership of democratic transitions in Asia'. *Pacific Affairs* 75, 4, pp. 535–555.

Thompson, Virginia. 1937. *French Indo-China.* London: Allen & Unwin.

Thomson, Andrew, Ken Cain and Heidi Postlewait. 2004. *Emergency sex (and other desperate measures).* London: Ebury Press.

Thomson, R.S. 1945. 'The establishment of the French Protectorate over Cambodia'. *Far Eastern Quarterly* 4, 4, pp. 313–340.

Toshiyasu Kato, Jeffrey A. Kaplan, Chan Sophal and Real Sopheap. 2000. *Cambodia: Enhancing government for sustainable development.* Manila: Asia Development Bank.

Tully, John A. 1994. 'Cambodia in the reign of king Sisowath (1904–1927): a study of colonialism and development'. PhD thesis, Monash University.

———. 2002. *France on the Mekong: A history of the Protectorate in Cambodia, 1863–1953*. Lanham, Maryland: University Press of America.

Ung, Loung. 2005. *Lucky child: A daughter of Cambodia reunited with the sister she left behind*. London; New York; Sydney; Auckland: Fourth Estate.

United Nations Cambodia. 2000. *Partners for the advancement of women*. Phnom Penh: United Nations Cambodia.

Vella, Walter F. 1957. *Siam under Rama III, 1824–1851*. Locust Valley, New York: J.J. Augustin.

Vickery, Michael. 1973. 'The Khmer inscriptions of Tenasserim: A reinterpretation'. *JSS*, 61, 1, pp. 51–70.

———. 1977. 'Cambodia after Angkor: The chronicular evidence for the fourteenth to sixteenth centuries'. PhD thesis, Yale University.

———. 1984. *Cambodia: 1975–1982*. North Sydney, NSW: Allen & Unwin.

———. 1985. 'The reign of Sūryavarman I and royal factionalism at Angkor'. *JSEAS* 16, 2, pp. 226–244.

———. 1986. *Kampuchea: Politics, economics and society*. Sydney; London and Boston: Allen & Unwin.

———. 1994. 'What and where was Chenla?'. In F. Bizot (ed.), *Recherches nouvelles sur le Cambodge*. Paris: EFEO. 197–212.

———. 1998. *Society, Economics, and Politics in Pre-Angkorian Cambodia: The 7th–8th Centuries*. Tokyo: The Center for East Asian Cultural Studies for UNESCO.

———. 2003–2004. 'Funan reviewed: Deconstructing the ancients'. *BEFEO* 90–91, pp. 101–143.

Viengkèo Souksavatdy. 1997. *L'Archaéologie des débuts de l'histoire khmère dans la région de Champassak*. Paris: DEA.

Viollis, Andrée. 1935. *SOS Indochine*. Paris: Gallimard.

Weiner, Annette B. 1976. *Women of value, men of renown*. Austin, Texas: University of Texas Press.

Wenk, Klaus. 1968. *The restoration of Thailand under Rama I, 1782–1809*, trans. Greeley Stahl. Tucson, Arizona: University of Arizona Press.

———. 1995. *Thai literature: An introduction*, trans. Erich W. Reinhold. Bangkok: White Lotus.

Whitworth, Sandra. 2004. *Men, militarism, and UN peacekeeping: A gendered analysis*. London: Boulder.

Wijeyewardene, Gehan. 1977. 'Matriclans or female cults: A problem in northern Thai ethnography'. *Mankind* 11, pp. 19–25.

Williams, Maslyn. 1969. *The land in between: The Cambodian dilemma*. Sydney; London: Collins.

Wolters, O.W. 1965. *Early Indonesian Commerce*. Ithaca, NY: Cornell University Press.

———. 1966. 'The Khmer king at Basan (1371–3) and the restoration of the Cambodian chronology during the fourteenth and fifteenth centuries'. *Asia Major*, n.s. 2, 1, pp. 44–89.

———. 1973. 'Jayavarman II's military power: The territorial foundation of the Angkor empire'. *JRAS*, 1, pp. 21–30.

———. 1974. 'North-western Cambodia in the seventh century'. *Bulletin of the School of Oriental and African Studies* 37, 2, pp. 355–384.

———. 1999. *History, culture, and region in Southeast Asian perspectives*, rev. ed. Ithaca, New York: Southeast Asia Program Publications, Cornell University; Singapore: Institute of Southeast Asian Studies.

Women's Media Centre. 2000. *Gender in election and female leadership at the communal level.* Phnom Penh: Women's Media Centre.

———. 2000. *Gender and behaviour towards love.* Phnom Penh: Women's Media Centre.

———. 2000. *Gender in writings.* Phnom Penh: Women's Media Center of Cambodia.

———. 2001. *Women's Media Centre of Cambodia* information leaflet. Phnom Penh: WMC.

Yoneo Ishii. 1986. *Sangha, state, and society: Thai Buddhism and history*, trans. Peter Hawkes. Honolulu: University of Hawai'i Press.

Zepp, Ray. 1997. *A field guide to Cambodian pagodas.* Phnom Penh: Bert's Books.

Zimmerman, Cathy. 1995. *Plates in a basket will rattle: Domestic violence in Cambodia.* Phnom Penh: Project Against Domestic Violence.

MATERIAL ONLINE

A true love stuns judges. 2003. *Koh Santepheap* newspaper, Phnom Penh, 4 September 2003, obtained from camnews@cambodia.org newsgroup.

Becker, Elizabeth. 2003. 'Khieu Ponnary, 83, first wife of Pol Pot, Cambodian despot, dies, 3 July 2003'. www.genocidewatch.org/CambodiaJuly3KhmerDies.htm.

'Cambodian women in the revolutionary war for the people's national liberation'. 1973. *Cambodian Genocide Program Resources*, www.yale.edu/cgp/kwomen.html.

Norodom Sihanouk. 2003. 'Charmante'. *Messages par Norodom Sihanouk*, www.norodomsihanouk.info/Messages, 6 August 2003.

———. 2003. 'Le problème de la prostitution au Cambodge'. *Études cambodgiennes*, 29 October 2003, www.norodomsihanouk.info/Messages/ec%200406.htm.

Puy Kea (comp.) 2002. 'Important events in Cambodia'. Cambodian People's Party. www.cambodianpeopleparty.org/29-02-00.htm.

Saumura, Tioulong. 2000. 'Gender, security and human rights: The case of Cambodia. Speech presented at the *14th Asia-Pacific Roundtable*, 3–6 June 2000, Kuala Lumpur'. Available at www.samrainsyparty.org/national_assembly/KL_ISIS_CONF_JUNE2000_ts_speech.html.

Vanthanouvong, Manila and Sak Linda. 2003. 'Women moving toward power'. *Light of the voters*, www.ijf-cij.org/folder_file_for_cambodia/8.htm

'Women leaders'. www.onlinewomeninpolitics.org/cambo/cmbdleads.html. Accessed 2003.

Vanphone Phomphipak and Sun Heng. 2003. 'Women's party takes single-minded approach to winning', *Light of the voters*, www.ijf-cij.org/folder_file_for_cambodia/9.htm.

Index

Khmer Rouge, 4, 6, 8, 11–13
  female leaders, 181
  gender policies, 218–220, 222, 225
  legacies in contemporary Cambodia,
    238, 243, 246, 255, 267, 276
  treatment of women, 227–233
  see also Democratic Kampuchea;
    education; marriage; morality
khsae (patron–client links), 7, 33, 84,
  132, 138, 261, 284
K'mouch (ghost), 196. *See also brai;*
  devata; female spirits
koan kroach (foetus talisman), 97, 135,
  140, 197, 228
komlang (strength), 6. *See also* power
Kossamak (Queen), 183–184, 197,
  199, 201, 210 n.4
Kulaprabhavati, 22–23, 32, 34

laws, 10, 13, 276, 278, 288
  colonial era, 167, 185–186
  nineteenth century, 117–119, 125,
    136–137, 143
  pre-modern period, 35, 87, 93–100
  Sangkum approach to, 191–192, 209
Leclère, Adhémard, 78, 121, 133, 135,
  151–152, 167, 173
Ledgerwood, Judy, 3–4, 32, 119, 246,
  251, 253
lesbianism, 153
Liu Ye, 19, 33, 37 f.n., 47–48

marriage
  classical Cambodia, 46–49, 54, 57,
    60, 66–68
  colonial period, 150–151, 155,
    158–159
  contemporary attitudes toward, 242,
    247, 253
  early Cambodia, 27–31, 33–35, 40
    n.36

early modern period, 88, 90–91, 93,
  96–97, 100–102
Khmer Rouge period, 223–224, 230
Sangkum period, 185–186, 188,
  192, 203
temporary, 99–100, 102, 150–151,
  173. *See also encongayment*
'traditional' approaches to, 111, 129,
  132–135, 138–139, 142
  see also concubine; sexual relations;
    virginity
matrilineal succession, 2, 31, 32, 35,
  55–56, 63, 69
Me Penh, 82
me sa (powerful female spirit), 142,
  153, 287. *See also* female spirits
meba (ancestral spirits), 6, 96–97, 99,
  133, 238, 192, 265, 288. *See also*
  female spirits
mediums. *See rup*
middle period, 10, 32, 74–108 *passim.*
  See also marriage; pre-modern
  period
midwives, 60–61, 140, 160–162, 168,
  176–177 n.30, 187, 211 n.17, 224
mise en valeur (development), 156
mit neary ('female comrade'), 204,
  219, 222–223, 229. *See also* Khmer
  Rouge
morality, 6, 192, 195, 200–201,
  208–209
  Buddhist, 121, 151
  contemporary attitudes toward, 268,
    278
  European, 159, 162, 166, 171–172
  Khmer Rouge, 222–223, 228–229
Muslims. *See* Islam

nationalism, 8, 13, 171–173, 178 n.55,
  278, 286

NIAS Press is the autonomous publishing arm of
NIAS – Nordic Institute of Asian Studies, a research institute
located at the University of Copenhagen. NIAS is partially funded by the
governments of Denmark, Finland, Iceland, Norway and Sweden
via the Nordic Council of Ministers, and works to encourage and
support Asian studies in the Nordic countries. In so doing, NIAS
has been publishing books since 1969, with more than two
hundred titles produced in the past few years.

COPENHAGEN UNIVERSITY

Nordic Council of Ministers